P9-DBZ-941

**Serving Gifted and Talented Students**

# Serving Gifted and Talented Students

❖ ❖ ❖

## A Resource for School Personnel

Edited by

**Judy L. Genshaft**
**Marlene Bireley**
**Constance L. Hollinger**

pro·ed

8700 Shoal Creek Boulevard
Austin, Texas 78757

**pro·ed**

© 1995 by PRO-ED, Inc.
8700 Shoal Creek Boulevard
Austin, Texas 78757-6897

All rights reserved. No part of the material protected by this
copyright notice may be reproduced or utilized in any form or by
any means, electronic or mechanical, including photocopying,
recording, or by any information storage and retrieval system,
without the prior written permission of the copyright owner.

**Library of Congress Cataloging-in-Publication Data**

Serving gifted and talented students : a resource for school personnel
/ edited by Judy L. Genshaft, Marlene Bireley, Constance L. Hollinger.
  p.    cm.
  Includes bibliographical references and index.
  ISBN 0-89079-605-X
  1. Gifted children—Education.   2. Educational counseling.
 I. Genshaft, Judy.   II. Bireley, Marlene.   III. Hollinger, Constance L.
LC3993.2.S47   1994
371.95—dc20                                                    94-9263
                                                                  CIP

This book is designed in New Century Schoolbook and Helvetica.

Production Manager: Alan Grimes
Production Coordinator: Adrienne Booth
Art Director: Lori Kopp
Reprints Buyer: Alicia Woods
Editor: Debra Berman
Editorial Assistant: Claudette Landry

**Publisher's Note:** This book was a joint effort of PRO-ED and the National Association of School Psychologists (NASP). Many individuals contributed to the development of this book; the efforts of Leslie Hale, Susan
Gorin, and the NASP Publications Board are greatly appreciated.

Printed in the United States of America

1   2   3   4   5   6   7   8   9   10     99   98   97   96   95

# Contents

Chapter 13
**Highly Gifted Children**   217
Linda Kreger Silverman


**PART IV** ❖ Personal, Interpersonal, and Cultural Issues   **241**

Chapter 14
**Impact of Family Patterns Upon the Development of Giftedness**   243
Sylvia B. Rimm

Chapter 15
**Stress and the Gifted**   257
Judy L. Genshaft, Steven Greenbaum, and Susan Borovsky

Chapter 16
**Stress as a Function of Gender: Special Needs of Gifted Girls and Women**   269
Constance L. Hollinger

Chapter 17
**Serving the Needs of Gifted Children from a Multicultural Perspective**   285
Deborah L. Plummer


**PART V** ❖ Intervention Strategies   **301**

Chapter 18
**Family Consultation as an Approach to Providing Psychoeducational Services to Gifted Children**   303
Gerald Porter and Joel Meyers

Chapter 19
**Counseling Academically Behaving Adolescents About Wellness**   323
Paul Michael Janos

Chapter 20
**Counseling Gifted Young Women About Educational and Career Choices**   337
Constance L. Hollinger

# *Preface*

◆　◆　◆

UNLIKE SPECIAL EDUCATION, gifted education has not been perceived as an important area of concern for support personnel practicing in school psychology, school counseling, school social work, and school nursing. As editors of this book, all of whom are school psychology trainers with a particular interest in gifted education, we believe that this is an oversight that diminishes the quality of service to gifted students and deprives support personnel of an important and fulfilling professional duty.

Most support professionals probably have little direct training in the needs of gifted students. Many, we surmise, believe the common myth that the gifted will "make it on their own" and, unlike disabled clients, have few needs that can be fulfilled by the professional. In a recent critical analysis of the field, however, Shore, Cornell, Robinson, and Ward (1991) concluded that, of the 101 recommended practices most often found in the literature on gifted students, about half concerned identification, assessment, or affective needs most often considered to be the area of expertise of these professional groups.

This book is our attempt to provide up-to-date information on the personal and educational needs of the gifted student, with particular emphasis on the roles that support staff can play. We solicited chapters from some of the best known professionals in the field of gifted education, most of whom also have a background in psychology and/or counseling. To a person, they responded with enthusiasm to the project, stating that this was a long "overdue" book. We hope you agree and that you will find it useful in your daily work.

We in the United States have historically "rooted for the underdog" and espoused an egalitarian orientation. On the other hand, we relish our position as "number one" in the world and are engaged in a far-reaching educational reform movement designed to maintain this excellence by improving our school systems. Encouraging our "brightest and best" means not only providing excellent academic opportunities, but nourishing their souls and their psyches, and recognizing that exceptional persons, even those with "good" exceptionalities, are at greater risk for feeling out of step with their peers. As noted by a number of authors, the asynchronous development of the gifted child should be of primary concern to all educators. The dissonance between the 10-year-old brain, the 7-year-old body, and the 6-year-old social response system, for example, is easily misunderstood by children and adults alike and fraught with psychological pitfalls. Such asynchrony in a mildly handicapped child would be readily recognized and merit concern and collaborative effort to minimize its effects on the child's education and development. We believe that a parallel need exists for the gifted child.

The design of this book is simple. We have identified the major issues in gifted education, presented the latest research and thinking of some of the country's most noted experts, and have ended many chapters with specific ways for practicing support staff to incorporate this information into their daily work. Part I provides a historical overview of the field placed in the societal context of the 20th century and a discussion of the particular needs of gifted children based upon disparate developmental patterns.

Part II discusses the issues of assessment and identification, the inevitable "Who are the gifted?" questions. As many of you know, a major contributor to our changing understanding of the nature of intelligence is Robert Sternberg. He presents an extension of his conception of intelligence into the specific realm of types of giftedness and describes his ongoing attempt to develop assessment procedures consistent with his theories. Several chapters explore the research base and traditional practice of the identification of the gifted through standardized measurements and preview the current trend toward portfolio development and authentic assessment. In this section and throughout the book, we tend to use the term *gifted* generically, to include the gifted, creative, and talented, more as a matter of editorial convenience than precision. In actual practice, the term *gifted* most often refers to those with academic and intellectual exceptionality, *creative* to innovative problem solvers, and *talented* to those with special abilities in the visual and performing arts. It is our intent that, unless the context demands otherwise, our readers will comprehend the word *gifted* within this broader meaning.

Educational services for the gifted student are in a state of flux, parallel to the inclusion movement in special education. The 1-day-a-week pull-out or resource room model has served as the primary focus of gifted education for the past 20 years. Educators are now recognizing the need to accommodate giftedness on a 5-day-a-week basis. Part III begins with Feldhusen and Moon's discussion of the full range of services that are now considered as appropriate models in gifted education. Their overview is followed by the presentation of a widely respected model of service, the Autonomous Learning Model developed by George Betts and his associates, a discussion of regular classroom interventions, and a vision of the role of technology in enhancing service to the gifted. These chapters are designed to expand the reader's knowledge of possible interventions and to enhance the repertoire of possibilities that support personnel can bring to a collaborative planning effort on behalf of a gifted student.

Gifted education shares with special and regular education the problem of identifying and providing programming for underserved populations. Readers who serve special students routinely will recognize the familiar needs of the underachieving and disabled groups, but may be less familiar with the unique problems of the dually labeled populations—that is, those who are both disabled and/or underachieving and gifted. It is in this area that we hope to have a direct and immediate impact upon your work because you are already serving these groups. The opposing forces that impact upon the dually labeled child are particularly devious and destructive. Legal mandates and common practice have pushed us to serve the disability; however, we need to heed the equally pressing mandate of acknowledging and serving the abilities of this group of children. Similarly, the highly gifted are a minority largely without voice. As different from their "average" gifted peers (those in the 130–150 IQ range) as the latter are from average children, their rarely found and highly divergent behaviors are often misdiagnosed and misunderstood. Silverman eloquently pleads their case and suggests several specific ways to accommodate their unusual learning needs.

The chapters in Part IV deal with issues familiar to support personnel: stress, gender issues, psychosocial needs, and career choices. Our intent has not been to cover old ground, but to build upon known concepts and to supply a new twist—the impact of giftedness upon these universal human issues. Superior intelligence can bring unique problem-solving skills to bear upon common life stressors, but these same abilities can add their own dimensions of stress in the form of higher societal, familial, or self-imposed expectations. The chapters in Part V are devoted to understanding these unique stressors and applying known skills, such as counseling, consultation, and collaboration, to alleviate their effect upon gifted individuals.

Finally, in Part VI, gifted education is discussed within the larger context of educational reform. Reis outlines the dimensions of gifted education that seem to have relevance for general education and for improving the excellence of schooling for all students. Indeed, gifted education may provide the best existing model for many of the visions that educators and politicians have put forth for the 21st century. At the same time, Dettmer cautions us to adapt from gifted education that which is appropriate for all children, but not to lose sight of the need for continued advocacy for flexibility and comprehensive service to our most able students.

Children and youth who are gifted, creative, and talented, like those with disabilities, are at risk when we consider the appropriateness of many of our current educational practices for their unique needs. We believe that school-based psychologists, counselors, social workers, and nurses should play a significant role in understanding and programming for this underserved group of students. We hope that the information this book provides will enhance your ability to achieve that goal.

# REFERENCE

Shore, B., Cornell, D., Robinson, A., & Ward, V. (1991) *Recommended practices in gifted education: A critical analysis.* New York: Teachers College Press.

# Editors and Contributors

Marlene Bireley
Psychoeducational Consultant
2242 Matrena Drive
Beavercreek, OH 45431

Judy L. Genshaft
Dean
School of Education 212
University at Albany
State University of New York
Albany, NY 12222

Constance L. Hollinger
Professor
Psychology Department
Cleveland State University
Euclid Avenue at East 24th
   Street
Cleveland, OH 44115

George T. Betts
Associate Professor
Division of Special Education
University of Northern Colorado
Greeley, CO 80639

Susan Borovsky
115 S. Columbia Avenue
Bexley, OH 43209

Carolyn M. Callahan
Professor
Department of Educational
   Studies
Curry School of Education
University of Virginia
Ruffner Hall
405 Emmet Street
Charlottesville, VA 22903-2495

Mary Ruth Coleman
Associate Director
Gifted Education Policy Studies
   Program
University of North Carolina at
   Chapel Hill
300 NCNB Plaza
Chapel Hill, NC 27514

Gary A. Davis
Professor
Department of Educational
    Psychology
Educational Sciences Building
University of Wisconsin
1025 West Johnson Street
Madison, WI 53706

Peggy Dettmer
Professor
Educational Psychology and
    Special Education
College of Education #304
Bluemont Hall
Kansas State University
Manhattan, KS 66506-5301

John F. Feldhusen
Distinguished Professor
Gifted Education–Resource
    Institute
Purdue University
South Campus Courts–G
West Lafayette, IN 47907

Dawn P. Flanagan
Assistant Professor of School
    Psychology
Department of Psychology
St. John's University
8000 Utopia Parkway
Jamaica, NY 11439

James J. Gallagher
Kenan Professor of Education
University of North Carolina at
    Chapel Hill
300 NCNB Plaza
Chapel Hill, NC 27514

Steven Greenbaum
19 Hampshire Place
Delmar, NY 12054

Michael J. Hoover
Adjunct Professor
Division of Special Education
University of Northern Colorado
Greeley, CO 80639

Richard D. Howell
Associate Professor
Special Education
Department of Educational
    Services and Research
College of Education
The Ohio State University
356 Arps Hall
Columbus, OH 43210

Paul Michael Janos
Psychologist
Northwest Youth and Family
    Services
8288 Lake City Way, NE
Seattle, WA 98115

Elizabeth Maxwell
Associate Director
Gifted Child Development
    Center
1452 Marion St.
Denver, CO 80218

Joel Meyers
Professor
Department of Educational
    Psychology and Statistics
School of Education 232
University at Albany, SUNY
Albany, NY 12222

Sidney M. Moon
Visiting Assistant Professor
Gifted Education
Resource Institute
Purdue University
South Campus Courts–G
West Lafayette, IN 47907

Beverly N. Parke
05-165-13-99
Bryan, OH 43508

Deborah L. Plummer
Assistant Professor
Department of Psychology
Cleveland State University
Euclid Avenue at East 24th
   Street
Cleveland, OH 44115

Gerald Porter
Assistant Professor
Department of Educational
   Psychology and Statistics
School of Education 232
University at Albany, SUNY
Albany, NY 12222

Sally M. Reis
Associate Professor
Department of Education
   Psychology
University of Connecticut
362 Fairfield Road, U-7
Storrs, CT 06269-2007

Sylvia B. Rimm
Founder
Family Achievement Clinic, S.C.
1227 Robruck Drive
Oconomowoc, WI 53066

Linda Kreger Silverman
Director
Gifted Child Development
   Center
1452 Marion St.
Denver, CO 80218

Robert J. Sternberg
IBM Professor of Psychology and
   Education
Department of Psychology
Yale University
Box 11A Yale Station
2 Hillhouse Avenue
New Haven, CT 06520-7447

# *Part I*

# Developmental Perspectives

# Chapter 1

# Gifted Education: Historical Perspectives and Current Concepts

Mary Ruth Coleman, James J. Gallagher

◆  ◆  ◆

SOCIETY HAS ALWAYS had mixed feelings about the importance of recognizing and developing talented individuals. Americans have vacillated between desire for equity and desire for excellence (Gallagher, 1984) in response to the social, political, and educational issues of the day. During perceived social crises, we seem to rally to the call for excellence and to invest more in the most capable students, with the hope that their leadership will carry us forward. When complacency resumes, however, the tendency is to emphasize equity, forsaking individual accomplishments for the "good of all."

To illustrate this, we have selected highlights of gifted education from the past several decades and tried to place them within the social and political context of their times. By understanding the past, professionals have an opportunity to shape the future for the nation's gifted students.

## WHERE HAVE WE BEEN?

A review of history indicates that, during times of outside threat, the nation has focused on excellence and programs for gifted students' benefit. When the country's energy has been focused on domestic issues, however, the main thrust has been equity, and programs for gifted students have taken a back seat. The following historical highlights illustrate this relationship.

During the first and second decades of this century, one focus in gifted education was on measuring intelligence, and several tests were developed. This effort was driven in part by the need to sort soldiers by intellectual capacity for duties in World War I (Stephens, 1992), but was furthered by efforts to assimilate large numbers of immigrants into the industrial labor force (Gallagher & Weiss, 1979). Lewis Terman (1916) refined the intelligence test for use with school children, and his method of assessing intelligence has shaped the field of gifted education, only recently becoming less influential.

Programs designed for gifted students also began to appear during this time. A national survey indicated that, in 1911, 6% of the cities had special classes for gifted students (Stephens, 1992). The primary strategy for program differentiation was acceleration; however, special classes and individualization were also used (Davis & Rimm, 1989).

In the 1920s, the country had survived World War I and was blissfully unaware that the Depression and another world war lay in its path. Although there was no apparent threat from a military standpoint, the country faced an ever-increasing wave of immigrants from middle and southern Europe. The resulting influx of children who initially had some difficulties coping with school and cultural changes created a demand for special services for gifted and talented children.

Gifted education saw the development of achievement tests; initiation of the *Genetic Studies of Genius* (Terman, 1925); establishment of the longest continuous program for gifted students, the Cleveland Major Works Classes; the first college course devoted to gifted students, taught by Leta Hollingworth at Columbia University; and the publication of the first textbook on gifted, *Education of Gifted Children*, by Stedman (Gallagher & Weiss, 1979; Stephens, 1992; Witty, 1951). During this time, women gained the right to vote and the Pan-American Treaty was signed to prevent further conflicts between nations. The decade, however, came to a crashing close on "Black Friday" as the U.S. Stock Exchange collapsed and the world faced economic crisis (Grun, 1979).

The 1930s were marked by the effort to survive the Depression, and by the escalating crises in Europe and the Pacific which would eventually carry the United States back into war (Grun, 1979). Hollingworth, perhaps more than any other leader in the field at this time, recognized the need to cultivate the potential of gifted students in order to "guide the people safely in a world where, without vision, more people will perish in more different ways than have ever perished before" (Pritchard, 1951).

The country was not far into the 1940s when once again it faced war. The nation rallied and special efforts were made to accelerate students so that they could serve their country. The use of tests to identify individuals with special talents and abilities was accepted as part of a patriotic duty, and special attention was given to students with extremely high IQs (Gallagher & Weiss, 1979). When the war ended in 1945, more than 1 million veterans headed to college under the GI Bill and the complacency of being victorious was nurtured by a thriving economy (Grun, 1979). During this period, programs for gifted children declined, and by 1948 less than 1% of larger school systems reported grouping students by ability levels for instruction (Gallagher & Weiss, 1979).

In the late 1950s, the country was rudely awakened by a blast from the Soviet Union as Sputnik was launched (Davis & Rimm, 1989). The focus immediately turned to the education system and the need to change the curriculum, particularly in the math and science areas, to ensure that the brightest students would be challenged (Davis & Rimm, 1989; Gallagher & Weiss, 1979). The wave of curriculum reform was funded by massive federal grants and was part of the country's overall defense strategy. Gifted students were one of the major beneficiaries, and for a short period of time teachers were encouraged to teach to the highest levels of student capacity instead of to the middle levels (Gallagher & Weiss, 1979).

New approaches to meet the needs of gifted students were initiated, including mentor programs, Saturday workshops, and special summer residential programs (French, 1964). The notion of radical acceleration was introduced to allow students to rocket through the standard curriculum, and ability grouping was widely used (French, 1964). The post-Sputnik period, from the late 1950s through the early 1960s, was perhaps the closest the country has come to addressing the education needs of gifted students on a national scale.

The 1960s and 1970s saw the escalation of the conflict in Vietnam and the Civil Rights movement, with a wave of legal and practical issues to work through in attempts to desegregate schools. Within gifted education, the Marland Report (Marland, 1972) offered the first national definition of gifted and presented a strong case for different educational programming to meet the needs of the gifted. In spite of the growth of programs that this report spurred, the needs of gifted students were still not being fully addressed at the end of the 1970s (Gallagher & Weiss, 1979).

As the country moved into the 1980s, education took a swing back to the basics. Minimum competency tests were developed for high school graduation, and textbooks moved back toward the "three R's." This movement, combined with detracking efforts (Oakes, 1985), eliminated some ability-grouped classes and created difficulty for gifted students who remained bored in their regular classrooms year after year.

The field of gifted education is currently undergoing many changes. Some of these are being driven by the growing understanding of intelligence—what it is, how it can be recognized, and how it can be developed. Other changes, however, are propelled by factors involved in the relationship of educational restructuring initiatives to a broader social and political context. In the next section, we take a look at the current state of gifted education in light of these issues.

# WHERE ARE WE NOW?

It is impossible to discuss the current status of gifted education in the United States without touching upon the larger forces at work in the academic community, the public schools, and the culture at large. We discuss three of these changes—the developing understanding of intelligence, the educational restructuring movement, and the social and political climate for excellence—in the following sections.

## Intelligence

For many years, psychologists and educators followed the rather circular definition that "intelligence is what an intelligence test measures." Unfortunately, intelligence tests were designed largely to measure aptitude for school and for a school program with a rather limited intellectual content. In the past decade, a number of theoreticians have emerged who wished to redefine intelligence to include the full range of human behavior and thought. In doing this, the concept of intelligence has taken on greater breadth (Gardner, 1983), including many dimensions that go beyond the standard verbal and mathematical skills that dominated the standard intelligence test (Wechsler, 1974). This redefinition incorporates the burgeoning interest in human information processing: How individuals solve problems, make decisions, and monitor their own intellectual behavior became important dimensions of these new models of intelligence (Sternberg, 1986). Finally, there was the "felt need," particularly in the sciences, to go beyond problem solving to include "problem finding," where the significance of identifying and selecting a meaningful problem to attack becomes more important (Gallagher, Stepien, & Rosenthal, 1992).

Perhaps of even greater significance was the change in the concept of intelligence to a continually evolving and developing process, rather than a "done deal" at conception. Although one needs to clearly acknowledge the genetic component in an individual's ability to learn (Plomin, 1989), it is equally clear that such native abilities must be nurtured and stimulated before they can crystallize into effective intellectual *behavior*. The last several decades have also indicated that many youngsters with outstanding talent have not had a favorable, or fertile, environment in which to develop their intellectual skills (Baldwin, 1987; Frasier, 1987). The consequence of this unfavorable environment has been that many students with outstanding potential have not been so identified. This has led many educators of gifted students to seek children with hidden talent and to look for alternative methods for the identification of gifted and talented students (Coleman & Gallagher, 1991). The effort to discover and nurture the hidden talents of students from culturally diverse backgrounds, gifted underachievers, or gifted children with disabilities (e.g., learning disabilities) has engaged many educators in the 1990s (see Coleman, 1992).

## Educational Reform and Restructuring

During the past 5 years, significant power sources and decision makers in the United States have made a major attempt to restructure the educational enterprise. They have based this effort mainly on the assumption that the educational system was a failing operation, turning out too many students of limited skills who could not compete successfully with other nations in many academic areas (*America 2000*, 1991; Coleman & Selby, 1986; Gardner, 1983). This restructuring movement underscores the classic conflict in American culture between two desirable goals: *excellence* and *equity*. The conflict is clearly visible in the national educational goals, approved in 1991 by the 50 governors and the president of the United States. The contrast between one of the goals stressing excellence, that *"we will be first in the world in mathematics and science by the year 2000,"* and another goal stressing equity, *"we will also graduate ninety percent of an age group from high school,"* is heightened by a new effort to educate all children in the same or a similar setting (full inclusion) (*America 2000*, 1991).

Some of the major manifestations of the educational restructuring movement are found in the middle school movement, cooperative learning, site-based management, and outcome-based education (Gallagher, 1991).

### Middle Schools

The middle school movement, designed to replace the typical junior high school, emphasizes affective education, interdisciplinary curriculum, the development of thinking skills, and the role of the teacher as a facilitator rather than a disseminator of knowledge. Many of these goals fit in admirably with the goals of educators of gifted students (Clark, 1989; Gallagher & Gallagher, 1994). Where the middle school and gifted programs depart is on the insistence of some of the leaders of the middle school movement (Oakes, 1985; Slavin, 1990a) on heterogeneous grouping as one fundamental element of the middle school. Such an insistence has resulted in some programs for gifted students being abandoned and an attitudinal gulf developing between educators of gifted students and middle school educators (Coleman & Gallagher, 1992). This focus on heterogeneous grouping highlights the concern for equity, while minimizing the call for excellence.

### Cooperative Learning

One significant instructional strategy of the past decade has been that of cooperative learning, a collection of approaches with many different interpretations and models, but that basically involves small groups of students attacking significant curriculum tasks or problems and, in the process, learning group dynamics such as working cooperatively with others and using the talents of others to enrich one's own problem-solving capabilities (Johnson & Johnson, 1990; Kagan, 1988; Slavin, 1990a, 1990b). Many of the goals stressed by cooperative learning advocates are similar to those of educators of gifted students, particularly those who emphasize independent learning and/or problem finding and problem solving. Once again, the concept of heterogeneous grouping has become a significant issue for educators of gifted students, and has led to polarized attitudes around the benefit of cooperative learning for gifted students (Gallagher, Coleman, & Nelson, 1993).

### Site-Based Management

Site-based management tries to bring significant educational decision making back to the local school, thus empowering local teachers and administrators to shape policy decisions that affect the well-being of their students. This movement was spawned in large measure by the dissatisfaction with decisions made at a distance from the school district administration—at the state or federal level. This long-distance decision making seemed, in many ways, inapplicable to the idiosyncratic nature of local conditions and individual students.

It is not yet certain how this movement will affect programs for gifted students. It runs the risk of having a shortage of people at the local school level who are knowledgeable about the special needs and special programming required for gifted students. Ironically, while *this* movement tries to empower local decision makers, another significant educational movement, the national standards movement, is taking away significant clements of local decision making (Levin, 1992). Once again, the political climate is having an effect on educational programs.

### Testing and Assessment

There is a significant movement afoot to create national tests to assess the knowledge and skills that students have mastered across the United States. At the same time, there is the recognition that these national assessments in content areas, such as mathematics or social studies, could well be the first step toward a national curriculum. The design of a national test leads quite logically to the development of a national curriculum, because the only way that teachers can be sure that their students will do well on these tests is to teach their students what will be on the test. With a national curriculum, teachers in New Mexico and New Hampshire will be teaching much the same content. There is not yet a consensus as to whether this is a good idea.

As part of this national testing movement, the nature of the assessments is changing from multiple-choice paper-and-pencil exams to performance or authentic assessments (Schnitzer, 1993). The enthusiasm over the replacement of multiple-choice questions with performance-based measures overlooks some of the difficulties with measuring performance. One problem is that performance measures often do not lend themselves to being generalized. Individual items or authentic measures often do not correlate well with each other, even though they are designed to test the same concepts (Shavelson & Baxter, 1992). The only way to truly improve reliability is to add more performance items to the test, and that means longer and longer tests (Linn, 1993).

If multiple-choice tests can be criticized on the grounds of fairness, one can imagine what will happen the first time performance-based measures are used as a "high-stakes" test, where important educational decisions will be made based on the results. Will students and parents be able to say that it was not fair because they were not taught what was on the test? Or that the persons who scored their tests were much tougher than the judges in other places? Although judges can be prepared to use comparable standards, such a task is neither easy nor inexpensive (Baker, Freeman, & Clayton, 1990).

On balance, the movement toward performance-based testing is probably favorable for gifted students, because it gives them the chance to reveal their full intellectual and academic gifts. For teachers who are trying to develop thinking students, such test items justify the extra time it takes for students to work on individual projects or design unique responses to problems, rather than simply memorizing facts.

Many questions have yet to be resolved, however. What will represent "passing grades" or "outstanding performance" in these performance based tests? If most students can pass the test, will it be challenging enough for gifted students? If it is a challenge for gifted students, how will the average student pass? Will there be different standards at different levels of performance? By abandoning the old multiple-choice tests, professionals have merely traded one set of problems for another. However, the emphasis on providing tests that require meaning and integration of knowledge, as opposed to mastery of isolated information, is a move in the right direction for all students, and may be particularly beneficial for gifted students.

## Social and Political Climate

Many observers believe the education of gifted students is held hostage to the love–hate relationship that American society has with special and unusual talent (Gallagher, 1984). On one hand, Americans are proud of the technological gains and the improvements that have been made by creative and gifted individuals which have strengthened the economy and made lives more interesting and pleasant. On the other hand, many persons view special provisions for gifted students as "elitist." That term is devastating when used to oppose programs for our most talented individuals. It is not made less so by the obviously enthusiastic support of an American "elite" in athletics, where special programs, extraordinary physical facilities, and special instruction are all made available without apology or even elaborate justification.

The truth is that Americans do not want a small cluster of people to be making decisions for everybody or to have the capability of shaping and directing the future. There appears to be an underlying societal fear that if we educate our best and brightest too extensively, we will allow them to take control of our lives.

On the other hand, there is a growing understanding that the self-interest of ordinary citizens can be directly connected to how effectively America educates *all* students, and that this is particularly the case with students who have special talents and gifts. There are only a few of us who will not need a good doctor, or a good lawyer, or a good psychiatrist, or a competent airplane pilot. Our increasingly complex technological society obviously has created heavy demands for extremely well-educated and talented individuals. If we fail to meet these demands, then we will inevitably fall behind in international economic competition, with devastating effects on our economy and way of life.

The other limiting political factor that shapes the education of gifted students is that programs of preserving intellectual resources, similar to those preserving environmental resources, are of a long-term nature, whereas the political system operates on short-term goals and actions. We have learned that our failure to take care of our water, air, and forests has had devastating consequences for both current and future generations. We have not yet begun to act at a societal level on the parallel problems of failing to nurture our scarce intellectual resources, and we are faced with consequences that may be even more serious.

# WHAT MIGHT THE FUTURE HOLD?

When we look to the future of gifted education, we once again need to keep in mind the context within which these events will unfold. It is always risky to predict what may happen; however, by failing to project ahead, we may find that we miss many opportunities to help shape the future. In this section, we present three issues—collaboration, personnel preparation, and technical assistance—that we feel are critical for the further development of gifted education.

## Collaboration

The days of gifted programs that can afford to operate in isolation have passed, and as America moves into the next decade, collaboration will become even more critical. Collaboration, or working jointly with others to achieve a shared goal, includes efforts within educational areas and those that reach outside to form partnerships with businesses and community members.

To achieve collaboration, the structure of the American educational bureaucracy must change (Fine, Grantham, & Wright, 1979; Hathaway, 1985). The old structures must give way to both new paradigms of thought and new arrangements of personnel and resources (Martinson, 1982; Scott & Smith, 1987). Team teaching, cross-disciplinary teaming, interagency coordination, and business partnerships are all examples of this type of shift.

Within the field of education, opportunities for collaboration abound (West, Idol, & Cannon, 1989). However, making the changes needed to initiate these efforts often meets with resistance (Fine et al., 1979). Services for gifted students need to be aligned with regular education to assist with appropriate curriculum differentiation and with other specialized education programs, such as those for bilingual and disabled students, to ensure that these gifted students' needs are being met (VanTassel-Baska, 1991a, 1991b). As school restructuring efforts move forward, gifted education can contribute with strategies to increase the challenge level that students experience, thus helping America reach the goal of excellence in educational outcomes (Lathlaen, 1990; Sicola, 1990). Many of the structural changes proposed by school reform should actually facilitate this collaboration (Gallagher et al., 1993).

These areas need to be explored further, but advocates for gifted students also need to work collaboratively within the educational policy-making arena to help shape decision making (Gallagher, 1988). Without active participation in the policy arena, the needs of gifted students may be overlooked.

The time is ripe for working collaboratively with business and community members (Jones & Maloy, 1988). The special needs of gifted students can be met in part through mentorships, scholarships, and other formalized relations with these communities.

## Personnel Preparation

We have all heard the adage "the army is only as good as the individual soldier," and this can apply to a school system as well. The individuals who make the decisions and those who directly touch the lives of gifted children all should be knowledgeable about these students' special needs. This will require a change from the traditional staff development approach. University and staff development personnel need to move from "teacher training" to a model that includes broad-based personnel preparation for teachers, administrators, and educational support staff, all of whom play a critical role in the quality of education for gifted students (Gallagher & Coleman, 1993). This system relies on an already strong preservice program for elementary and secondary teachers.

Personnel preparation should be tailored both to the target audience (e.g., school counselors, school social workers) and to the level of knowledge needed, ranging from introductory and basic awareness through advanced strategies. The current use of "one-size-fits-all" staff development needs to give way to flexible models that can accommodate a variety of needs (Coleman, Harrison, & Howard, 1993).

## Technical Assistance

Even with the best personnel who are collaborating well, creating optimal "systems" takes further support (Clifford & Trohanis, 1980). The many attempts at school reform over the years are a testament to the difficulty of the change process (Cuban, 1990; Guskey, 1986). The literature on effecting lasting "change" suggests that minor modifications and short-term commitments are not enough (Tushman & Romanelli, 1985). The provision of technical assistance (TA) to create and sustain the needed changes in education, and the education of gifted children in particular, is an area for development (Gallagher, 1974).

Technical assistance differs in four main ways from the traditional expert consultant relationship that has often been established with school systems. The support provided through TA (a) is client driven and directed, (b) is responsive to situational needs, (c) does not push a "product" for sale, and (d) is long term and tied to specific outcomes (Gallagher & Coleman, 1993). Each of these characteristics makes TA an ideal vehicle for accomplishing change through establishing ownership and outcomes (Gallagher & Coleman, 1993).

Although TA has been used in several other educational areas (Trohanis, 1986), it has never been applied specifically to gifted education. This application, at this time, may be the essential next step to ensure that the needs of gifted students are addressed in a comprehensive and integrated way within American schools. The establishment of TA services will also facilitate the need for personnel preparation and collaborative efforts.

# CONCLUSION

Although there is no way to know specifically what the future holds, we can, if we study the past and current situations, forecast some of the issues that will face us. The major dilemma we will face is that of providing a competent, competitive cadre of young graduates who can fulfill leadership roles. This must be juxtaposed against the growing numbers of students in our schools who come from populations that have been traditionally at risk for school failure. This struggle between excellence and equity must be resolved. As a society, we will need to find the balance that allows all children to grow to their full capacity. With the economic and political interest currently focused on education, and the threat of outside force minimized, we may have a golden opportunity to achieve this balance.

We have attempted to highlight some of the important events of the past, present, and future, and to place these in the social and political context of the times. As with any overview, much has been left out as we tried to select those issues that may be most essential to the unfolding of gifted education. Where American education will be 10 or 20 years from now is impossible to say. However, through studying history and actively shaping the present, we have the opportunity to help create the future.

# REFERENCES

*America 2000.* (1991). Washington, DC: U.S. Department of Education.

Baker, E., Freeman, M , & Clayton, S. (1990). *Cognitive assessment of subject matter: Understanding the matter of psychological theory and educa-*

*tional policy in achievement testing.* Los Angeles: UCLA Center on Research in Education.

Baldwin, A. (1987). Undiscovered diamonds. *Journal for the Education of the Gifted, 10,* 271–286.

Clark, B. (1989). *Growing up gifted* (3rd ed.). Columbus, OH: Charles H. Merrill.

Clifford, R., & Trohanis, P. (Eds.). (1980). *Technical assistance in educational settings.* Columbus: Ohio State University Press.

Coleman, M. R. (1992). A comparison of how gifted/LD and average/LD boys cope with school frustration. *Journal for the Education of the Gifted, 15*(3), 239–265.

Coleman, M. R., & Gallagher, J. (1991). *State policies on the identification of gifted students from special populations: Three states in profile.* Chapel Hill: University of North Carolina, Gifted Education Policy Studies Program.

Coleman, M. R., & Gallagher, J. (1992). *Middle school survey report: Impact on gifted students.* Chapel Hill: University of North Carolina, Gifted Education Policy Studies Program.

Coleman, M. R., Harrison, A., & Howard, J. (1993). Personnel preparation: Academically Gifted Plan accepted by the North Carolina State Department of Education.

Coleman, W. J., & Selby, C. (1983). *Educating Americans for the 21st century.* Washington, DC: National Science Board Commission on Precollege Education in Mathematics, Science, and Technology.

Cuban, L. (1990). Reforming again, again, and again. *Educational Researcher, 19,* 3–13.

Davis, G., & Rimm, S. (1989). *Education of the gifted and talented* (2nd ed.). Englewood Cliffs, NJ: Prentice-Hall.

Fine, M., Grantham, V., & Wright, J. (1979). Personal variables that facilitate or impede consultation. *Psychology in the Schools, 16,* 533–539.

Frasier, M. (1987). The identification of gifted black students: Developing new perspectives. *Journal for the Education of the Gifted, 10*(3), 155–180.

French, J. (Ed.). (1964). *Educating the gifted.* New York: Holt, Rinehart & Winston.

Gallagher, J. (1974). Technical assistance: A new device for quality education services for the gifted. *TAG Newsletter, 16,* 5–8.

Gallagher, J. (1984). Excellence and equity—A worldwide conflict. *Gifted International, 2,* 1–11.

Gallagher, J. (1988). An issue of survival: Education of gifted children. In R. Haskins & D. Macrae (Eds.), *Policies for America's public schools: Teachers, equity, and indicators* (pp. 171–193). Norwood, NJ: Ablex.

Gallagher, J. (1991). Educational reform, values, and gifted students. *Gifted Child Quarterly, 35,* 12–19.

Gallagher, J., & Coleman, M. R. (1993). *A collaborative statewide gifted education technical assistance program* (Proposal to J. K. Javits Grants, submitted to U.S. Office of Education). Chapel Hill: University of North Carolina, Gifted Education Policy Studies Program.

Gallagher, J., Coleman, M. R., & Nelson, S. (1993). *Cooperative learning as perceived by educators of gifted students and proponents of cooperative education*. Chapel Hill: University of North Carolina, Gifted Education Policy Studies Program.

Gallagher, J., & Gallagher, S. (1994). *Teaching the gifted child* (4th ed.). Needham Heights, MA: Allyn & Bacon.

Gallagher, J., & Weiss, P. (1979). *The education of gifted and talented students: A history and prospectus* (Occasional Paper 27). Washington, DC: Council for Basic Education.

Gallagher, S., Stepien, W. J., & Rosenthal, H. (1992). The effects of problem-based learning on problem solving. *Gifted Child Quarterly, 36*, 195–200.

Gardner, H. (1983). *Frames of mind: The theory of multiple intelligences*. New York: Basic Books.

Grun, B. (1979). *The timetables of history: A horizontal linkage of people and events*. New York: Simon & Schuster.

Guskey, T. (1986). Staff development and the process of teacher change. *Educational Researcher, 15*, 5–12.

Hathaway, W. (1985). "Model for school–university collaboration: National and local perspectives on collaboratives that work." Material prepared for a symposium presented at the annual meeting of the American Educational Research Association.

Johnson, D., & Johnson, R. (1990). Social skills for successful group work. *Education Leadership, 47*, 29–32.

Jones, B., & Maloy, R. (1988). *Partnerships for improving schools*. New York: Greenwood Press.

Kagan, S. (1988). *Cooperative learning: Resources for teachers*. Riverside: University of California.

Lathlaen, P. (1990). The national board for professional teaching standards and possible implication for gifted education. *Journal for the Education of the Gifted, 14*, 50–65.

Levin, R. (1992). *Educational assessment: Expanded expectations and challenges*. Los Angeles: UCLA Center on Research in Evaluation.

Linn, R. L. (1993). Educational assessment: Expanded expectations and challenges. *Educational Evaluation and Policy Analysis, 15*(1), 1–16.

Marland, S. (1972). *Education of the gifted and talented: Volume 1. Report to the U.S. Congress by the U.S. Commissioner of Education*. Washington, DC: Government Printing Office.

Martinson, M. (1982). Interagency services: A new era for an old idea. *Exceptional Children, 48*, 389–394.

Oakes, J. (1985). *Keeping track*. New Haven, CT: Yale University Press.

Plomin, R. (1989). Environment and genes: Determinants of behavior. *American Psychologist, 44*, 105–111.

Pritchard, M. (1951). The contributions of Leta S. Hollingworth to the study of gifted children. In P. Witty (Ed.), *The gifted child* (p. 84). Boston: D. C. Heath & Company.

Schnitzer, S. (1993). Designing an authentic assessment. *Educational Leadership, 50*, 32–35.

Scott, J., & Smith, S. (1987). *Collaborative schools*. Paper prepared for ERIC Clearinghouse on Educational Management.

Shavelson, R., & Baxter, G. (1992). What we've learned about assessing hands-on science. *Educational Leadership, 49*, 20–25.

Sicola, P. (1990). Where do gifted students fit? An examination of middle school philosophy as it relates to ability grouping and the gifted learner. *Journal for the Education of the Gifted, 14*(1), 37–49.

Slavin, R. (1990a). Ability grouping, cooperative learning and the gifted. *Journal for the Education of the Gifted, 14*(1), 3–8, 28–30.

Slavin, R. (1990b). Research on cooperative learning: Consensus and controversy. *Educational Leadership, 47*, 52–54.

Stephens, T. (1992). The shadow of the future: Serving Ohio's gifted students. In *Challenges in Education*. Columbus: Ohio Department of Education.

Sternberg, R. (1986). *Beyond IQ: A teacher's theory of human intelligence.* Cambridge, England: Cambridge University Press.

Terman, L. (1916). *The measurement of intelligence.* Boston: Houghton Mifflin.

Terman, L. (1925). *Mental and physical traits of a thousand gifted children* (Vol. 1). Stanford, CA: Stanford University Press.

Trohanis, P. (Ed.). (1986). *Improving state technical assistance programs.* Chapel Hill, NC: The Technical Assistance Personnel Preparation System.

Tushman, M., & Romanelli, E. (1985). Organizational evolution: A metamorphosis model of convergence and reorientation. *Research in Organization Behavior, 7*, 171–222.

VanTassel-Baska, J. (1991a). Gifted education in the balance: Building relationships with general education. *Gifted Child Quarterly, 31*, 26–35.

VanTassel-Baska, J. (1991b). Serving the disabled gifted through educational collaboration. *Journal for the Education of the Gifted, 14*(3), 246–266.

Wechsler, D. (1974). *Manual for the Wechsler Intelligence Scale for Children–Revised.* San Antonio: Psychological Corporation.

West, J., Idol, L., & Cannon, G. (1989). *Collaboration in the schools.* Austin, TX: PRO-ED.

Witty, P. (Ed.). (1951). *The gifted child.* Boston: D.C. Heath.

# Chapter 2

# The Changing Developmental Needs of the Gifted: Birth to Maturity

**Elizabeth Maxwell**

◆ ◆ ◆

TO MANY PEOPLE, the term *giftedness* implies superior ability found in individuals who are otherwise like everyone else. We expect the emotional needs, developmental stages, and life experiences of these individuals to be "within normal limits" and to follow the same patterns as with the great majority of other human beings. This might be called the Fairy Godmother Theory of Giftedness: A lucky Cinderella here or Pinocchio there is touched with magic, but basically only wants to meet her prince or to be a real boy like everyone else.

Thus, it is said that gifted children are children first and gifted second and that, in the basic, human things that count, we are all alike. Undoubtedly there *is* a great pool of human experience that we all share, and there are truly important ways in which we *are* alike, as Maslow (1954), with his hierarchy of needs, for instance, has pointed out. However, this global view may not yield as helpful or clear a picture of the differences and real needs of actual gifted individuals as does a developmental point of view. When we investigate the experience of gifted persons, we see giftedness as much more complex. It permeates the whole being and alters life experience in ways that are important to consider. Understanding qualitative differences in the lives of the gifted not only helps us understand the population better, but it enriches and broadens our understanding of human nature in general.

## A DEVELOPMENTAL DEFINITION

A new definition of giftedness, which recognizes the complexity and the vulnerabilities of giftedness, is coming to the fore:

> Giftedness is asynchronous development in which advanced cognitive abilities and heightened intensity combine to create inner experiences and awareness that are qualitatively different from the norm. This asynchrony increases with higher intellectual capacity. The uniqueness of the gifted renders them particularly vulnerable and requires modifications in parenting, teaching and counseling in order for them to develop optimally. (The Columbus Group, 1991)

These two basic components—the *complexity* of experiencing different mental, emotional, social, and physical ages, which must somehow be integrated, together with that *intensity* so noticeable in the gifted—combine in ever more intricate ways to create experience that is different. This difference is more likely to increase with maturation, although proficiency in masking it may make it less noticeable as life experience is gained.

Giftedness, especially in terms of advanced cognitive development, has two sides to it, in that gifted children experience different needs as well as the positives that go with the territory. In this chapter, I examine some of these needs, using a developmental framework. The realization that a child can be many ages at the same time may also alert those who work with the gifted that the usual developmental stages and timetables are probably not especially helpful in dealing with this population.

# EARLY CHILDHOOD

## Advanced Cognition

Even in infancy, developmental differences are often detectable (Lewis & Brooks-Gunn, 1981; Storfer, 1990; Tannenbaum, 1992). Many parents of gifted children report that, almost from birth, their youngsters exhibited greater intensity and awareness. Their babies smiled early and recognized caregivers early. They reacted with greater intensity to noises, frustration, and stimulation (Rogers, 1986). They were prone to colic. They napped less frequently and were harder to put to sleep (Munger, 1990).

Ear infections are common in the lives of many young children, whether gifted or not. Not so common is the realization that these infections can have serious aftereffects, especially if chronic during those months when the child is learning to talk (Feagans, 1986). Because so many gifted children develop language early, at a time when the immune system is still building resistance to infection, it is highly possible that ear infections and language acquisition will coincide. A strong correlation exists between chronic ear infections and later problems with auditory processing (Downs & Blager, 1982). Following oral directions and explanations, sequencing, and time management may be impaired. However, these problems are often masked by the intact acuity and impressive vocabularies of gifted children. Also, the children's puzzle-solving ability may fill in the gaps in what they hear if contextual clues allow. Unless specific testing is done for auditory processing problems, the condition may go undetected. The "spacey," disorganized child who is bright but nonproductive may be a victim of ear infections that have caused a real disability (Silverman, 1989). Parents and pediatricians need to be alert to this danger. Causes of infection, such as possible allergies, should be investigated. Also, tubes should be considered for children with chronic ear infections, as they decrease the risk of aftereffects (Downs & Blager, 1982).

Advanced cognition also may lead to particular emotional difficulties. Morelock (1992a, 1992b) explained that children are usually protected from a too-early brush with reality both by their parents' "omnipotence" and by their own magical thinking. Most young children unconsciously accept the omnipotence of their parents, who can fix all hurts and make everything better. Gifted children, however, can discern the mistakes of adults around them from a very early age. They can reason that illness or death is possible for *anyone*, and the magic invulnerability that most children enjoy vanishes. Adding to the fear that such realizations bring is powerful imagination that contributes to dark and fearsome pictures. Such children may be extremely difficult to console. They *know* they and those they love are at risk. It is helpful for them to feel that their parents and other adults in their lives take their fears seriously and respect the depth of their concerns.

Our society likes to group children by age. There is a belief that children move through developmental stages at roughly the same time and that the age gauge works. This practice can make for difficult social situations for gifted children whose asynchrony places them on a different timetable. Often these children have a strong preference for play with older children or holding serious conversations with adults. Their interests and vocabulary are likely to be different from those of their age-mates (Hollingworth, 1931). If gifted children are expected to spend time with children their own age, particularly in a play group or prekindergarten situation, they are likely to act out their frustration or withdraw; then they are seen as antisocial. If placed with older children or with equally advanced children, however, gifted children bloom socially.

A look at the stages of moral development as set forth by Lawrence Kohlberg further illustrates differences between gifted and nongifted children. Through empirical studies involving moral issues, Kohlberg

(1984) noted six stages of moral growth. Gifted children usually do not respond well to the first stage, which is based on reward and punishment. Although they themselves may be excellent manipulators, they resist being manipulated, and are more likely to operate at the second stage of bargaining. Then, when other children their age may be into bargaining, they may well have advanced to the rule-bound law-and-order stage, and expend much energy trying to get their playmates to play by an elaborate set of rules, which they just happen to have memorized. This usually does not make for popularity. Then, when age-mates do become interested in the challenge of playing by the rules, gifted children have moved ahead to a realization of the complexity of life and see rules as two-dimensional and silly. All along the line, they are "out of sync" with their age-mates. Their asynchrony and ill fit with social norms increase their vulnerability to the belief that something is wrong with them.

## Overexcitabilities

Intensity is an outstanding characteristic of the gifted, becoming heightened in proportion to the degree of cognitive development (The Columbus Group, 1991; Morelock, 1992b; Silverman, 1993a). Noted by parents and many who work with this population (Piechowski, 1991a, 1991b), intensity permeates the lives of the gifted, showing up in strong concentration, deep emotional sensitivity, persistent curiosity, elation or anguish, enthusiasm or inhibition (Piechowski, 1979). A theory of emotional development that takes note of such intensity was delineated by Polish psychologist and psychiatrist Kazimerz Dabrowski (1902–1980), who recognized such intensity in school children he observed, as well as in creative artists who were his clients. He theorized that this intensity signaled a strong potential to reach advanced levels of development (Dabrowski, 1964, 1972). His Polish term for these energies translates into *overexcitabilities*, a superabundance of responsiveness to stimuli in five dimensions: psychomotor, sensual, emotional, imaginative, and intellectual. Gifted individuals may display intensities in some or all of these five dimensions, with some channels more active than others. In general, they demonstrate drive toward action; deep and rich response to sensory stimuli; intense feelings, fears, joys, and caring; vivid and extensive fantasy life; and a mind that simply will not quit because there are too many fascinating things that compel investigation.

Research comparing overexcitabilities (OEs) has found a greater incidence of OEs in gifted children and adults than in comparison populations, such as graduate students in counseling psychology or chemical engineers or even artists (Felder, 1982; Gallagher, 1985; Miller, Silverman, & Falk, in press; Piechowski & Colangelo, 1984; Piechowski, Silverman, & Falk, 1985). Particularly noticeable were heightened emotional overexcitabilities—the capacity for strong feelings, for empathy, compassion, and recognition of relationship. It is important to realize that deep emotionality, moral sensitivity, and powerful imagination often coexist with advanced cognition. It is the whole person who is gifted, and the whole personality is qualitatively changed.

Overexcitabilities and intensities can startle and even alarm others. These behaviors are not easy to live with, although they do make life interesting. Nevertheless, the intensity of overexcitabilities—intense caring, strong frustration at limitations, immersion in some project or area of investigation, a rich fantasy life that can even mix fact and fiction, inconsolable grief at a pet's death, total delight in the shape of a snowflake—is normal for gifted children. These behaviors do not need to be "fixed." Great care needs to be taken to sort out real psychological problems, which certainly occur in all populations, from the natural heightened intensity and sensitivity that correlate positively with the degree of giftedness.

## Self-Esteem Issues

Many people are surprised that gifted children tend to have lower self-esteem than would be expected. Often the greater the degree of giftedness, the lower the self-esteem. Poor environmental feedback is an important factor in this phenomenon. An individual's self-concept and self-respect are based in large part on how others accept and respond to him or her. Although most parents of gifted children provide them with love, appreciation, and advocacy, other children, the school, and the community at large may be giving quite different feedback. Where there is a poor fit between the child and a given group, the child often receives feedback that he or she does not fit, that he or she needs to change, *that it is not all right to be oneself.* It is not the differences caused by asynchrony that are the problem—these undoubtedly are noticed and questioned at an early age by bright minds. The problem is that differences are not accepted and that the child's self is not accepted.

Gifted children also feel estranged when the easy camaraderie of shared experience, likes and dislikes, jokes and humor is missing. Such camaraderie is difficult where vocabulary, humor, and ideas go over the heads of other children and sometimes even of teachers or other important adults. A child in such a position has the choice to pull back and not really share or to maintain integrity and become a loner. One of the major benefits of placement in a gifted program is the positive feedback and reassurance that one is all right as a self and a human being (Higham & Buescher, 1987). This benefit is even more important than the challenge given to intellectual growth. Gifted children, with their emotional overexcitability, need deeply caring friends who can match their complexity, enjoy the fantasy, and catch allusions on the fly. Parents, counselors, and teachers need to remember that gifted children are sensitively vulnerable to the feedback of others, and that this vulnerability increases with the degree of giftedness.

## Other Common Characteristics

### Stubbornness

One type of gifted child is often labeled stubborn and willful. Such children begin very early to know exactly what they want and to go after it. Usually, they will not be deflected from their goal by some diversionary tactic. They may throw tantrums and display intense frustration when they are not allowed to do what they choose; however, they rarely are being naughty or willfully difficult. They simply have the mental ability to concentrate on a goal and not let go until it is accomplished. Their persistence is remarkable. Often they are quite capable of achieving sought-after goals, having skills and abilities that parents do not acknowledge because the children are considered "too young" to be able to do what they actually can do.

### Perfectionism

Gifted children often are perfectionistic, as well. Undoubtedly, it is difficult to live with perfectionists. It is hard to watch their frustration and emotional intensity when they insist that no errors are allowable. These children may anguish over coloring gone awry, tear up the paper, and start over yet again, or maybe smash the clay figure because the shape their fingers form simply will not equal the shape pictured in their mind's eye. Some shy away from attempting anything that they fear they cannot do perfectly from the start, thus severely hampering their ongoing learning. Outsiders may judge that parental standards are too high, and parents, aware of their own perfectionism, may take this to heart, but in most cases, the high expectations lie within the child and are not imposed by the parents (Kerr, 1991; Silverman, 1983). These children have the intellectual capacity to compare the picture in their head with the product botched by their motor skills. Their asynchrony is jarring them. Because of their advanced cognitive abilities, they feel more on a par with adults and expect adult-like results, but their bodies will not cooperate.

How can adults help gifted children who are perfectionistic? Both parents and teachers need to understand that excellence *does* matter to the child. Adults can soothe some of the pain by letting the child know they appreciate the fine picture in the mind. They can also share that many creative people endure the same problem. Perfectionism is the hallmark of giftedness (Silverman, 1983). It stands out as a characteristic of gifted children and adults, and the pain of perfective endeavors is part of being gifted.

### Sensitivity

Emotional sensitivity may also be seen as a problem for gifted children. The child is said to be "too thin-skinned" or "overreacting." The stratospheric highs and abysmal lows may lead to some fear of bipolar disorder. Although this disorder is a possibility, the situation needs to be closely examined because intense emotions are normal for gifted children. These reactions are at the other end of the continuum from stolidity, callousness, and dullness. Emotionality is a natural overexcitability. It holds promise that this child is capable of becoming a caring adult, able to be compassionate and committed to responsive and responsible action in the world. Gifted children need to be reassured that feelings are important, and that many things the world values most—art, literature, social reform, and the ability to nurture—grow out of feelings deeply held. Dabrowski (1994) spoke of such "heroism of sensitivity" that has the power to bring about real changes in an often unfeeling world.

## Dealing with Gifted Children's Differences: Reframing

We have been looking at ways in which gifted children are different from other children and showing how these differences have legitimacy. They stem from the innate dynamics of the children's development. The powerful tools that are the natural possessions of these children—powerful tools such as abstract reasoning, nonstop curiosity, goal orientation, and the visualization of excellence—must and do create different successes and different problems. Part of these problems stem from the interpretation put upon their differences by others. Adults who care about these children can learn to see them in the best light. Where adults understand the dynamics at play, there can be real acceptance. Then there can be effective problem solving that still respects who the child is and his or her right to be that way.

Viewpoints and attitudes can be enlightened through *reframing*, a technique used by many psychologists and refined within Neuro-Linguistic Programming (Bandler & Grinder, 1979, 1982). Reframing changes either the content or the meaning of a situation to align with the positive intention involved. Reframing can diminish some of the power struggles and attempts to change the innate nature of children. Seen positively, this nature becomes an ally in seeking win–win situations.

Reframing sees sensitivity as a precursor of empathy and understanding that is more than skin deep. It notes the drive toward excellence at the heart of perfectionism and helps the gifted child prioritize what is best perfected. Positive reframing acknowledges the inner-directedness and goal orientation of gifted children as a strength. The children are accepted as having the focus, concentration, and ability to plan and carry out skilled action. They are tomorrow's leaders, who may be difficult to live with today, but who already possess skills that many adults would like to have. Positive reframing more readily gives them the early responsibility that they crave and often handle well.

## LATER CHILDHOOD

Asynchrony does not lessen as gifted children mature. Usually it deepens. These children tend to become better at the things they do well and to fall farther behind in weaker skills. The internal disparity increases as mental ability leaps ahead while emotional age ranges from adult wisdom to infantile playfulness and petulance. Social, physical, and chronological ages still differ. Parts of the child will be out of sync with other parts, and the whole child will be out of sync with age-mates. The child's feeling that something is wrong with him or her is likely to increase.

Gifted children may try to fit in by holding back their abilities. They may become antisocial, or develop coping skills and strategies that partially meet their needs and partially leave needs unmet. Where their environment allows them to be part of a group of similar children, where their mental need for complexity and challenge is met, where they feel it safe to allow their feelings to show, gifted children thrive and blossom. This usually does not make life any simpler for themselves and for parents, teachers, or other significant adults, but it makes life positive, exciting, and full of growth.

Both boys and girls who are gifted are highly sensitive. Both also often have good ideas and may find themselves trying to direct others, because their leadership just makes sense to them. Often, we encourage sensitivity in girls and leadership in boys, but not the other way around. It is very important to nurture and promote both qualities in boys and girls alike. Boys have a right to their emotionality, and need not to be seen as immature because they feel deeply. Especially, they should not be held back from early entrance or acceleration on such grounds. A year of boredom at tasks they have grown beyond will not change their emotional sensitivity. Girls, on the other hand, have a right to try out their leadership skills without being discriminated against as being "bossy," a term seldom applied to boys (Silverman, 1993b).

Friendship is another area in which developmental differences may cause problems. Gifted children may have expectations about friendship that are in line with their emotional overexcitability and their tendency to operate at a higher moral level. Consequently, they may be seeking a different kind of friendship and be repelled by the power plays and shifting alliances that are a familiar part of childhood. Many gifted children, for all their intellectual ability, simply do not understand what all this jockeying for favor is about. They give and look for trust and open sharing, and often when they find a similar companion, make a friend for life. In the absence of such a true friend, they may need help understanding the concept of having different kinds of friends for different situations: neighborhood play friends, school friends, chess club friends, and so forth (Roedell, 1985).

Asynchronous development continually pressures gifted children to balance inner complexity, as well as to deal with a sometimes bewildering environment. The ambiguity the environment can present to a mind that perceives possibilities on many levels is unsettling. It necessitates a sorting-out process: What kind of a response is expected on what level and in how much depth? Small talk and social ritual are particularly treacherous. It is difficult to think of what to say that is appropriately trivial when a mind is filled with interesting ideas bursting to be shared. Some gifted children learn to play the social game at an early age, but many struggle for years to be socially savvy.

# ADOLESCENCE

Adolescence is well known as a stormy time of life. This is no less true for the gifted adolescent, already working to cope with inner and outer complexity. The gifted adolescent has to contend with the common adolescent issues of finding one's own identity and establishing intimacy, in addition to others, such as making career choices in the light of multiple potential, or leaving home early because of acceleration.

Paradoxically, adolescent issues often surface early in gifted children. Leta Hollingworth (1931) observed that when children reach a mental age of 12, which might be anywhere from age 6 to 10 for a gifted or highly gifted child, questions arise concerning religion, morality, sexuality, and existential issues. Gifted children may have been reading on an adult level for years and struggling to comprehend adult mores. At the same time, many gifted adolescents go through a period of trying to hold on to childhood. Although they have mentally rehearsed the issues before them, they may be more fully aware of the hazards and difficulties ahead than are others their age, and may shrink from leaving the caring intimacy of their families.

Adolescence poses special problems for girls. Gilligan (1991) noted that, with the onset of adolescence, girls tend to lose their former self-confidence and to speak their thoughts and opinions far less frequently, especially in coeducational situations. They realize that it is no longer socially safe. For gifted girls it is doubly unsafe. It is well known that the number of girls in gifted classes declines in junior high and high school (Read, 1987), although in elementary school there tends to be an equal number of boys and girls in such classes. The gifted girls have gone underground. They have begun "degifting" themselves, closing doors for themselves. In adulthood they may genuinely think that their earlier abilities were fleeting. It is extremely important that gifted girls come in contact with empowered gifted women who can serve as life models for them (Hollinger, 1991; Phelps, 1991).

Gifted adolescents of both sexes are generally more resistant to peer pressure. They reason well and are able to envision the outcomes of their actions. Their emotional intensity and their moral sensitivity may, however, bring them face-to-face with philosophical and psychological issues that stress them exceedingly. They are vulnerable to existential depression and even to suicide (Delisle, 1990; Kerr, 1991; Webb, Meckstroth, & Tolan, 1982), and any indicators of such pain should be taken extremely seriously. A group of peers or a sympathetic mentor who will listen and discuss on an adult level will be invaluable.

# ADULTHOOD

The results of the asynchronous experience do not go away upon reaching adulthood. People cannot unlearn what they know or change the experiences they have had. The richness, the complexity, the interior struggle, the depth of perception, and the intensity that characterized the growing up years remain a part of the gifted person. The realization of differences from many others in the environment and consequent self-doubt will likely remain, although there is more freedom to seek out truly compatible friends and co-workers.

On the positive side, the gifted adult is likely to have a more acutely aware consciousness, partly the result of years of concerted effort to balance conflicting energies. It is quite possible that gifted individuals tend to relegate less to habit and to remain more consciously alert and more keenly perceptive than those who lead less emotionally strenuous lives. They have the potential to be more focused and alive. This may be a compensatory reward for asynchronous experience. It holds the possibility of leading a more examined life, of being less prey to introjections and programming, and of being a few steps further on the way to inner authority and authenticity. The challenge of becoming authentic and of actualizing their own potential will continue to be an intense, compelling, difficult, and creatively rewarding enterprise for gifted adults for the rest of their lives.

# EFFECTIVE INTERVENTION

Both preventive and therapeutic interventions are based on recognition of needs. Most fundamental is the need for gifted individuals to be seen and recognized in a positive light—the same enhancement of self-esteem that nourishes all people. Positive reframing of otherwise negatively viewed traits, such as perfectionism, intensity, sensitivity, and love of complexity, is really just reflecting acceptance of gifted individuals' right to be who they are. Because gifted youngsters are acutely and vulnerably aware of their differences, such acceptance is both nurturing and therapeutic. Support personnel have an important role to play in interpreting the traits and behaviors of gifted children to teachers, administrators, and parents, and to the children themselves. An understanding of overexcitabilities (Dabrowski, 1964, 1972) or of being a step ahead in Kolhberg's (1984) levels of moral development can further a whole new approach on the part of teachers and parents. Also, counseling that begins with positive reframing aimed at helping a gifted child feel understood has a greater chance of being effective.

Support personnel familiar with disabilities are positioned to investigate underachievement associated with such conditions as auditory processing problems or visual-motor difficulties. It is important they recognize that gifted children may also be learning disabled. Even though the disabilities of gifted children may not be severely below grade level, when viewed in relation to abilities, a whole new picture may emerge regarding behavior or emotional problems of this population (Silverman, 1989). Professionals who understand the developmental differential of gifted children are in a better position to detect disabilities behind "spaciness" or "laziness" or "tuning out."

Support personnel, administrators, and teachers can work together to ensure that gifted children will have a true peer group, even if small, within their classrooms. The policy of distributing very bright children among many classrooms on the theory that they should learn to fit in may result in painful isolation. Given their asynchrony and their resulting vulnerability, gifted children truly need to share with mental-age peers. Self-contained gifted classes meet this need best. Other solutions may be cross-age grouping, ad hoc project groups, acceleration, or even lunchtime discussion groups that meet informally with a teacher or counselor (Peterson, 1990). The truth that developmentally appropriate peers for gifted children are other gifted children or mental-age peers should be central to placement policy.

# CONCLUSION

Support personnel, along with other educators and parents, play crucial roles in helping gifted children develop into the highly complex, caring, perceptive, responsive, and responsible leaders of tomorrow that they show promise of becoming. Adults' positive feedback, respectful engagement in collaborative problem solving, and enlightened advocacy are truly needed by these children. Recognition of the needs of gifted individuals commensurate with their asynchronous growth can make a real difference in how fully they express their potential in the future.

# REFERENCES

Bandler, R., & Grinder, J. (speakers). (1979). *Frogs into princes: Neurolinguistic programming* (Transcript of audiotapes edited by J. O. Stevens, Ed.). Moab, UT: Real People Press.

Bandler, R., & Grinder, J. (1982). *Reframing.* Moab, UT: Real People Press.

Columbus Group. (1991, July). Unpublished transcript of the meeting of the Columbus Group, Columbus, OH.

Dabrowski, K. (1964). *Positive disintegration.* London: Gryf.

Dabrowski, K. (1972). *Psychoneurosis is not an illness.* London: Gryf.

Dabrowski, K. (1994). Heroism of sensitivity (E. Hyzy-Strzekecka, Trans.). *Advanced Development, 6,* 87–92.

Delisle, J. R. (1990). The gifted adolescent at risk: Strategies and resources for suicide prevention among gifted youth. *Journal for the Education of the Gifted, 13,* 212–228.

Downs, M., & Blager, F. B. (1982). The otitis prone child. *Developmental and Behavioral Pediatrics, 3,* 106–109.

Feagans, L. (1986). Otitis media: A model for long term effects with implications for intervention. In J. Kavanaugh (Ed.), *Otitis media and child development.* Parkton, MD: York Press.

Felder, R. F. (1982, October). *Responses of gifted education and chemical engineering graduate students on the OEQ and DRI*. Paper presented at the National Association for Gifted Children Conference, New Orleans.

Gallagher, S. A. (1985). A comparison of the concept of over-excitabilities with measures of creativity and school achievement in sixth grade students. *Roeper Review, 8,* 115–119.

Gilligan, C. (1991). Women's psychological development: implications for psychotherapy. In C. Gilligan, A. G. Rogers, & D. L. Tolman (Eds.), *Women, girls and psychotherapy: Reframing resistance* (pp. 5–31). New York: Haworth Press.

Higham, S. J., & Buescher, T. M. (1987). What young gifted adolescents understand about feeling "different." In T. M. Buescher (Ed.), *Understanding gifted and talented adolescents: A resource guide for counselors, educators and parents* (pp. 26–30). Evanston, IL: Center for Talent Development, Northwestern University.

Hollinger, C. L. (1991). Facilitating the career development of gifted young women. *Roeper Review, 13,* 135–139.

Hollingworth, L. S. (1931). The child of very superior intelligence as a special problem in social adjustment. *Mental Hygiene, 15,* 1–6.

Kerr, B. A. (1991). *A handbook for counseling the gifted and talented*. Alexandria, VA: American Counseling Association.

Kohlberg, L. (1984). *The psychology of moral development*. New York: Harper & Row.

Lewis, M., & Brooks-Gunn, J. (1981). Visual attention at three months as a predictor of cognitive functioning at two years of age. *Intelligence, 5,* 131–140.

Maslow, S. H. (1954). *Motivation and personality*. New York: Harper & Row.

Miller, N. B., Silverman, L. K., & Falk, R. F. (in press). Emotional development and intellectual ability. *Journal for the Education of the Gifted*.

Morelock, M. J. (1992a, February). *The child of extraordinarily high IQ from a Vygotskian perspective*. Paper presented at the Esther Katz Rosen Symposium on the Psychological Development of Gifted Children, University of Kansas, Lawrence.

Morelock, M. J. (1992b). Giftedness: The view from within. *Understanding Our Gifted, 4,* 1, 11–15.

Munger, A. (1990). The parent's role in counseling the gifted: The balance between home and school. In J. VanTassel-Baska (Ed.), *A practical guide to counseling the gifted in a school setting* (2nd ed., pp. 57–65). Reston, VA: Council for Exceptional Children.

Peterson, J. S. (1990, July/August). Noon-hour discussion: Dealing with the burdens of capability. *G / C / T, 13*(4), 17–22.

Phelps, C. R. (1991). Identity formation in career development for gifted women. *Roeper Review, 13,* 140–141.

Piechowski, M. M. (1979). Developmental potential. In N. Colangelo & R. T. Zaffrann (Eds.), *New voices in counseling the gifted* (pp. 25–57). Dubuque, IA: Kendall/Hunt.

Piechowski, M. M. (1991a). Emotional development and emotional giftedness. In N. Colangelo & G. Davis (Eds.), *A handbook of gifted education* (pp. 285–306). Boston: Allyn & Bacon.

Piechowski, M. M. (1991b, May). *Giftedness for all seasons; Inner peace in a time of war*. Presented at the Henry B. and Jocelyn Wallace National Research Symposium on Talent Development, University of Iowa, Iowa City.

Piechowski, M. M., & Colangelo, N. (1984). Developmental potential of the gifted. *Gifted Child Quarterly, 28*, 80–88.

Piechowski, M. M., Silverman, L. K., & Falk, R. F. (1985). Comparison of intellectually and artistically gifted on five dimensions of mental functioning. *Perceptions and Motor Skills, 60*, 539–549.

Read, C. R. (1987). *Gender distribution in programs for the gifted: A national survey of the proportions of boys and girls in public school programs for the gifted in 1985–1986*. Unpublished doctoral dissertation, University of Denver, Denver, CO.

Roedell, W. C. (1985). Developing social competence in gifted preschool children. *Remedial and Special Education, 6*, 6–11.

Rogers, M. T. (1986). *A comparative study of developmental traits of gifted and average children*. Unpublished doctoral dissertation, University of Denver, Denver, CO.

Silverman, L. K. (1983). Personality development: The pursuit of excellence. *Journal for the Education of the Gifted, 6*(1), 5–19.

Silverman, L. K. (1989). Invisible gifts, invisible handicaps. *Roeper Review, 22*, 37–42.

Silverman, L. K. (1993a). The gifted individual. In L. K. Silverman (Ed.), *Counseling the gifted and talented* (pp. 3–28). Denver, CO: Love.

Silverman, L. K. (1993b). Social development, leadership and gender issues. In L. K. Silverman (Ed.), *Counseling the gifted and talented* (pp. 291–327). Denver, CO: Love.

Storfer, M. (1990). *Intelligence and giftedness*. San Francisco: Jossey-Bass.

Tannenbaum, A. J. (1992). Early signs of giftedness: Research and commentary. *Journal for the Education of the Gifted, 15*, 104–133.

Webb, J. T., Meckstroth, E. A., & Tolan, S. S. (1982). *Guiding the gifted child: A practical source for parents and teachers*. Columbus: Ohio Psychology.

# *Part II*

# Assessment, Identification, and Evaluation Issues

# Chapter 3

# Changing Conceptions of Intelligence and Their Impact Upon the Concept of Giftedness: The Triarchic Theory of Intelligence

**Robert J. Sternberg**

◆   ◆   ◆

PEOPLE TEND to think of intelligence as analogous to temperature—as something that is quantifiable as a one-dimensional construct. Although a thermometer may be a more valid and reliable instrument for measuring temperature than is a conventional intelligence test for measuring intelligence, the basic idea is often viewed as the same.

I would like to argue, in contrast, that intelligence is more analogous to weather. Knowing the temperature gives us one piece of information—an important one—regarding the weather as a whole, but it does not tell us everything we want to know. Some of the other aspects of weather are fairly easily quantifiable: air pressure, wind speed, humidity, and so on. Others, however, are quantifiable only with difficulty and imprecision: amount and type of cloud cover, for example. The same is true for intelligence.

Moreover, although there are certainly differences across regions in weather, just as there are across people in intelligence, the weather does not remain totally the same in a given region and may even shift over time, just as intelligence can fluctuate in a person from time to time. Intelligence is not stable, but is subject to change and even, like weather, to human intervention. Following this analogy, the gifted individual's intelligence might be analogous to the weather in the nicest parts of California!

# THE TRIARCHIC THEORY OF INTELLIGENCE

According to the triarchic theory of intelligence, three features of intelligence are particularly worthy of note, but within each of these three features are more specific aspects important in themselves (Sternberg, 1985, 1988). The aspects differ in how easily measurable they are, but all are important. In the following sections, I consider each subtheory of the triarchic theory.

## The Componential Subtheory

### Components and Feedback from Them

The general structure of the triarchic theory of intelligence is shown in Figure 3.1. The theory posits three basic kinds of information-processing components: metacomponents, performance components, and knowledge-acquisition components.

*Metacomponents* are the higher order, executive processes used to plan what one is going to do, monitor it while it is being done, and then evaluate it after it is finished. For example, if a child attempts to solve a mathematical word problem involving percentages, the child uses metacomponents to decide on the steps needed to solve the problem, to monitor the solution along the way (ensuring, e.g., that an answer that is to be expressed as a percentage does not exceed 100), and to evaluate the solution after it is reached (ensuring, e.g., that the percentage— say an interest rate—makes sense, given what the child knows about interest rates).

*Performance components* are the lower order, nonexecutive processes used to carry out the steps planned by the metacomponents, such as reading all of the problem before attempting its solution, multiplying a decimal answer by 100 to obtain a percentage, and the like. The performance components, then, actually get the work done.

*Knowledge-acquisition components* are the lower order, nonexecutive processes used to learn how to solve the problem in the first place. For example, in a percentage problem, they are the processes the student once used to learn the algorithms for solving percentage problems. They may also be used in solving the current problem if it has novel aspects that one must learn in order to reach a solution.

Metacomponents activate performance and knowledge-acquisition components, which in turn provide feedback to the metacomponents. For example, after deciding how to solve the problem (via metacomponents), the child goes ahead and solves it (via performance components). If the algorithm the child is using does not work, however, the feedback to the metacomponents indicates the need for a different algorithm, which the child then tries. If nothing the child knows works,

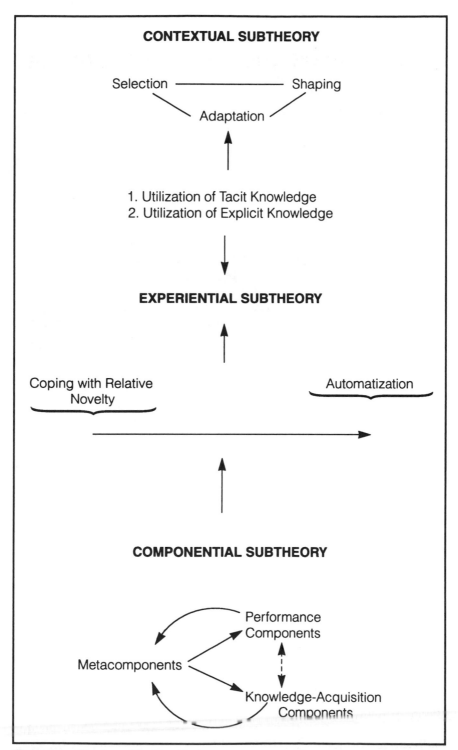

**Figure 3.1.** Structure of the triarchic theory.

then the metacomponents may direct the child to learn how to solve problems of this kind, thereby activating the knowledge-acquisition components.

### Implications for Giftedness

The componential subtheory suggests at least three potential sources of giftedness. The first is in the metacomponents: A person gifted in a metacomponential sense would be exceptionally adept at planning strategies for solving problems, representing information about problems, allocating resources in problem solving, monitoring work while solving problems, and evaluating problem solution after it is done. Several theories of giftedness, including my own, have emphasized the importance of metacomponential functioning in giftedness (e.g., Borkowski & Peck, 1986; Jackson & Butterfield, 1986; Sternberg, 1986). I personally believe that excellence in metacomponential functioning comes rather close to the psychometric notion of general intelligence (Spearman, 1927), measured by conventional intelligence tests.

A second source of giftedness would be in performance-componential functioning. Excellence in this area would be in actually executing steps, whether in solving mathematics problems, as in the above example, or in reading, writing, or other intellectual endeavors. This aspect of giftedness is not identical to the metacomponential one. Many of us have known students (or adults) who are very good at planning what they want to do, but not nearly as good at actually getting it done. Students who think well but make computation mistakes in mathematics, or who have good ideas but write poorly, are those whose metacomponential abilities exceed their performance-componential abilities.

A third source of giftedness is in knowledge-acquisition components. The notion that gifted children are fast learners is certainly an entrenched one in the giftedness literature (e.g., Stanley & Benbow, 1986). In the present view, however, not all gifted students are rapid learners and, moreover, those who are rapid learners are not necessarily the ones who are best able to use what they have learned. For example, a fast learner may be able to memorize material quickly but unable to exploit the material. This child might get an "A" in a foreign language or mathematics course, but still be unable to apply what was learned in the course.

The person who is strong in metacomponential, performance-componential, and knowledge-acquisition componential functioning in typical academic settings is referred to in the triarchic theory as *analytically gifted*. This is the most common form of giftedness seen in the schools. The typical analytically gifted student does well on tests, writes good papers, gets good grades, and generally conforms to the pattern that schools value. This type of child is the type most likely to be identified through conventional gifted identification procedures.

## The Experiential Subtheory

Components are always applied to experience. As shown in Figure 3.1, this experience varies from extremely novel to extremely familiar. In other words, some tasks that students confront are common (e.g., learning a list of spelling words), whereas other tasks are unusual (e.g., learning a new alphabet, such as the Cyrillic one). The experiential subtheory highlights that different aspects of intelligence are involved in learning at different points on the experiential continuum. It is important to note that these aspects of intelligence are probably somewhat domain specific. One may be good at coping with novelty in mathematics but not in verbal domains, or vice versa.

### Coping with Relative Novelty

According to the triarchic theory, problems that are relatively novel provide an excellent basis for measuring intelligence. If a problem is too novel, it does not provide a good measurement of intelligence because the student has nothing to bring to bear on the problem. Because they are too novel, calculus problems would not provide a good measure of intelligence for first graders. If a problem is routine, however, it does not provide the kind of challenge that is provided by something that is not only new, but new in kind.

### Automatization

Automatization occurs when a skill that was at one time conscious, controlled, and effortful becomes unconscious, automatic, and essentially effortless. A child who is first learning to read is likely to sound out syllables and words, but after a while, reading becomes effortless and automatic. The same applies when the child learns a foreign language. Similarly, when a person first learns to drive, the act of driving requires a great deal of attention; eventually, the person can drive, talk, and listen to the radio at the same time.

According to the triarchic theory, the ability to automatize is a second critical aspect of experiential intelligence. People need to automatize major portions of their behavior so that they have the mental resources left over to cope with what is new in their experience. Because mental resources are limited, the more people can automatize, the more they can process what is new, because they are consuming only minimal resources in executing automatized behavior.

### Implications for Giftedness

The experiential subtheory implies two additional kinds of giftedness: giftedness in coping with novelty and giftedness in automatization. The former is seen in insightful and flexible people. Again, extant theories of giftedness have recognized the importance of coping with novelty (see, e.g., Davidson, 1986; Feldhusen, 1986; Gruber, 1986; Sternberg, 1986); however, children who are strong in this area are not necessarily appreciated by schools, nor identified as gifted by conventional assessment procedures. Many of the types of problems appearing on typical ability tests are anything but novel, and tend to benefit the more prototypically gifted child who is good at remembering facts and analyzing arguments.

Giftedness in automatization is seen in a variety of ways that, on the surface, may appear to be quite unrelated. People who are gifted in learning and using foreign languages, or in dance, or in tennis, or in mathematical computation, may all be displaying, in different ways, very high levels of automatization in specialized domains. Note that, with regard to dance or tennis, the giftedness is not in the physical strength involved, but rather in the automatization of steps.

People who are gifted in coping with novelty are not necessarily gifted in automatization, and vice versa. Someone may be highly insightful, for example, but not a particularly fast reader or researcher. Similarly, some of the most automatized people are among the least able to cope with novelty. Indeed, too much emphasis upon automatization can lead to inflexibility and rigidity in one's approach to solving problems.

Someone who is strong in both of these aspects of experiential intelligence would be referred to in the triarchic theory as *synthetically* or *creatively gifted*. This person is good at coming up with new ideas and at seeing old problems in new ways. The most creative people have to have automatized a fairly large base of knowledge, because to go beyond where things are, one has to know where they are. Otherwise, one risks "reinventing the wheel." Creative people need to free their minds of the routine in order to be able to open their minds to the extraordinary.

In my opinion, creative giftedness is the most neglected asset of gifted children. Teachers never view themselves as devaluing creativity, but often they do little to foster it, or even to recognize it when it occurs. In this respect, they are no different from people in other occupations. Teachers, like lawyers or business managers, often have a set way in mind for things to be done, and come to expect that things be done this way. The problem is that, unlike lawyers or business managers, teachers are in an ideal position to be identifying and fostering creativity.

I believe that the problem with tests of creativity, such as the *Torrance Tests of Creative Thinking* (Torrance, 1966), that measure creativity in a relatively domain-free way, is that creativity virtually always occurs in a domain. People's creative abilities may differ vastly from one domain to another, although the evidence collected to date suggests at least some correlation between creative abilities across domains (Sternberg & Lubart, 1991).

## The Contextual Subtheory

### Adaptation to, Shaping of, and Selection of Environments

The contextual subtheory specifies that the components of intelligence are applied to experience so as to serve one of three functions in the environment: adaptation to existing environments, shaping of existing environments so as to change their form, and selection of new environments.

In adaptation, one changes oneself to fit into the environment as it exists. Institutions, including schools, tend to value people who adapt well, as they are the people who are seen as "fitting in." The consummate adapter learns how a system works, and then plays it to the hilt. Such adaptation requires one to learn the "tacit knowledge" of the system, or those facts about the system in which one works that are almost never directly taught and that usually are not even verbalized (Wagner & Sternberg, 1986).

In shaping, one changes the environment to suit oneself. One almost never encounters the "perfect" environment, whether as a student, a teacher, or a support professional. Children try to shape the behavior of other children, of their parents, and of their teachers to make the environment closer to what they ideally would like it to be.

In selection, one seeks out a new environment. Often, selection occurs when attempts at both adaptation and shaping have failed. For example, the child may be sent to a private school after all attempts to make the public school "work" for him have been futile. Or a psychologist may leave a school system because of the view that what is expected of her does not fit her idea of what a psychologist should do (e.g., doing nothing but IQ testing all day!).

### Implications for Giftedness

Practical giftedness is so little recognized in the context of the school that often it is not even seen as a form of giftedness at all. The future entrepreneur or chief executive officer is often seen as someone who was only an average student without any exceptional qualities. Unfortunately, the student is likely to remember the way he or she was viewed in school when it comes time to allocate money to the school system!

People who are excellent in applying their intelligence in context are not necessarily the same as those who are excellent in applying their intelligence abstractly. Any number of studies have suggested that people who are very successful in practical settings are not necessarily very successful in academic ones (e.g., Ceci & Liker, 1986; see essays in Sternberg & Wagner, 1986).

The consummate adapter in the school system is not necessarily an adapter outside of it, and vice versa. Especially in urban settings, the demands of the environment outside the school may be antisocial—for example, via gang activity or selling drugs—so that a juvenile who is running a successful business may be failing math in school. Often, such a youth needs to go outside the context of the school to have his or her giftedness recognized.

I believe that excellence in shaping is, if anything, more important than excellence in adaptation. The shaper is the potential leader in a field of endeavor—the person who convinces others to follow his or her path. The so-called greats in any field of endeavor—people like Picasso in art, or Hemingway in literature, or Einstein in science—are almost always shapers, in that the fields in which they work have borne their imprint. The field is no longer the same for their having worked in it. In contrast, most fields would change little if a typical contributor to them had decided to follow a different career.

Finally, knowing when to select a new environment is critical as well. Many people who show giftedness at one stage of their career, but then fade, are people who do not know when it is time to move on. The "near-misses," such as Donald Trump or Robert Maxwell, who gain and squander fortunes, almost never seem to know how to quit when they are ahead or to move on to some other kind of enterprise. Of course, there are people in my own profession of psychology who are the same way: Having proposed a theory early in their career, they can never leave it behind, no matter how much evidence may be adduced to refute it!

The *practically gifted person*, ideally, would be strong in all three aspects of adaptation, shaping, and selection, but I suspect that such individuals are rare. Most people who are adapters, for example, are not shapers, and vice versa. Thus, we need a concept of practical giftedness-ness that is not so restricted as to require a combination of skills that is extremely rare.

I believe that a more realistic take on practical giftedness is that the practically gifted person is someone who knows his or her strengths as well as limitations, and then capitalizes on strengths and compensates for weaknesses. In other words, the person knows in what areas he or she excels, and makes the most of these strengths. The person also recognizes areas of weakness and finds ways around these weaknesses, including having other people do what he or she does not do well. Thus, the practically gifted person is not necessarily good at everything, but is very good at something, and makes the most of that.

## ASSESSMENT OF TRIARCHIC ABILITIES

How does one identify the gifted using the triarchic theory of intelligence? There are basically two options. The first is to construct a test on the order of a conventional test, but broader. I have pursued this option, with a test described in Sternberg (1991). The test, comprising 12 subtests, is group administered. The 12 subtests are a cross between four aspects of information processing (componential-analytic, creative-synthetic, automatization, practical-contextual) and three different kinds of contents (verbal, quantitative, figural). Levels of the test range from the primary grade levels to college level.

Unfortunately, the test is still in preliminary form. We have a satisfactory form at the high school level (currently being construct validated), which we have been using for identification of the gifted for a summer program we are running, the results of which are described in the next section. We use the test in this case to distinguish between those who are more gifted in an analytic, synthetic, or practical sense, or who are balanced (high but not necessarily extremely high in all three). In general, the best use of the test is for obtaining not a single score, but rather scores representing a profile of abilities.

Although the exact kinds of items within a subtest vary by level, I provide examples here for the high school level. Each section is considered in turn.

The componential section is the most like a standard test of intelligence. The verbal subtest requires learning meanings of words from context, as when an unknown word is presented in the context of a paragraph; the quantitative subtest, completing number series; and the figural subtest, solving figural matrix problems. Note that verbal ability is measured by learning from context rather than by vocabulary, because we are more interested in the processes than the products of verbal abilities. In fact, most vocabulary is learned from context (Sternberg, 1987).

The coping-with-novelty section introduces items more unusual for an intelligence test. The verbal subtest consists of novel reasoning items. The subject is presented with a verbal analogy, but is asked to solve the analogy as though a particular presupposition were true. Half of the presuppositions are factual (e.g., canaries sing songs), and half are counterfactual (e.g., canaries play hopscotch). Those taking the exam must solve the analogies as though the presuppositions are true, whether or not they are. The quantitative subtest consists of number matrices with novel symbols. For example, the number 4 might be represented by a symbol such as ˆ , or the + operator might be represented by a symbol such as @. Subjects then need to complete the matrices, which mix familiar with novel symbols. The figural subtest consists of figural series that map symbols from a familiar to an unfamiliar domain. For example, the series might start off with a sequence of triangles, but then switch to circles. The student would have to complete the sequence with the circles.

The automatization section consists of verbal, quantitative, and figural items in which one must recognize two different symbols or sets of symbols (letter, numbers, abstract symbols) as belonging to either a single category or two different categories. For example, in the verbal subtest, one might have to recognize whether two different letters are both vowels.

The practical section also contains three subtests. The verbal section requires informal reasoning about advertisements, slogans, propaganda, and the like. For example, one boy might say to another that every member of one baseball team is better than every member of another team, and that therefore the first team is better than the second. Exam takers have to recognize whether there is an error of logic. The quantitative subtest involves practical mathematics. For example, children solve problems involving menus, bus schedules, train schedules, ticket purchases, and the like. The emphasis is not on what is known, but on how well what is known can be used in practical problem solving. Finally, the figural subtest requires route planning: Students see a map, and need to plan an efficient route to get certain things done in the geographic area represented by the map.

A second option for assessing triarchic abilities is to construct one's own tests, based upon the precepts of the theory. The only limitations for such testing are in the imagination of whomever devises the testing.

For example, componential abilities can be measured by essays that require analysis, comparing and contrasting, evaluation, and judgment. One might compare two literary characters, or analyze what makes things "valuable," or evaluate the strengths and weaknesses of various political views, and so on.

Synthetic abilities can be measured by creative essays, projects, inventions, compositions, and the like. One might ask children to write a short story, or an essay on what the world will be like in 500 years, or to design a small experiment, or to invent something, or to create a work of art.

Practical abilities can be measured by having students do leadership activities or projects that involve work in the school or community, or propose interventions to solve everyday problems. Even an essay addressed to a practical problem, such as how to improve our schools or how to solve problems of hunger, can provide a useful assessment of practical abilities.

I believe that tests of these kinds provide a useful supplement to the more conventional kinds of multiple-choice tests that we have traditionally used to assess abilities. I do not see them as replacing multiple-choice tests. Rather, different children excel in different kinds of testing media. To ensure that we are getting the best possible measurement of abilities without regard to testing medium, it is best to use "converging operations" and assess abilities through a variety of testing media.

# TEACHING OF TRIARCHIC ABILITIES

All of the abilities in the triarchic theory are teachable, to gifted as well as to other students. Teaching these abilities does not remove individual differences, in our experience (Davidson & Sternberg, 1984), but rather brings both gifted and nongifted groups to higher levels of functioning.

We have conducted programs that explicitly train componential abilities (Sternberg, 1987), insight abilities (Davidson & Sternberg, 1984), and practical abilities (Sternberg, Okagaki, & Jackson, 1990). In all cases, we have had considerable success: Experimental (trained) groups have gained significantly more from pretest to posttest than have control (untrained) groups.

Currently, we are engaged in our most ambitious project yet, which involves a combination of identification, training, and assessment. High school students are being identified as highly gifted in either the componential, the synthetic, or the practical domain, or in a balance of the three (i.e., not extremely high in any one, but rather high in all three), using the full set of tests described above. They are then being randomly assigned to a psychology course that emphasizes either analytical thinking (e.g., analyzing and comparing psychological theories), creative thinking (e.g., designing experiments), or practical thinking (e.g., designing community interventions and using psychology in everyday life). Finally, all students are assessed by tests measuring all of these aspects of abilities. The logic of the study is one of aptitude–treatment interaction—to determine whether by identifying, teaching, and assessing gifted students in ways that capitalize upon their strengths, we can obtain better educational outcomes than are currently being achieved.

In the summer of 1992, we ran a pilot program of 60 high school students. One-third were identified as analytically gifted, one-third as creatively gifted, and one-third as practically gifted via the multiple-choice and essay procedures described above. Although the pilot sample was small, the results were interesting. First, although the three subscores (analytic, creative-synthetic, practical) were correlated, the correlations were well below the reliabilities, so that we were able to identify distinct groups. Second, the proportion of minority students identified was higher than would typically be identified through only conventional tests of the more analytical abilities. Third, children in the analytic, synthetic-creative, and practical sections of the psychology course, overall, did equally well. Fourth, they differed, however, in what they did well. High creatives in the creative section did better on the creative assessments than did members of any other ability-treatment group, whereas low creatives in the creative section did worse on the creative assessments than did members of any other group. In other words, high creatives were able to benefit from the teaching, whereas low creatives probably would have better exploited the high abilities they had (analytical or practical) if they had been placed in a section that matched their abilities. High practicals in the practical section did better on the practical measures than did members of any other ability-treatment group. Interestingly, however, high analyticals did not do particularly well in the analytical section. In fact, the low analyticals did better! Why? Follow-up questioning revealed that the children identified as high analyticals were children who had always done well in school, many of them with very little work. They came into the summer course expecting to get by with very little work, and discovered that they were wrong!

These pilot results suggest that matching children in a way that enables them to capitalize upon their strengths and to compensate for or remediate their weaknesses makes practical as well as theoretical sense. Unfortunately, very few schools take this positive step toward helping children make the most of their abilities.

The need for more innovative forms of testing, such as those described in this chapter, is also shown by a study we recently completed on the predictive validity of the *Graduate Record Examination* (GRE) in the graduate psychology program at Yale. We found that, for students matriculating in this program over a period of 12 years, the GRE provided modest to moderate prediction of first-year (but not second-year) graduate grades. No surprise there, as many other studies have found the same. However, when the tests were used to predict graduate faculty ratings of students' analytic, creative, practical, overall research, and overall teaching abilities, prediction was trivial, with the possible exception of the analytic test. Moreover, what prediction was obtained for the analytic test was significant only for men, not for women. These results suggest that the "high-IQ" types who are so often identified as gifted may in fact get better grades throughout schooling, but may not be any better when it comes to the kinds of meaningful performances that matter in careers. Interestingly, a similar study in the economics department yielded almost identical results.

# CONCLUSION

The triarchic theory of intelligence serves as a basis for understanding, assessing, and teaching of gifted children. We are actively using the theory in our own research and intervention efforts and, of course, hope others will consider using it as well. Our goal, which follows directly from the theory, is to help gifted students do something that does not always come easily in schools as we now know them: to capitalize upon their strengths and compensate for or remedy whatever weaknesses they might have.

# ACKNOWLEDGMENTS

The work reported herein was supported under the Javits Act Program (Grant No. R206R00001) as administered by the Office of Educational Research and Improvement, U.S. Department of Education. The findings and opinions expressed in this chapter do not reflect the position or policies of the Office of Educational Research and Improvement or the U.S. Department of Education.

Thank you to Susan Papa for editorial assistance in preparation of this chapter.

# REFERENCES

Borkowski, J. G., & Peck, V. A. (1986). Causes and consequences of metamemory in gifted children. In R. J. Sternberg & J. E. Davidson (Eds.), *Conceptions of giftedness* (pp. 182–200). New York: Cambridge University Press.

Ceci, S. J., & Liker, J. (1986). Academic and nonacademic intelligence: An experimental separation. In R. J. Sternberg & R. K. Wagner (Eds.), *Practical intelligence* (pp. 119–142). New York: Cambridge University Press.

Davidson, J. E. (1986). The role of insight in giftedness. In R. J. Sternberg & J. E. Davidson (Eds.), *Conceptions of giftedness* (pp. 201–222). New York: Cambridge University Press.

Davidson, J. E., & Sternberg, R. J. (1984). The role of insight in intellectual giftedness. *Gifted Child Quarterly, 28,* 58–64.

Feldhusen, J. F. (1986). A conception of giftedness. In R. J. Sternberg & J. E. Davidson (Eds.), *Conceptions of giftedness* (pp. 112–127). New York: Cambridge University Press.

Gruber, H. E. (1986). The self-construction of the extraordinary. In R. J. Sternberg & J. E. Davidson (Eds.), *Conceptions of giftedness* (pp. 247–263). New York: Cambridge University Press.

Jackson, N. E., & Butterfield, E. C. (1986). A conception of giftedness designed to promote research. In R. J. Sternberg & J. E. Davidson (Eds.), *Conceptions of giftedness* (pp. 151–181). New York: Cambridge University Press.

Spearman, C. (1927). *The abilities of man.* New York: Macmillan.

Stanley, J. C., & Benbow, C. P. (1986). Youths who reason exceptionally well mathematically. In R. J. Sternberg & J. E. Davidson (Eds.), *Conceptions of giftedness* (pp. 361–387). New York: Cambridge University Press.

Sternberg, R. J. (1985). *Beyond IQ: A triarchic theory of human intelligence.* New York: Cambridge University Press.

Sternberg, R. J. (1986). A triarchic theory of intellectual giftedness. In R. J. Sternberg & J. E. Davidson (Eds.), *Conceptions of giftedness* (pp. 223–243). New York: Cambridge University Press.

Sternberg, R. J. (1987). Most vocabulary is learned from context. In M. G. McKeown & M. E. Curtis (Eds.), *The nature of vocabulary acquisition* (pp. 89–105). Hillsdale, NJ: Erlbaum.

Sternberg, R. J. (1988). *The triarchic mind: A new theory of intelligence.* New York: Viking-Penguin.

Sternberg, R. J. (1991). Theory-based testing of intellectual abilities: Rationale for the Triarchic Abilities Test. In H. Rowe (Ed.), *Intelligence: Reconceptualization and measurement* (pp. 183–202). Hillsdale, NJ: Erlbaum.

Sternberg, R. J., & Lubart, T. I. (1991). An investment theory of creativity and its development. *Human Development, 34,* 1–31.

Sternberg, R. J., Okagaki, L., & Jackson, A. (1990). Practical intelligence for success in school. *Educational Leadership, 48,* 35–39.

Sternberg, R. J., & Wagner, R. K. (Eds.). (1986). *Practical intelligence: Nature and origins of competence in the everyday world.* New York: Cambridge University Press.

Torrance, E. P. (1966). *Torrance Tests of Creative Thinking.* Bensenville, IL: Scholastic Testing Service.

Wagner, R. K., & Sternberg, R. J. (1986). Tacit knowledge and intelligence in the everyday world. In R. J. Sternberg & R. K. Wagner (Eds.), *Practical intelligence: Nature and origins of competence in the everyday world* (pp. 51–83). New York: Cambridge University Press.

# Chapter 4

# *Identifying High Ability/High Achievement Giftedness*

**Marlene Bireley**

◆ ◆ ◆

ALTHOUGH GIFTEDNESS occurs surprisingly frequently, many school support personnel have little training in identifying, programming, and serving the needs of this large population. Sattler (1988), for example, commited only 16 pages to this topic in his book *Assessment of Children*. Nearly three-fourths of surveyed National Association of School Psychologists members reported that they received little or poor training on tests of creativity, and nearly one-half reported they did not know enough about using tests to make placement decisions for children who are both gifted and learning disabled. Members reported a wide variety of training (from none to excellent) in the placement of gifted children, compared with consistently excellent training in the placement of children with learning disabilities (Klausmeier, Mishra, & Maker, 1987).

In a survey regarding current state practices in educating the gifted (Adderholdt-Elliott, Algozzine, Algozzine, & Haney, 1991), state consultants for the gifted reported a 26% "strong agreement" with the statement that school psychologists participate in identifying gifted students, while they strongly agreed that regular teachers and teachers of the gifted participate in this process 69% and 72%, respectively. About half of these same consultants reported that gifted students were identified by group achievement and ability tests, whereas slightly less than one-third reported primary use of individual tests for these purposes.

From the viewpoint of the practicing school psychologist, it is easy to understand these figures. Because federal and state mandates require primary attention to disabled students, psychologists are less likely to be directly involved in identifying gifted students. Additionally, the presumed good test-taking abilities of gifted students raise the question of the time and cost efficiency of individually assessing potential students in this population, especially in school districts where screening procedures might uncover as many as 5% to 20% of the total population as possible candidates for gifted programming.

My experience in both school psychology and gifted education has led me to believe that it is not necessary to test each gifted child individually. Neither do I believe that this population is served well when the entire responsibility for screening and identification is given to gifted education consultants, some of whom may have no direct training in tests and measurements. A typical consultant undertakes the identification task with trepidation and relatively unsophisticated skills.

Consequently, this process requires a middle-ground approach. Appropriate initial screening may be undertaken by using district group tests, but either school psychologists or school counselors need to assist novice gifted education consultants in acquiring and interpreting such results. Although the term "multifactored evaluation" is seldom used in the gifted education literature, gathering information from multiple sources is recommended. Integrating and interpreting quantifiable data with other information, such as teacher, parent, peer, or self-recommendations, or factoring in portfolio assessments or creativity tests or checklists, makes a formidable decision-making task. Similarly, underserved gifted populations require additional expertise. As discussed here and elsewhere in this book, unique measurement and programming problems that require input from assessment and exceptional population specialists are presented by underachieving, disadvantaged, disabled, and/or minority gifted; the highly gifted; and, in some cases, gifted females. When school psychologists and counselors are not in the decision-making loop, these underserved groups are less likely to be included in gifted education programs.

An extensive survey (Richert, Alvino, & McDonnel, 1982) of the identification practices of seven different groups of gifted education leaders and practitioners uncovered widespread misuse of instruments. Certain procedures were used to identify types of giftedness in ways in which the procedures were not intended. In some cases, instruments were used on inappropriate subpopulations, resulting in cultural bias. In other cases, instruments with inadequate ceilings were used. Richert et al. concluded, "Apparently, the state of the art of identification of gifted and talented youth is in some disarray" (p. 39). There is little reason to believe that the situation has improved dramatically in the decade since this study was completed.

# A SIDE ISSUE: THE CHANGING CONCEPT OF INTELLIGENCE

How do professionals differentiate the "good test taker" from the "truly gifted" individual? Present thinking clearly demands that assessment specialists examine long-held concepts of intelligence and, logically, those instruments that have been used to define intellectual behavior. A choice must be made. If professionals are to accept current theories—such as those of Sternberg (1988); Gardner (1983), who identified seven "intelligences"; or Naglieri and Das (1990), who believe that their PASS (planning–arousal–simultaneous–successive) cognitive processes can serve as a model for intelligence—traditional assessment procedures must eventually be broadened or replaced. Development of the prototypes is under way. They may hold the key to differentiating the good test taker from the truly gifted or, more specifically, the "knowledge-acquisition" gifted from the gifted executive planner and decision maker.

In the meantime, a body of literature exists that reveals certain patterns of test behavior when individual intelligence instruments are used with high-ability students. Knowing these patterns can serve as a useful backdrop for decision making regarding students who have been individually tested.

# SELECTING THE INSTRUMENT

Most state definitions of giftedness are direct adaptations or edited versions of the federal definition of giftedness (Marland, 1972) that includes demonstrated or potential high performance in the areas of general intellectual ability, specific academic aptitude, creative or productive thinking, leadership ability, or ability in the visual or performing arts. Problems abound in assessing these categories. Davis, in Chapter 5, discusses some of the approaches and problems in determining "creativity" in children. Identifying leadership ability presents even greater problems. Although not discussed in detail in this book, the responsibility for identifying the talented performer or artist has been given with increasing success to the teachers of these arts. In collaboration with gifted educators, such teachers are using auditions, portfolios, and various creativity tests and checklists to identify the gifted.

In the areas of general intellectual ability and specific academic aptitude, the challenges are to identify *potential* when ability is not clearly demonstrated, to balance the needs of the underserved gifted against those of other mandated demands upon the time of the school professionals, and to train support personnel to recognize and serve the needs of the gifted population with the same expertise that they demonstrate with other exceptional, and even average, populations. Part of this training may be simply to overcome that pervasive and erroneous stereotype that gifted children and youth are more than capable of "making it on their own" and therefore do not need special services.

To help meet these challenges, support personnel need to learn how to use results of individually administered intelligence tests. Research data exist regarding the applicability of each popular individual intelligence assessment to the gifted population and certain subpopulations. Test ceilings and test content become particularly critical issues with the gifted, as Silverman clearly demonstrates in Chapter 13. If the underserved populations described above are targeted for individual testing, test patterns, subtest spread, and cultural bias are important issues. A brief review of the literature regarding the use of major individual assessment instruments with the gifted follows.

## Kaufman Assessment Battery for Children

The *Kaufman Assessment Battery for Children* (K-ABC) (Kaufman & Kaufman, 1983) has two apparent, related weaknesses. Comparative studies with *The Stanford–Binet Intelligence Scale, Fourth Edition* (Stanford–Binet IV) (Thorndike, Hagen, & Sattler, 1986) or *The Stanford–Binet Intelligence Scale Form L-M* (Terman & Merrill, 1973) and the *Wechsler Intelligence Scale for Children–Revised* (WISC-R) (Wechsler, 1974) reveal consistently lower scores on the K-ABC (Hayden, Furlong, & Linnemeyer, 1988; McCallum, Karnes, & Edwards, 1984). Hayden et al. found nearly an 8-point discrepancy between the *Stanford–Binet IV* and the K-ABC and concluded that, for nearly half of their gifted subjects, six or more of the eight subtests had an inadequate ceiling. McCallum et al. (1984) found that children who had a mean score of 119.2 on the K-ABC Mental Processing Composite had previous mean WISC-R scores of 132 or mean *Stanford–Binet L-M* scores of 130.9.

Hessler (1985) cited several characteristics of the K-ABC that raise questions of its appropriateness with the gifted population. In addition to the low ceiling, he questioned if the reduction of cultural bias might be attributed to the lack of "important complex intellectual content," and hypothesized that the absence of the assessment of verbal reasoning and problem solving abilities and the lack of a comprehensive measure of achievement diminished its usefulness for this group.

## Stanford–Binet

Historically, the *Stanford–Binet* and gifted children have been linked, largely because of the relationship of Lewis Terman to both the *Stanford–Binet* and his epic longitudinal study of the gifted (Terman, 1925). The superiority of the *Stanford–Binet L-M* for early identification and the lack of an adequate ceiling for gifted adolescents were noted above. The heavy verbal weighting on this test tends to favor the "typical" gifted child and, when compared with the broader based *Stanford–Binet IV* and the WISC-R or WISC-III, higher IQs may result for this population. Silverman and Kearney (1992) recommended the continued use of the *Stanford–Binet L-M*, especially for younger and highly gifted children. (See Chapter 13 for an elaboration on these points.) On the other hand, Robinson (1992) contended that the updated norms and factorial structure of the *Stanford–Binet IV* outweigh its disadvantages, which, according to her, include less interesting material for younger students, a move from a developmental to a psychometric perspective, and inadequate ceilings for gifted populations.

Kluever and Green (1990) found significantly different results on the two tests when 51 gifted children were tested on both the *Stanford–Binet L-M* and the *Stanford–Binet IV*. The Abstract Reasoning score (121) was significantly lower than either the Verbal Reasoning or the Quantitative Reasoning score (135 and 132, respectively). These authors concluded that the *Stanford–Binet IV* would exclude from programs many children who were found eligible on the basis of a *Stanford–Binet L-M* score. They hypothesized that these differences might be accounted for by the inclusion of an area (visual reasoning) that can be considered a fluid ability rather than the "traditional" concept of giftedness as a combination of well-developed, crystallized abilities and precocious linguistic development. If the *Stanford–Binet IV* is used for identification, Kluever and Green suggested that eligibility requirements for gifted programs should be redefined and that the resulting group of identified children may have different characteristics and may need a different kind of curriculum.

In a comparison of the *Stanford–Binet L-M*, the *Stanford–Binet IV*, and two widely used group tests, the *Otis–Lennon Mental Ability Test* and the *Cognitive Abilities Test*, Tyler-Wood and Carri (1991) found that only 5 of 21 children met state criteria for the gifted on all four measures. Other findings were that the *Stanford–Binet L-M* tended to give the highest scores, nonverbal scores were significantly higher than verbal scores on the *Cognitive Abilities Test*, and the *Otis–Lennon* scores were significantly lower than scores on the *Stanford–Binet L-M*. This latter finding was supported by Linn and Lopatin

(1990), who found that the *Otis–Lennon* underestimated the *Stanford–Binet* IQ, with the difference becoming greater at higher levels.

In a study that compared scores for gifted students on the *Stanford–Binet IV*, the WISC-R, and the *SRA Educational Ability Series*, Carvajal and McKnab (1990) found a 10-point difference between the two individual tests, with higher scores on the WISC-R. In evaluating the group test for screening purposes, they found a .66 correlation between the SRA and the *Stanford–Binet IV* and concluded that, if a cutoff of 115 were used, the SRA was an adequate screening instrument.

### Slosson Intelligence Test

The *Slosson Intelligence Test* (SIT) (Slosson, 1971) is used by many consultants who wish to test beyond the group results but who do not have access to psychological services. A number of studies suggest, however, that the SIT may not have any great advantage over the group results. Karnes and Brown (1979) found a .48 correlation between the SIT and the WISC-R and concluded that, "at the lower end, SIT IQs tend to underestimate the WISC-R Full Scale IQ, while at the upper end they tend to overestimate the WISC-R Full Scale IQ" (p. 481). Clark, McCallum, Edwards, and Hildman (1987) found that the SIT had only "moderately" achieved the goal of increased concurrent validity with gifted children when the criterion was correlation with the *Stanford–Binet L-M* and the WISC-R. The publication of new versions of all three of these tests may have changed this situation somewhat, but the trend with the SIT appears to be that it produces scores lower than either the *Stanford–Binet* or the WISC.

### Wechsler Preschool and Primary Scale of Intelligence

The original and revised editions of the *Wechsler Preschool and Primary Scale of Intelligence* (WPPSI and WPPSI-R) (Wechsler, 1967, 1989) have received little attention in the assessment of the gifted, compared with the other major individual intelligence tests. One study (Speer, Hawthorne, & Buccellato, 1986) described the WPPSI patterns for 306 private school candidates in Atlanta. Like older children tested with various forms of the WISC, these subjects tended to have higher Verbal than Performance scores. The highest three scores were on the Vocabulary, Similarities, and Comprehension subtests (mean subscale scores ranged from 16.65 to 15.82) and the lowest three were on the Mazes, Animal House, and Block Design subtests (means ranged from 14.16 to 13.66). The authors concluded that the verbal superiority of gifted children was evident at an early age, but the performance score (overall mean of 129.56) could by no means be considered a weakness in this group.

## Wechsler Intelligence Scale for Children

The recent publication date of the *Wechsler Intelligence Scale for Children–Third Edition* (WISC-III) (Wechsler, 1991) limits the data available on this test. The WISC-III manual reports one small study that supports the conclusion that the new version may test lower than the WISC-R (Wechsler, 1974). For a small group of 23 children identified as gifted by "independent evaluations," the Verbal, Performance, and Full Scale IQs of the WISC-III are 5.8, 1.1, and 4.9 points lower than the respective scores on the WISC-R. The manual underscores the wider variability of the Processing Speed scale and notes that the Processing Speed and Freedom from Distractibility scores are not as highly related to general intelligence as are the Verbal Comprehension and Perceptual Organization scales.

Possibly because of the WISC-R's general popularity and the trend in gifted education to extend identification to populations beyond the "typical" gifted child, much of the recent research in this area has focused on the WISC-R. Comparing the patterns of subtest strengths and weaknesses and interpreting Verbal–Performance discrepancies are two areas of interest.

In a factor analytical study with a gifted population, Brown and Yakimowski (1987) uncovered four factors, which they labeled Perceptual Organization, Verbal Comprehension, Acquisition of Knowledge, and Spatial Memory. The latter two did not appear in a similar analysis of an average group. Brown and Yakimowski concluded that the gifted children processed information differently from average students, and they hypothesized that the gifted children might apply problem-solving strategies differently, resulting in different subtest patterns. The gifted group was superior in Verbal Comprehension, with the highest scores in Similarities, Comprehension, and Vocabulary. The other three factors were approximately equivalent.

Silver and Clampit (1990) used the statistical theory and data from the WISC-R manual to devise a table of theoretical occurrences of Verbal–Performance discrepancies that illustrates that wide discrepancies are common and less "pathological" in high-ability children than in the total normative sample. They were able to compare the theory with the data from the actual sample and found a close correspondence between the two. For instance, one-half of all children with IQs above 132 have a Verbal–Performance discrepancy of 12 to 14 points and one-fourth have a 19- to 23-point discrepancy. By comparison, an "all children" table would have labeled a 21-point discrepancy as occurring in 2% to 5% of cases.

A third issue of interpretation of the WISC-R and gifted children is that of response speed. Many gifted children are perfectionists and planners. They "think twice" before responding. Reams, Chamrad, and Robinson (1990) found no difference in speed of response between average and high-ability children on the Picture Arrangement and Object Assembly subtests, but a slight advantage for the high-ability group on the Block Assembly subtest ($p < .02$). They believe that speed as a component of general intelligence is of limited utility and that "tests of higher-order capabilities which permit children to use their preferred problem-solving styles, be those rapid or cautious, would seem to make more sense" (p. 110).

# ASSESSING ACHIEVEMENT

Assessing achievement may be less complicated and controversial than assessing ability. Group achievement tests are given periodically in many school systems. High-achieving gifted children who are good test takers will reveal themselves through these tests, and it is neither necessary nor efficient for school support personnel to participate in this process unless they have responsibility for administering or interpreting the group tests.

The decision-making process becomes more difficult when the child in question has a specific academic aptitude in the midst of other academic abilities that range from average to gifted. The issue of programming becomes more critical than identification because a specific aptitude will manifest itself without formal testing. For example, not long ago, I assessed a 5-year-old kindergartner and a 6-year-old first grader, both of whom were testing at the seventh-grade level in reading decoding and at fourth grade in reading comprehension. The kindergartner was a physically large, but emotionally immature, child whose aggressiveness caused frequent problems with her classmates. The first grader, a boy, was physically small, but emotionally mature. His reading prowess was matched by a similar gift in playing piano and good emerging math skills. He was an "ideal gifted" student.

Needless to say, neither these children nor their parents came to me so that I could tell them that the children were good readers. Issues of placement, acceleration versus enrichment options, private versus public school, and ways of coping with the uneven developmental skills of their children were very much on the minds of these two families. The psychological implications of the educational decisions being made for these children were of primary concern to both sets of parents. How could their child fit in without hiding his or her gifts? How could they keep their child from feeling different when such obvious differences existed? Would the teachers demand that their child do the repetitive and low-level tasks of the primary grades when the children had already mastered them? How could these parents advocate for their child without being labeled "difficult"?

In the case of the kindergartner, the child was placed for the last grading period in a first-grade classroom with a teacher trained in individual instruction. The girl was given additional assistance in learning manuscript writing and rewarded for doing seatwork by being given time in the school's reading room. The transition was supported by several conferences that included the parents, the teachers, the gifted education consultant, the school counselor, and myself (functioning as a private psychologist). At the end of school, the problems of peer interaction had not been solved, but the acceleration was alleviating some of the child's academic unrest. The decision was made to promote her to the second grade.

In the second case, the child's needs were outlined very specifically to the parents, who were urged to discuss them with the staff of his parochial school and with the gifted education coordinator of the public school system. The coordinator was able to offer a program in the boy's home school with a specifically selected teacher skilled in both whole language and Talents Unlimited (a higher level thinking program incorporated within the regular curriculum) (Schlichter, 1986). The boy will transfer into this school for second grade, with the possibility of acceleration to be considered later.

These two cases illustrate the complex needs of the high-achieving child, the need for flexibility in developing adequate placements, and the myriad problems that may accompany decision making for these students. Assessment of their achievement was a straightforward and simple task; however, for the underserved groups of children discussed below, assessment may be more problematic. As noted in that discussion, honoring cultural differences and using subjective as well as objective data are critical if we are to include children with gifted potential. Designing an appropriate education for gifted students requires the same degree of team planning that is necessary for disabled students.

# ASSESSING UNDERSERVED POPULATIONS

The unique problems of testing atypical populations are well known. Underinclusion of students in gifted programs is as much a problem as possible overinclusion in programs for the disabled. Following their survey of existing practices, Richert et al. (1982) recommended the use of individual intelligence tests to get "disadvantaged" students into the talent pool, the use of both "standardized" intelligence and achievement tests to match ability and certain types of programs, and the use of achievement tests for evaluating academic progress.

## A Study in Identifying Underserved Gifted Students

Recently, I had the opportunity to serve as the assessment consultant on a project for identifying and serving potentially gifted third-grade students from the four most disadvantaged schools in a small midwestern city. The project was designed to develop identification procedures and intervention strategies to help children decrease the discrepancy between their potential and current performance. After much discussion, we developed a "wide-net" approach for identification. Candidates for the program were nominated by teachers who were given an inservice workshop on underserved gifted and a checklist describing characteristics of such subpopulations as the gifted with learning disabilities, the disadvantaged gifted, minority gifted, and underachieving gifted. These children were tested using the WISC-R. The inclusion criteria were set as 115 on any of the three IQs or a mean scaled score of 11.5 on any of the three Kaufman factors of Verbal Comprehension, Perceptual Organization, or Freedom from Distractibility. Twenty-one children met the criteria, but this represented only 54% of those referred by the teachers, leading us to conclude that the checklist was more useful for raising awareness about underserved populations than as an identification instrument. We then scanned the group scores of the remaining third graders and tested the 9 who had standard scores of 110 or more and had an erratic grade pattern. Eight additional children were identified, representing 89% of this second pool, a much better "hit rate." The conclusion was that, unless students' cumulative educational data are computer based, finding this population may involve laborious and inefficient searching of records (Springfield City Schools, 1991).

The promising news is that 27 of the 29 identified students were served in a second-year remediation program that consisted of "gifted" thematic teaching, some prescriptive teaching of basic skills, and major emphasis on increasing self-esteem through a variety of affective activities. At the end of the second year, the students' WISC-R IQs (treating Verbal, Performance, and Full Scale scores separately) increased significantly ($p < .05$), but a significant increase did not occur on the group-administered *Cognitive Abilities Test*. On the *Iowa Test of Basic Skills*, their achievement test scores increased dramatically ($p <$

.01 level); however, all but four of these scores continued to be below the 115 standard score level and would not have identified the students had only group scores been used. It was the opinion of the project teacher, an experienced gifted educator, that after this short intervention, 9 of the group could integrate successfully into any gifted program, 11 could integrate after longer or more intensive intervention, and 6 had multiple problems that required other kinds of service (Springfield City Schools, 1991).

This experience reinforced my belief that school support personnel, particularly school psychologists, must be involved in identifying such populations and that, once identified, the curriculum for these students must contain as much emphasis on the affective as on the cognitive. The potential role of school psychologists, counselors, and social workers in the latter is endless and obvious.

## Minority Gifted Students

The issues of being gifted and from a minority are discussed in detail in Chapter 17. In relation to identification, however, Frasier (1987) suggested that schools should adopt practices that honor diversity, support inclusion rather than exclusion, use multiple criteria from both objective and subjective sources, and use culturally relevant indicators as well as general identification procedures. She similarly stressed the need to acknowledge the heterogeneity within minority groups based on socioeconomic status. In disadvantaged children, accepted indicators of potential giftedness include such traits as alertness; curiosity; retaining, using, and generalizing from new information; original and creative thinking; and resourceful problem solving.

Building upon some of the same principles, Woods and Achey (1990) described a project in Greensboro, North Carolina, in which the minority representation in their gifted program was raised after 3 years from 13% to 28% in a district with a 55% minority population. Their procedures included reviewing the group intelligence and achievement scores of all minority children in Grades 2 through 5 (the target group had to score at or above the 85th percentile in two or three achievement subtests depending upon grade level), parent meetings describing the program prior to continuing evaluation, the administration of a second set of group intelligence and achievement tests, and, finally, the K-ABC and, to a random group, the WISC-R. In comparing the latter, it was found that the K-ABC Achievement scale of 86th percentile was a good predictor of qualifying WISC-R scores, and the use of only the K-ABC Achievement followed by the WISC-R became the standard procedure. The Full Scale IQ was used unless there was greater than a 12-point spread; then the higher of the Verbal or the

Performance IQ was used. Using this system, two-thirds of those referred by the K-ABC Achievement/WISC-R scores qualified for the program. This qualification was determined by placing these scores in a matrix identification system, which equated percentile scores and grades with points and required 98 points for admission, but no single cutoff score was required for a particular test.

In support of Frasier's (1987) plea for adding culturally relevant criteria, Tonemah (1987) described a Tribal–Cultural checklist that was developed by Indian educators, then ranked for appropriateness by noneducator tribal people. The checklist includes four categories encompassing acquired skills (traditional academic subjects), personal–human qualities (e.g., inquisitive, individualistic, self-disciplined), tribal–cultural understanding (e.g., knowledge of tribal history and culture, respect for tribal elders), and aesthetic abilities (e.g., artistic, dance, music, drama ability). Tonemah expressed the tribal concern that those best able to maintain the Native American traditions may not be identified and encouraged to develop their potential when the formal assessments of the majority culture are used as the sole criteria for identifying gifted and talented students. He is continuing his work to refine procedures to address this cultural need.

One model to identify Hispanic children has been developed in the Rural and Migrant Gifted Project in Fresno County, California (Ortiz & Gonzalez, 1991). The multistep project includes (a) referral by teachers of students with potential in the areas of academics, intellectual ability, and creativity; (b) the administration in both Spanish and English of a short-form WISC-R validated by Ortiz and Gonzalez (1989); (c) achievement records; and (d) "behavior and motivation factors." The short-form WISC-R comprises the Similarities, Vocabulary, Picture Arrangement, and Block Design subtests. Students who score between the 85th and the 94th percentiles are considered accelerated, and those in the 95th percentile and above are considered gifted. After identification, students in this project are enrolled in a program that has a curriculum devised to meet the needs of the Hispanic population. It emphasizes language learning through the study of literature and oral discussions and language-based study in all curricular areas, hands-on math, career awareness, and a parallel parent training program.

Unlike other minority groups, the stereotypical status of Asian-Americans tends to be that of high achievers. In fact, some backlash has occurred toward Asian-Americans and their seeming superiority in achievement. Equating Asian heritage with academic prowess may lead to serious underidentification under certain circumstances. Woliver and Woliver (1991) warned against perceiving Asians and Pacific Islanders as a homogeneous group, and pointed out that individual differences exist within groups and families based on such variables as time and reason for immigration, and socioeconomic status before and afterward. For instance, the first wave of Vietnamese who entered the United States as a result of the Vietnam War generally were more affluent and educated than the later immigrants and, as a group, assimilated more easily.

Of greatest significance for those trying to identify Asian-American children are those traits that may differentiate Asians and Pacific Islanders from American children of European heritage and may serve to mask their ability in the identification process, especially if teacher referral is the first step in this process. These traits include a hesitancy to speak unless spoken to; indirectness; the belief that expressing one's opinion is impolite; the tendency to be self-critical and perfectionistic (the "shame" of being wrong may limit risk taking); continued sex-role differentiation and male dominance; and the desire to achieve for a group, rather than for oneself as an individual. Strengths include a valuing of education, respect for elders, and an ability to listen and follow directions (Woliver & Woliver, 1991). Acknowledgment of these traits should be built into the process when identifying Asian-American and Pacific Islander children who are gifted.

Other underserved populations present their own unique problems. These are discussed in Chapters 11, 12, 13, and 16.

## CONCLUSION AND RECOMMENDATIONS

The research discussed in this chapter has a number of recurring themes. The most useful summary statements appear to be the following:

1. Changing concepts of intelligence may have an impact upon the future definition and identification of the gifted population in a number of critical ways, especially in the need to resolve the mismatch between the content of existing instruments and the new theories of intelligence.

2. It is not necessary to assess individually all candidates for gifted programs, but it is imperative if those candidates are among the underserved populations.

3. Gifted programs could be enhanced if school psychologists, whether or not they assess individual students, would share knowledge about the interpretation of group tests, collaborative consultation and program planning, and their skills for counseling gifted students.

4. If individual testing does occur, gifted patterns may be somewhat different from those reported for normative groups. For instance, discrepancies of 12 points or more between Verbal and Performance IQs on the WISC-R occurred in half of the gifted population (Silver & Clampit, 1990).

5. The broader content of the WISC-III and the *Stanford– Binet IV* tends to lower the scores of gifted children whose strengths have been traditionally recognized in the linguistic and abstract reasoning areas. Using these newer instruments may change the nature of children who are identified as gifted, with consequent curricular implications for gifted programs.

6. Preschool and highly gifted children may be best identified by continued use of the *Stanford–Binet L-M* (see Chapter 13 for a complete discussion of this issue).

7. A deliberate cognitive style and slow response speed may cause some gifted children to score poorly on timed tests or subtests.

8. Identification procedures for children from underserved populations must include both objective and subjective criteria, must acknowledge cultural or socioeconomic differences, and should include individually administered intelligence tests.

9. Ideally, identification of students for gifted programs serving high ability/high achievement gifted students will be undertaken in a process that includes the following steps:

   a. Provide inservice training of all referring staff (and ideally parents) on the characteristics of typical and underserved gifted populations. Solicit recommendations for students whose grades may not support the teacher's "intuitive" hunch about their true ability or who seem to have an observable, if undefinable, "spark."

   b. Gather teacher and parent recommendations (sometimes supplemented by peer and self-nominations).

   c. Scan group ability and achievement data.

   d. Prepare an identification matrix involving the quantifiable data.

   e. Examine available portfolio data.

f. Present a list of candidates to a selection committee consisting of representatives from each school, psychologists, and/or counselors.

g. Select the "clearly" eligible students (those with high scores on the matrix on the basis of multiple criteria).

h. Develop a list of potentially eligible students who have one or more deficits, and test these students individually. (While the start-up time commitment for such a process may be a problem, once under way, the majority of the candidates thus identified should come from the lowest grade served by the program and fall within manageable limits.)

Other pragmatic considerations must be faced in such a process. What if the number of "clearly" gifted students equals or exceeds the number of available slots? (In states without service mandates, local districts may not be obligated to provide programs for all identified gifted children.) Should underserved groups be included at the exclusion of "more qualified" students? The issues of equity and discrimination in gifted programs parallel in many ways those issues in special education (although underinclusion, rather than overinclusion, of minorities is the critical issue). I believe that affluent, primarily Caucasian, suburban schools should maintain at least 10% of their slots for underserved groups and that schools with large minority and/or disadvantaged populations should adapt guidelines used for achieving equity in other programs to assure broad representation in the gifted and talented programs. If schools are to move the process of identification and programming for all gifted children from one of "disarray" to that of a full and appropriate educational experience, it is imperative that the skills of school support personnel be added routinely to the team that serves these children.

# REFERENCES

Adderholdt-Elliott, M., Algozzine, K., Algozzine, B., & Haney, K. (1991). Current state practices in educating students who are gifted and talented. *Roeper Review, 14*, 20–23.

Brown, S. & Yakimowski, M. (1987). Intelligence scores of gifted students on the WISC-R. *Gifted Child Quarterly, 31*, 130–134.

Carvajal, H., & McKnab, P. (1990). Relationships between scores of gifted students on Stanford-Binet, IV, and the SRA Educational Ability Series. *Gifted Child Quarterly, 34*, 80–82.

Clark, P., McCallum, R. S., Edwards, R., & Hildman, L. (1987). Use of the Slosson Intelligence Test in screening of gifted children. *Journal of School Psychology, 25*, 189–192.

Frasier, M. (1987). The identification of gifted black students: Developing new perspectives. *Journal for the Education of the Gifted, 10*, 155–180.

Gardner, H. (1983). *Frames of mind.* New York: Basic Books.

Hayden, D., Furlong, M., & Linnemeyer, S. (1988). A comparison of the Kaufman Assessment Battery for Children and the Stanford-Binet, IV, for the assessment of gifted children. *Psychology in the Schools, 25*, 239–243.

Hessler, G. (1985). Review of the Kaufman Assessment Battery for Children: Implications for assessment of the gifted. *Journal for the Education of the Gifted, 8*, 133–148.

Karnes, F., & Brown, K. E. (1979). Comparison of the SIT with the WISC-R for gifted students. *Psychology in the Schools, 16*, 478–482.

Kaufman, A., & Kaufman, N. (1983). *Kaufman Assessment Battery for Children, interpretive manual.* Circle Pines, MN: American Guidance Service.

Klausmeier, K., Mishra, S., & Maker, C. J. (1987). Identification of gifted learners: A national survey of assessment practices and training needs of school psychologists. *Gifted Child Quarterly, 31*, 135–137.

Kluever, R., & Green, K. (1990). Comparing scores on the Stanford-Binet 4th edition and Form LM for identifying gifted children. *Roeper Review, 13*, 16–20.

Linn, M., & Lopatin, E. (1990). A simultaneous screening/assessment procedure for identifying the gifted student. *Psychology in the Schools, 27*, 303–310.

Marland, S., Jr. (1972). *Education of the gifted and talented. Report to the Congress of the United States by the U.S. Commissioner of Education.* Washington, DC: U.S. Government Printing Office.

McCallum, R., Karnes, F., & Edwards, R. (1984). The test of choice for assessment of children: A comparison of the K-ABC, WISC-R, and Stanford-Binet. *Journal of Psychoeducational Assessment, 2*, 57–63.

Naglieri, J., & Das, J. P. (1990). Planning, attention, simultaneous, and successive (PASS) cognitive processes as a model for intelligence. *Journal of Psychoeducational Assessment, 8*, 303–337.

Ortiz, V., & Gonzalez, A. (1989). Validation of a short form of the WISC-R with accelerated and gifted Hispanic students. *Gifted Child Quarterly, 33*, 152–154.

Ortiz, V., & Gonzalez, A. (1991). Gifted Hispanic adolescents. In M. Bireley & J. Genshaft (Eds.), *Understanding the gifted adolescent: Educational, developmental, and multicultural issues* (pp. 240–247). New York: Teachers College Press.

Reams, R., Chamrad, D., & Robinson, N. (1990). The race is not necessarily to the swift: Validity of the WISC-R bonus points for speed. *Gifted Child Quarterly, 34*, 108–110.

Richert, E. S., Alvino, J., & McDonnel, R. (1982). *National report on identification: Assessment and recommendations for comprehensive identification of gifted and talented youth.* Sewell, NJ: Educational Information and Resource Center.

Robinson, N. (1992). Stanford-Binet IV, of course! Time marches on! *Roeper Review, 15,* 32–34.

Sattler, J. (1988). *Assessment of children* (3rd ed.). San Diego, CA: Author.

Schlichter, C. (1986). Talents Unlimited: An inservice model for teaching thinking skills. *Gifted Child Quarterly, 30,* 119–123.

Silver, S., & Clampit, M. (1990). WISC-R profiles of high ability children: Interpretation of Verbal–Performance discrepancies. *Gifted Child Quarterly, 34,* 76–79.

Silverman, L., & Kearney, K. (1992). The case for the Stanford-Binet L-M as a supplemental test. *Roeper Review, 15,* 34–37.

Slosson, R. L. (1971). *Slosson Intelligence Test (SIT).* East Aurora, NY: Slosson Educational Publications.

Speer, S., Hawthorne, L., & Buccellato, L. (1986). Intellectual patterns of young gifted children on the WPPSI. *Journal for the Education of the Gifted, 10,* 57–62.

Springfield City Schools. (1991). *Helping underachieving gifted students: A guide to implementation.* Springfield, OH: Springfield City Schools.

Sternberg, R. (1988). *The triarchic mind: A new theory of intelligence.* New York: Viking-Penguin.

Terman, L. (1925). *Genetic studies of genius: Vol. 1. Mental and physical traits of a thousand gifted children.* Stanford, CA: Stanford University Press.

Terman, L., & Merrill, M. (1973). *The Stanford–Binet Intelligence Scale: Manual for the Third Revision Form L-M.* Boston: Houghton-Mifflin.

Thorndike, R. L., Hagen, E. P., & Sattler, J. M. (1986). *The Stanford–Binet Intelligence Scale, Fourth Edition: Guide for administering and scoring.* Chicago: Riverside.

Tonemah, S. (1987). Assessing American Indian gifted and talented students' abilities. *Journal for the Education of the Gifted, 10,* 181–194.

Tyler-Wood, T., & Carri, L. (1991). Identification of gifted children: The effectiveness of various measures of cognitive ability. *Roeper Review, 14,* 63–64.

Wechsler, D. (1967). *Manual for the Wechsler Preschool and Primary Scale of Intelligence.* San Antonio, TX: Psychological Corporation.

Wechsler, D. (1974). *Manual for the Wechsler Intelligence Scale for Children–Revised.* San Antonio, TX: Psychological Corporation.

Wechsler, D. (1989). *Manual for the Wechsler Preschool and Primary Scale of Intelligence–Revised.* San Antonio, TX: Psychological Corporation.

Wechsler, D. (1991). *Manual for the Wechsler Intelligence Scale for Children–Third Edition.* San Antonio, TX: Psychological Corporation.

Woliver, R., & Woliver, G. (1991). Gifted adolescents in the emerging minorities: Asians and Pacific Islanders. In M. Bireley & J. Genshaft (Eds.), *Understanding the gifted adolescent: Educational, developmental, and multicultural issues* (pp. 248–257). New York: Teachers College Press.

Woods, S., & Achey, V. (1990). Successful identification of gifted racial/ethnic group students without changing classification requirements. *Roeper Review, 10,* 21–26.

# Chapter 5

# *Identifying the Creatively Gifted*

**Gary A. Davis**

◆　◆　◆

IN GIFTED EDUCATION, creativity plays a key role in defining giftedness, formulating program objectives, identifying gifted and talented students, and planning acceleration and enrichment activities that enhance students' creative potential. School personnel want both to locate creative students for programs for the gifted and talented (G/T) and to offer G/T programs that promote creative growth. Advocates for gifted programs proclaim that "tomorrow's leaders are in today's schools," referring to students as future professionals who will be uniquely able to make technical and creative contributions to society.

There are many ways to identify creativeness in students. For convenience, these may be categorized as formal or informal, depending upon whether the identification is based on objective test scores or on subjective opinions of teachers, parents, peers, or students themselves. Somewhere between formal and informal lies a gray area in which objective-looking questionnaires and inventories are used to record subjective impressions of students' creative abilities, personality characteristics, or quality of past creative activities.

Before looking at formal and informal ways to puzzle out which students have unusual creative potential, it is helpful to consider several complications regarding creativity. First, and obviously, creativity is complex in its many processes and forms (e.g., Davis, 1989b). For example, creativity can be forced, as in brainstorming sessions, or it can happen spontaneously and unpredictably. It involves rational and logical thinking as well as irrational thinking, such as fantasy, play, and analogical thinking. Creativity can result from hard work and deliberate planning or from insight and chance. Creative capability is partly innate, and partly learned. It requires certain personality traits, high motivation, relevant cognitive and information-processing abilities, and applicable experience. Creativity also takes innumerable forms. Although people quickly associate the word *creativity* with innovation in the arts and sciences, there are unlimited personal, educational, and professional areas for creative thinking and expression. Creative thinking and innovation are found in every facet of human activity. As discussed by Torrance (1979), people can be creative in an infinite number of ways.

Second, creativity is often considered a capability with values of 1 and 0; a person is either "creative" or "uncreative." Like other abilities, however, creative potential is normally distributed. Some students labeled creative will be only noticeably above average, some will be definitely creative, a few will be outstanding, and the rare Mozart or Gauss will be profoundly creative, usually in visible ways.

Third, although creativity and intelligence are separate constructs, they are related. Many bright, grade-getting students are too conforming and insecure to even think about creative and unconventional activities. At the same time, highly creative persons virtually always are above average in intelligence (e.g., Sternberg, 1988; Walberg & Herbig, 1991). The accepted relationship between creativity and intelligence has been dubbed the "threshold concept" (MacKinnon, 1961, 1978a): A base level of intellectual ability is essential for creative productivity. Above that threshold, there is virtually no relationship between measured intelligence and creativity. The brightest students are not necessarily the most creative, and the most creative are not necessarily the brightest. Some common characteristics and behaviors of creative students—for example, unconventionality and indifference to conventions—are inconsistent with the conformity needed for pleasing teachers and earning high grades.

In the following sections, I discuss informal ways to identify creative students and review formal creativity testing. Those gray-area inventories and questionnaires appear in both spots.

# INFORMAL IDENTIFICATION OF CREATIVE TALENT

## Biographical Information: Creative Activities

This statement is self-evident to the point of triviality, but to locate creative students at any grade level, school personnel need merely to look for persons who have been doing creative things, based on their background of creative activities. Does the elementary child constantly make or build things? Does he or she have wide interests, unusual hobbies, or unique collections—magic, juggling, Nordic gods, prehistory, Charlie Chaplin impressions, a collection of oboe and bassoon reeds? Does the child have an unusually strong background in art, photography, poetry, creative writing, handicrafts, music, dance, computer programming, or a science area? Perhaps the child is a "photography kid" or knows more about Picasso, Hemingway, or Maya Angelou than do the teachers. One way for school personnel to learn of these interests is to create a self-report inventory, or an inventory to be filled in by parents, that simply asks about the student's artistic, musical, writing, scientific, handicraft, or other interests or hobbies (Figure 5.1).

Another subtle but strong predictor of creativeness is whether the person had an imaginary playmate as a child. Unusually creative secondary students and adults may laughingly say, "I still do." Typically,

---

### List of Creative Interests and Hobbies

In the space below, list any hobbies, collections, or strong interests you [your child may] have in art, music, writing, science, handicrafts, or other areas. For example, have you been [is your child] interested in magic, space travel, theater, doll collecting, or some type of animal, or do you [does your child] have other hobbies? If so, list them.

_____

_____

_____

_____

_____

_____

_____

_____

_____

---

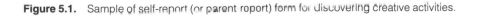

**Figure 5.1.** Sample of self-report (or parent report) form for discovering creative activities.

the imaginary friend disappears shortly after children enter kinder-garten (Somers & Yawkey, 1984). Students who report having had an imaginary playmate or pretend animal friends will show further per-sonality or background traits of creativity.

For high school students and adults, another sure identifier of creativity is a background in theater. Students involved in theater show virtually all the biographical and personality traits of creative persons (described later), and their creativity spills over into nonthea-ter areas.

Some biographical data may be indicators of, but not strongly re-lated to, creativeness. For example, Schaefer (1969, 1970) found that creative high school students were more likely to have friends younger and older than themselves, rather than the same age. They also were more likely to have lived in more than one state, may have traveled outside the United States, and were not particularly interested in sports. High school girls who were creative writers were significantly more likely to own a cat.

## Personality Characteristics of Creative Persons

Much research and no small amount of opinion exist on the topic of personality characteristics of creative persons. I have been convinced for some years that characteristics such as confidence, independence, open-mindedness, high energy, risk taking, curiosity, humor, a toler-ance for complexity and ambiguity, and particularly a "creativity con-sciousness" are absolutely essential enabling traits of virtually all cre-ative people (e.g., Davis, 1975, 1989a, 1991). Many students have the necessary underlying abilities, but they are not predisposed to engage in creative thinking and activities.

A short time ago (Davis, 1992), I tallied up slightly over 100 adjec-tives and short phrases used to describe characteristics of creative persons, drawn, for example, from Barron (1969, 1978, 1988), Davis (1975; Davis & Bull, 1978; Davis, Peterson, & Farley, 1973; Davis & Rimm, 1982), Lingemann (1982), MacKinnon (1978a, 1978b), Perkins (1988), Simonton (1988), Sternberg (1988; Tardif & Sternberg, 1988), Torrance (1962, 1981a, 1987, 1988), and Walberg (1988; Walberg & Herbig, 1991). An "eyeball factor analysis" placed the traits in a sur-prisingly small 12 categories, although some categories were much larger (i.e., approximate synonyms were cited by many more authors) and more important than others. The 12 categories, with a few repre-sentative synonyms, are as follows:

1. *Aware of creativeness*—is creativity conscious, values orig-inality and creativity, values own creativity.

2. *Original*—is a "what if?" person; is imaginative, flexible in ideas and thought, resourceful, nonconforming, unconventional; challenges assumptions.

3. *Independent*—is self-confident, internally controlled, individualistic, self-accepting, unconcerned with impressing others; sets own rules; may resist societal demands.

4. *Risk taking*—does not mind consequences of being different; is not afraid to try something new; is willing to cope with hostility, willing to cope with failure, optimistic.

5. *Energetic*—is adventurous, sensation seeking, enthusiastic, excitable, spontaneous, impulsive; exhibits driving absorption; goes beyond assigned tasks.

6. *Curious*—is questioning, experimenting, inquisitive; has wide interests; is open to new experiences and growth.

7. *Sense of humor*—is playful; plays with ideas; demonstrates childlike freshness in thinking.

8. *Attracted to complexity*—is attracted to novelty, the mysterious, the asymmetrical; is a complex person; tolerates ambiguity, disorder, incongruity; tends to believe in psychical phenomena, flying saucers.

9. *Artistic*—has artistic and aesthetic interests.

10. *Open-minded*—is receptive to new ideas, receptive to other viewpoints, open to new experiences and growth, liberal, altruistic.

11. *Needs time alone*—needs privacy; is reflective, introspective, internally preoccupied, sensitive; may be withdrawn; likes to work by himself or herself.

12. *Intuitive*—is perceptive, sees relationships, uses all senses in observing.

An awareness of such traits can help school personnel and parents informally recognize creative potential. Inventories and rating scales are available in both self-report forms and forms that can be used by teachers or others (who know a student well) to rate creativity characteristics. One brief but well-conceived rating scale is Renzulli's (1983) Creativity Characteristics scale, shown in Figure 5.2. The scale evaluates central, intuitively sound, and empirically validated traits of creative children, adolescents, and adults.

Torrance (1981a) listed additional "nontest indicators of creativity"

## *Creativity Characteristics*

**Scoring Weights: 1 = Seldom or never; 2 = Occasionally; 3 = Considerably; 4 = Almost always.**

|  | 1 | 2 | 3 | 4 |
|---|---|---|---|---|
| 1. Displays a great deal of curiosity about many things; is constantly asking questions about anything and everything. | ____ | ____ | ____ | ____ |
| 2. Generates a large number of ideas or solutions to problems and questions; often offers unusual ("way out"), unique, clever responses. | ____ | ____ | ____ | ____ |
| 3. Is uninhibited in expressing opinion; is sometimes radical and spirited in disagreement; is tenacious. | ____ | ____ | ____ | ____ |
| 4. Is a high risk taker; is adventurous and speculative. | ____ | ____ | ____ | ____ |
| 5. Displays a good deal of intellectual playfulness; fantasizes; imagines ("I wonder what would happen if . . ."); manipulates ideas (i.e., changes, elaborates upon them); is often concerned with adapting, improving, and modifying institutions, objects, and systems. | ____ | ____ | ____ | ____ |
| 6. Displays a keen sense of humor and sees humor in situations that may not appear to be humorous to others. | ____ | ____ | ____ | ____ |
| 7. Is unusually aware of his or her impulses and more open to the irrational in himself or herself (freer expression of feminine interest for boys, greater than usual amount of independence for girls); shows emotional sensitivity. | ____ | ____ | ____ | ____ |
| 8. Is sensitive to beauty; attends to aesthetic characteristics of things. | ____ | ____ | ____ | ____ |

**Figure 5.2.** Renzulli's Creativity Characteristics rating scale. From "Rating the Behavioral Characteristics of Superior Students" by J. S. Renzulli, 1983 (September/October), *G/C/T*, pp. 30–35. Reprinted by permission.

9. Is nonconforming; accepts disorder; is not interested in details; is individualistic; does not bear being different.

    \_\_\_\_ \_\_\_\_ \_\_\_\_ \_\_\_\_

10. Criticizes constructively; is unwilling to accept authoritarian pronouncements without critical examination.

    \_\_\_\_ \_\_\_\_ \_\_\_\_ \_\_\_\_

Total Score _____

**Figure 5.2.** continued

that included, for example, high verbal and conversational fluency; irritation and boredom with the routine and obvious; enjoyment of pretending; experimentation with familiar objects to see if they will become something other than what they were intended to be; and enjoyment over telling about his or her discoveries or inventions.

Creative children and adolescents also may demonstrate *negative* traits that a teacher or parent may not like. Examples from Torrance (1981a) and Smith (1966) include indifference to conventions and courtesies, uncooperativeness, capriciousness, cynicism, sloppiness with details and unimportant matters, tendencies to question rules and authority, egocentrism, forgetfulness, and sometimes being temperamental, emotional, and overactive physically and mentally. Alarming numbers of creatively gifted children are diagnosed as having attention deficit hyperactivity disorder and are placed on Ritalin® (Davis & Rimm, 1994).

Despite recurring commonalities in personality traits, not all creative students show all traits. Furthermore, creative students differ dramatically from each other. Some are high achievers whose artistic or scientific creativity takes socially valued forms. Others are more unconventional in appearance and behavior. Many creative students are energetic, outgoing, confident, and comical. Some, perhaps artistic and poetic ones, are introverted, withdrawn, and anxious.

## Creative Abilities

The creative process may be outlined as follows: (a) becoming motivated to solve a problem or create something artistic, scientific, or otherwise useful; (b) simplifying the "mess," clarifying the facts, separating relevant from irrelevant, and understanding the solution requirements; (c) thinking of many possibilities, including original ones, and reducing them to one or more workable solutions; and (d) carrying out the solution ideas, solving many subproblems in the process, and (e) evaluating the final solutions or products. With this description, which is not much different from those of Wallas (1926), Parnes (1981), or Torrance (1988), it is difficult to think of cognitive abilities that would not be involved in creativity. However, some cognitive and information-processing abilities seem more central than others, and I examine examples of these.

Many abilities interweave closely with creative personality traits—for example, originality, humor, perceptiveness, reflectivity, spontaneity, risk taking, and being artistic. School personnel should consider these abilities, in addition to the creative personality traits, when informally identifying creative students.

Barron (1988) entirely avoided the distinction between personality traits and cognitive abilities, listing only six "ingredients of creativity": (a) recognizing patterns, (b) making connections, (c) taking risks, (d) challenging assumptions, (e) taking advantage of chance, and (f) seeing in new ways.

Davis (1992), drawing from many sources, itemized the creative abilities listed in Table 5.1. Included are the four scores of the *Torrance Tests of Creative Thinking* (Torrance, 1966), *fluency, flexibility, originality*, and *elaboration*; Bloom, Englehart, Furst, Hill, and Krathwohl's (1956) higher level thinking skills of *analysis, synthesis*, and *evaluation*; Guilford's important *transformation*, the ability to look at one thing and perceive other possibilities; the pivotal ability to think *analogically*, enabling one to draw innovative ideas from comparison sources (e.g., Gordon & Poze, 1986); and the ability to *regress*, to play with ideas and think like a child with fewer restrictions from habits, rules, and conformity pressures, which even Sigmund Freud recommended as a route to imagination. Table 5.1 also includes *sensitivity to problems*, which can be subdivided into the abilities to detect diffi-

**TABLE 5.1. Creative Abilities**

| | |
|---|---|
| Fluency | Analysis |
| Flexibility | Synthesis |
| Originality | Evaluation |
| Elaboration | Ability to predict outcomes, consequences |
| Transformation | |
| Sensitivity to problems | Logical thinking |
| Ability to define problems | Ability to regress |
| Visualization, imagination | Intuition |
| Analogical/metaphorical thinking | Concentration |

**TABLE 5.2.  Information-Processing Traits**

Uses existing knowledge as basis for new ideas

Avoids perceptual sets and entrenched ways of thinking

Questions norms and assumptions

Builds new structures instead of using existing structures

Uses wide categories; sees "forest" instead of "trees"

Thinks metaphorically

Thinks logically

Makes independent judgments

Is alert to novelty and gaps in knowledge

Copes well with novelty

Finds order in chaos

Uses internal visualization

May prefer nonverbal communication

Is flexible and skilled in decision making

Adapted from "What Do We Know About Creativity?" by T. Z. Tardif and R. J. Sternberg, in *The Nature of Creativity* (pp. 429–440) by R. J. Sternberg (Ed.), 1988, New York: Cambridge University Press. Adapted by permission.

culties, detect missing information, and ask good questions; and *problem-defining abilities*, which includes the abilities to identify the "real" problem, simplify it, eliminate irrelevancies, identify sub-problems, and perhaps define problems more broadly to open up new solutions. *Intuition* is an ill-defined, yet central ability that some have explained as the perceptive ability to make intellectual leaps—to see relationships or reach conclusions based on sketchy information.

Tardif and Sternberg (1988) produced a list of information-processing traits of creative persons, which appear in a modified form in Table 5.2. These also seem to be reasonably central capabilities that could aid educators or parents in identifying creative students.

# FORMAL IDENTIFICATION: CREATIVITY TESTS

Because of the complexity and many forms of creativity, validity of creativity tests necessarily is limited. An exception to the so-so validity of virtually all creativity tests might be questionnaires that directly assess a student's background of creative activities and products.

As a general rule, I recommend using at least two criteria of creativeness. For example, a G/T program coordinator might use any of the following: nominations (or ratings) by two teachers, one of whom might be an art, science, or drama teacher; a teacher nomination plus parent, peer, or self-reports of creative involvement; a teacher nomination plus scores from one creativity test or inventory; or scores on two creativity tests, preferably one personality inventory and one divergent thinking test. If a given student receives high scores on both creativity criteria, the coordinator can be reasonably confident about having identified a creatively gifted student.

Creativity tests are divided into the two main categories of *divergent thinking tests* and *personality/biographical inventories*. Most divergent thinking tests assess a (small) sample of creative abilities by asking students to respond with as many answers as they can to an open-ended question or problem, such as the 90-year-old "List unusual uses for a brick." The tests typically are scored at least for ideational *fluency* (the total number of relevant ideas) and *originality* (the uniqueness or statistical infrequency of each idea). Personality/biographical inventories evaluate personality, motivational, attitudinal, and biographical traits common to creative persons. Both types of tests work reasonably well, despite built-in psychometric difficulties. Divergent thinking tests take longer to administer and score.

## Divergent Thinking Tests

Among divergent thinking tests, the industry standard is the *Torrance Tests of Creative Thinking* (Torrance, 1966). They are available in four test booklets, Thinking Creatively With Words (verbal) and Thinking Creatively With Pictures (nonverbal, figural), Forms A and B. The verbal battery includes seven subtests, which require students, for example, to ask questions about a strange picture, list unusual uses for a cardboard box or tin can, list improvements for a stuffed elephant or monkey, and list consequences of an unlikely event (e.g., clouds having strings attached to them). The figural battery includes three subtests, all of which present an incomplete or abstract sketch that students transform into a meaningful picture. As noted earlier, four basic scores are derived, representing four important creative abilities: *fluency* (number of ideas), *flexibility* (number of categories of ideas, approaches to the problem), *originality* (statistical infrequency), and *elaboration* (in the figural forms, number of details beyond the basic picture).[1]

---

1. A comparatively new streamlined scoring system, for figural tests only, is intended both to speed up scoring and assess a total of 18 creative abilities (see Torrance & Ball, 1984).

The Torrance tests may be used at any grade level, although administration must be individualized below third grade. Torrance (1977) noted that the nonverbal, figural tests are more culture-fair. According to Torrance (1984),

> The basic battery of the Torrance tests has been used in over 1,000 published research studies. These tests have been translated into over 30 different languages and have been published and standardized in France, Italy, Czechoslovakia, and Taiwan. . . . According to the best estimates available, about 150,000 children and adults are being tested with these instruments each year. (p. 3)

Several other published batteries of divergent thinking tests are available. Two of these, the Getzels and Jackson (1962) tests and the Wallach and Kogan (1965) tests, appear only in their books and apparently may be used without charge. Tests available for purchase are the *Monitor Test of Creative Potential* (Hoepfner & Hemenway, 1973; for age 7 and older), *Exercise in Divergent Thinking* (Williams, 1980), *Thinking Creatively in Action and Movement* (Torrance, 1981b), and *Thinking Creatively with Sounds and Words* (Torrance, Khatena, & Cunnington, 1973).

Torrance's *Thinking Creatively in Action and Movement* is unique in that it was designed for very young children. One subtest, for example, asks children to demonstrate as many ways as they can to put a paper cup in the wastebasket. *Thinking Creatively with Sounds and Words*, available in forms for children and adults, includes two different subtests. The test taker is asked to write ideas stimulated by four abstract sounds in Sounds and Images and by 10 word stimuli (e.g., *zoom, boom, fizzy, jingle*) in Onomatopoeia and Images. Unlike most divergent thinking tests, students write only one response per stimulus, which is scored for originality. Sounds and Images could use updated scoring norms to accommodate contemporary associations to the sounds. For example, "Mount St. Helens erupting" and "racquetball" are very common responses to two sounds, yet they earn maximum originality points according to the 1973 scoring guide.

I recommend the Torrance Tests, which were 10 years in development, have the most complete administration and scoring guides and norms, and have an extensive, even longitudinal validation history (e.g., Torrance, 1984, 1988). The streamlined scoring evaluates many more creative abilities than do other batteries, although some rarely appear in students' tests. One minor irritation with the Torrance Tests is that one figural test, Picture Construction, as originally published in 1966, included a pastel-colored, peel-off, egg-shaped or sausage-shaped sticker that could be placed on another page in any orientation and decorated. In the current, cheaper version, the egg or sausage is printed in solid black and can be neither rotated nor written on, yet scoring guides and norms have not been changed to accommodate this substantial difference.

## Personality/Biographical Inventories

Creativity inventories evaluate the extent to which the test taker possesses personality, motivational, and biographical traits known to characterize creative persons.[2] They may be efficiently administered and scored. Renzulli's (1983) rating scale, used by teachers to rate the creativeness of students of any age, appeared in Figure 5.2. One need look no further.

My *How Do You Think* (HDYT) test (Davis, 1975; Davis & Subkoviak, 1978) was developed with college students and validated against actual creative writing, art, and invention projects required for a creativity class.[3] The test also works well with high school students. Offspring of HDYT are the *Group Inventory for Finding Interests* (GIFFI) I and II for middle and high school, respectively (Davis & Rimm, 1982). HDYT less directly influenced the *Group Inventory for Finding Creative Talent* (GIFT) for elementary students (Rimm & Davis, 1976) and the *Preschool and Kindergarten Interest Descriptor* (PRIDE) (Rimm, 1983), which parents fill out to describe their young child. GIFFI I and II, GIFT, and PRIDE must be scored by the publisher, which increases costs.

Four additional published creativity inventories include, for elementary children, Schaefer's (1971) *Creativity Attitude Survey* and Williams's (1980) *Exercise in Divergent Feeling*. Khatena and Torrance's (1976) *Something About Myself* and *What Kind of Person Are You?* are for adolescents and adults. A good unpublished elementary school creativity inventory is available from John Feldhusen at Purdue University.

As a final note on testing, myriads of unpublished creativity tests exist, some of which are intended to evaluate creativity in specific subject areas. For example, the *Judging Criteria Instrument* (Eichenberger, 1978) is used by peers and oneself to evaluate creativity in a physics class, using rating scales that evaluate fluency, flexibility, originality, elaboration, usefulness, worth to science, and social acceptance. The *Detroit Public Schools Creativity Scales* (Parke & Byrnes, 1984) are based on factors used by experts to evaluate creativity in art,

---

2. Exceptions are inventories that evaluate only the person's background of creative activities. To my knowledge, none currently is commercially available.

3. Tests and a manual, with scoring and subscale scoring guides, are available from the author. See the list of contributors near the front of this book for the mailing address.

music composition, music performance, dance, drama, poetry, short story and novel writing, and speech.

Some older lists of unpublished creativity tests appear in Davis (1971, 1973), Kaltsoonis (1971, 1972), and Kaltsoonis and Honeywell (1980). As a sample of the variety, the lists include a creative writing evaluation form, a scale that measures the capacity to empathize with story characters, a preference for polygons task, a motor creativity test, several math creativity tests, a chemistry creativity test, a creative background inventory, an "experiential curiosity measure," and a "choice dilemma questionnaire." An ERIC search would add more recent examples.

# CONCLUSION

Creative students exist, and the more school personnel and parents become acquainted with characteristics of creativity, the more easily they can recognize them. As with all students, creative students will differ among themselves as well as from others.

Identification may be informal, based on students' visible display of creative personality and motivational characteristics or their background of creative activities. Imaginary playmates and, in secondary school, a background in theater are certain giveaways. Identification at all school levels also may be formal. Divergent thinking tests evaluate some—but by no means all—creative abilities. Personality/biographical inventories assess whether students possess traits known to characterize creative persons. Due to the complexity and variety of forms of creativity, no one test can ever be highly valid, except perhaps a trustworthy report of a student's creative accomplishments. I strongly recommend that at least two criteria of creativity be used. A person scoring high on both almost always has creative potential and therefore is a good candidate for a G/T program.

# REFERENCES

Barron, F. (1969). *Creative person and creative process*. New York: Holt.

Barron, F. (1978). An eye more fantastical. In G. A. Davis & J. A. Scott (Eds.), *Training creative thinking*. Melbourne, FL: Krieger.

Barron, F. (1988). Putting creativity to work. In R. J. Sternberg (Ed.), *The nature of creativity* (pp. 76–98). New York: Cambridge University Press.

Bloom, B. S., Englehart, M. D., Furst, E. J., Hill, W. H., & Krathwohl, D. R.

(1956). *Taxonomy of educational objectives: Handbook I. Cognitive domain*. New York: McKay.

Davis, G. A. (1971). Instruments useful in studying creative behavior and creative talents: Part II. *Journal of Creative Behavior, 5*, 162–165.

Davis, G. A. (1973). *Psychology of problem solving*. New York: Basic Books.

Davis, G. A. (1975). In furious pursuit of the creative person. *Journal of Creative Behavior, 9*, 75–87.

Davis, G. A. (1989a). Gary Davis speaks to teachers: Objectives and activities for teaching creative thinking. *Gifted Child Quarterly, 33*, 81–84.

Davis, G. A. (1989b). Testing for creative potential. *Contemporary Educational Psychology, 14*, 257–274.

Davis, G. A. (1991). Teaching creative thinking. In N. Colangelo & G. A. Davis (Eds.), *Handbook of gifted education* (pp. 236–244). Needham Heights, MA: Allyn & Bacon.

Davis, G. A. (1992). *Creativity is forever* (3rd ed.). Dubuque, IA: Kendall/Hunt.

Davis, G. A., & Bull, K. S. (1978). Strengthening affective components of creativity in a college course. *Journal of Educational Psychology, 70*, 833–836.

Davis, G. A., Peterson, J. M., & Farley, F. H. (1973). Attitudes, motivation, sensation seeking, and belief in ESP as predictors of real creative behavior. *Journal of Creative Behavior, 7*, 31–39.

Davis, G. A., & Rimm, S. (1982). Group Inventory for Finding Creative Interests (GIFFI) I and II: Instruments for identifying creative potential in the junior and senior high school. *Journal of Creative Behavior, 16*, 50–57.

Davis, G. A., & Rimm, S. B. (1994). *Education of the gifted and talented* (3rd ed.). Needham Heights, MA: Allyn & Bacon.

Davis, G. A., & Subkoviak, M. J. (1978). Multidimensional analysis of a personality-based test of creative potential. *Journal of Educational Measurement, 12*, 37–43.

Eichenberger, R. J. (1978). Creativity measurement through use of judgment criteria in physics. *Educational and Psychological Measurement, 38*, 221–227.

Getzels, J. W., & Jackson, P. W. (1962). *Creativity and intelligence*. New York: Wiley.

Gordon, W. J. J., & Poze, T. (1986). *The new art of the possible* (rev. ed.). Cambridge, MA: SES Associates.

Hoepfner, R., & Hemenway, J. (1973). *Monitor Test of Creative Potential*. Hollywood, CA: Monitor.

Kaltsoonis, B. (1971). Instruments useful in studying creative behavior and creative talents: Part I. Commercially available instruments. *Journal of Creative Behavior, 5*, 117–126.

Kaltsoonis, B. (1972). Additional instruments useful in studying creative behavior and creative talents: Part III. Noncommercially available instruments. *Journal of Creative Behavior, 6*, 268–274.

Kaltsoonis, B., & Honeywell, L. (1980). Additional instruments useful in studying creative behavior and creative talent: Part IV. Noncommercially available instruments. *Journal of Creative Behavior, 14*, 56–67.

Khatena, J., & Torrance, E. P. (1976). *Manual for Khatena–Torrance Creative Perceptions Inventory.* Chicago: Stoelting.

Lingemann, L. S. (1982). *Assessing creativity from a diagnostic perspective: The creative attribute profile.* Unpublished doctoral dissertation, University of Wisconsin, Madison.

MacKinnon, D. W. (1961). Creativity in architects. In D. W. MacKinnon (Ed.), *The creative person* (pp. 291–320). Berkeley: University of California, Institute of Personality Assessment Research.

MacKinnon, D. W. (1978a). Educating for creativity: A modern myth? In G. A. Davis & J. A. Scott (Eds.), *Training creative thinking.* Melbourne, FL: Krieger.

MacKinnon, D. W. (1978b). *In search of human effectiveness: Identifying and developing creativity.* Buffalo, NY: Creative Education Foundation.

Parke, B. N., & Byrnes, P. (1984). Toward objectifying the measurement of creativity. *Roeper Review, 6,* 216–218.

Parnes, S. J. (1981). *Magic of your mind.* Buffalo, NY: Bearly Limited.

Perkins, D. A. (1988). The possibility of invention. In R. J. Sternberg (Ed.), *The nature of creativity* (pp. 362–385). New York: Cambridge University Press.

Renzulli, J. S. (1983, September/October). Rating the behavioral characteristics of superior students. *G/C/T,* 30–35.

Rimm, S. B. (1983). *Preschool and kindergarten interest descriptor.* Watertown, WI: Educational Assessment Service.

Rimm, S. B., & Davis, G. A. (1976). GIFT: An instrument for the identification of creativity. *Journal of Creative Behavior, 10,* 178–182.

Schaefer, C. E. (1969). Imaginary companions and creative adolescents. *Developmental Psychology, 1,* 747–749.

Schaefer, C. E. (1970). *Biographical Inventory—Creativity.* San Diego, CA: Educational and Industrial Testing Services.

Schaefer, C. E. (1971). *Creativity Attitude Survey.* Jacksonville, IL: Psychologists and Educators.

Simonton, D. K. (1988). Creativity, leadership, and chance. In R. J. Sternberg (Ed.), *The nature of creativity* (pp. 386–426). New York: Cambridge University Press.

Smith, J. M. (1966). *Setting conditions for creative teaching in the elementary school.* Needham Heights, MA: Allyn & Bacon.

Somers, J. V., & Yawkey, T. D. (1984). Imaginary play companions: Contributions of creativity and intellectual abilities of young children. *Journal of Creative Behavior, 18,* 77–89.

Sternberg, R. J. (1988). A three-facet model of creativity. In R. J. Sternberg (Ed.), *The nature of creativity* (pp. 125–147). New York: Cambridge University Press.

Tardif, T. Z., & Sternberg, R. J. (1988). What do we know about creativity? In R. J. Sternberg (Ed.), *The nature of creativity* (pp. 429–440). New York: Cambridge University Press.

Torrance, E. P. (1962). *Guiding creative talent.* Englewood Cliffs, NJ: Prentice-Hall.

Torrance, E. P. (1966). *Torrance Tests of Creative Thinking.* Bensenville, IL: Scholastic Testing Service.

Torrance, E. P. (1977). *Creativity in the classroom*. Washington, DC: National Education Association.

Torrance, E. P. (1979). *The search for satori and creativity*. Buffalo, NY: Creative Education Foundation.

Torrance, E. P. (1981a). Non-test ways of identifying the creatively gifted. In J. C. Gowan, J. Khatena, & E. P. Torrance (Eds.), *Creativity: Its educational implications* (2nd ed.). Dubuque, IA: Kendall/Hunt.

Torrance, E. P. (1981b). *Thinking creatively in action and movement*. Bensenville, IL: Scholastic Testing Service.

Torrance, E. P. (1984). Some products of twenty-five years of creativity research. *Educational Perspectives, 22*, 3–8.

Torrance, E. P. (1987). *The blazing drive: The creative personality*. Buffalo, NY: Bearly Limited.

Torrance, E. P. (1988). The nature of creativity as manifest in its testing. In R. W. Sternberg (Ed.), *The nature of creativity* (pp. 43–75). New York: Cambridge University Press.

Torrance, E. P., & Ball, O. E. (1984). *Torrance Tests of Creative Thinking: Streamlined (revised) manual, figural A and B*. Bensenville, IL: Scholastic Testing Service.

Torrance, E. P., Khatena, J., & Cunnington, B. F. (1973). *Thinking creatively with sounds and words*. Bensenville, IL: Scholastic Testing Service.

Walberg, H. J. (1988). Creativity and talent as learning. In R. J. Sternberg (Ed.), *The nature of creativity* (pp. 340–361). New York: Cambridge University Press.

Walberg, H. J., & Herbig, M. P. (1991). Developing talent, creativity, and eminence. In N. Colangelo & G. A. Davis (Eds.), *Handbook of gifted education* (pp. 245–255). Needham Heights, MA: Allyn & Bacon.

Wallach, M. A., & Kogan, N. (1965). *Modes of thinking in young children*. New York: Holt.

Wallas, G. (1926). *The art of thought*. New York: Harcourt, Brace & World.

Williams, F. (1980). *Creativity assessment packet*. Buffalo, NY: DOK.

# Chapter 6

# *Evaluating Instructional Outcomes for Gifted Students*

Carolyn M. Callahan

◆ ◆ ◆

IN EFFORTS to serve gifted students, school personnel often become so engaged in debate over identification, grouping, and curriculum issues that they fail to consider their ultimate goals and to develop plans that evaluate the outcomes of their endeavors. This shortcoming applies at both the program and the individual student levels. Hence, school personnel seriously impair opportunities to use data for clear feedback to students and parents about the student's growth and accomplishments and for program development.

Of course, determining the effectiveness of educational services and programs for the gifted is predicated on the assumptions that school personnel (a) know what to look for as reasonable indicators of success, (b) know how to assess change on those indicators, and (c) know how to interpret that change when it does occur. The lack of direction and the dearth of exemplary practice on these assessment issues continue to plague gifted program administrators, teachers, evaluators, and parents.

## ASSESSMENT ISSUES

### The Limitations of Standardized Instruments

One of the lingering problems facing those who attempt to determine the effectiveness of programs for the gifted is the selection or construction of instruments that will yield reliable and valid information. A second, related problem is the determination of indicators of success acceptable to those who must rely on the information for decision making.

These problems stem from several sources, primarily the mismatch between existing standardized instruments and the goals and objectives of gifted programs. Existing standardized achievement instruments have been criticized for their narrowness, lack of validity in assessing the goals of gifted programs, and potential ceiling effects (e.g., Callahan, 1983; Carter, 1986).

### Narrowness of Assessed Knowledge and Skills and the Related Validity Issue

Standardized group achievement tests are designed to assess the traditional curriculum. Test developers go to great lengths to ensure that standardized tests reflect the predominant curricular goals at the appropriate grade level. This results in assessment across traditional curricular areas within a narrow range of expectations. The selection of both the content and the level of thinking required to answer the questions on such tests reflects the aim of assessing those areas most students are exposed to in school. This stands in contrast to the broad and extended goals of programs for the gifted. These goals encompass such skills as the development of creative and critical thinking, development of independent learning skills, and advanced content knowledge. In addition, the content of most gifted programs falls under the rubric of "enrichment"—content not normally included within the traditional course of instruction.

This narrowness of assessment leads to a validity issue. Validity is simply a term use to describe the degree to which a test assesses what it is intended to assess. A test may be valid for one purpose, but not another. Standardized tests are an excellent example of this tenet. That is, standardized tests might be quite accurate in assessing the outcome of the traditional program because the items closely match the goals and objectives of that program; however, they may be very invalid for assessing the goals of a gifted program because of the mismatch described above. Even when the standardized tests propose to assess the thinking skills that are now being integrated into all curricular areas, caution must be exercised. Too often, the level of thinking required is still very low and does not reflect the objectives of gifted programs.

When students are in a gifted program based on an acceleration model, the use of standardized tests may be justified if there is a close match between the test chosen and the content to be taught. However, even when the curriculum offered to gifted students is accelerated, the use of standardized assessments presents very particular problems. If on-grade assessments are used, the range of items presented to students will fail to assess accelerated goals and objectives because few items will go beyond the traditional grade level. If out-of-level assessment is done, the use of new types of answer sheets, the type face and size, the density of problem presentation, and even the length of the test may interfere with the assessment process.

### Ceiling Effects

Standardized tests are also limited because of the insufficient number and variety of items in the advanced, more difficult ranges of the tests, making it impossible to fully assess student growth. This is particularly a problem when students are identified for placement in a gifted program on the basis of high scores on one of these tests. If a student earns a score between the 95th and the 99th percentile on a standardized achievement test, that student has most probably responded correctly to nearly all of the items prior to any instruction at all. Thus, if these instruments are used to measure change, there is simply no way for change to be demonstrated because there are not enough items at an advanced enough level to be sensitive to that change.

### Regression to the Mean

High scores on a pretest also will result in a statistical phenomenon known as regression to the mean. This effect occurs because all test scores contain some random error; that is, on any given day, a student may earn a higher or lower score, not because of what he or she knows or can do, but because the student guessed correctly, or marked an answer incorrectly, or misread a question, or any other reason. For students who earn high scores, the error factor was most likely in their favor that day. Thus, when they take the test again, the error may then work against them and lower their scores (i.e., cause their scores to regress to the mean).

## The Lack of Suitable Measures Addressing the Outcomes of Gifted Programs

Although some measures of critical thinking skills and creativity have been used in assessing the effectiveness of programs for the gifted, these measures are usually limited in scope and address only a small number of the many goals of gifted programs. For example, although the *Torrance Tests of Creative Thinking* (TTCT) (Torrance, 1966) are considered reasonable measures of the specific skills of fluency, flexibility, and originality, many experts question whether scores on this test are suitable for the assessment of the larger construct labeled creativity. Furthermore, many of these instruments (e.g., the TTCT, the *Ross Test of Higher Cognitive Processes* [Ross & Ross, 1976], the *New Jersey Test of Reasoning Skills* [Shipman, 1985]) are used in the identification process and the students are selected on the basis of high scores on the tests. Thus, if these same instruments are used for assessing change, ceiling effects and regression to the mean effects may interfere with the assessment of true change.

The numbers of such instruments are also very limited, which is not surprising in light of the complexities of gifted programs and the drawbacks of developing instruments for such programs. Test development and publication is extremely expensive, requiring considerable distribution to warrant the investment. The market does not exist for instruments designed to assess the outcomes of gifted programs. There are no "national" or "state" curricula or even objectives for gifted programs. Even in those areas where professionals agree on general goals, such as the development of creativity or higher level thinking skills, there is little commonality in definition and little agreement about the appropriateness of a given skill for a given grade level. Also, absolutely no common content base exists except in some acceleration programs and in advanced placement courses. In many programs based on individual programming models and independent study, there may not even be a common set of goals for all students served by the gifted program.

## Locally Developed Assessment Instruments

Locally developed instruments are one logical alternative. Unfortunately, few school-level personnel have expertise in instrument construction. The result is failure to create quality assessment tools with appropriate evidence of reliability or validity and failure to establish reasonable norms and standards. Finally, in programs that are individualized in nature, it is nearly impossible to identify one instrument that will assess the myriad goals that might be part of the educational programs of even a small number of students.

## Lack of Attention to Affective Concerns

One of the most serious concerns of parents and teachers of gifted students is appropriate development of the gifted child's social skills and satisfactory adjustment. These areas of concern have been raised repeatedly in the literature on acceleration and even in the literature on enrichment programs (e.g., Adderholdt-Elliot, 1991; Cornell, Callahan, Bassin, & Ramsay, 1991; Hoge & Renzulli, 1991). Nevertheless, relatively little effort is made to assess or document the effects of a particular gifted program on the affective development of the students in that program. Although educators have definite opinions about such practices as acceleration (Southern, Jones, & Fiscus, 1989), these opinions are not necessarily research based. These judgments are most often based on one negative, aberrant case, and tend to ignore the successful cases because those cases failed to generate the publicity that surrounded the negative case. The research literature is not conclusive about the effects of these educational practices (e.g., Cornell, Callahan, Bassin, & Ramsay, 1991; Shore, Cornell, Robinson, & Ward, 1991). It is more important in the evaluation of gifted students that each child be assessed relative to how a given educational practice is impacting him or her than to rely on unsubstantiated generalizations (Hunsaker & Callahan, 1991).

Finally, it is important for educators, parents, and psychologists to remember that, when no special program is implemented, they are not absolved from the responsibility of assessing the cognitive and affective development of gifted students. The regular education program *is* a program and school personnel should be constantly evaluating its impact on these special children.

# ALTERNATIVE STRATEGIES

Individual evaluation and program evaluation are, of course, closely related. The evaluation of student outcomes is ultimately one of the concerns of the program evaluator, who is concerned with the impact of the program on students in general. The teacher, the parent, and the psychologist are concerned with the individual student. Some of the concerns with outcome evaluation and strategies for dealing with those concerns are common to both groups.

## Out-of-Level Assessment

As suggested above, to assess a program that is based on acceleration, school personnel may be able to use an out-of-level, standardized test effectively. The more advanced standardized test should be used only when the objectives assessed by the level of the instrument selected match instructional objectives. However, even when that match is clear, care must be taken at certain grade levels to ascertain that the format of the test does not interfere with performance. For example, in testing second graders on upper level forms of the *Iowa Test of Basic*

*Skills* (Hieronymus, Hoover, & Lindquist, 1990) at the National Research Center on the Gifted and Talented, we found that the format of answering on separate answer sheets was new, confusing, and ultimately inhibiting to performance. Some standardized tests use much less "white space" on upper level tests, and younger students may find the page layout very distracting. We have also found that students accustomed to being able to answer all or nearly all items on a test can become very frustrated with a test that has more difficult items. All of these issues suggest that careful examination of the test objectives, format, instructions, and length must precede use of the instrument or school personnel may misinterpret scores.

## Assessment in Nontraditional Areas and in Traditional Areas Using Nontraditional Means

Issues of validity and reliability often dictate that the instruments that are used to assess gifted students' growth and performance must be locally developed. A wide variety of instruments have been constructed for this purpose, including

- Surveys and questionnaires
- Rating scales or checklists to evaluate student products and performances, attitudes, behaviors, and so forth
- Standardized achievement tests
- Standardized self-inventories of adjustment, attitudes, interests
- Interview protocols
- Teacher-made or evaluator-constructed achievement tests (objective and subjective)

The current movement in educational assessment of student outcomes is away from a total focus on standardized, multiple-choice tests toward assessment of student performance through examination of students' products in portfolios and exhibitions, student performances, and the processes that students use to complete projects, and even process portfolios (Gardner, 1980). In some disciplines, the use of any standardized instrument, especially any standardized paper-and-pencil assessment, is unwarranted. These include the visual and performing arts and leadership. Such assessment also is inappropriate for certain goals and objectives within the traditional academic areas of science, mathematics, social studies, language arts, and foreign language. Of particular concern are areas where the goals and objectives of instruction go beyond the simple acquisition of knowledge to the application, analysis, and evaluation of concepts from a discipline and areas where creative production are the focus of instruction.

The development of portfolio and performance assessment tools is critical to fair and authentic assessment in these areas. Assessment tools can relate to processes involved in creation or execution in any discipline or to products that are produced. In either case, the development of these portfolio or product and performance tools requires careful examination of goals, careful delineation of categories or behaviors for rating or evaluation, and extremely careful selection and training of raters. A machine can score a correctly marked answer sheet; experts must rate portfolios and products. The expertise must be of two sorts: (a) expertise in judging the kind of product or performance and (b) expertise in the assessment of the work of students of the particular age group assessed.

Use of product evaluation and performance evaluation is becoming much more prevalent, and school personnel need to draw on the technology that is being developed for general assessment to improve instruments in this arena. For example, the performance assessment program in Connecticut has included attempts to assess many outcomes that are parallel to those of gifted programs (products that reflect real-life solutions to problems, creative solutions to problems, etc.) (Collison & Greig, 1990). These assessments are designed to "approximate real-life, authentic situations with integrated complex, and challenging tasks . . . more appropriate to use to assess individual achievement and higher level thinking skills" (Zimmerman, 1991). Hence, they have potential for the assessment of many of the goals and objectives common in programs for the gifted.

The criteria for tasks used in such assessment programs are suggestive of the kinds of outcomes expected from the activities considered important in a differentiated curriculum. For example, the first criterion that Zimmerman (1991) listed for successful performance evaluation is evaluating students on tasks that approximate disciplined inquiry (synthesized by Zimmerman from Archbald and Newman, 1988, and Wiggins, 1989). This closely matches the goal of many gifted programs of having students produce "real-life products" or demonstrate in-depth understanding of the discipline. Considering knowledge holistically, rather than in fragmented parts, matches concerns for the use of broad-based themes, integrated curriculum, and so on, advocated in programs for the gifted (Kaplan & Gould, 1987). Valuing student achievement, in and of itself and apart from whether it is being assessed, is closely aligned to the notions of autonomous and self-directed learning (Betts, 1986; Treffinger, 1986), as is the criteria of educating students to assess their own achievements in conjunction with assessments by others. Attending to both process and products of teaching and learning is closely aligned to concerns in gifted education with developing the processes of production, and even more specifically to Renzulli and Reis's (1985) notions of practicing the discipline as professionals practice the discipline. Finally, expecting students to present and defend their work in written or oral form and publicly is reminiscent of Renzulli and Reis's notion of presenting work to a real-life audience.

Product and performance assessment, however, is of no value if inappropriately implemented. Unfortunately, carelessly developed authentic assessments have too often been substituted for carefully developed standardized assessment, while the importance of reliability, validity, and comparability to all assessment tools is ignored. Donahue (1992) also noted other impediments to appropriate use of authentic assessment. First, all assessment is time-consuming, but performance assessment is tremendously time-consuming across the stages of instrument development, administration, and scoring. Second, proper implementation of authentic assessment requires intensive and extensive teacher training and staff development. Finally, the seeming validity from the appearance of items is often substituted for careful sampling of the domain of behaviors to be assessed and careful examination of the validity of decisions based on these assessments.

Stiggens (1987) provided guidelines and a carefully developed teaching module for those interested in construction of performance assessments. Briefly, the steps include the following:

1. Clarify the reason for assessment (specify decisions to be made, specify decision makers, specify use to be made of results, describe students to be assessed)

2. Clarify performance to be evaluated (specify the content or skill focus, select the type of performance to be evaluated, list performance criteria)

3. Design exercises (select form of exercises, determine obtrusiveness of assessment, determine the amount of evidence to be gathered)

4. Design performance rating plan (determine the type of scores needed, determine who is to rate performance, clarify score recording method to be used)

Stiggens stressed the importance of maximizing validity by carefully considering purpose, being explicit about student characteristics to be observed and evaluated, choosing and clearly explicating a continuum along which behaviors will be rated, and comparing ratings to other performance indicators. Reliability comes from using carefully defined criteria with clear explanations; having thoroughly trained raters; planning and using appropriate scoring procedures; sampling the full range of performance contexts and behaviors; minimizing rater bias by careful training in cultural awareness; providing clear, unbiased criteria; and training and providing for standardized and uniform assessment conditions when appropriate.

## Multiple Assessment

One of the strategies used to garner more credibility for any assessment of programs or individuals is *triangulation*. This technique is used when school personnel recognize that they do not have a perfectly controlled design, a perfect instrument, or perfectly unbiased sources of information. The term evolves from the strategy used to locate a position or point when surveying. The essential principle is to use multiple indicators from multiple sources to assure consensus on the finding. In assessing student outcomes, professionals can apply this concept by thinking in terms of multiple assessment strategies, multiple measures, and multiple scorers or raters. For example, in assessing the student outcomes in a program that emphasizes creativity, school personnel might use a standardized measure such as the *Torrance Tests of Creative Thinking* (Torrance, 1966) (assuming it was not used for identification) to assess some of the related skills that are specifically addressed in the program, a product rating scale used by experts in the discipline of the product with a dimension specifically focused on characteristics of student products that are creative in nature, a process rating scale upon which the teacher rates the steps engaged in by the students in creative production, and a self-rating scale on creativity completed by the students. Using all these data points would provide the best possible assessment of the student's overall performance.

## Assessing Affective Outcomes

The literature includes few systematic efforts to monitor the social and emotional adjustment of students in gifted programs (Hunsaker & Callahan, 1991). The most frequent method for monitoring students seems to be sole reliance on teacher observations. One exception is the Early Entrance Program (EEP) at the University of Washington (Janos et al., 1988; Robinson, 1983). In that program (for students age 14 or younger and/or who have not yet entered the 10th grade), students are assigned departmental and college advisors, and they must with an EEP counselor to check their program and any changes to it. Group meetings are held twice weekly. A mid-quarter interview is conducted with each student to monitor progress and resolve problems.

The Program for the Exceptionally Gifted at Mary Baldwin College requires that residence advisers keep daily logs on students, noting any indicators that might require monitoring, such as emotional indicators and behavioral misconduct (Cornell, Callahan, & Loyd, 1991).

Many programs have monitored groups of students and tried to assess the overall program effects on affective variables. The instruments that have been used include standardized group assessments, such as the *California Psychological Inventory* (Gough, 1987), the *Harter Self-Perception Profile for Adolescents* (Callahan, Cornell, & Loyd, 1992), the Cattell *Sixteen Personality Factor Questionnaire* (Institute for Personality and Ability Testing, 1980), and the *Adjective Checklist* (Brody & Benbow, 1987). In addition, some studies have used individual personality assessments such as the Rorschach (Callahan et al., 1992; Loftus, 1989), sociometric data, comparisons of referral data for emotional problems (Hobson, 1948), teacher rating scales (e.g., Klausmeier, 1963; Klausmeier, Goodwin, & Ronda, 1968), assessments of involvement in extracurricular activities (e.g., Alexander & Skinner, 1980), and specially constructed questionnaires (e.g., Brody & Benbow, 1987; Richardson & Benbow, 1990). See Table 6.1 for a listing of the types of tools that have been used to assess the outcomes of gifted programs.

One of the critical issues reflected by the listing of possible assessment tools is the lack of a clear criterion of "appropriate adjustment." Although there is agreement that any clinical adjustment problem is problematic, there is little agreement about the appropriate indicators of "good adjustment." One of the predominant and widely accepted variables considered in assessment of adjustment is healthy self-concept. The often-used assessments of extracurricular involvement, sociometric data, and friendships are less clearly related to adjustment and perhaps reflect more of the "average person's" conception of what should be, rather than what the child might find acceptable and, in fact, desirable. It is critical in evaluating the adjustment of the child that the child's happiness and satisfaction with life take precedence over artificial criteria professionals might create. (This does not, however, preclude concerns over the rights and happiness of other children or adults in the gifted child's sphere.)

# THE STANDARDS ISSUE

Even when school personnel have managed to find appropriate instruments, have been able to assess change over time, and are comfortable with the reliability of the assessments, several nagging problems re-

## TABLE 6.1. Types of Assessment Tools Used in Evaluation Studies

| Type of Question Asked | Kinds of Instruments or Data Used |
|---|---|
| *What is the immediate impact of the program on the students' achievement?* | • Standardized achievement tests—generic and specific<br>• Grades in courses or classes—current<br>• Teacher and principal ratings of student success in school<br>• Self-report of success through questionnaire<br>• Interviews with students, parents, and teachers<br>• SAT scores<br>• Surveys/ratings by professors<br>• Aptitude tests<br>• Specialized tests of creativity, problem solving, critical thinking, etc.<br>• Product/performance assessment |
| *What is the long-term impact of acceleration on the students' achievement?* | • Grades in later courses; high school grade point average; college grade point average; college matriculation and completion; retentions<br>• Honors and awards<br>• Number and place of college admissions<br>• Self-report<br>• *Scholastic Aptitude Test* scores; *Graduate Record Examination* scores<br>• Number of advanced placement exam credits earned<br>• Participation in honors courses or other advanced classes<br>• Participation in extracurricular activities<br>• Career choice |
| *What is the immediate impact of acceleration programs on social adjustment?* | • Parent ratings<br>• Teacher ratings<br>• Self-report on questionnaires<br>• Sociometric data<br>• Personality tests (objective and projective)<br>• Referrals for emotional problems<br>• Participation in extracurricular activities<br>• Standardized behavioral ratings<br>• Conformance to school rules and regulations |

main in judging those outcomes. Are the student outcomes achieved better than "nothing," better than other gifted programs, meeting the standards set for gifted students in the programs, or meeting the highest criteria set in the field? The assumption that a "gifted program" is being compared with "no program" is always unfounded. Gifted students will always be in *some* educational program, whether it is a special program or the existing regular school program. It is easy to assume that, in evaluating a new reading program, if this program is not continued, then another will be adopted. Some educators often assume, however, that if they have no gifted program, they have no program. In reality, the question of whether the program is better than nothing does not make sense. The gifted students will still be in the school in *some* educational program, even if the formal gifted program does not exist. Thus, the question is whether to compare the effectiveness of a program to other gifted programs, to outcomes of the regular curriculum, or to a set of standards (criteria). To what degree do educators hold the program responsible for meeting the standards of "the field" and to what degree do they hold the program responsible only for achieving preset goals, even if these goals are considered inadequate for gifted students and their education?

## The Minimum Standard Screen

One of the current trends in the education reform movement is toward setting national standards for achievement. Many states have already set minimum standards for advancement to high school or for graduation from high school, and several officials of the U.S. government are proposing national examinations. The potential danger of this movement is that the minimum standards set by such tests will come to be seen as acceptable for all when, in fact, these standards and examinations fall far short of assessing the predominant goals and objectives for gifted students. The current formats do not even provide a reasonable benchmark against which to assess educational achievements of gifted programs. It is the clear responsibility of educators in gifted programs to look beyond such standards and measures for gifted student assessment.

## Grade Equivalency Scores

Parents, teachers, counselors, and psychologists often misinterpret the scores of gifted students. Teachers often say that a grade equivalent score of 5.3 in reading means that the child is reading at the fifth-grade level. In fact, it means that the child earned the same number of points as the average child in the third month of fifth grade, which may or may not reflect fifth-grade–level performance as defined by the curriculum of that school. It is tempting to use changes in grade equivalency scores on standardized tests as standards for gifted program assessment. Aside from the validity issues raised above, it is important to recognize that grade equivalency has little meaning for academically gifted students. The concept of grade equivalency is based on differences between the scores of average students across grades, not gifted students. We have no index for what a reasonable change in grade equivalent scores would be for gifted students across the period of an academic year—whether or not in gifted programs.

## Control Groups

When trying to assess the effectiveness of educational programs, educators have traditionally compared the achievement of students receiving special services with those who do not receive those services. This problem has been discussed in many articles on gifted program evaluation. There is simply no way educators have been able to (or should) restrict access to gifted programs by gifted students. Solutions to this problem have focused on two strategies: using students as their own controls and using matching control groups. Typically, using students as their own controls involves single-subject designs which gather baseline data on outcome measures, institute instructional intervention and measure outcomes, stop interventions to measure outcomes, repeat the intervention, and so on. This kind of assessment might be used in evaluating models such as the "Revolving Door" component of Renzulli and Reis's (1985) Schoolwide Enrichment Model. Comparing projects completed while the student is "revolved in" with projects completed as part of regular classroom instruction (using criteria established as goals for the model) allows educators to demonstrate the differences in types of projects produced within the special classroom setting and also the influence of the program on other projects.

# PROFESSIONAL AND PARENT ROLES

## The Role of the School Psychologist and Counselor

The school psychologist and counselor play critical roles in helping both the gifted child and the child's parents understand the data that are provided through testing and other assessments. Not only should the psychologist and counselor be available to help explain such data, they should also be prepared to help interpret the gifted child's behaviors in terms of both the expected behaviors for children of that age and for gifted children of that age. For example, it is not unusual for a gifted child to wonder about death or worry about social injustices at an earlier age than average students. Parents need to understand that this is not an indication of impending depression. The school counselor and psychologist must also be prepared, however, to help assess when behavior does seem unusual. More in-depth assessment of a child's adjustment or achievement may be required to recommend appropriate interventions or placements or to assess the effectiveness of a current placement.

## The Role of the Teacher

The teacher's role in constructing appropriate academic assessment tools has been discussed above. However, the teacher also has the responsibility for continuous behavioral assessment of the child's adjustment to school, peers, and the curricular and programming options. Teachers also need to be wary of imposing artificial criteria. For example, Klausmeier (1963) found that teachers often judged young students to be having problems with adjusting to an acceleration program when they did not sit in their seats for extended periods of time "like the other children did" or if they had "poor handwriting." However, these children were, in fact, able to remain in their seats as long or longer than same-age peers and had motor skills as good as those of age-mates. *The teacher* was the one who was not able to adjust to the age differences in children.

## The Role of the Parents

Parents provide a unique and valuable perspective in evaluating the outcomes of gifted programs. Their input should be sought in helping to evaluate the outcomes of instruction, particularly as they relate to boredom or frustration on the negative side and new interests, projects, and enthusiasm on the positive side. Parents also play a role in helping determine when students are developing competitive or even perfectionist behaviors that may threaten self-concept or self-esteem. A parent may observe the child exhibiting behaviors that lead to inability to complete a task because of perceived inadequacy (when the effort does seem sufficient and the product seems to meet the task requirements), or may see the child having an excessively unhappy response to a less-than-perfect performance, an instance in which he or she was not best or first, and so on. If this seems to be a pattern, then the parent should raise this concern with the teacher.

Parent information about positive outcomes can also be useful to teachers and program administrators, but parents often neglect to share this information. A new interest generated by a school activity or an extracurricular activity may be useful in helping the teacher expand on the student's knowledge and skills in that area.

## CONCLUSION

It is popularly assumed that "the gifted child will make it" and that nobody needs to be overly concerned about that child's success. However, ample evidence indicates that often these children do not realize their potential because the educational system fails to meet their academic or adjustment needs. Unfortunately, this realization may come too late. A carefully planned effort on the part of psychologists, counselors, teachers, and parents can be effective in monitoring the effects of educational decisions on the lives of these children and help provide the necessary data to inform decision making in the most positive way.

## ACKNOWLEDGMENT

Preparation of this chapter was supported by the National Research Center on the Gifted and Talented under the Jacob K. Javits Gifted and Talented Students Education Act (Grant No. R206R00001) and administered by the Office of Educational Research and Improvement, U.S. Department of Education. However, grantees undertaking such projects are encouraged to express freely their professional judgment. This report, therefore, does not necessarily represent the position or policies of the government, and no official endorsement should be inferred.

## REFERENCES

Adderholdt-Elliot, M. (1991). Perfectionism and the gifted adolescent. In M. Bireley & J. Genshaft (Eds.), *Understanding the gifted adolescent* (pp. 65–75). New York: Teachers College Press.

Alexander, P. J., & Skinner, M. E. (1980). The effects of early entrance on subsequent social and academic development. *Journal for the Education of the Gifted, 3*, 147–150.

Archbald, D. A., & Newman, F. M. (1988). *Beyond standardized testing: Assessing achievement in the secondary school.* Reston, VA: National Association of Secondary School Principals.

Betts, G. T. (1986). The autonomous learning model for the gifted and talented. In J. S. Renzulli (Ed.), *Systems and models for developing programs for the gifted and talented* (pp. 27–56). Mansfield Center, CT: Creative Learning Press.

Brody, L. E., & Benbow, C. P. (1987). Accelerative strategies: How effective are they for the gifted? *Gifted Child Quarterly, 31,* 105–110.

Callahan, C. M. (1983). Issues in evaluating programs for the gifted. *Gifted Child Quarterly, 27,* 3–7.

Callahan, C. M., Cornell, D. G., & Loyd, B. L. (1992). The academic development and personal adjustment of high ability young women in an early college entrance program. In N. Colangelo (Ed.), *Proceedings of the Henry B. and Jocelyn Wallace Nation Symposium on Talent Development* (pp. 248–260). Unionville, NY: Trillium.

Carter, K. (1986). Evaluation design: Issues confronting evaluators of gifted programs. *Gifted Child Quarterly, 30,* 88–95.

Collison, J., & Greig, J. (1990, April). *Samples of COMPACT performance tasks in mathematics and science.* Paper presented at the annual meeting of the American Educational Research Association, Boston.

Cornell, D. G., Callahan, C. M., Bassin, L. E., & Ramsay, S. G. (1991). Affective development in accelerated students. In W. T. Southern & E. D. Jones (Eds.), *The academic acceleration of gifted children* (pp. 74–101). New York: Teachers College Press.

Cornell, D. G., Callahan, C. M., & Loyd, B. L. (1991). Socio-emotional adjustment of adolescent girls enrolled in a residential accelerated program. *Gifted Child Quarterly, 35,* 58–66.

Donahue, M. (1992, April). *Performance assessment: Implementation issues.* Paper presented at the annual meeting of the National Council on Measurement in Education, San Francisco.

Gardner, H. (1980). Multiple intelligences: Implications for art and creativity. In W. J. Moody (Ed.), *Artistic intelligences: Implications for education* (pp. 11–27). New York: Teachers College Press.

Gough, H. G. (1987). *California Psychological Inventory, 1987 Revised Edition.* Palo Alto, CA: Consulting Psychologists Press.

Hieronymus, A. N., Hoover, H. D., & Lindquist, E. F. (1990). *Iowa Test of Basic Skills.* Chicago: Riverside.

Hobson, J. R. (1948). Mental age as a workable criterion for school admission. *Elementary School Journal, 48,* 312–321.

Hoge, R. D., & Renzulli, J. S. (1991). *Self-concept and the gifted child.* Storrs, CT: The National Research Center on the Gifted and Talented.

Hunsaker, S. L., & Callahan, C. M. (1991). Student assessment and evaluation. In W. T. Southern & E. D. Jones (Eds.), *The academic acceleration of gifted children* (pp. 207–222). New York: Teachers College Press.

Institute for Personality and Ability Testing. (1980). *Sixteen Personality Factor Questionnaire.* Champaign, IL: Author.

Janos, P. M., Robinson, N. M., Carter, C., Chapel, A., Cufley, R., Curland, M., Daily, M., Guilland, M., Heinzig, M., Kehl, H., Lu, S., Sherry, D.,

Stoloff, J., & Wise, A. (1988). A cross-sectional developmental study of the relations of students who enter college early. *Gifted Child Quarterly, 32,* 210–215.

Kaplan, S. N., & Gould, B. T. (1987). *Developing competencies related to a differentiated curriculum for the gifted / talented.* Ventura, CA: Office of the Ventura County Superintendent of Schools.

Klausmeier, H. J. (1963). Effects of accelerating older elementary pupils: A follow-up. *Journal of Educational Psychology, 54,* 165–171.

Klausmeier, H. J., Goodwin, W. L., & Ronda, T. (1968). Effects of accelerating bright, older elementary school pupils: A second follow-up. *Journal of Educational Psychology, 59,* 53–58.

Loftus, K. A. (1989). Rorschach measures of identity development in academically talented female adolescents. *Dissertations Abstracts International, 50,* 5324B.

Renzulli, J. S., & Reis, S. M. (1985). *The schoolwide enrichment model: A comprehensive plan for educational excellence.* Mansfield Center, CT: Creative Learning Press.

Richardson, T. M., & Benbow, C. P. (1990). Long-term effects of acceleration on the social–emotional adjustment of mathematically precocious youth. *Journal of Educational Psychology, 82,* 464–469.

Robinson, H. B. (1983). A case for radical acceleration: Programs of the Johns Hopkins University and the University of Washington. In C. P. Benbow & J. C. Stanley (Eds.), *Academic precocity: Aspects of its development* (pp. 139–159). Baltimore: Johns Hopkins University Press.

Ross, J., & Ross, C. (1976). *Ross Test of Higher Cognitive Processes.* Novato, CA: Academic Therapy Publications.

Shipman, V. (1985). *New Jersey Test of Reasoning Skills.* Montclair, NJ: Montclair State College, Institute for the Advancement of Philosophy for Children.

Shore, B. M., Cornell, D. G., Robinson, A., & Ward, V. S. (1991). *Recommended practices in gifted education: A critical analysis.* New York: Teachers College Press.

Southern, W. T., Jones, E. D., & Fiscus, E. D. (1989). Practitioner objections to the academic acceleration of young gifted children. *Gifted Child Quarterly, 33,* 29–35.

Stiggens, R. J. (1987, Fall). Design and development of performance assessments. *Educational Measurement: Issues and Practices,* pp. 33–42.

Torrance, E. P. (1966). *Torrance Tests of Creative Thinking.* Bensenville, IL: Scholastic Testing Service.

Treffinger, D. J. (1986). Fostering effective, independent learning through individualized programming. In J. S. Renzulli (Ed.), *Systems and models for developing programs for the gifted and talented* (pp. 429–461). Mansfield Center, CT: Creative Learning Press.

Wiggins, G. (1989). Teaching to the (authentic) test. *Educational Leadership, 47*(7), 41–47.

Zimmerman, E. (1991). *Authentic evaluation of progress and achievement of artistically talented students from diverse backgrounds.* Unpublished manuscript, Indiana University, Bloomington.

# Part III

# Educational Services

# Chapter 7

# The Educational Continuum and Delivery of Services

**John F. Feldhusen, Sidney M. Moon**

◆　◆　◆

GIFTEDNESS CAN BE defined in a number of ways. Some professionals define giftedness based on performance on tests of intelligence, achievement, or aptitude. For instance, a minimum IQ of 130, achievement test scores at or above the 90th percentile, or Scholastic Aptitude Test scores (in seventh or eighth grade) above 500 verbal or quantitative might be used as criteria. Others define giftedness as special characteristics such as those assessed by the *Scales for Rating the Behavioral Characteristics of Superior Students* (Renzulli, Smith, White, Callahan, & Hartman, 1976) or the *Purdue Academic Rating Scales* (Feldhusen, Hoover, & Sayler, 1990). These scales include such items as "is a keen and alert observer" or "organizes ideas and sequences well." Still another way of defining giftedness is to delineate special needs (VanTassel, 1979). According to this approach, the gifted are children who have special needs to be challenged in thinking, in project activity, and in subject matter learning. Giftedness may also be defined as superior ability in any worthwhile area of human endeavor (DeHaan & Havighurst, 1957; Witty, 1951).

The major definition of giftedness prevailing in the United States and adopted in many other countries derives from the Marland report to the U.S. Congress in 1972:

> Gifted and talented children are those identified by professionally qualified persons who by virtue of outstanding abilities are capable of high performance. These are children who require differentiated educational programs and services beyond those normally provided by the regular school program in order to realize their contributions to self and society.

The report delineated the following categories of giftedness:

1. General intellectual ability
2. Specific academic aptitude
3. Creative or productive thinking
4. Leadership ability
5. Visual and performing arts
6. Psychomotor ability (pp. 13–14)

Our own conception of giftedness emphasizes "talent" as the definer of giftedness (Feldhusen, 1992b). The field of gifted education has long used the terms *gifted, creative,* and *talented* as virtually synonymous. Feldhusen (1992b) urged that it would be much more productive for the education of highly able youth to focus on identification of special talents and aptitudes. Feldhusen (1992b) and Treffinger (1988) also suggested that developmental efforts should be focused on students' special talents, aptitudes, and abilities, not on general gifted treatments.

Our own definition, then, is as follows: Talented youth are those who have especially high aptitude, ability, or potential in any worthwhile area of human endeavor as determined by tests, rating scales, behavioral observations, or assessment of past performance in authentic learning activities and in comparison with a normative peer group. Thus, children might be judged talented if they score at 127 on an intelligence test or the 96th percentile in language arts on a standardized achievement test, are rated very high on the "mathematics scale" of the *Purdue Academic Rating Scales,* or have a portfolio of highly creative writings and essays.

The talent, once identified, represents precocity and potential. The student's performance is far ahead of age peers and exhibits potential for continued superior achievements. That momentum is best sustained by continuing opportunities to surge ahead, to develop the talents to the highest degree through accelerated and enriched learning experiences that maintain academic challenge and motivation to achieve (Feldhusen, 1986a). Peers, parents, and teachers often urge the talented child to slow down, adapt to the norm, and be like everybody else. Thus, the talent momentum may be lost. In special classes and with teachers' and parents' encouragement, however, youth can experience the joy of accomplishment, the satisfaction of self-fulfillment that comes from a sense of using and developing one's special aptitudes to the fullest.

School services and programs must be adapted and adjusted to the special needs and characteristics of talented youth. Maker (1982) proposed that modifications of the school experience for talented youth should come through the curriculum, especially in alterations of the content, the processes of learning, the products of learning experiences, and the learning environment. The content should be higher level, more complex, and more extensive. The processes of learning should involve much more and higher level thinking and conceptualization. The products such as project reports and performances should reach higher levels of excellence such as one might expect of talented adults. Finally, the learning environment should be open, creative, and challenging.

Feldhusen (1994) presented the following as guidelines for curriculum modifications necessary for talented learners:

1. Focus on major ideas, issues, themes, problems, concepts, and principles.
2. Emphasize the need for a large knowledge base.
3. When possible, use an interdisciplinary approach.
4. Emphasize in-depth research and independent study with original and high-level products or presentations.
5. Teach research skills and thinking skills as metacognitive processes.
6. Incorporate higher level thinking skills in content study—in discussions, independent study, research, and writing.
7. Increase the level, complexity, and pace of the curriculum to fit the precocity of the students.
8. Teach methods for independence, self-direction, and self-evaluation in learning. (p. 113)

All of these modifications should involve acceleration and enrichment (Shore, Cornell, Robinson, & Ward, 1991); that is, talented learners need learning activities at a level, pace, and breadth that matches their readiness or levels of precocity.

School programs, however, usually focus on instruction for the majority of youth who are at the normative level and on youth who have handicaps or disadvantages. In many schools, there is little or no attention to the special, high-level needs of talented youth. There are ridiculous myths that circulate among school personnel that talented youth will suffer from "pressure" to achieve at higher levels, that they will suffer early "burnout," or that they will become "social misfits" (Southern & Jones, 1991). Although good research refutes these myths (Robinson & Noble, 1991), they continue to be promulgated in schools, and talented youth suffer as a result.

Appropriate education for talented youth must provide enriched and accelerated curricula, classroom experiences that are challenging and open to discussion, opportunities to work with talented peers and project activity with high-level expectations, and a striving for excellence (Feldhusen, 1986b). How to provide the range and types of school services to meet the needs of talented youth is the subject of the next section of this chapter.

# RANGE AND TYPES OF SERVICES

A wide variety of school activities, programs, and curricula can be adapted or used directly as services to meet the needs of talented youth (Feldhusen, 1983a). It is a serious mistake to assume that only specifically delineated models labeled "gifted programs" can meet their needs. Although a variety of models have been set forth as programs for the gifted (Juntune, 1986; Renzulli, 1986), they are often eclectic in nature and present little evidence of effectiveness when compared with one another. Stanley (1980) advocated a "smorgasbord" of opportunities as the ideal approach to meeting the needs of talented youth. The smorgasbord can include a broad range of school and community offerings. Feldhusen (1986b) presented an extensive list of in-school alternatives, as shown in Table 7.1. Feldhusen et al. (1990) advocated that schools begin by doing an inventory of all the potential resources and activities that are already in place and might be useful in meeting the needs of talented youth for stimulating, enriched, and accelerated instruction.

Colleges and universities are rich potential sources of educational experiences for talented youth. Many offer Saturday and summer programs for both residential and community students (Feldhusen, 1983b, 1991b). High school students can begin to take regular college courses for credit on a part-time basis or elect to enter college early (Stanley, 1991). A number of colleges and universities in the United States now offer special services to facilitate early admission of talented or highly able youth (Sayler, 1990).

The community at large can also be a rich source of opportunities for talented youth. Community programs such as 4-H clubs and scouts can provide talented youth with opportunities to develop task commitment and leadership abilities. Special classes are often offered at museums, art institutes, and science centers. The history of a community can be a valuable area of study for some talented youth through both library research and visits to historical sites. Laboratories and research centers often open their doors to internships or mentoring experiences for talented youth. Musical and drama organizations also wel-

**TABLE 7.1.   The Continuum of Services at Various Age Levels**

| Elementary Services | Junior High or Middle School Services | High School Services |
|---|---|---|
| 1. Full-time classes | 1. Counseling<br>  a. *Group*<br>  b. *Individual* | 1. Counseling<br>  a. *Group*<br>  b. *Individual* |
| 2. Pull-out program | | |
| 3. Cluster grouping | 2. Honors classes | 2. Honors classes |
| 4. Individualized Education Programs | 3. Future problem solving | 3. Advanced placement classes |
| 5. Junior Great Books | 4. Junior Great Books | 4. Foreign languages |
| 6. Future problem solving | 5. Odyssey of the Mind | 5. Seminars |
| 7. Odyssey of the Mind | 6. Career education | 6. Mentorships |
| 8. Career explorations | 7. Seminars | 7. Internships |
| 9. Mentors | 8. Mentors | 8. Concurrent college enrollment |
| 10. Saturday classes<br>  a. *Arts*<br>  b. *Academics*<br>  c. *Enrichment topics* | 9. Advanced placement or college classes | 9. College classes in high school |
| 11. Summer programs | 10. Special opportunities<br>  a. *Art*<br>  b. *Music*<br>  c. *Drama*<br>  d. *Dance* | 10. Special opportunities<br>  a. *Art*<br>  b. *Music*<br>  c. *Drama*<br>  d. *Dance* |
| 12. Foreign language | 11. Acceleration | 11. Special projects for vocationally talented |
| 13. Early admission | 12. Special projects for vocationally talented | 12. Debate |
| 14. Grade advancement | 13. Foreign language | 13. Correspondence study |
| 15. Math Olympiad | 14. Correspondence study | 14. Independent study |
| 16. Counseling | 15. Independent study | 15. Early entrance to college |
| 17. Special library access | 16. Math contests | |

Adapted from a figure that first appeared in "A New Conception of Giftedness and Programming for the Gifted" by J. F. Feldhusen, 1986, *Illinois Council for the Gifted Journal, 5,* pp. 2–6. Adapted by permission.

come youth in apprenticeship roles. Counselors, parents, and teachers can serve as the stimuli and guides to these services for talented youth.

We turn next to specific types of services that are appropriate at different age-grade levels. Although the general guidelines set forth previously are applicable across levels, some special considerations are applicable within the four major time frames: preschool, elementary, middle school, and high school.

## Preschool

Some talented youth show extreme precocity prior to entering school. They may be able to read, do arithmetic, or speak fluently and logically as early as $2\frac{1}{2}$ or 3 years of age (Gross & Feldhusen, 1990). The momentum in learning can be sustained only by continuing opportunities to read, do arithmetic, and talk with intelligent adults. Some children will have access to excellent and challenging preschool programs. Others will have to depend on their parents to provide the resources, stimulation, and experiences to sustain their momentum and growth. Dunn, Dunn, and Treffinger (1992), in their book *Bringing Out the Giftedness in Your Child,* have offered an abundance of ideas and suggestions for developing giftedness in preschool children.

Early admission to school is another excellent option for highly precocious children. Proctor, Feldhusen, and Black (1988) reviewed the literature on early admission and found that it is a sound approach if guidelines they offer are followed for assessing and placing such children in school.

## Elementary

At the elementary level, a common form of enrichment programming for talented youth is the pull-out/resource room (Cox, Daniel, & Boston, 1985; Gallagher, Weiss, Oglesby, & Thomas, 1983). The value of pull-out enrichment has been vigorously debated in the field of gifted education (Renzulli, 1987a, 1987b; VanTassel-Baska, 1987a, 1987b). Strengths of the model include the opportunities it creates for implementation of a differentiated curriculum by specially trained teachers in an intellectually stimulating environment conducive to the development of creativity (Cox et al., 1985; Renzulli, 1987a, 1987b). Weaknesses include disruption of regular classroom routines, missed instruction in the regular classroom, and the small amount of total time spent in the program (Belcastro, 1987; Cox et al., 1985; VanTassel-Baska, 1987a). Research indicates that pull-out programs have been effective in enhancing the cognitive skills, affective development, and achievement of gifted youth (Moon, Feldhusen, & Dillon, 1994; Renzulli & Reis, 1994; Vaughn, Feldhusen, & Asher, 1991).

Feldhusen (1991a) and Feldhusen and Sayler (1990) advocated full-time, self-contained classes for gifted and talented youth at the elementary level, based on their studies of the effects and value of such classes. These classes offer excellent opportunities to provide for advanced and accelerated curricula and instruction for talented youth, to give them the benefits of stimulation by intellectual peers, to challenge and motivate them to high-level achievement, and to sustain the momentum of their intellectual development.

The elementary school years are also an ideal time to grade advance highly talented children. Feldhusen, Proctor, and Black (1986) reviewed the literature on grade advancement of talented youth and concluded that, contrary to the myth that predicts social and emotional damage, the effects are, in reality, almost always positive. Feldhusen (1992a) presented guidelines to help support personnel and parents make sound decisions on grade advancement of talented youth. Those guidelines also are presented later in this chapter.

## Middle School

When talented youth reach the middle school years, it is vital that they have challenging learning experiences, especially in their talent strength areas (Bloom & Sosniak, 1981), and instruction delivered by highly competent teachers (Bloom, 1982). They also need powerful support and facilitation of their talent development from parents (Bloom, 1985; Feldman, 1986). In school, they need honors classes, opportunities to take advanced mathematics and science courses early, counseling that recognizes and helps them clarify their special talents, and a variety of extracurricular opportunities such as Math Olympiad, Junior Great Books, language clubs, and so on. Bloom (1985) noted that, in the middle stage of talent development, those youth who go on to high-level, creative achievement developed strong motivation to achieve in their talent strength area. He also noted that these were the years when youth were expected by teachers and parents to be participating in recitals, contests, and showings and to become increasingly independent in guiding their own intellectual or artistic development. He summarized, "A long-term commitment to the talent field and an increasing passion for the talent development are essential if the individual is to attain the highest levels of capability in the field" (Bloom, 1985, p. 538).

Gagne (1985) suggested that the pattern of development of talent is from broad general abilities or gifts to ever more specific talent strengths. The mediating processes between the general abilities and specific talents, as shown in Figure 7.1, are family, school, and the community, as well as the talented child's own personality dimensions, especially interests, attitudes, and motivations. This view is consistent with Feldhusen's (1992b) assertion that talent develops in a pattern from the broad, general intelligences presented by Gardner (1983) to the specific talent domains presented by Renzulli and Reis (1985). A

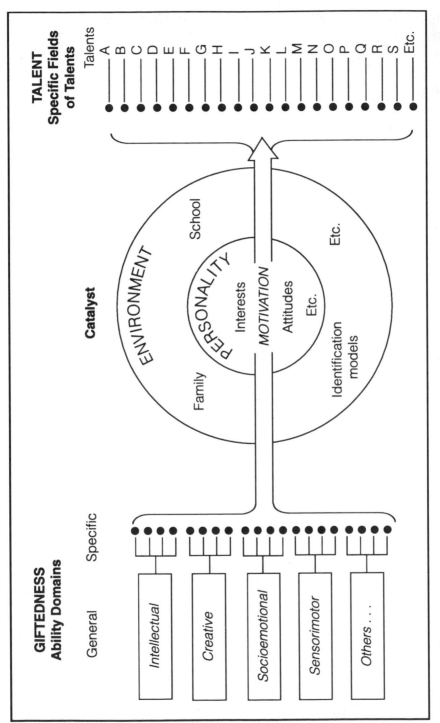

**Figure 7.1.** Gagne's (1985) model of talent development. From "Giftedness and Talent: Reexamining a Reexamination of the Definitions," by F. Gagne, 1985, *Gifted Child Quarterly, 29,* pp. 103–112. Reprinted by permission.

wide variety of stimulating, challenging, accelerated, artistic, intellectual, and affective experiences in schools, home, and community are essential elements in the development of talent.

## High School

The high school years represent the final preparation for the intellectual challenges of college. The school experience should include a diversity of intellectual and aesthetic learning opportunities, as shown in Figure 7.2. Above all, there should be counseling services in both group and individualized forms for talented youth delivered by professionals who understand their special capabilities. Feldhusen and Robinson (1986) suggested that group counseling should be used to help talented youth clarify their career goals and plan long-range educational programs.

College Board Advanced Placement classes, honors classes, and seminars are vital parts of a sound academic program (Feldhusen & Reilly, 1983), as is acceleration to higher level courses in mathematics and science. Career education, especially with mentoring opportunities (Haeger & Feldhusen, 1989), can be linked to the counseling function discussed above. The fundamental career development needs of talented youth are knowledge of the nature of high-level creative occupations and understanding of the educational route to those occupations, combined with a strong commitment to attain them.

Exposure to the arts is essential for aesthetic development of all talented youth, aiding them to develop an aesthetic way of knowing and understanding the world of experience (Eisner, 1985). For those who are talented in art, the school art program must provide high-level, challenging studio experiences with highly talented artists. It should also provide advanced instruction in art history and art criticism.

The importance of extraschool learning experiences in the community and at colleges and universities has been discussed earlier in this chapter. These experiences are akin to the extraschool cultural experiences that should introduce talented youth to the world of classical music, drama, opera, art, dance, and sculpture, broadening the aesthetic experience that is vital to the life fulfillment of talented youth.

Foreign language learning is also a vital and productive experience for talented youth (Garfinkel & Prentice, 1985; VanTassel-Baska, 1981). Verbal capacities are sharpened, a sense of cultural differentiation emerges, world knowledge grows, and academic discipline emerges through foreign language learning. Many talented youth will become members of a broader professional world than that represented by national boundaries.

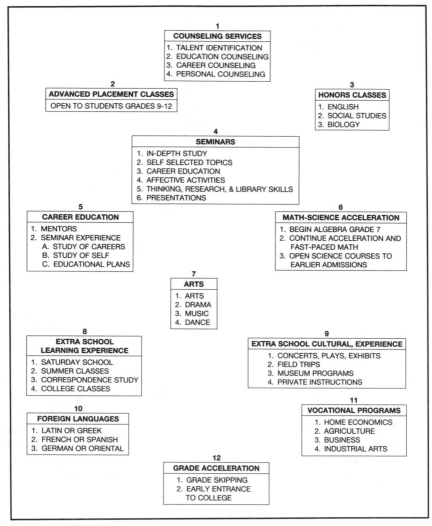

**Figure 7.2.** Secondary program options. Adapted from "The Purdue Secondary Model for Gifted and Talented Youth" by J. F. Feldhusen and A. W. Robinson, in *Systems and Models for Developing Programs for the Gifted and Talented* (p. 158) by J. S. Renzulli (Ed.), 1986, Mansfield Center, CT: Creative Learning Press. Copyright 1986 by Creative Learning Press. Adapted with permission.

Finally, there are domains of talent in the vocational program areas (Feldhusen et al., 1990). High-level, creative, professional careers are now available in agriculture, industry, home economics, and business. Koopman-Dayton (1986) showed that talent in these domains manifests itself in the middle and high school years and is well recognized by teachers in the vocational areas.

Accelerative options are also desirable during the high school years. They include compacting the 4 years of high school to 3 years, taking college courses while in high school, concurrent high school and college enrollment, and entering college early. All these options may be essential to sustaining the momentum and motivation to achieve.

Thus, the high school years represent a time of powerful development for talented youth, with ever closer identification of their ultimate career goals and the educational routes to their attainment. Self-fulfillment of all one's potential is the ultimate goal.

# GUIDELINES FOR SUPPORT PERSONNEL

How can school support personnel facilitate the delivery of educational services to gifted and talented youth? The framework we use in answering this question is the systems-ecological perspective (Fine & Carlson, 1992). This framework suggests that the education of gifted children involves the family, the school, and the community. All three of these systems can offer educational opportunities to the gifted child.

In the section that follows, we discuss ways in which school support personnel can facilitate the delivery of educational opportunities to gifted and talented youth by (a) matching student needs with appropriate services, (b) facilitating grade acceleration, and (c) serving as a catalyst for the development of appropriate educational services in systems where none currently exist.

## Matching Student Needs with Educational Services

Once student needs have been identified, school support personnel can help meet those needs by suggesting appropriate educational services to gifted children and their families. One way to accomplish this matching process is through the development of individual learning plans (Betts, 1985, 1986; Feldhusen et al., 1990; Renzulli & Reis, 1985). These plans can be broad or narrow in scope. At a macro level, learning plans enable students to set and carry out their own learning goals, utilizing the resources of the home, school, and community systems. In fact, one of the best ways to develop a broad program of services for talented youth is through a counseling program that engages talented youth in goal-setting activities, study of higher level careers, and educational routes to those careers, and in the planning of personal odysseys to attain the goals. Feldhusen et al. (1990) advocated specific planning of this nature for talented youth culminating from time to time in an individualized growth plan (Figure 7.3).

## Growth Plan

Name _____ Phone ( _____ ) _____

Grade level _____

Current courses _____ _____

_____ _____

_____ _____

Clubs, organizations _____ _____

_____

Awards, honors _____ _____

_____

Test scores _____ _____

_____

Prior experience in gifted program _____

_____

Interest analysis _____ _____

_____ _____

Learning styles _____ _____

_____ _____

| *Student's own goals* | *Recommended classes for next year* |
|---|---|
| *Recommended activities in school* | *Recommended extraschool activities* |

Final plan _____

**Figure 7.3.** Individualized growth plan for talented youth.

A growth plan includes assessment information, student-generated goals, and recommended activities for accomplishing those goals. In developing a growth plan for a talented child, it is important to involve the child in the process. The purposes of the planning process are to help the child learn to establish his or her own goals and to find ways to accomplish those goals using the resources of the home, the school, and the community. School support personnel can play the role of facilitator. They can help to gather the assessment information, facilitate the goal-setting process, and provide information about options in the school and community that might help the student accomplish his or her goals. Through such careful planning and commitment to a set of goals, talented youth can achieve the autonomy, self-direction, and independence advocated by Betts (1986) in his Autonomous Learner Model. As the student grows, he or she should take an increasingly active role in this process. Eventually, the student should be able to develop his or her own growth plans without the assistance of adults.

Learning plans also can provide guidance to teachers on how to compact the existing curriculum to avoid needless repetition of mastered material and make more room for accelerated or enriched learning experiences. Renzulli and Reis (1985) provided extensive guidance on the compacting process. Recent research on the compacting process is presented by Reis in Chapter 22 of this volume. Support personnel can help teachers with the compacting process by meeting with students and teachers to identify curriculum areas to be considered for compacting and by suggesting appropriate acceleration or enrichment activities.

The process of matching student needs with educational services can occur in many ways, both formal and informal. However it happens, it is important to (a) empower the student to set his or her own goals, (b) maximize the use of existing resources, (c) consider multiple educational options both in and out of school, (d) be creative and flexible, and (e) involve all interested persons in the planning process.

## Facilitating Grade Acceleration

Another appropriate consultant role for school support personnel is facilitating collaborative decision making on grade acceleration. Feldhusen and Kroll (1985, 1991) showed that boredom in school due to low-level, unchallenging, and repetitive curriculum is a major problem for talented youth. Grade advancement is one possible solution to this problem, especially for highly able youth. Feldhusen et al. (1986) reviewed the research on acceleration of gifted children and developed the following guidelines for support personnel to use in making decisions about grade advancement of precocious children:

1. There should be comprehensive psychological evaluation of the child's intellectual functioning, academic skill levels, and social–emotional adjustment. The assessment should not only be concerned with potential risks but also with recognition that failure to advance a precocious child may result in poor study habits, apathy, lack of motivation, and maladjustment.

2. Intellectually, the child should have an IQ of 125 or higher or have a level of mental development at or above the mean of the grade he or she desires to enter.

3. Academically, the child should demonstrate skill levels at or above the mean of the grade desired. If the child is high in several skill levels but low in only one, the child may be advanced to the appropriate grade if private tutoring is provided in the area of weakness.

4. Socially and emotionally, the child should be free of any serious adjustment problems.

5. Physically, the child should be in good health.

6. Support personnel should determine that the child does not feel unduly pressured by the parents to advance.

7. The receiving teacher or teachers should have positive attitudes toward the acceleration and be willing to help the child adjust to the new situation.

8. Efforts should be made to have grade advancement occur at natural transition points, such as the beginning of a new school year. However, mid-year advancements may sometimes be desirable because the new teacher and the teacher the child is leaving may more easily confer about how best to help the child make a smooth transition.

9. All cases of grade advancement should be arranged on a trial basis. The child should be aware that if it does not go well, he or she may request to be returned to the original grade.

10. Care should be exercised not to build up excessive expectations from grade advancement. The child should not be made to feel he or she is a failure if it does not go well. (pp. 26–27)

Potential benefits of grade acceleration include higher levels of academic achievement, recognition of accomplishment, exposure to a new peer group, increased time for careers at the end of schooling, and administrative economy (Kulik & Kulik, 1984; Shore et al., 1991; Southern & Jones, 1991). Grade acceleration is an inexpensive way for school systems to provide more challenging instruction for highly able learners. When acceleration is practiced wisely, accelerated students have been found to maintain their interest in school, excel academically, and complete higher levels of education sooner than the norm (Feldhusen et al., 1986).

As noted earlier in this chapter, highly motivated students who are excelling in all areas at the high school level are also good candidates for early entrance to college (VanTassel-Baska, 1991). Early entrants to college may leave high school one or several years early without ever graduating from high school. However, several states now offer early college admission programs in which students earn dual credits toward high school graduation and a college degree and are awarded a high school diploma after a year or two of college work. Such students are usually highly intellectually gifted and extremely motivated to pursue advanced coursework and degrees.

Because grade acceleration involves complex issues, it is important that the decision-making process be collaborative. All persons affected by the decision should be included on the decision-making team. At the elementary level, the team might include the school psychologist, the child, the family, teachers, and coordinators of the gifted, classroom teachers and the building principal. At the high school level, essential individuals would be the student, the parents, and a professional with training in differentiated education and career development for the gifted (school psychologist, career counselor, and/or gifted teacher or coordinator).

## Support Personnel as Catalysts

Finally, support personnel are in a unique position to serve as catalysts for educational change in both the home and the school systems. Most families of the gifted function quite well (Jenkins-Friedman, 1992). However, parents of the gifted have a number of unique concerns (Hackney, 1981; Keirouz, 1990; Silverman, 1991). For example, parents may wonder how much stimulation they should provide for their child at home or they may feel inadequately prepared to raise an exceptional child. Support personnel can implement parent education programs to help parents support the development of their gifted children. Parent education programs can provide information on the needs and characteristics of gifted children and create a supportive environment in which parents can share their concerns with other parents who are struggling with similar issues. These programs can also inform parents about the variety of educational options available to their children in the school and community.

When the educational problems of gifted children have their roots in family dysfunctions, school support personnel may need to intervene more actively. They can provide family counseling in a school setting if they have appropriate training (Fine & Holt, 1983; Frey & Wendorf, 1985). If the school professional is not equipped to provide such counseling, the family can be referred to a community counselor who is trained in both family counseling and the special needs and characteristics of the gifted. The goal should be to help the family learn more appropriate ways of interacting so members can serve as a resource rather than a stressor for the child.

School support personnel can also facilitate change in school systems. They can provide information on the strengths and weaknesses of existing educational programs for the gifted. They can participate in planning efforts by local schools on behalf of gifted students. Using Table 7.1 as a guide, they can suggest additional services that might be developed to increase the educational options available to these students. They can advocate for specific educational services, acceptance of accelerative options, and differentiated career development.

# CONCLUSION

The special characteristics and needs of gifted youths call for special and differentiated types of services. School support personnel can help provide many of these services. Support personnel should collaborate with teachers, administrators, parents, and gifted youth to assure that a full continuum of services is available and used. Then gifted youth will be able to develop their talents to the highest possible level and experience a sense of fulfillment through a creative and productive adulthood.

# REFERENCES

Belcastro, F. P. (1987). Elementary pull-out program for the intellectually gifted—Boon or bane? *Roeper Review, 9*, 208–212.

Betts, G. T. (1985). *Autonomous learner model for the gifted and talented.* Fort Collins, CO: Alps.

Betts, G. T. (1986). The autonomous learner model for the gifted and talented. In J. S. Renzulli (Ed.), *Systems and models for developing programs for the gifted and talented* (pp. 27–56). Mansfield Center, CT: Creative Learning Press.

Bloom, B. S. (1982). The master teachers. *Phi Delta Kappan, 63*, 664–668, 715.

Bloom, B. S. (1985). *Talent development.* New York: Ballantine Books.

Bloom, B. S., & Sosniak, L. A. (1981). Talent development. *Educational Leadership, 39*, 86–94.

Cox, J., Daniel, N., & Boston, B. O. (1985). *Educating able learners.* Austin: University of Texas Press.

DeHaan, R. F., & Havighurst, R. J. (1957). *Educating gifted children.* Chicago: University of Chicago Press.

Dunn, R., Dunn, K., & Treffinger, D. (1992). *Bringing out the giftedness in your child.* New York: Wiley.

Eisner, E. (1985). Aesthetic modes of knowing. In E. Eisner (Ed.), *Learning and teaching: The ways of knowing* (Eighty-fourth yearbook of the National Society for the Study of Education, Part II, pp. 23–36). Chicago: University of Chicago Press.

Feldhusen, J. F. (1983a). Eclecticism: A comprehensive approach to education of the gifted. In C. P. Benbow & J. L. Stanley (Eds.), *Academic precocity: Aspects of its development* (pp. 192–204). Baltimore: Johns Hopkins University Press.

Feldhusen, J. F. (1983b). University services for highly gifted youth. *The College Board Review, 129,* 18–22.

Feldhusen, J. F. (1986a). A conception of giftedness. In R. J. Sternberg (Ed.), *Conceptions of giftedness* (pp. 112–127). New York: Cambridge University Press.

Feldhusen, J. F. (1986b). A new conception of giftedness and programming for the gifted. *Illinois Council for the Gifted Journal, 5,* 2–6.

Feldhusen, J. F. (1991a). Full-time classes for gifted youth. *Gifted Child Today, 14,* 10–13.

Feldhusen, J. F. (1991b). Saturday and summer programs. In N. Colangelo & G. A. Davis (Eds.), *Handbook of gifted education* (pp. 197–208). Boston: Allyn & Bacon.

Feldhusen, J. F. (1992a). Early admission and grade advancement. *Gifted Child Today, 15,* 45–49.

Feldhusen, J. F. (1992b). *Talent identification and development in education (TIDE).* Sarasota, FL: Center for Creative Learning.

Feldhusen, J. F. (1994). Developing units of instruction. In J. VanTassel-Baska (Ed.), *Comprehensive curriculum for gifted learners* (2nd ed., pp. 91–128). Boston: Allyn & Bacon.

Feldhusen, J. F., Hoover, S. M., & Sayler, M. F. (1990). *Identifying and educating gifted students at the secondary level.* Monroe, NY: Trillium Press.

Feldhusen, J. F., & Kroll, M. (1985). Parent perceptions of gifted childrens' educational needs. *Roeper Review, 7,* 249–252.

Feldhusen, J. F., & Kroll, M. D. (1991). Boredom or challenge for the academically talented in school. *Gifted Education International, 7,* 80–81.

Feldhusen, J. F., Proctor, T. B., & Black, K. N. (1986). Guidelines for grade advancement of precocious children. *Roeper Review, 9,* 25–27.

Feldhusen, J. F., & Reilly, P. (1983). The Purdue secondary model for gifted education: A multi-service program. *Journal for the Education of the Gifted, 6*(4), 230–244.

Feldhusen, J. F., & Robinson, A. W. (1986). The Purdue secondary model for gifted and talented youth. In J. S. Renzulli (Ed.), *Systems and models for developing programs for the gifted and talented* (pp. 152–179). Mansfield Center, CT: Creative Learning Press.

Feldhusen, J. F., & Sayler, M. F. (1990). Special classes for academically gifted youth. *Roeper Review*, *12*, 244–249.

Feldman, D. H. (1986). *Nature's gambit.* New York: Basic Books.

Fine, M. J., & Carlson, C. (Eds.). (1992). *The handbook of family–school intervention: A systems perspective.* Boston: Allyn & Bacon.

Fine, M. J., & Holt, P. (1983). Intervening with school problems: A family systems perspective. *Psychology in the Schools*, *20*, 59–66.

Frey, J., & Wendorf, D. J. (1985). Families of gifted children. In L. L'Abate (Ed.), *The handbook of family psychology and therapy* (pp. 781–809). Homewood, IL: Dorsey Press.

Gagne, F. (1985). Giftedness and talent: Reexamining a reexamination of the definitions. *Gifted Child Quarterly*, *29*, 103–112.

Gallagher, J. J., Weiss, P., Oglesby, K., & Thomas, T. (1983). *The status of gifted / talented education: United States survey of needs, practices and policies.* Los Angeles: Leadership Training Institute.

Gardner, H. (1983). *Frames of mind.* New York: Basic Books.

Garfinkel, A., & Prentice, M. (1985). Foreign language for the gifted: Extending cognitive dimensions. In P. Westphal (Ed.), *Meeting the call for excellence* (pp. 43–49). Lincolnwood, IL: National Textbook.

Gross, M. U., & Feldhusen, J. F. (1990). The exceptionally gifted child. *Understanding Our Gifted*, *2*, 1, 7–10.

Hackney, H. (1981). The gifted child, the family, and the school. *Gifted Child Quarterly*, *25*, 51–54.

Haeger, W. W., & Feldhusen, J. F. (1989). *Developing a mentor program.* East Aurora, NY: DOK.

Jenkins-Friedman, R. (1992). Families of gifted children and youth. In M. J. Fine & C. Carlson (Eds.), *The handbook of family–school intervention: A systems perspective* (pp. 175–187). Boston: Allyn & Bacon.

Juntune, J. J. (1986). *Successful programs for the gifted and talented.* St. Paul, MN: National Association for Gifted Children.

Keirouz, K. S. (1990). Concerns of parents of gifted children: A research review. *Gifted Child Quarterly*, *34*, 56–63.

Koopman-Dayton, J. (1986). *A study of vocationally talented youth.* Unpublished masters thesis, Purdue University, West Lafayette, IN.

Kulik, J. A., & Kulik, C. C. (1984). Effects of accelerated instruction on students. *Review of Educational Research*, *54*, 409–425.

Maker, C. J. (1982). *Curriculum development for the gifted.* Rockville, MD: Aspen.

Marland, S. P. (1972). *Education of the gifted and talented: Report to the Congress.* Washington, DC: U.S. Government Printing Office (Document 72–5020).

Moon, S. M., Feldhusen, J. F., and Dillon, D. R. (1994). Long-term effects of an enrichment program based on the Purdue Three-Stage Model. *Gifted Child Quarterly*, 38, 38–48.

Proctor, T. B., Feldhusen, J. F., & Black, K. N. (1988). Guidelines for early admission to elementary school. *Psychology in the Schools*, 25, 41–43.

Renzulli, J. S. (Ed.). (1986). *Systems and models for developing programs for gifted and talented.* Mansfield Center, CT: Creative Learning Press.

Renzulli, J. S. (1987a). The positive side of pull-out programs. *Journal for the Education of the Gifted*, *10*, 254–255.

Renzulli, J. S. (1987b). The difference is what makes differentiation. *Journal for the Education of the Gifted, 10*, 265–266.

Renzulli, J. S., & Reis, S. M. (1985). *The schoolwide enrichment model: A comprehensive plan for educational excellence.* Mansfield Center, CT: Creative Learning Press.

Renzulli, J. S., & Reis, S. M. (1994). Research related to the Schoolwide Enrichment Triad Model. *Gifted Child Quarterly, 38*, 7–20.

Renzulli, J. S., Smith, L. H., White, A. J., Callahan, C. M., & Hartman, R. K. (1976). *Scales for rating the behavioral characteristics of superior students.* Mansfield Center, CT: Creative Learning Press.

Robinson, N. M., & Noble, K. D. (1991). Social–emotional development and adjustment of gifted learners. In M. C. Wang, M. C. Reynolds, & H. J. Walberg (Eds.), *Handbook of special education: Research and practice* (pp. 57–76). New York: Pergamon.

Sayler, M. F. (1990). *Early college entrants at Purdue University: A study of their academic and social characteristics.* Unpublished doctoral dissertation, Purdue University, West Lafayette, IN.

Shore, B. M., Cornell, D. G., Robinson, A., & Ward, V. S. (1991). *Recommended practices in gifted education: A critical analysis.* New York: Teachers College Press.

Silverman, L. K. (1991). Family counseling. In N. Colangelo & G. A. Davis (Eds.), *Handbook of gifted education* (pp. 307–320). Boston: Allyn & Bacon.

Southern, W. T., & Jones, E. D. (1991). Academic acceleration: Background and issues. In W. T. Southern & E. D. Jones (Eds.), *The academic acceleration of gifted children* (pp. 1–28). New York: Teachers College Press.

Stanley, J. C. (1980). On educating the gifted. *Educational Researcher, 9*, 8–12.

Stanley, J. C. (1991). A better model for residential high schools for talented youth. *Phi Delta Kappan, 72*, 471–473.

Treffinger, D. J. (1988, April). Cultivating potentials—Beyond "the gifted program." *Teaching pre K-8*, pp. 54–57.

VanTassel, J. (1979). A needs assessment for gifted education. *Journal for the Education of the Gifted, 2*(3), 141–148.

VanTassel-Baska, J. (1981). *Results of a Latin-based experimental program for the verbally precocious.* Unpublished doctoral dissertation, University of Toledo, Toledo, OH.

VanTassel-Baska, J. (1987a). The ineffectiveness of the pull-out program model in gifted education: A minority perspective. *Journal for the Education of the Gifted, 10*, 255–264.

VanTassel-Baska, J. (1987b). Response to Renzulli: Advocating the pull-out model. *Journal for the Education of the Gifted, 10*, 267–269.

VanTassel-Baska, J. (1991). Identification of candidates for acceleration: Issues and concerns. In W. T. Southern & E. D. Jones (Eds.), *The academic acceleration of gifted children* (pp. 148–161). New York: Teachers College Press.

Vaughn, V. L., Feldhusen, J. F., & Asher, W. J. (1991). Meta-analysis and review of research on pull-out programs in gifted education. *Gifted Child Quarterly, 35*, 92–98.

Witty, P. (1951). *The gifted child.* Boston: D. C. Heath.

# Chapter 8

# Developing Curricular
# Interventions for the Gifted

**Beverly N. Parke**

◆  ◆  ◆

THE CONTINUING questions of "What should be taught to gifted and talented students?" and "How should instruction be delivered?" have taken on new dimensions as schools are being restructured and renewed emphasis is being placed on matters of excellence and equity. Although these questions have long elicited discussion, consensus has never been established. For years, the debate between the false dichotomy of acceleration versus enrichment raged. This was followed by right brain versus left brain and content versus product deliberations. All have highlighted issues that are pieces of the puzzles involved in delivering appropriate educational instruction and service to gifted and talented students. Unfortunately, they seem to have over-shadowed larger problems in service delivery and have *not* resulted in anything close to full or appropriate service for the vast majority of this population (Westberg, Archambault, Dobyns, & Salvin, 1993).

There is greater hope for the paradigm shift currently taking place within the field of gifted child education. It has simply refocused the issue of service from "programs for the gifted and talented" to "programs *involving* the gifted and talented" (The Association for Gifted, 1989). Alteration of one word has prompted a thunderous change in perspective on the range of service delivery. Where planning once concentrated on distinct program options for these students (resource rooms, advanced placement, honors classes), planners and policymakers are now refocusing their efforts on students. Regardless of the school setting, service must follow students. Personnel in *all* components of the educational system must be accountable for and involved in creating appropriate learning environments and experiences for each individual student. Rather than leaving the business of educating gifted and talented (G/T) students solely to a G/T resource teacher, every member of the educational staff—regular classroom teachers, special educators, administrators, and support personnel—has a responsibility and voice in the planning and delivery of instruction as each has gifted and talented students within his or her caseload or classroom. These students carry their abilities with them throughout the school day and to all activities in which they are engaged. It is every educator's job to assure that those abilities are accommodated each step of the way.

# INTERVENTION DECISIONS

Curricular and programmatic interventions for G/T students are required when general education curricular or program offerings do not meet the needs of these students. Although it is possible to develop a general education program so rich that further modification is not needed, it is highly unlikely that such a program is in place. Therefore, program planners should take into account two basic sets of variables when developing a program or curricular design: (a) the nature and abilities of the population to be served and (b) the resources available or able to be marshalled.

## Student Factors

Lists of characteristics of G/T students exist throughout the literature on this population (Gallagher, 1985; Martinson, 1974; Renzulli, Smith, White, Callahan, & Hartman, 1976). Although no list is inclusive, authors generally agree that G/T students have three defining characteristics that underlie their need for differentiated service (Parke, 1992b): Gifted students (a) learn at an accelerated pace, (b) have the capacity to understand in greater depth or complexity, and (c) have interests that vary from their age peers (Maker, 1982). These characteristics often lead to situations where what is being taught in the classroom is subject matter already mastered by the students (Taylor & Frye, 1988) and is, therefore, inappropriate. When this occurs and modification is needed, program planners should also attend to (a) the intensity of student need (the degree to which each student differs from the norm), (b) the scope of student need (e.g., academic, personal, nonacademic, remediation), and (c) the areas of student need (content areas, interpersonal relationships, study habits, etc.). These variables, which pinpoint learning objectives and the type(s) of intervention(s) needed for student growth, are the basis for writing student profiles of need. Profiles include assessment data, student objectives, and recommended interventions.

## Resource Banks

The profiles of student need and objectives can then be compared with the resources available to the school system. Planners should broadly consider their resource options and not be limited to such conventional alternatives as advanced courses, independent studies, grade acceleration, or cross-grade groupings. Although these options are meritorious, the possibilities are far greater. Rather than looking for gifted programs and curricula, attention should turn to programs and curricula that serve the gifted and talented well. Options might include student council, journalism, vocational or technical education, mentoring, prescribed special education, peer counseling, internships, simulations, academic competitions, student courts, dual enrollment, original research, and community service projects. The resource bank should include options that address each of the defining characteristics of this population; that is, program and curricular options should be available to respond to flexible pacing, in-depth learning, and varying student interest (see Table 8.1). When options are not available that correspond to the needs and objectives listed on the student profiles, program and curricular development is needed.

## Placement Decisions

When possible, program and curricular decisions are best made by placement and/or curriculum teams composed of G/T specialists,

**TABLE 8.1. Sample Programs By Modification Area**

| Flexible Pacing | In-depth Learning | Student Interests |
|---|---|---|
| Fast-paced classes | Questioning | Guest lectures |
| Curriculum compacting | Skill groups | Advanced seminars |
| Self-instruction | Internships | Future problem solving |
| Advanced materials | Simulations | Madrigal choir |
| Early admission | Junior Great Books | Journalism |
| Multiage groups | Original research | Mentorships |
| Continuous progress | Independent studies | Interest groups |
| Dual enrollment | Peer coaching | Student council |

grade-level specialists, content specialists, policymakers, support personnel, parents, and individual students directly affected. This process of matching student need and learning objectives to system resources results in students having a program or curriculum geared to individual profiles. No one program or curriculum can meet all the varying needs that G/T students bring to the educational process. Rather, a mosaic of program and curricular options is necessary from which individual programs can be tailored to meet individual need. With a variety of options, full service becomes a far greater possibility.

# MOSAIC OF CURRICULAR OPTIONS

Professionals who are developing a full-service curriculum for G/T students in general or special educational settings need to keep in mind guiding curricular principles specifically suited to this population. Kaplan (1989) offered the following:

1. The curriculum should be responsive to the needs of the gifted student as both a member of the gifted population who requires specific, differentiated learning and as a member of the general population who requires the societally defined learning all individuals are expected to master.
2. The differentiated curriculum should include or subsume aspects of the regular curriculum.
3. The curriculum should provide gifted students with opportunities to exhibit those characteristics that were instrumental in their identification as gifted individuals.
4. The curriculum for gifted students . . . should not academically or socially isolate these students from their peers.
5. The differentiated curriculum should not be used as either a reward or punishment for gifted students. (p. 170)

Coupling these principles with individual student objectives provides the basis for curricular practice and development. A curriculum can be modified in four areas (Maker, 1982): content of instruction, process or method of instruction, products developed by students, and environment in which learning occurs. Individual students may require some curricular modification in all or some of these areas. It is the accomplished teacher who has the flexibility and skill to manage a classroom in which many curricular configurations may be occurring at the same time.

## Modifying Curricular Content

The content of curriculum is the subject matter that is taught. Because many G/T students are identified by their advanced ability to comprehend information beyond what is expected for their ages and their vast storehouses of knowledge, content of instruction is often an important issue with this group. Teachers often hear G/T students complain that they already know the skills being taught. In addition, these students can learn at accelerated paces and often complete assignments ahead of their age peers.

Curricular modifications to content may include such alterations as introducing content that is more advanced, sophisticated, complex, or unique. Advanced materials, cross-level grouping patterns, independent research studies, grade skipping, flexible pacing, curriculum compacting, and management systems are among the strategies that assist in the delivery of appropriate, meaningful, and challenging content.

In one of the more intriguing strategies being used to address content issues, students are asked to go beyond the content being presented and to learn to think like a professional in that field. How do mathematicians think? Do they think differently from the way historians think? What does it mean to have "math sense"? How does this affect the way various people attack a mathematical problem? Considering such questions opens the content area (in this case mathematics) to unique and challenging areas of learning and discussion.

## Modifying the Process of Instruction

The manner in which content is presented is another aspect of differentiating curricular practice. As G/T students have unbridled curiosity, the capacity to learn in greater depth, and an unyielding desire to delve into problems or see how things work, the methods of instruction become integral to providing challenging and meaningful curricula. Basic lecture or read-and-discuss formats, although far and away the most frequently used strategy with this population (Archambault et al., 1993), are woefully inadequate to fully address the needs of these students. Traditional approaches should be coupled with more active approaches, such as independent investigations, cooperative learning, enrichment centers, peer coaching, simulation gaming, and internships. In this way, students have a structure built around the content, which allows in-depth investigation of problems, manipulation of ideas, hands-on learning, asking of pointed questions, peer or self-instruction, and self-directed learning. Hopefully, this will result in motivated students with sufficient skills to be active and lifelong learners.

## Modifying Products of Learning

The third facet of curricular practice that can be differentiated is the products of learning. This area can be considered from two points of view. First, learner outcomes may be varied based on individual student abilities and needs. Second, the work students generate may differ based on objectives, interests, assignments, creative perspective, and preference.

Alternative learner outcomes are seen by VanTassel-Baska (1992) as "necessary in order for gifted students to be appropriately challenged" (p. 3). She stated that learner outcomes for the gifted "lie in the scope of the outcome, the stage of development at which it is expected, and the implicit proficiencies necessary to achieve it at an exemplary level" (p. 3). Thus, teachers of G/T students, as well as regular classroom teachers, may have students working not only in different materials or in various ways, but with individually crafted purposes.

Divergence naturally becomes part of curricular practice when students have an opportunity to express themselves in many ways. It is that divergence that allows students to respond to ideas or assignments at a level that is appropriate to their level of expertise. Teachers can institute one strategy by simply offering choices in how an assignment is carried out. By allowing students to select from three alternative assignments, as long as the teacher's purpose is consistent throughout the three options, the teacher should see varying ways to approach the same information in what students produce. To extend this idea, a fourth option—permitting students to create their own alternative assignment subject to approval from the teacher—may be offered.

## Modifying Learning Environment

Establishing an environment in which learning is encouraged and enhanced is essential to the differentiation process. If students do not feel it is safe to be adventurous in their thinking and aggressive in their pursuit of learning, they will conform to a standard they feel is acceptable. Teacher attitude is central to creating a classroom in which individual learners feel safe. Verbal and nonverbal expression must convey a respect for individuals and what they can accomplish. Difference must be celebrated rather than discouraged.

With this attitudinal environment in place, the structure of a classroom and the physical layout can be modified. A student-centered environment, in which students are partners in decision making, is optimal. Students are given an opportunity to take responsibility for their learning and to develop lifelong learning skills. Contracts, conferencing, peer coaching, learning centers, management sheets, and learning packets can all assist in helping students learn how to manage their own learning. "By opening up the classroom to students, the students are given a chance to take responsibility for their own learning and the teachers [can] focus on the learning of individual students" (Parke, 1989, p. 67).

The physical layout of the student-centered classroom should facilitate and encourage learning. Furniture is arranged to accommodate small- and large-group instruction, activity is everywhere and noise levels are reasonable, materials are accessible without teacher assistance, and everyone in the classroom has responsibility for one another and the environment in which they work.

## Assembling the Mosaic

A mosaic of curricular possibilities emerges from this convergence of learner need, distinguishing characteristics, program options, and curricular modifications (see Table 8.2). The central organizational point, however, remains the student profiles of ability and need. These profiles drive the direction of curricular practice and development. Skilled instructional staff, in cooperation with students, work from

**TABLE 8.2. Relationship Between Curricular Modification and Sample Program Options**

| | *Curricular Modification* | | | |
|---|---|---|---|---|
| ***Program Option*** | ***Content*** | ***Process*** | ***Product*** | ***Environment*** |
| Self-instruction | | X | X | X |
| Contracts | | X | X | X |
| Simulation | X | X | X | X |
| Fast-paced classes | X | | X | |
| Mentorships | X | X | X | X |
| Independent studies | X | X | X | X |
| Early admission | X | | | |
| Future problem solving | | X | X | X |

this base to develop the mosaic of options from which curricular plans for individual students can be drawn. It is unlikely that any two students will have identical plans or that options chosen will remain constant across students or instructional years. The flexibility of the mosaic concept gives teachers and students the necessary latitude to provide full and appropriate service plans.

# REVIEW OF RELATED RESEARCH

In reviewing research on curricular interventions for G/T students, a few troubling findings quickly emerge. Most significantly, very little research exists. Mostly what is found is evaluative in nature, and even that is far less than comprehensive. Individual theorists have developed research bases to document their work (Meeker, 1969; Renzulli, Smith, & Reis, 1982; Slavin, 1980), but little work has been done across intervention strategies or combinations. What *has* become well documented over the past 15 years is the consistent lack of programs and curricular interventions for G/T students (Council for Exceptional Children, 1978; Council of State Directors of Programs for the Gifted, 1990). These students are spending most of their instructional time in regular classroom settings (Cox, Daniel, & Boston, 1985). Unfortunately, what is happening in those classrooms rarely is at the students' level of instruction or challenge. Very little modification of instruction is taking place (Archambault et al., 1993; Westberg, Archambault, Dobyns, & Salvin, 1993). The danger in this situation is that students who do not receive educational experiences at their instructional levels may become more like their age peers in terms of achievement levels (Ness & Latessa, 1979). Comparative international studies consistently highlight the extent to which students in the United States fall behind their age and ability peers throughout the industrialized world (Callahan, 1990) across every curricular area investigated.

# ISSUES RELATIVE TO CURRICULAR INTERVENTIONS

## Full Service

Clearly, the biggest issue facing curriculum and program planners for G/T students is how to achieve full service and what Sellin and Birch (1980) referred to as service "invulnerability." The Association for Gifted (1989) took a big step in this effort by issuing *Standards for Programs Involving the Gifted and Talented*. This document outlines, for the first time, standards for practice in assessment, program development, curricular planning, and personnel. In addition, the reinstatement of a federal Office for Gifted and Talented and development of a national research center reinforce the need for continued attention and development in the field of gifted child education. Nevertheless, with school restructuring and fiscal constraints, programs serving this population are continually vulnerable to policymakers' red pencils. Programs and provisions are still seen as frills due to a misunderstanding of student need. Gifted students do not "make it on their own." The waste in talent potential is not measurable, but nonetheless is apparent in student attitudes, achievement scores, and parent frustrations.

Collaborative problem solving, frequently absent, is essential for full service to be a reality (Parke, 1992a). All members of the educational community must share a common purpose to bring appropriate service to all students, including the gifted and talented; then they can join together to determine how this purpose can best be accomplished in their particular circumstances. Experts in gifted child education should meet with administrators, parents, support personnel, special class teachers, general education teachers, and other support staff to develop a systemwide integrated approach to full service. Without collaboration, full service is impossible to mount or sustain.

## Assessment-Supported Decision Making

Educational decision making is bolstered by the appropriate use of assessment data. Within the realm of educating the gifted and talented, there is no exception—only unique challenges. To accurately determine such factors as achievement or ability levels, assessment must occur that includes sufficient range to measure high response levels. Too often, assessments or instruments are tied to grade levels, resulting in ceiling effects that negate accurate measurement of G/T students' levels.

This problem is compounded by a lack of instruments in non-academic areas and minimal use of criterion-referenced measures. When the assessment goal is to measure distinct skill mastery, it is difficult to attain resources outside of mainstream content areas. Unfortunately, a bias against the use of criterion-referenced measures for program placement and curricular planning leaves planners with little data upon which to base decisions. The result is that many educational decisions for G/T students are made on intuition or standard practice. Teachers and professionals in areas dealing with assessment could facilitate full service through the development, standardization, and use of appropriate measurement tools.

Invulnerability also becomes a measurement issue, as little documentation of student growth and program effectiveness is generated in most districts. Thus, when the policymakers are asked to make decisions about program viability, little support documentation exists. Program personnel do not know how the students are different as a result of their participation in a program. Little data exist about student outcomes. Programs that are assessment driven can generate such information as part of evaluation designs. Progress monitoring through the joint use of student data, program data, comparative data, parent surveys, and so forth can result in powerful statements for program continuity as well as program design.

## Role of Support Personnel

In the system described in this chapter, everyone is a member of a support team to student programs. In a more traditional sense, support personnel can be defined as the nonclassroom-based educators (psychologists, counselors, speech therapists, social workers, etc.). While often left to deal with the most extreme cases of student exceptionality, these professionals bring valuable skills to everyday program delivery and decision making. Not only do they hold expertise on such thorny matters as out-of-level testing, dealing with perfectionism, and home schooling, they can combat the impression that high-ability students are problem free. The problems of the gifted are real; they may simply differ from those seen in age peers or other students in the school population.

The challenge is to get the support personnel invited into the planning and decision-making process or into the classrooms where they can interact with students. If administrative structures governing the programs are inclusive, this issue is less difficult to tackle. Where no collaborative structure exists, it is almost impossible to accomplish. At the least, support personnel can view the challenge of providing full service to the gifted and talented students as part of their list of responsibilities and not that of someone else. This alone would be a giant step toward assuring that these students receive educational experiences that are challenging and fruitful as they progress toward the world of work.

# CONCLUSION

The changing nature of education of the gifted and talented—from a narrow range of program options to a broad-based perspective on curricular modification—necessitates a similar broadening of the team that develops the individualized education plan for each student. The decisions to be made require expertise concerning gifted and normal child development, affective needs, assessment-supported planning, and curriculum modification. As has happened in other areas of exceptionality, it is time to develop and/or expand the collaborative efforts of classroom educators, educational consultants, and support personnel, so that these new directions in gifted education can be achieved with optimum benefit to the students being served.

# REFERENCES

Archambault, F. X., Westberg, K. L., Brown, S. W., Hallmark, B. W., Zhang, W., & Emmons, C. L. (1993). Classroom practices used with gifted third and fourth grade students. *Journal for the Education of the Gifted, 16,* 13–28.

Association for Gifted, The. (1989). *Standards for programs involving the gifted and talented.* Reston, VA: Council for Exceptional Children.

Callahan, C. M. (1990). *A commissioned paper on the performance of high ability students in national and international tests.* Unpublished paper, University of Virginia, Charlottesville.

Council for Exceptional Children. (1978). *The nation's commitment to the education of gifted and talented children and youth.* Reston, VA: Council for Exceptional Children.

Council of State Directors of Programs for the Gifted. (1990). *The 1990 state of the states gifted and talented education report.* Augusta, ME: Council of State Directors of Programs for the Gifted.

Cox, J., Daniel, N., & Boston, B. (1985). *Educating able learners.* Austin: University of Texas Press.

Gallagher, J. J. (1985). *Teaching the gifted child* (3rd ed.). Boston: Allyn & Bacon.

Kaplan, S. N. (1989). Language arts for gifted learners. In R. M. Milgram (Ed.), *Teaching gifted and talented learners in regular classrooms* (pp. 169–178). Springfield, IL: Charles C. Thomas.

Maker, C. J. (1982). *Curriculum development for the gifted.* Austin, TX: PRO-ED.

Martinson, R. A. (1974). *The identification of the gifted and talented.* Ventura, CA: Office of the Ventura County Superintendent of Schools.

Meeker, M. N. (1969). *The structure of intellect.* Columbus, OH: Charles E. Merrill.

Ness, B. J., & Latessa, E. (1979). Gifted children and self-teaching techniques. *Directive Teacher, 2,* 10–12.

Parke, B. N. (1989). *Gifted students in regular classrooms.* Boston, MA: Allyn & Bacon.

Parke, B. N. (1992a). Collaboratively planning and delivering services to gifted and talented students. In Ohio Department of Education (Ed.), *Chal-*

*lenges in gifted education* (pp. 73–79). Columbus: Ohio Department of Education.

Parke, B. N. (1992b, October). Meeting the challenge of gifted students in regular classrooms. *ERIC Bulletin*, pp. 1–2. Reston, VA: The Council for Exceptional Children.

Renzulli, J. S., Smith, L. H., & Reis, S. M. (1982). Curriculum compacting: An essential strategy for working with gifted students. *The Elementary School Teacher, 82*(3), 185–194.

Renzulli, J. S., Smith, L., White, A., Callahan, C., & Hartman, R. (1976). *Scales for rating the behavioral characteristics of superior students*. Mansfield Center, CT: Creative Learning Press.

Sellin, D., & Birch, J. (1980). *Educating gifted and talented learners*. Rockville, MD: Aspen Systems.

Slavin, R. E. (1980). Cooperative learning. *Review of Educational Research, 50*, 315–342.

Taylor, B. M., & Frye, B. J. (1988). Pretesting: Minimizing time spent on skill work of intermediate readers. *The Reading Teacher, 42*, 100–103.

VanTassel-Baska, J. (1992, October). Developing learner outcomes for gifted students. *ERIC Bulletin*, pp. 2–4. Reston, VA: Council for Exceptional Children.

Westberg, K. L., Archambault, F. X., Dobyns, S. M., & Salvin, T. J. (1993). The classroom practices observation study. *Journal for the Education of the Gifted, 16*, 29–56.

# Chapter 9

# Encouraging Lifelong Learning Through the Autonomous Learner Model

George T. Betts, Michael J. Hoover

◆  ◆  ◆

## HISTORICAL DEVELOPMENT

RARELY DO EDUCATORS have the opportunity to develop programs based upon the needs of students who are successful and those who are not successful without the major restrictions of curriculum guidelines or district policy. During the 1970s, teachers and administrators at Arvada West High School in Jefferson County, Colorado, were given the opportunity to develop a cadre of programs for such students. Communication classes were developed, support groups for students were established, and a teaching position to facilitate new classes was established. The process of change was accepted and rewarded throughout the school, beginning with the administration.

### Successful Students

A program for seniors, entitled Senior Seminar, was established to provide opportunities for students outside of the school. Students were involved in community service and occupational activities in Denver, the suburbs, the Rocky Mountains, and the deserts of the Southwest. Students visited college campuses and learned more about the worlds of higher education and work. Challenges were established to help students after they had left high school.

### Nonsuccessful Students

Another program identified first-semester sophomores who were having difficulty with school and might drop out. These students attended two or three regular classes per day in the morning. During the afternoon, they were involved in a 2-hour block that was designed to provide emotional and social support, as well as academic intervention. Teachers, support personnel, and administrators worked together to support students who might have fallen through the cracks. Many of these students were in the process of dropping out of school, and others had already done so. When asked if they felt as though they dropped out or were pushed out, many responded that they were "left out."

As this program was being developed and implemented, it became evident to the teachers that many of these students might be gifted. This seemed incongruous because the unwritten definition at the time described gifted students as those who were very bright, good students with straight "A" averages—in other words, those students who had mastered the system and would go on to outstanding achievement in the future. Other students, especially those who were not successful in school, had never been perceived as gifted.

As the program developed, it became evident that many of these students had learning difficulties, whereas others had emotional, social, and behavioral challenges. However, in some, abilities were observed that had not been detected or reinforced in the school system. Could it be that these students might be gifted? Could the emphasis of the program shift from stressing only the students' limitations to also emphasizing their strengths? A shift in philosophy occurred, which encouraged teachers to look at both strengths and weaknesses. This was a major change in the program, one that ultimately led the educators to new attitudes toward students. Instead of focusing only on the limitations, strengths were discovered and enriched, leading to an entirely different experience. Students were more determined to be successful, to learn, and to grow. The students who were once viewed as "at risk" were now becoming successful.

## Training of Educators

By 1976, the educators at Arvada West were convinced that many of their students who had been unsuccessful in school were also very bright, and possibly gifted. At this time, the Jefferson County Public Schools began a program with Dr. Irving Sato of the National/State Leadership Training Institute for the Gifted. Schools that wanted to explore gifted education became pilot schools for the district. Each school sent a team of teachers, administrators, counselors, and school psychologists to learn about gifted children and youth over a period of 3 years.

Training was provided by national leaders in the field of gifted education. Included was information on definitions, characteristics, identification, curriculum, programs, and assessment. The training was a life-changing event for many of the educators because it allowed them to see their students and themselves in a different light. They learned approaches that looked at the potential of students whose needs were not being met in the regular classroom. Tannenbaum (1983) introduced a philosophy that would provide the opportunity for students to go beyond the normal role of "consumers" to "producers" of knowledge. For those of us involved with gifted education at Arvada West High School, this concept of moving a student from the role of a consumer to that of a producer had a profound impact on our program development. We asked questions to define what a producer actually was, and what modifications to guidelines and curriculum would have to be made by schools to develop producers. Eventually, the planning that grew from this process became the Autonomous Learner Model (ALM) (Betts, 1985a; Betts & Knapp, 1981).

## A Community-Wide Support Team

Today, education is more than classrooms and a school building. To be effective in any reform movement, educators must reach out to parents, community leaders, and businesses. A key to success in the ALM in each participating school and in our district was the development of a community-wide support team. Membership was open to all groups within the community. Letters were sent to parents, community leaders, and a variety of service groups.

The support team had the following roles:

1. To become knowledgeable about the definitions, characteristics, and needs of gifted children and youth.

2. To develop an approach that describes what it is that gifted children may become if the appropriate educational opportunities are present.

3. To become knowledgeable about the programming options available to gifted students within the school and the community.

4. To provide advocacy for programming development.

5. To develop a community resource pool for students to contact people concerning speakers, places to visit, and ongoing mentorships.

6. To act as a resource when programming changes were necessary to continue the effectiveness of the approach.

The members of the community-wide resource team included school administrators, the school coordinator of gifted education, regular classroom teachers, the school counselor, the school psychologist, and several members of the community who were dedicated to education. It is imperative to include the counselor and the psychologist in such a group to ensure that programming options for gifted students go beyond cognitive needs and include emotional and social development. A basic understanding of the total child is essential for this support group.

# AUTONOMOUS LEARNER MODEL
# LEARNER OUTCOMES

According to Rogers (1983), teachers need to become aware of the conditions that are necessary to facilitate learning, personal growth, and new ways to produce lifelong learners. He wrote:

> We are, in my view, faced with an entirely new situation in education where the goal of education, if we are to survive, is the facilitation of change and learning. The only man who is educated is the man who has learned how to learn; the man who has learned how to adapt and change; the man who has realized that no knowledge is secure, that only the process of seeking knowledge gives a basis for security. Changingness, a reliance on process rather than upon static knowledge, is the only thing that makes any sense as a goal for education in the modern world. (p. 120)

Using this philosophy as a basis of our approaches to meeting the diversified needs of gifted and talented students, we developed student/learner goals (Betts, 1985a) for use within the ALM. According to these goals, students/learners will

- Develop more positive self-concepts.

- Comprehend their own giftedness in relationship to self and society.

- Develop the skills appropriate to interact effectively with peers, siblings, parents, and other adults.

- Increase their knowledge in a variety of subject areas.

- Develop their thinking, decision-making, and problem-solving skills.

- Participate in activities selected to facilitate and integrate the cognitive, emotional, and social development of the individual.

- Demonstrate responsibility for their own learning in and out of the school system.

- Ultimately become responsible, creative, independent learners. (p. 4)

# DEFINING THE GIFTED AND TALENTED

Who are the gifted and the talented? Are these students the same or different? What about students who are creative? Are their needs being met in the school? Are all students gifted? What definition is being used? Should quantitative or qualitative data be used? Or both? These questions and many more needed to be answered by the community-wide support group.

While one goal of the selection of gifted and talented students was to discover and identify students whose abilities and needs were such that they required differentiated programming opportunities, another goal was to look closely at *all* students and include them in different enrichment options within the school and community. Enrichment became part of the school plan for all students. With the inclusion of enrichment for all students, many students who would have been missed for the programming options for the gifted were included.

Schools and school districts that now use the Autonomous Learner Model are identifying and serving the intellectually gifted, the creatively gifted, and the talented. Also, many districts are now using the model with underachieving and nonproducing students. Rimm (1986) developed a method to identify students who are underachieving in the public schools, and Delisle (1992) went beyond this definition and identified students as "nonproducers" rather than as underachievers. All of these students could be included in gifted programming based on the ALM.

As a result of looking closely at the behavior and feelings of students who participated in the model, Betts and Neihart (1988) developed an approach that provided profiles of six types of gifted and talented students. This approach focused on the emotional and social development of each individual in terms of behavior and feelings.

Most other approaches at the time were concerned primarily with cognitive development and used standardized tests as the major components of the identification approach. The profiles approach provided additional information concerning the "total" child. Betts and Neihart (1988) reported that many students identified for the program had Type One behavior and feelings, which meant that they were the successful students in school, whereas those with Type Two behavior and feelings were those who "acted out" in class, were in trouble much of the time, and were not identified for gifted programs unless teachers and administrations saw beyond the acting out of students whose needs were not being met in school. Those with Type Three behavior and feelings (the underground) did not want teachers to know they were gifted. They hid their abilities so that they could be like everyone else. Students with Type Four behavior and feelings were the dropouts. They were angry and wanted out. School was no longer something that they valued. Type Five students had mixed behavior and feelings. They were the "twice exceptional" because they had been identified by their weaknesses and provided special education services, but it was time to look at their strengths through the use of the ALM.

As noted above, schools are more typically producing "students" rather than "learners" (Betts, 1985b). A major goal for the ALM model and, we believe, for all education is to develop students who become lifelong learners. These students (Type Six) have become learners and are seen as independent and self-directed. They will be capable of being involved in the changing world around them as they continue into adulthood. Much is written about the adult as a self-directed, lifelong learner (Cafferela, 1983; Candy, 1991), but only a few educational leaders are writing about students and their potential of becoming lifelong learners while they are still in school (Betts, 1985c; Betts & Knapp, 1981; Betts & Neihart, 1988; Rogers, 1983).

Thus, it is essential that schools "cast a wide net" so that students will not be left out of the process of selection for enrichment and programming for the gifted. Many districts identify only the intellectually gifted who are already achieving because that task is easiest to do. To find the others, schools must have a flexible selection system that is needs based and includes the creatively gifted as well as the talented students.

# THE SELECTION PROCESS OF THE GIFTED AND TALENTED

In many districts throughout the United States, the process of identifying the gifted was developed to look closely for gifted students at one time. In many school systems, this time was the third grade. Now, practices are changing and the gifted are being identified earlier, although an ongoing process that is in effect each school year is still not common. The ideal approach is ongoing and considers abilities and needs of students instead of only traditional information (e.g., test scores) and teacher recommendations.

The ALM selection process begins at the start of each school year and continues until June. School personnel look for behavior of students that might be missed if the process is limited to one time per year or to a 1-year approach. The process requires districts to consider the issues discussed in the following sections.

### Definition

As the ALM model has been adopted across the country, we have found that the selected definition varies from state to state and district to district, but we recommend that a broad definition is the most effective for finding diversified gifted and talented students. Regardless, the selection process must be congruent with the selected definition. If not, major errors might occur.

### Staff Development

It is essential that an ongoing staff development program be developed for educators, parents, and involved community and business members. Initially, support personnel who design the program need to present information on the different types of gifted students. In our project, a combination of lectures and case studies was used. To reinforce the initial training, specific activities were given to the regular classroom teachers that assisted them in selecting students for the project.

One observation tool that we found useful is the *Kingore Observation Inventory* (Kingore, 1990). Characteristics of the gifted are included in the inventory, and teachers are asked to keep track of each time these characteristics are seen in children in the regular classroom. This adds a performance component to the process.

### Nomination Pool

After staff development has been completed concerning definitions, characteristics, needs, and behavior, nominations are requested through teacher nominations, parent nominations, peer and self-nominations, test scores, and nominations from additional nontraditional sources, such as community leaders and other people who are involved directly with students outside of school. Nominations are sought for students who have the potential of being selected for programming for the gifted. Information is necessary for each element of the following formula for selecting students:

$$\text{Attitudes} + \text{Abilities} + \text{Passions} + \text{Behavior}$$
$$= \text{Needs of the Students}$$

### Data Gathering

Depending upon the selected definition, additional quantitative and qualitative information may be collected. This information may be necessary to better determine the needs of the students.

A major component of the selection process for ALM programming is the interview of students and, when needed, interviews of parents, teachers, and additional resource people who represent the student. The interview is usually a one-to-one experience and lasts approximately 15 to 20 minutes. Answers to interview questions provide additional information concerning elements of the above formula. This information is then used to determine the unique needs of the individual student.

Schools then must determine whether something was missed. Do school personnel need to look deeper to find more information? Are there additional family or community members who can provide more information? For example, sometimes the coordinator of the youth center or the corner grocer can add information about behaviors that may not be evident in the school. At this time, it is appropriate for teachers who are convinced that a student should be selected, but are lacking some information, to become a teacher advocate and present additional information in support of the student.

### The Selection Process

Final selection for involvement in the ALM is based upon the intellectual, emotional, and social needs that have been identified through the process of looking closely at each nominated student. These selected students will be involved in the ALM for a minimum of 3 years and, hopefully, for 5 to 6 years. Developing autonomous learners is a process that takes time, energy, and alternative learning experiences.

The selection of students for ALM programming is an ongoing process. Information should be kept on each student who is not selected, and new information should be added in the following weeks, months, and years. Parents and students have the right to add information, which is given to the support team that reviews the information for possible changes in the decisions.

# THE AUTONOMOUS LEARNER MODEL FOR THE GIFTED AND TALENTED

## Basic Principles

The Autonomous Learner Model for the Gifted and Talented was designed not by teachers, but by students. The teachers became facilitators and directed many questions to the students: If you could change school in any way, how would you change it? What is missing in this school? What do you want to accomplish outside of school? What do you want this program to be? Why did you decide to be part of this approach? What is the purpose of gifted education from your point of view? Are you gifted? Why were you selected for this approach?

All of these questions and more were presented to the students. The teachers did it *with* the students, not *to* them! In other words, the approach belonged to the students, not to the teachers. The students decided what they wanted to do and then how to do it. This was a very radical idea for a school to accept and facilitate!

The support started with the principal of Arvada West High School. He addressed the group of students by stating that he believed that it was up to them to design a program that was based on their needs, abilities, and content areas, not on teachers' perceptions of their needs, abilities, and content areas.

From 1976 until 1980, the students and teachers worked together to develop a unique approach to identify achieving, underachieving, and nonproducing gifted and talented students and to provide them with new, exciting, and enriching experiences. Lifelong learning became a theme that was slowly understood by all the participants.

Different directions were followed over the 4-year period with some successes and some failures, but autonomy, creativity, and self-selection of topics or areas became consistent. Out of this approach came some of the basic principles that are the foundations of the Autonomous Learner Model (Betts, 1985b):

- Emphasis is placed on the emotional, social, and cognitive development of the individual.
- Self-esteem is encouraged and facilitated.
- Social skills are developed and enhanced.
- Curriculum is based on the interests of the students.
- Students are involved in guided, open-ended learning experiences.

- Responsibility for learning is placed on the student/learners.

- Students need experiences that allow them to become lifelong learners.

- Teachers are facilitators of the learning process as well as dispensers of knowledge.

- Learning is cross-disciplinary.

- Students develop a wider area of basic skills.

- Higher level thinking skills are integrated, reinforced, and demonstrated in the learning process.

- Students develop appropriate questioning techniques.

- Varied responses are sought from the students.

- Content topics are broad-based, with emphasis on major themes, problems, issues, and ideas.

- Time and space restrictions for schools are removed for in-depth learning.

- Students develop new and unique products.

- Students use varied resources in the development of in-depth studies.

- Mentorships provide adult role modeling, active support, and individual instruction and facilitation.

- Completion and presentation of in-depth studies are integral in the learning process.

A school or district that commits to implementing the ALM must look closely at the basic principles to see if it is possible to follow or complete them. Community-wide resource team members are asked to discuss the above principles. The more the ALM principles can be followed, the better the chance that the implementation of the ALM will be successful.

## Dimensions of the ALM

As discussed in detail below, the ALM comprises five separate dimensions: orientation, individual development, enrichment activities, seminars, and in-depth study (see Figure 9.1). The model (Betts, 1985a; Betts & Knapp, 1981) is designed to meet the diversified cognitive, emotional, and social needs of gifted and talented students, although it is now beginning to be used successfully with students whose

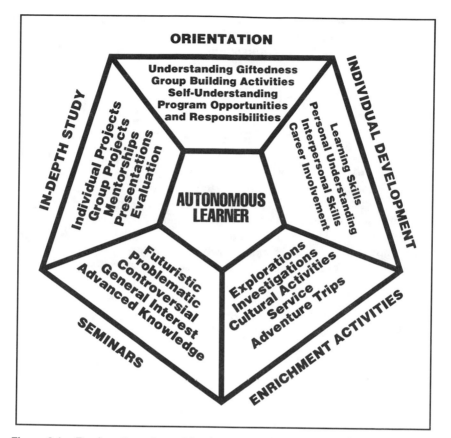

**Figure 9.1.** The five dimensions of the Autonomous Learner Model. From *The Autonomous Learner Model for the Gifted and Talented* (p. 2) by G. T. Betts, 1985, Greeley, CO: Autonomous Learning Publications and Specialists. Copyright 1985 by Autonomous Learning Publications and Specialists. Reprinted by permission.

abilities and characteristics are not as strong as those of gifted and talented students. The model is a process that moves the student from the role of student to that of learner, while the teacher moves from the role of teacher to the role of facilitator.

Besides becoming a facilitator, the educator should spend time each day becoming or functioning as a lifelong learner, being involved with the process of the ALM in the same manner as that of the students. In other words, if the students are working on developing better interviewing skills or completing individual explorations, the teachers need to spend some time each week being involved in the same activities. Modeling is a key component in the use of the ALM. It provides for a process that is completed *with* the students, not done *to* the students.

The teacher is only part of the team that should serve the students at this time. Involvement of school psychologists, counselors, and/or social workers is extremely important because of their knowledge of the development of the affective domain.

### Orientation

The first dimension of the ALM is orientation, which provides a *foundation* for students, educators, parents, and community members. Although many programming approaches for gifted and talented students begin with skill development, such as critical or creative thinking, or with specific content areas that may lead to independent work, the orientation dimension is essential. It contains four areas: understanding giftedness, group building activities, self-understanding, and program opportunities and responsibilities. The respective goal of each component is to enable the students to learn about the concepts of giftedness, intelligence, creativity, and potential; to learn more about themselves and others with particular emphasis on group roles and functioning; to promote self-understanding about their own unique abilities; and to delineate program expectations and help them to begin to formulate individual goals that will culminate in the development of a student/learner growth plan or guide for further participation in the model.

### Individual Development

The second dimension of the ALM is individual development (see Figure 9.2), which is designed to give students the appropriate skills, concepts, and attitudes for lifelong learning—in other words, to help them become autonomous learners. The individual development dimension of the model is divided into the four areas of learning skills, personal understanding, interpersonal skills, and career involvement. Major topics include the following:

- Intellectual skills
- Organizational skills
- Personal understanding
- Communication skills
- Discussion skills
- Career awareness and involvement

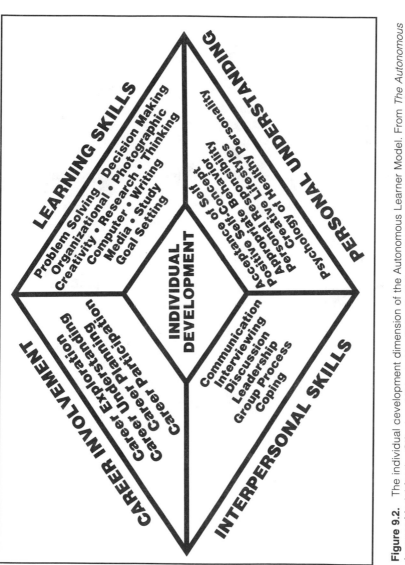

**Figure 9.2.** The individual development dimension of the Autonomous Learner Model. From *The Autonomous Learner Model for the Gifted and Talented* (p. 3) by G. T. Betts, 1985, Greeley, CO: Autonomous Learning Publications and Specialists. Copyright 1985 by Autonomous Learning Publications and Specialists. Reprinted by permission.

This dimension provides for the basic skills and understanding necessary to proceed within the model. To skip this dimension would weaken the effectiveness of the model.

### Enrichment Activities

The major goal of the enrichment activities dimension is to develop "student-based content" as opposed to "prescribed content" developed primarily by educators. Many different approaches are used to allow the student/learners to become more aware of what is "out there" to be learned. They are given the opportunity to decide what they want to study and how they want to study their selected topics. The different approaches include the following:

- *Explorations*—What do I want to study? Some students have many ideas, but others do not know where to start. Explorations provide opportunities for students to learn what is out there in the schools, homes, and community. These are usually 1- or 2-day activities. A series of these is completed before involvement takes place in investigations.

- *Investigations*—An investigation is a mini in-depth study. Students go more in-depth into their individual or small-group projects. A beginning contract is developed and students research their topics for 2 to 3 weeks. A short presentation is included at the end of each investigation.

- *Cultural activities*—With other students, the entire class, or their families, cultural activities are completed so that students learn about concerts, museums, speeches, or other cultural events. This approach requires students to make arrangements to "go beyond" the event and learn how it is developed and presented.

- *Service*—This is a nonnegotiable component. Each student must give of himself or herself and time for direct involvement with people who need help. Activities might include working with the elderly, raising food for shut-ins, or working for community agencies.

- *Adventure trips*—Students organize, finance, and implement trips that provide emotional, social, and/or physical challenges for their group. Trips can include adventures into large cities, national parks, or other environments selected by the students.

### Seminars

By the time the students have reached the seminars dimension of the ALM, emphasis is placed on "production" of ideas and topics. Students are now operating as learners instead of as students. More and more responsibility is placed on them. Also, more opportunities are available.

Learners, who work together in small groups, select a topic, research the topic, and plan and implement a seminar with three phases: presentation of factual information, group discussions and/or activities, and closure. Seminars are selected from five major areas:

1. Futuristic

2. Problematic

3. Controversial

4. General interest

5. Advanced knowledge

At the end of each seminar, the learners and facilitators evaluate the concept and effectiveness of the seminar.

### In-Depth Study

The main goal of the ALM is for the learners to attain autonomous learning skills. The in-depth study dimension is designed to allow the students to use these learning skills in an in-depth study. Either independently or in small groups of two or three, the learners develop an in-depth study contract, which outlines a description of the study, the objectives and activities, the questions to be answered, a timeline, a list of human and material resources, and a plan for ongoing and final presentations.

An in-depth study is the most demanding and challenging dimension in the ALM. Once the learners have developed the contract, they are able to participate in their studies. Most studies require 2 months to $2\frac{1}{2}$ years to complete. Learners are responsible for their own progress and receive support from mentors and their teacher/facilitators.

## THE ROLE OF SUPPORT PERSONNEL IN THE ALM

Support personnel play an extremely valuable role when a school adopts the Autonomous Learner Model. They are able to provide expertise in the identification and selection of students for the program. Too frequently, the selection team focuses on the cognitive aspects and does not see the other areas of giftedness addressed in the model. Familiarity with producing profiles of individual learners is critical to ensuring that deserving individuals are included.

Professionals must be skilled in identifying those individuals who are able to think "outside of the paradigm." Those individuals who are capable of looking at life from another viewpoint should not be overlooked. The low or nonproducing student merits the same consideration as the high excelling student.

Skills in the area of facilitation are crucial. Support personnel must serve collaboratively with teachers, parents, administrators, and students. As a consultant to teachers, the effective practitioner can assist in reducing the fear and insecurity in guiding the learning of the gifted and talented student. Many times, highlighting effective teaching practices currently in use can aid in the empowerment of the instructional staff.

With the current national emphasis placed on the inclusion of all students in the regular education program, support personnel can act as an advocate, resource, and facilitator for the gifted and talented student. These high ability students have traditionally been ignored due to the emphasis placed on the needs of students with cognitive deficits, physical impairments, and mild to moderate learning disabilities. In many inclusive settings, the gifted and talented are left to fend for themselves, because they can usually survive (if not thrive) without assistance. Being autonomous learners does not negate the need for specialized programming, including educators and community members who serve as mentors and advocates.

As a facilitator, the practitioner can act as a coordinator with the various disciplines that provide services to the student. Support personnel are logical individuals to facilitate collaboration among the curricular, programmatic, and support services, and all persons delivering the services to the student.

Support personnel serving a traditional role in the public school system typically have had limited experiences with gifted and talented students. It is essential that these professionals receive additional training in working directly with gifted and talented students. Many times, this additional training can be accomplished through Saturday and summer programs. In relationship to the ALM, the Summer Enrichment Program at the University of Northern Colorado has provided opportunities for psychologists and counselors to experience working with gifted and talented students on a daily basis while observing and participating in activities that exemplify their unique needs and talents. (Although this experience was planned for these two groups, it could have served others interested in the affective domain equally well.) The 4-week program attracted gifted students from all over the nation and consisted of both formal classroom and extracurricular experiences. The milieu was designed for exceptional students, but many of the experiences are applicable to general public school situations. The role of the psychologist and counselor in the summer program was more experiential and less formal, and provided valuable experience in interacting with this area of exceptionality.

The summer program also allowed the opportunity for facilitating a group of students identified as leaders by their staff and peers. (The role of the group facilitator can be both demanding and rewarding when the group is made up of "leaders.") This leadership group was not involved in formal classroom activities. They met to learn leadership qualities and styles that are effective in dealing with their chosen goals. The goal was to allow students to explore their areas of interest and discomfort. The activities included communications-skill building, a ropes course, guided visualization, assistance in classroom activities with younger students, and group performances.

The most dramatic dynamic observed was the struggle for leadership among a group of leaders. No one leader emerged, but situational leadership prevailed. By providing varied activities, individuals were allowed to experience their "day in the sun." At times, some learners demonstrated effective leadership by being effective followers.

The goal of the group was to establish a sense of community. This feeling evolved only as the need for individuality was met and each student was able to express and establish the particular skill and/or talent he or she possessed. When each individual had established his or her role, cohesion developed. An enlightening aspect verbalized by the students themselves was that initially they were not a cohesive group, or even friends. As time progressed, they acquired an appreciation for each other's uniqueness, and the feeling of community evolved.

The professional created an environment in which participants felt comfortable in exposing their unique talents and accepting others. This environment was created by providing varied experiences and promoting accepting behaviors within the group. By demonstrating acceptance of uniqueness and allowing individuality, group cohesion could develop.

An area of increasing demand is that of providing crisis intervention to the gifted and talented student. Providing educational programming for gifted and talented students in a summer setting has demonstrated that this population requires intervention services in approximately the same frequency as in a regular school program. The fact that nearly every state in the nation was represented by summer program participants created a situation in which many students were a long distance from their nuclear families. In addition, the group was represented by approximately the same socioeconomic levels and family dynamics and status as in the typical population.

At times during the summer program, the teachers, counselors, and psychologists needed to deal with the threat of suicide, drug abuse, eating disorders, and self-abusive behavior in the gifted and talented students. At these times, psychologists and counselors had both ethical and legal responsibilities in providing prevention, intervention, and postintervention services. In providing these services, strategies for successful involvement and interventions in the summer program included the following:

- The need to help students focus on the critical areas of concern.

- The need to assist students in understanding their own giftedness.

- The use of problem-solving techniques that are taught to solve problems both now and in the future.

- The concept of developing an internal locus of control. Gifted students are sensitive and need to learn to rely on their own instincts and choices.

- The value of seeing the uniqueness of the learner. Rejection may occur as a result of being gifted, and techniques must be taught to help students value and accept themselves.

- The ability to become tolerant of the differences of others.

Sometimes crisis interventions can extend to the student's family. Support personnel can assist the family in crisis by:

1. Giving the student the permission to be "not perfect." Too frequently, the family perceives the student as being perfect and cannot tolerate such "flaws" as the stresses associated with growing up.

2. Helping the family to realize that being gifted does not eliminate traumatic situations that lead to stress disorders. These may include rape, abuse, and witnessing traumatic events.

3. Allowing the family to problem solve as a group. This is another area where the facilitation skills are critical.

# CONCLUSION

The ALM is flexible, fluid, and facilitative. It can be used in the regular classroom, the resource room, special classes, summer programs, and a variety of individual and small-group cluster settings. The goal is to develop an environment that is conducive to meeting the diversified intellectual, emotional, and social needs of gifted and talented students.

Support personnel are key members of the educational community in facilitating the growth of autonomous learners. Betts (1985c, p. IV) defined what the gifted may become in the following poem:

Some people have the ability
to create excitement in their lives.

They are the ones who strive,
who grow,
who give and share,
They are the ones who love . . .

They possess passion . . .
for themselves, others,
Nature and experiences.

They have the ability
to see beyond today,
to rise above the hectic pace,
to strive for their own perfection . . .

And they are gentle,
for they love themselves,
and they love others . . .

Through their living
they create peace and contentment.

At the same time
they create excitement,
for there is always another mountain,
a deeper joy,
a new dawn . . .

# REFERENCES

Betts, G. (1985a). *Autonomous learner model for the gifted and talented.* Greeley, CO: Autonomous Learning Publications and Specialists.

Betts, G. (1985b). *An introduction to the autonomous learner model for the gifted and talented.* Greeley, CO: Autonomous Learning Publications and Specialists.

Betts, G. (1985c). *Some people have the ability* . . . Greeley, CO: Autonomous Learning Publications and Specialists.

Betts, G., & Knapp, J. (1981). Autonomous learning and the gifted: A secondary model. In A. Arnold (Ed.), *Secondary programs for the gifted* (pp. 29–36). Ventura, CA: Office of the Ventura Superintendent of Schools.

Betts, G., & Neihart, M. (1988). Profiles of the gifted. *Gifted Child Quarterly, 32,* 248–253.

Cafferela, R. S. (1983). Fostering self-directed learning in post-secondary education: The use of learning contracts. *Life-long learning: An omnibus of practice and research, 7,* 7–10, 25–26.

Candy, P. C. (1991). *Self-direction for lifelong learning: A comprehensive guide to theory and practice.* San Francisco: Jossey-Bass.

Delisle, J. (1992). *Guiding the social and emotional development of gifted youth: A practical guide for educators and counselors.* New York: Longman.

Kingore, B. W. (1990). *The Kingore Observation Inventory (KOI).* Des Moines, IA: Leadership Publishers.

Rimm, S. B. (1986). *Underachievement syndrome: Causes and cures.* Watertown, WI: Apple Publishing.

Rogers, C. (1983). *Freedom to learn for the 80's.* Columbus, OH: Charles E. Merrill.

Tannenbaum, A. (1983). *Gifted children: Psychological and educational perspective.* New York: Macmillan.

# Chapter 10

# *Technological Innovations in the Education of Gifted and Talented Students*

**Richard D. Howell**

◆　◆　◆

CHILDREN WHO ARE gifted and talented, as well as those with various other special needs, can benefit from innovative technological developments. Whereas the severely disabled can profit from the use of extensive assistive and prosthetic technological aids to achieve their highest potential, the gifted student may benefit from the expansive, almost limitless, intellectual and aesthetic horizons offered by new technological tools and techniques. This chapter examines the patterns that have resulted from both historical and contemporary applications of technology in the education of gifted and talented students. In addition, a strategy for the integration of technologies into gifted curricula and classrooms is proposed. Finally, a future vision is articulated of the educational potential inherent in new, highly interactive multimedia and multiple, reality-based simulations.

Instructors of gifted students must deal with both conceptual and practical issues as they plan for the integration of technology into their instruction. Instructors must first have a clear idea of their own curricular focus and the aspects of technology that they wish to use if they are to enhance the understanding and use of this information. This is primarily a matching process between the conceptual information and the best manner of presenting and manipulating this information using a technological tool. The result of this process should be a conceptual framework involving instruction and identification of the technological methods and tools that will be used in instructional delivery.

Contrary to commercial claims, most aspects of using technologies involve complex, cognitive phenomena and require continuous training for teachers and other personnel in the schools. Both formal and informal instruction for teachers in the use of technologies should be sought to increase one's knowledge and competence in these issues. Teachers need to recognize that it takes time and effort to learn to use new tools and then to integrate them into their personal instructional patterns.

Finally, implementing technology into a gifted classroom is a dynamic and flexible merger of known concepts and skills with the unknown capabilities and liabilities that accompany new technologies. The constant interaction and friction within this lively environment results in the particular technology utilization scenario that each teacher eventually develops. These scenarios can range from simple word processing or computer-assisted instruction to a fully integrated multimedia, telecommunications, and simulation development capability in the gifted classroom.

# APPLICATIONS OF TECHNOLOGY FOR GIFTED STUDENTS

Technological utilization in programs for the gifted has generally followed the pattern of regular education programs with the usual array of tools for science, mathematics, and writing (i.e., scientific measurement devices, calculators, tape recorders, typewriters). The relative lack of technological innovation within programs for the gifted and talented probably arises from two sources: (a) untrained teacher educators in colleges and universities who are unable to effectively model new technological tools and methodologies to preservice teachers and (b) the inability of schools to provide adequate funding and support to update the hardware and software needs for classrooms. Luckily, even though the problem is widespread, many individual teachers of the gifted have achieved a high level of expertise in new technologies and have assembled the basic tools and materials needed to use them.

## Historical Applications

The literature contains remarkably little general discussion or research concerning any aspect of technological utilization with students who are gifted. A content analysis of the literature on giftedness from January 1975 to December 1986 located a total of 39 publications (out of 3,220 possible citations) concerning either computers or some other new technology (Rogers, 1989). Of this number, 37 articles discussed non–research-based applications of technologies in gifted and talented settings, and only two articles dealt with a research-based use of technology. One of the earliest analyses of computer-based instruction

(Kulik, Bangert, & Williams, 1983) isolated one of the few definitive findings concerning the use of computer-assisted instructional software with gifted students. Kulik et al. stated that "the effects of computer-based teaching seem especially clear in studies of disadvantaged and low aptitude students . . . whereas effects appeared to be much smaller in studies of talented students" (p. 22). The implications of this study are that computer-assisted instruction may be inappropriate or inadequate for use within classrooms for the gifted.

In a more recent study that provided some support for Kulik et al.'s findings, Kanevsky (1985) investigated the influence of three instructional factors in the use of computers by gifted and talented students. Forty elementary school students in third and fourth grades were assigned to one of three treatment groups: competitive, cooperative, or traditional instructional interventions. Both the competitive and the cooperative groups received computer-assisted instruction (CAI) in basic math operations, which involved finding as many solutions to blank equations as possible (a fluency procedure). The traditional group received group flash card drills on the math operations for 15 minutes per day for 10 consecutive school days, the same amount of time that the two comparative groups received CAI instruction. The results indicated that the CAI and the flash card presentations of math drills were "significantly and equally effective in increasing gifted students' performance on tests of basic math operations" (p. 239). The use of competitive or cooperative group structure in the learning experiences that involved CAI had no effect on gifted students' speed or accuracy in basic math operations. This study's results indicate that there is no advantage to the use of computer-assisted instruction over traditional instructional strategies in the development of fluency in basic math skills for young children identified as gifted in public schools. Although the study may have called into question the appropriateness of using standard CAI software with gifted students, it did not evaluate the effectiveness or productivity of students using more advanced software and the impact of new developments in multimedia and telecommunications.

## A Conceptual Framework for Technology Utilization

A coherent and forward-looking discussion of technological innovation and integration in an age of educational reform was articulated by David Barr (1990). He asserted that, for all practical purposes, "new technology remains a solution in search of a problem" (p. 00). His main premise was that the potential of new technologies is basically unrealized because of a lack of systematic thinking about which instructional problems are amenable to, or will be enhanced by, the application of new technological tools. However, systematic thinking is especially important as the teacher attempts to integrate technology into the instructional program of a gifted classroom because some of the more common (and available) applications, such as CAI, are generally inappropriate for use with gifted students.

Finally, Barr discussed five goals for meaningful change in educational practice that involve using new technologies to make learning (a) more independent, (b) more individualized, (c) more interactive, (d) more interdisciplinary, and (e) more intuitive. These goal areas are of particular use to gifted educators who seek to match the capabilities of gifted students with specific technological applications because student learning needs can be merged with specific types of technological innovations.

### Independent Learning

A substantial amount of both research-based and anecdotal information asserts that independent learning behaviors are highly desirable for gifted students to develop and practice. Independent learning implies the ability of the student to explore, create, and discover information primarily by himself or herself. Some of the qualities that students must develop and maintain are the abilities to motivate, direct, and monitor their own learning. The most obvious example of curricular activities used to develop independent learning is the venerable "independent research project." New technologies can be incorporated to make this an exciting and rewarding learning experience.

An example of independent learning might involve a student who wants to conduct a study and then write a research report by using electronic databases (e.g., NSF-NET, ERIC, DIALOG, BRS) or by accessing mass storage devices such as Compact Disk–Read Only Memory (CD-ROM) and Compact Disk–Interactive (CD-I). Other students can use computers as probes and measuring tools when conducting scientific experiments. Students can then use the computer to analyze the resulting data through both qualitative and quantitative programs. These programs provide for the ordering and exposition of written observational data and for the manipulation of statistical data through software packages (e.g., MiniTab, SPSS-X, SYSTAT 5.0). Finally, the results of the analysis can be merged into a word processing program that allows for the integration of numeric, graphic, and textual information into a single presentation format. In this way, students can produce research documents that embody excellent inquiry methods, tool use, and information presentation.

### Individualized Learning

New technological applications are now sufficiently diverse in style and function to assist teachers who are trying to meet the demands of students with widely varying instructional needs. The applications range from content-based solutions (e.g., computer-assisted instruction) to mutimedia-based presentations (e.g., hypertext, hypermedia) that allow students to tailor their products more closely to their own aesthetic ideals. The basic instructional demands on students include developing their ability to work at their own pace and their ability to select appropriate materials.

An example of more individualized learning using technological tools is linked to the emergence of "object-oriented programming languages." This new class of software allows persons with no formal programming knowledge or training to create sophisticated personalized programs. The commercial authoring programs (e.g., *LinkWay*, *HyperCard*) allow for computer, video, CD-ROM, and other peripherals to be used interactively to create instructional or demonstration programs on almost any subject. This new class of software goes far beyond the limitations of typical CAI by providing multiple stimulus events, response variety, and feedback options—all within the context of a single program. They provide flexible development tools with a minimum amount of instructional overhead in the form of knowledge or skill requirements by either teachers or students.

### Interactive Learning

Another important component of the successful education of gifted students involves the development of increasingly complex communication skills involving inquiry, feedback, and ongoing collaboration among individuals. These interactions can originate from teachers, peers, mentors, parents, and, importantly (in this context), a machine—the computer/video system. This area will offer the most visible example of student ideas and effort, extending the common one-dimensional presentation of ideas in classrooms to more multidimensional and dynamic audio, visual, and textual information resources. Some of the new tools that are available to students and teachers are video production/projection systems, expert systems, interactive videodisc, and telecommunications networks.

One of the most powerful, and visible, uses of technology is as a means of presenting the student's ideas. Technology can be used to design, store, and present the student's work in ways that have never been possible. Proper use of this technology can result in a meaningful achievement for the student. For example, the student may do independent research on the Civil War, create and organize the presentation text or slides and graphics, and then store them all on the computer. When ready to present the project, the student uses the computer system to control the process and visual display as he or she is talking to classmates.

### Interdisciplinary Learning

Klein (Barr, 1990) defined interdisciplinary learning as "the exploration of the fundamental assumptions, problems, perspectives, methodologies, problem-solving techniques, historical evolution, and habits of mind of more than one discipline and which focuses attention on the similarities and differences between these disciplines" (p. 89). This type of learning will be particularly important in the future if the projections of increasingly complex workplaces, frequent and evolving careers, and the continuing intrusion of new technologies become a reality. Students will be required to learn how to work and learn with others so that they understand how to create solutions to problems in a cooperative environment. The highly interactive nature of future society will require a commensurate increase in the ability of students to create interdisciplinary answers to the complex problems that they will face. The computer will be able to assist in this endeavor by providing a powerful work area that allows for gathering, analysis, and reporting of information by students. In addition, the use of advanced commercial and self-generated simulations will help students learn to work in complex, interrelated worlds that involve decision making at many levels.

Examples of interdisciplinary learning can be seen every day at the Apple Classroom of Tomorrow (ACOT) at West High School in Columbus, Ohio. In one situation, students in the journalism class had initially created a newsletter for a local business organization that was very well received by the business owners and their customers. Eventually, the students were contracted for the ongoing publication of the newsletter because of the high quality that was the result of the combination of student creativity and their use of sophisticated desktop publishing hardware and software. These students confronted and solved a multitude of practical and conceptual problems that faced them in the real-world design and production of the newsletter.

### Intuitive Learning

Intuitive learning is difficult to describe because it involves experiences that might be seen as having nonrational, vicarious, and/or unintended learning outcomes. These types of experiences will become more available as a number of multidimensional, all-encompassing simulation programs are developed using virtual reality and other types of sophisticated software programs. The use of new visualization techniques, sophisticated branching and intelligence within software programs, and increasingly malleable mental environments will allow for the development of computer-based experiences that are barely imaginable at this time.

New tools that might facilitate intuitive learning include graphing and modeling programs, advanced simulations, and virtual reality devices. An example of this type of learning results from the increasing use of realistic science and social studies simulation programs that rely on both competitive and collaborative learning schemes. These programs allow for long-term, complex interactions with the concepts and materials that are involved in the social or natural sciences. Students benefit from the highly realistic interactions, alternating between computer or video information and their peers in an engaging and motivating manner.

## Contemporary Applications

Technological tools and techniques are increasingly available for use with gifted students. Technology is affecting the learning of many subjects taught in school, including language arts, mathematics, sciences, and fine arts.

### Language Arts

An increasing variety of reading simulation programs (see Table 10.1 for a partial list) provide opportunities for gifted students to increase their ability to reflect upon, analyze, and organize their reading activities (Hanson, 1992; Perry, 1989). Writing and publishing projects have traditionally been a part of gifted education programs, but the advent of desktop publishing and new video capturing techniques promise a future rich with expressive potential (see Table 10.1). Of course, at each level of innovation, there is a commensurate increase in demands for greater technological acumen and skill on the part of both teachers and students. Wall and Taylor (1982) advocated using interactive writing programs to increase higher cognitive thinking skills in young gifted students. They asserted that, "When the young child learns spoken language, three interaction processes have been shown to influence increases in new information to be learned. These are modeling, expansion and reinforcement (when it is linked to getting the message across)" (p. 14). An innovative writing program for gifted students will attempt to create both computer- and noncomputer-based activities that incorporate these interactional patterns.

## TABLE 10.1. Suggested Software for Gifted Students

| Curricular Area | Software Title | Grades | Producer |
|---|---|---|---|
| Reading | Reader Rabbit | K–1 | Learning Company |
| | The Playroom | K–1 | Brøderbund Software |
| | Talking Classroom | K–2 | Orange Cherry Software |
| | Expanded Books (Series) | All ages | Voyager Company |
| | Silwa Literature Series | 9+ | Queue, Inc. |
| | Review of American Literature | 10–college | Queue, Inc. |
| Writing and desktop publishing | Bilingual Writing Center | 2+ | Learning Company |
| | Children's Writing and Publishing Center | 2+ | Learning Company |
| | Kidworks | K–4 | Davidson and Associates |
| | Pagemaker | 4+ | MacWarehouse |
| Mathematics | In the Neighborhood | 2+ | Critical Thinking Press |
| | Math Blaster Mystery | 1+ | Davidson and Associates |
| | NumberMazes | K–6 | Great Wave Software |
| | Operation Neptune | 4+ | Learning Company |
| | The King's Rule | 4+ | Wings for Learning |
| | Excel | 6+ | MacWarehouse |
| | Lotus 1, 2, 3 | 6+ | MacWarehouse |
| Science | All About Science (series) | 4–8 | Ventura Educational |
| | Destination: MARS! | 5–12 | Compu-Teach |
| | McGraw-Hill Science and Technical Reference Set | 9+ | McGraw-Hill |
| Fine arts | Kid Pix | K–6 | Brøderbund Software |
| | Fractal Design Painter | 4+ | Fractal Design |

(*continues*)

**TABLE 10.1.**  (*Continued*)

| Curricular Area | Software Tile | Grades | Producer |
|---|---|---|---|
| | Intervals, Melodies, Chord Qualities, Harmonies, Rhythms | 6+ | University of Delaware |
| *Multimedia Tools* | HyperCard 2.2 | 4+ | Claris |
| | Adobe Premier | 6+ | MacWarehouse |
| | Director 3.1 | 6+ | MacWarehouse |

### Key to Companies

Brøderbund Software
PO Box 12947
San Rafael, CA 94913-2947

Claris Corporation
440 Clyde Avenue
Mountain View, CA 94943

Compu-Teach
78 Olive Street
New Haven, CT 06511

Critical Thinking Press & Software
PO Box 448
Pacific Grove, CA 93950

Davidson and Associates, Inc.
19840 Pioneer Avenue
Torrance, CA 90503

Fractal Design
335 Spreckels Drive, Suite F
Aptos, CA 95001-2380

Great Wave Software
5353 Scotts Valley Drive
Scotts Valley, CA 95066

The Learning Company
6493 Kaiser Drive
Freemont, CA 94555

MacWarehouse
PO Box 3013
1690 Oak Street
Lakewood, NJ 08701-3013

McGraw-Hill Publishing Company
11 W. 19th Street
New York, NY 10011

Orange Cherry Software
Box 390 Westchester Avenue
Pound Ridge, NY 10576-0390

Queue, Inc.
338 Commerce Drive
Fairfield, CT 06430

Ventura Educational Systems
3440 Brokenhill Street
Newbury Park, CA 91320

Voyager Company
1351 Pacific Coast Highway
Santa Monica, CA 90401

University of Delaware
Office of Computer Based
  Instruction
Willard Hall Education Building
Newark, DE 19716

Wings for Learning
1600 Green Hills Road
PO Box 660002
Scotts Valley, CA 95607-0002

### Mathematics

The use of technologies in mathematics education is a natural marriage between tools and conceptual information (see Table 10.1). The National Council of Teachers of Mathematics (1989) views mathematics as an active and investigative discipline used for problem solving, reasoning, and communication. Grandgenett (1991) discussed some of the areas in mathematics that are particularly amenable to technological integration, including the following:

- *Symbolic processing*—New software programs that display visual representations of complex mathematical equations greatly increase the accessibility of symbolic processing concepts to students. For example, the automatic recalculation features of electronic spreadsheets allow for mathematical models to become dynamic and to change as new numeric values are entered into the equations. Gifted students are thus able to spend more time on problem solving through actual applications of the mathematical concepts as opposed to working out lengthy problems in algebra, trigonometry, or calculus using pencil and paper.

- *Numeric processing*—The use of spreadsheets also allows gifted students to experiment with advanced mathematical concepts, such as financial modeling, matrix theory, and approximation theory. A number of basic statistical packages also have powerful numerical processing capabilities that allow students to model and create simulations of real-life, dynamic numerical analyses.

- *Geometric and spatial concepts*—Gifted students need to design and use sophisticated graphing programs that allow for the gradual development of both geometric and spatial skills, including such concepts as symmetry, rotations, tessellations, transformational geometry, and two- and three-dimensional problem solving. The current emphasis on two-dimensional graphing is primarily a result of the dependence on paper-and-pencil tools to do graphing. Computers allow for complex three-dimensional graphics that can be rotated and resized automatically through the input of new functions.

- *Computer-aided design (CAD)*—CAD programs allow the student to create what are known as "intelligent drawings" that are automatically responsive to adjustments entered by the student (Grandgenett, 1991). This creates a highly sensitive design environment that is much more responsive to students' imaginations. These individualized design environments allow students to perform a number of "what-if" analyses of their own work and to incorporate geometric principles into the overall application.

### Science

Slavkin and Slavkin (1988) asserted, "Science curriculum content for the late 20th and early 21st century requires major re-assessment, novel re-integration of disciplines, significant updating in rapidly expanding scientific advancement area, and vertical integration into the teaching of science" (p. 36). The teaching of the scientific method involves the *entire* process of observation, hypothesis generation and testing, exploration through experimentation, and accurate reporting. One of the most often cited strategies for teaching and learning scientific concepts or skills is the collaborative or peer tutoring technique. This is a very desirable approach to teaching scientific concepts, information, methodology, and thinking skills at all grade levels for gifted students. Technology can be infused throughout this entire process using software simulations for concept building, database programs for storage and analysis, and probes and measurement devices for data gathering and analysis.

Science simulation programs (see Table 10.1) allow gifted students the unique ability to explore a variety of scientific phenomena within a cost-effective yet rich experimental environment (Perry, 1989). These types of programs create situations in which gifted students can advance past the simple acquisition of facts and toward the active exploration, testing, and experimentation associated with actual scientific inquiry.

### Fine Arts

Even though a controversy continues within the art community as to whether computer-generated art is "real art," there is no doubt that gifted students and their teachers can create beautiful and creative images using computers. In addition to providing the aesthetic environment of fine art, the computer is also useful for creating practical graphics using computer-assisted design and desktop publishing programs. It is important to provide gifted students with aesthetic options that extend their expressive abilities, and the computer provides an easily accessible platform for a variety of creative activities (see Table 10.1). Recent advances in the development of Musical Interface Digital Interfaces (MIDIs) have brought a variety of aspects of music performance within reach of an untrained public. These new music development and generation programs provide students with access to various aspects of music, including appreciation, history, theory, and performance.

## Other Software Programs for Gifted Students

### Hypermedia

Hypermedia is an umbrella term for a variety of interactive video and multimedia programs that mix textual, audio, and visual information for educational purposes. It is important to remember that, regardless of all the "bells and whistles" that seem to be hung on multimedia and hypermedia software programs, their primary utility lies in their ability to communicate the embedded learning objectives effectively. In this respect, the real tests of hypermedia programs are whether they are built around identifiable objectives and whether they are ultimately successful in facilitating students' achievement of these objectives.

Hypermedia programs have a number of potentially useful applications, including the ability (a) to involve peers and others in the activities, thus increasing the potential for collaborative learning; (b) to explore a variety of pathways and come to understand that few real-world problems have only one answer or solution strategy; and (c) to serve as a powerful tutor and information resource (see Table 10.1).

### Programming Languages

Programming languages may assist students in using both logic and creativity via step-by-step sequencing, long-range planning, branching, exploration, and creative problem solving (Perry, 1989). Seymour Papert (1980) wrote, "A programming language is like a natural human language in that it favors certain metaphors, images, and ways of thinking" (p. 3). Thus, a programming language can be made accessible to students while at the same time retaining its inherent complexity as an abstract phenomenon. Papert inferred that learning computer languages might affect students substantially in terms of their perspective as active learners. He stated that he could "see how children who had learned to program computers could use very concrete computer models to think about thinking and to learn about learning and in doing so, enhance their powers as psychologists and as epistemologists" (p. 5).

Regardless of the rhetoric surrounding the use of programming languages, they should not be used by all gifted students or in all gifted programs. It takes a great deal of knowledge on the part of the instructor to understand, much less accurately use, programming languages. This means that gifted students who desire to learn programming methods in gifted classes often must do so independently of their teachers. Concerns that should be addressed when considering using programming languages in gifted classrooms are that it is possible to learn poor solution strategies, or not be exposed to critical concepts when learning a programming language in isolation.

# MANAGEMENT OF THE TECHNOLOGY-BASED CLASSROOM

## Software Selection and Acquisition

Identifying appropriate software for a gifted classroom depends on the curricular goals developed by the teacher for a particular student. If the demand is to build research and scientific inquiry skills, then the best software might be simulations, database systems, interactive videodisc programs, and possibly spreadsheets. If the curriculum focuses on expressive writing, then the use of word processing, desktop publishing, and graphics software would be appropriate.

Perry (1989) provided several selection criteria to be applied when previewing educational software for use in gifted education. Selected software should (a) provide for different levels of ability; (b) include branching capabilities; (c) be reusable, allowing students to profit from using the software more than one time; (d) have an evaluation component; (e) be challenging for students; and (f) have accurate and up-to-date content.

## Configurations, Scheduling, and Access

A number of computer configurations could be used in educational settings with gifted students. Educators need to remember that the equipment location and configuration basically determine the level of student access and the curricular content that can be accommodated. The types of configurations possible in educational settings include the following:

1. *Saturated classrooms*—The saturated classroom generally approximates a one-to-one ratio of computers to students, and often includes a variety of other new technological tools, such as scanners, digitizers, laser printers, telecommunications, interactive videodisc, and CD-ROMs. There may be anywhere from 15 to 25 computers in these classrooms.

2. *Mini-labs in classrooms*—The mini-lab is basically a local area network in a classroom with 3 to 5 computers in the network and the space being shared among several teachers in a building.

3. *School laboratories*—The limited access and highly structured nature of the laboratory setting are not amenable to many of the programmatic needs of gifted students. Typical school labs have 20 to 25 computers in a standard row arrangement. The teacher must schedule his or her class into such labs along with all the other classes in a school building, meaning that only a single period during any given week is usually available.

4. *Stand-alone computers*—The "typical" configuration in classrooms for the gifted is to have one or two stand-alone computers. This arrangement has the distinct advantage of being under the control of the teacher and thus creates a high degree of flexibility. However, it also limits access to only one or two students at a time, and tends to be used for self-instruction rather than as a vehicle for small-group or collaborative learning situations.

# NEW AND EMERGENT TECHNOLOGIES FOR GIFTED EDUCATION

## Intelligent Computer-Assisted Instruction

Intelligent computer-assisted instruction (ICAI) is designed to analyze and interpret student responses and then present new information to learners which is modeled after their own cognitive strengths and weaknesses. The critical difference between ICAI and traditional CAI programs is in ICAI's ability to collect diagnostic information and to act on it. Basically, it "learns" from the user's responses. In addition, these programs are able to modify their instructional strategies based upon the patterns of information they gather from student responses.

An example of an ICAI program might be a math tutor that initially presents a group of mathematics problems at a defined difficulty level to a student. After the student responds to the initial set of problems, the program analyzes the response patterns and sets a starting point within a sequenced set of problems for the learner. The student then begins working on this first set, with the ICAI program analyzing the correct solutions and, most importantly, the types and patterns of errors the student makes. The program utilizes these error patterns to create expert models that will progressively guide the student through problem solution, providing hints and directional cues upon student errors. The program thus monitors, evaluates, and constructs problem solutions for each individual user.

## Virtual Reality

Virtual reality simulations are three-dimensional experiences that provide opportunities for creative development and the exploration of both real and imaginary mental environments. This software will help to "concretize" formerly highly abstract concepts (Papert, 1980) and thus allow for earlier and more powerful instructional interventions with gifted students. An example of an educational application of virtual reality might be a social studies simulation of a medieval village. The student would access the virtual "medieval world" through the computer-based simulation and a helmet that transmits the sounds and images to the user. A data-glove or joystick allows a limited response capability in order to manipulate "objects" in the village/world. The student can walk through the streets up to the castle, enter the castle, and take part in a grand feast in the main hall. The food, entertainment, and interactions can all be modeled in the virtual world to closely approximate those revealed in historical documents and paintings. The student can come to know and experience the reality of medieval life in a manner that is both encompassing and educational.

There may also be a "dark side" to virtual reality, however, which has not been fully articulated in the rush to bring the product into the recreational and entertainment marketplaces. Access to a variety of virtual worlds has the potential to be so engrossing that students would reject other types of learning or play experiences in favor of using the systems. The potential danger is that children might become isolated within these mental environments, which are so easily molded to meet their desires, and forsake the somewhat "messy" real world in which one must work at relationships and life.

## Electronic Communities

Developments in telecommunications will allow for greater interactions and sharing among gifted students from across the world. The distant interactions will provide new impetus for students to continue their studies, and perhaps to reach out and assist in the process of globalizing education for the future. A number of distance learning projects have already been initiated throughout the United States linking students from across the world with one another. The curricular focus of these projects ranges from second-language learning to social studies and language arts. However, their most important contribution to learning may be in the areas of cultural understanding and interpersonal communications. Students may be able to more fully realize and deal with the realities of a global community through such learning opportunities. The world grows smaller through such contacts, and understanding of different cultures and peoples will serve to prepare students better to deal with both global competition and cooperation as they mature into adulthood.

# CONCLUSION

The primary uses of technology in the education of gifted students involve computer and video tools in independent research, writing, art, and telecommunications. Computers can be great tools for facilitating cooperative learning in independent learning situations. They can be used as *exploration tools* when students are carrying out personal research projects or as *data storage and manipulation tools* when students use databases, spreadsheets, and statistical software. Finally, computers can be used as *presentation tools* to display the results of the creative process.

Both students and teachers should make use of these tools in an interactive and collaborative manner to increase their effectiveness and overall utility for both learning and management of the classroom. Becoming adept at using a technological tool involves gaining knowledge and skills in both technology and pedagogy. It takes time, patience, and, most importantly, practice with the hardware and software to develop a reasonable level of comfort with technologies. Actually achieving this type and level of usage, however, will demand a commitment from schools, teachers, and students to engage in training, budgeting, evaluation, and maintenance. This commitment will determine the individual and collective success of the effort to integrate technology into gifted education.

# REFERENCES

Barr, D. (1990). A solution in search of a problem: The role of technology in educational reform. *Journal for the Education of the Gifted, 1*(14), 79–95.

Grandgenett, N. (1991). Roles of computer technology in the mathematics education of the gifted. *GCT, 4,* 38–39.

Hanson, S. (1992). Writing with computers: Imagineering. *GCT*, *4*, 38–39.

Kanevsky, L. (1985). Computer-based math for gifted students: Comparison of cooperative and competitive strategies. *Journal for the Education of the Gifted*, *8*(4), 239–255.

Kulik, J. A., Bangert, R. L., & Williams, C. W. (1983). Effects of computer-based teaching on secondary school students. *Journal of Educational Psychology*, *75*, 19–26.

National Council of Teachers of Mathematics. (1989). *Curriculum and evaluation standards for school mathematics*. Reston, VA: Author.

Papert, S. (1980). *Mindstorms*. New York: Basic Books.

Perry, M. (1989). *Using microcomputers with gifted students*. Bloomington, IN: Phi Delta Kappa Educational Foundation.

Rogers, K. (1989). A content analysis of the literature on giftedness. *Journal for the Education of the Gifted*, *13*(1), 78–88.

Slavkin, H. C., & Slavkin, L. E. (1988). Science curriculum and teaching for the 21st century. *Journal for the Education of the Gifted*, *9*(2), 35–61.

Wall, S. M., & Taylor, N. E. (1982). Using interactive computer programs in teaching higher conceptual skills: An approach to instruction in writing. *Educational Technology*, *22*, 13–17.

# Chapter 11

# Underachievement Syndrome in Gifted Students

### Sylvia B. Rimm

◆  ◆  ◆

GIFTEDNESS, IN ITSELF, does not assure educational or creative productivity or success. Risks and pressures that often accompany high intelligence can detour potentially high achieving children toward defensive and avoidance patterns (Rimm, 1987b). Whether gifted children move toward high achievement or underachievement appears to be related to their home, school, and/or peer environments (Rimm, 1986b; Steinberg, Dornbusch, & Brown, 1992).

In *A Nation at Risk: The Imperative for Educational Reform*, the National Commission on Excellence in Education (1984) stated that one-half of gifted children do not perform to their tested abilities. Studies indicate that 10% to 20% of high school dropouts are in the gifted range (Davis & Rimm, 1994). One of the most shocking findings is that 40% of the top 5% of this country's high school graduates do not complete college (DeLeon, 1989).

School support personnel are in an excellent position to help prevent and reverse underachievement in gifted students and may even be able to prevent post–high school underachievement. They may be able to recommend classroom curriculum changes and can understand and interpret psychological issues involved in giftedness within the child, family, and peer group.

School support personnel will have to redefine their roles in schools in two important ways. First, they will want to expand their relationship with exceptionality to include both extremes of the normal curve. Although in some states this concept is already acceptable, in many states giftedness is not included within exceptional education. Second, school support personnel, particularly psychologists and counselors, while continuing to be involved in assessment, will want to include intervention strategies such as individual or small group therapy, collateral therapy with parents, and consultation with teachers.

# CHARACTERISTICS OF UNDERACHIEVEMENT

Incomplete assignments are the first symptoms of underachievement. Other symptoms include poor study habits, lack of interest in school learning, disorganization, and a tendency to blame teachers or parents. Boredom is a frequent explanation or excuse. Uneven abilities, specific learning style preferences, and high creativity often contribute to the problem. Perfectionism may also lead to later underachievement when students are challenged and perfection is unattainable.

Two underlying characteristics seem to be the most important in leading to the psychological defense mechanisms that make up the underachievement syndrome. First, students have a low sense of control over their own lives (Rimm, 1986b). If they fail at a task, they blame their lack of ability; if they succeed, they may attribute their success to luck. Thus, they may accept responsibility for failure but not for success (Felton & Biggs, 1977).

This attribution process has been related to the original theory of learned helplessness advanced by Seligman (1975). If children do not see a relationship between their efforts and the outcomes, they are likely to exhibit characteristics of learned helplessness and will no longer make efforts to achieve. Weiner (1974, 1980) also emphasized that children's subsequent performance will be strongly influenced by whether they attribute success and failures to ability, effort, task difficulty, or luck. Attributing success to effort leads to further effort, whereas attributing success to task ease or luck does not. Laffoon, Jenkins-Friedman, and Tollefson (1989) also found a lack of internal locus of control in their research with underachievers and commented on these children's lack of ability to persevere.

The second important factor seems to be related to the inability to function in competition (Davis & Rimm, 1994). The main competitive pressures that gifted children feel include (a) the need to be extraordinarily intelligent and/or perfect; (b) the wish to be extremely creative and unusual, which they may translate as nonconformity; and (c) the concern with being "most" well adjusted and, therefore, being popular (Rimm, 1987b). Obviously, these pressures conflict during varying developmental stages.

Although parents are often accused of pressuring their gifted children, typically these pressures arise, at least partially, because of their children's giftedness. These children may have internalized this sense of stress because multiple adults in their environments have admired them for their academic accomplishments, their unusual ideas, and/or their appearance. The profuse praise that they receive not only reinforces their motivation but, when too extreme or frequent, may cause them to feel pressured to accomplish the goals that are so admired or valued by important others. Not only may they feel pressured to achieve, but they may acquire a dependence on attention that is much like an addiction. Thus, they find it difficult to function without continuous praise and reinforcement. Their intrinsic reinforcement is thus diminished by their dependence on extrinsic reinforcement (Deci, 1986; Hom, Gaskill, & Hutchins, 1988).

If school and home environments foster appropriate relationships between effort and outcomes, it is more likely that children will manage the internalized pressures and will incorporate them as motivations toward achievement. Figure 11.1 illustrates four potential relationships between effort and outcomes (Rimm, 1987b). These will be explained further in the section on school and home causes of underachievement.

When school and home environments do not foster achievement, and students protect themselves psychologically, defense mechanisms exhibit themselves in mainly dependent or dominant directions. By adolescence, children's defenses usually are a combination of both dependence and dominance (Cornale, 1988). Some children actually exhibit both directions from the start. Figure 11.2 shows these two directions.

Conforming underachievers differ from those in the nonconforming category by their visibility and extensive use of defense mechanisms.

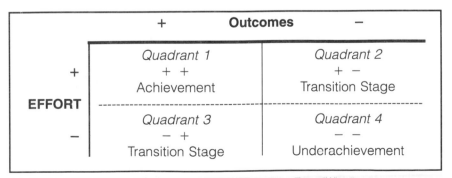

**Figure 11.1.** Relationship between effort and outcomes. From "Why Do Bright Children Underachieve? The Pressures They Feel" by S. B. Rimm, 1987 (November/December), *Gifted Child Today*, p. 34. Reprinted by permission.

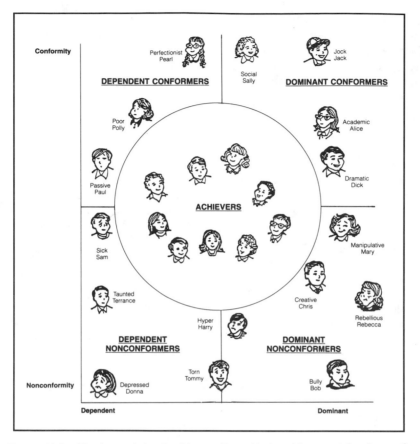

**Figure 11.2.** The inner circle of achievers. From *Underachievement Syndrome: Causes and Cures* (p. 141) by S. B. Rimm, 1986, Watertown, WI: Apple Publishing Co. Copyright 1986 by Apple Publishing Co. Reprinted by permission.

That is, conforming dependent and dominant students have the characteristics that may lead to greater underachievement problems, but their underachievement is not yet as serious or apparent as that of nonconforming dependent and dominant underachievers. The prototypical names used in Figure 11.2 (Passive Paul, Rebellious Rebecca, etc.) are not intended as labels for children but are used to emphasize the main characteristics of underachievers. Any one underachiever typically exhibits a group of these symptoms.

Rimm (1986b) emphasized that typical adult intuitive responses to these psychological defense mechanisms have seemed only to reinforce the patterns. Counterintuitive responses appear to be more effective in reversing underachievement.

# HOME, SCHOOL, AND PEER CAUSES
# OF UNDERACHIEVEMENT

## Home Risks

The family characteristics of underachievers have been described in several studies (Frazier, Passow, & Goldberg, 1958; French, 1959; Whitmore, 1980; Zilli, 1971). Rimm and Lowe (1988) targeted some critical differences between the families of 22 gifted underachievers and the findings from family studies of achievement and eminence. These are described in Chapter 14 of this text. Families with economic disadvantages and cultural divergence may also unintentionally move their children toward underachievement. Preoccupation with basic economic needs often prevents these families from providing the cultural enrichment that fosters a love for intrinsic learning. Parents themselves have often had negative school experiences as children. Identification of giftedness among culturally diverse students is notoriously inefficient. Richert (1987) estimates a 30% to 70% underrepresentation of minority students in gifted programming throughout the nation. Although some creative efforts are being made to identify and program for disadvantaged gifted children, progress has been slow (Baldwin, 1984; Davis & Rimm, 1994; Frasier, 1991; Matthew, Golin, Moore, & Baker, 1992; Smith, LeRose, & Clasen, 1991).

## School Environments

Quadrants 2 and 3 in Figure 11.1 provide the paradigms for classroom environments that encourage underachievement. There are classroom mismatches between effort and outcomes, which, if continued, will be likely to result in a loss of personal locus of control and are, therefore, likely to lead to underachievement.

School environments that foster Quadrant 2 (+ −) transitions toward underachievement patterns would be those that either do not value high achievement outcomes or conversely set achievement outcomes impossibly high. Thus, children may initially make appropriate efforts but do not gain the satisfactions from their successful efforts. Some school environments that do not value excellent school achievement include the following:

- An anti-intellectual school atmosphere that sets high priorities for athletics or social status but not for intellectual attainment or preparation for higher level education.

- An antigifted atmosphere that considers gifted programming to be elitist and emphasizes the importance of all students

adjusting and fitting into a mold. Many schools have eliminated homogeneous grouping despite its effectiveness for
gifted students (Kulik, 1992).

- A rigid classroom environment that encourages all children
to study identical materials at similar speeds or in similar
styles (Whitmore, 1980).

- Rigid teachers who do not see the quality of children's work,
either because of different values, personal power struggles,
or cultural or racial prejudice, which may cause children to
feel unable to accomplish goals despite their best efforts
(Davis & Rimm, 1994; Rimm, 1980).

- Heterogeneously grouped, cooperative education in which
gifted children often take the responsibility for much of the
group's work and feel continually frustrated by lack of cooperation or are expected to do the tutoring (Rimm, 1992).

School environments that lead to Quadrant 3 (−+) underachievement would be those that value the children's accomplishments but do
not provide them with challenging tasks that encourage sustained efforts. Thus, in effect, the work is too easy. The schools value good
grades and performance and, initially, grades reflect excellent performance. Children tend to feel positive about school, but they are not
sufficiently challenged. Children learn that achievement is easy, that
success is readily attainable, and that learning and study are effortless. Occasionally, they may comment about boredom or the lack of
challenge, but as long as grades continue to be high, they exhibit no
problem behaviors.

When the curriculum becomes more complex or when students
enter higher grades, where their peer populations are more intellectually competitive, they feel that they are not as intelligent as they
believed they were earlier. Some learn more appropriate study habits.
Others hide from their threatening feelings. They worry that they are
not as smart as they would like to be, and they invent or discover a
whole group of rituals and excuses that prevent them from making
further effort.

Bias among teachers against accelerated curriculum often prevents schools from challenging gifted students. Rimm and Lovance
(1992a, 1992b) found that grade and subject skipping were helpful in
preventing this problem by giving highly gifted children the opportunity to experience challenges, and thus preventing and even reversing underachievement. After surveying parents of 14 students who
were grade skipped and interviewing the students themselves, the

authors found that all students had made excellent adjustments. Numerous other studies have found acceleration to be successful in providing gifted students with challenge (Rogers, 1990; Stanley, 1978; Stanley & Benbow, 1986; Swiatek & Benbow, 1991).

## Peer Pressure

Although, subjectively, educators have always been aware of peer pressure on students to avoid the reputation of being "brainy," two pieces of research have closely identified the anti-intellectual pressure on achieving students. Brown and Steinberg (1990) found in a sample group of 8,000 high school students that only 10% were willing to acknowledge association with a "brain" crowd, and Steinberg, Dornbusch, and Brown (1992) found peer groups to be mediators between parenting influence and actual achievement. Thus, adolescents who came from effective families and associated with antilearning peer groups often underachieved, whereas those who associated with achieving peer groups often reversed the negative effects of poor parenting.

Research on the peer effects of achievement is in early stages. However, school psychologists and counselors should become increasingly aware of how peers may apply counterproductive pressure on those underachievers whom the psychologists may be counseling.

# REVERSAL OF UNDERACHIEVEMENT

## The TRIFOCAL Model

The underachieving gifted child continues to underachieve because the home, school, and/or peer environments unintentionally support that underachievement. The student is no longer motivated to achieve, and working below one's ability affects both immediate educational success and eventual career achievement.

Although it is difficult to reverse a long-standing pattern of underachievement, Rimm's (1986b) TRIFOCAL Model was found to be successful for 80% of her clients. She has found that the treatment of underachievement involves the collaboration of school and family in the implementation of six steps that provide the framework for change:

1. Assessment

2. Communication

3. Changing expectations

4. Role model identification

5. Correction of deficiencies

6. Modifications of reinforcements

### Assessment of Skills, Abilities, and Types of Underachievement

The first step in the underachievement reversal process is an assessment that involves the cooperation of the school psychologist, classroom teacher, teacher of the gifted, counselor, and parents. Because the school psychologist already has a solid background in measurement, he or she mainly needs to be aware of the special characteristics of gifted and creative children.

An individual intelligence test is a highly recommended first assessment instrument. That venerable IQ number has the potential to communicate important expectations about children's abilities. Because these children have not been motivated, it is likely that group intelligence test scores have underestimated their intellectual potential. The underachievement may even have had a depressing effect on scores from individual testing. It is helpful to look at past tests, which may give a more accurate picture of a child's abilities. *The Wechsler Intelligence Scale for Children–Revised* (WISC-R) (Wechsler, 1974) or the *Stanford–Binet L-M* (Terman & Merrill, 1960) can be individually administered by a psychologist. Although these tests have some disadvantages related to their out-of-date publication, they seem to be much more effective for identifying giftedness than *The Wechsler Intelligence Scale for Children–Third Edition* (WISC-III) (Wechsler, 1991) or the *Stanford-Binet, Fourth Edition* (Thorndike, Hagen, & Sattler, 1986). These last two tests do not discriminate well among highly gifted children and significantly underestimate test scores compared with early measures (Silverman & Kearney, 1992). If the student achieves scale scores of 19 in several subtests of the WISC-R, the Stanford-Binet L-M can be used to better estimate the student's verbal ability. Students who score in the 140 IQ range of the WISC-R Verbal test may score between 140 and 200 on the Stanford–Binet L-M. The greater range is important in making decisions for acceleration.

Intelligence testing should be followed by individually administered oral achievement tests to clearly assess strengths and deficits in basic skills, particularly reading and math. Because many under-achieving students have writing problems, tests that involve writing may actually underestimate these students' reading and math skills (Rimm, 1985).

A creativity test or inventory, which can be administered by the teacher or a psychologist, should also be part of the assessment. This instrument produces not only a norm-referenced creativity score, but also descriptions of abilities, characteristics, and interests that are relevant to understanding the child's personality, creative potential, and learning style. The *Group Inventory for Finding Creative Talent* (GIFT) (Rimm, 1976) and *Group Inventory for Finding Interests* (GIFFI) (Rimm & Davis, 1979) tests include dimension scores, such as Independence, Self-Confidence, Imagination, Interests, and Challenge–Inventiveness, that provide important insights for understanding the student.

*Achievement Identification Measure* (AIM) (Rimm, 1986a), *Group Achievement Identification Measure* (GAIM) (Rimm, 1987a), and *Achievement Identification Measure–Teacher Observation* (AIM-TO) (Rimm, 1988) are inventories developed for identifying children's characteristics related to achievement or underachievement. GAIM can be administered to students in Grades 5 through 12 (with parent permission), AIM is to be completed by parents, and AIM-TO is a teacher observation instrument. The latter two instruments can be completed for any school-age student. The scores provide a description of the extent and type of the child's underachievement. Dimension scores reveal whether the student exhibits mainly dependent or dominant characteristics or a combination of both. Scores also provide insights into parent consistency regarding messages about achievement. A description of the dimension scores is provided in Table 11.1.

Finally, parent and student interviews are very helpful in identifying underachieving patterns unintentionally maintained at home and school (see Appendix A for student and Appendix B for parent interview forms) (Rimm, Cornale, Manos, & Behrend, 1989). Ideally, both parents should be interviewed. If only one parent is interviewed, it is important to ask about the other parent's relationship to the child. Overall, the analysis of student abilities and home and school reinforcement contingencies is critical to the second step of the underachievement modification program.

### Communication

Communication between parents and teachers is vital to the cure for underachievers. Either a parent or the teacher may initiate the

**TABLE 11.1. Dimension Scores for *Achievement Identification Measure*, *Group Achievement Identification Measure*, and *Achievement Identification Measure–Teacher Observation***

*Competition*—High scorers enjoy competition whether they win or lose. They are good sports and handle victories graciously. They do not give up easily.

*Responsibility*—High scorers are responsible in their home and schoolwork. They tend to be well organized and bring activities to closure. They have good study habits and understand that their efforts are related to their grades.

*Achievement Communication*—Children who score high are receiving clear and consistent messages from parents about the importance of learning and good grades. Their parents have communicated positive feelings about their own school experiences, and there is consistency between mother and father messages of achievement.

*Independence/Dependence*—High scorers are independent and understand the relationship between effort and outcomes. They are able to share attention at home and in the classroom.

*Respect–Dominance*—High scorers are respectful toward their parents and teachers. They are reasonably well behaved at home and school. They value education. They are not deliberately manipulative.

From *Guidebook—Underachievement Syndrome: Causes and Cures* (pp. 102–103) by S. B. Rimm, M. Cornale, R. Manos, and J. Behrend, 1989, Watertown, WI: Apple Publishing Co. Copyright 1989 by Apple Publishing Co. Reprinted by permission.

first conference. The school psychologist or counselor could coordinate the conference in the hope of providing support for home and school, rather than placing blame. If it appears to the psychologist or counselor that the parents are not interested in, or capable of, working with him or her, a child advocate in the school can coordinate the process. A school psychologist, counselor, gifted coordinator, or resource teacher can be an excellent advocate. Reversing the pattern without parent assistance is not as efficient, but it is possible.

The discussion between parents and teachers should include an assessment of abilities and achievements, as well as formal and informal evaluations of the child's expressions of dependence or dominance. School personnel should be careful to communicate in clear English and avoid jargon, which mystifies all intelligent adults who are not educators.

Accountability will be an important part of continued communication. Some examples of forms to be used for accountability are the daily and weekly evaluation forms in Appendix C (Rimm et al., 1989).

### Changing the Expectations of Important Others

The expectations of parents, teachers, peers, and siblings are difficult to change. As noted above, IQ scores, if higher than anticipated, are very effective in modifying expectations. Anecdotal information can also provide convincing evidence of the child's abilities. For example, a teacher, in convincing parents of their child's mathematical talent, can explain that the child solves problems in an unusually clever way or seems to learn math concepts more quickly than anyone else in the class. A psychologist, in trying to convince a teacher that a child has unusual talent, can describe the unusual vocabulary or problem-solving skills that the child revealed during testing.

It is very important to underachieving children that parents and teachers be able to honestly say to them that they believe in their ability (Perkins & Wicas, 1971). The expectations of these important others are basic to the change in self-expectations that is necessary to convert underachievement to high achievement. Jackson, Cleveland, and Mirenda (1975) indicated in their longitudinal research with bright fourth-, fifth-, and sixth-grade underachievers that positive expectations by parents and teachers had a significant long-range effect on achievement in high school. Bloom's (1985) studies of talent development found that parents of research neurologists and mathematicians always expected their children to be very good students.

The following interesting, true story emphasizes the role of teacher expectation for achievement: It was the first parent–teacher conference of the new school year, a time when teachers may not yet know all the parents of their students. Ms. Dunn, a fourth-grade teacher, had two Janets in her class. One was an excellent student, positive and well adjusted; the second had multiple problems and was very negative. When the second Janet's parents came for the conference, Ms. Dunn mistook them for the first Janet's parents. She welcomed them with an enthusiastic description of their daughter's positive attitude, only to be greeted by their shocked expressions. She immediately realized her mistake, but rather than embarrass herself and the parents, she continued her discussion about a "few areas" where Janet needed improvement.

The parents left the conference more positive about their daughter than ever before and conveyed this excitement to their child. The next day, to Ms. Dunn's surprise, Janet entered school with a big smile and positive attitude. Her self-confidence and her school efforts were completely transformed. She ended the school year with "B"s instead of the

"D"s that had been typical of earlier report cards. A chance faux pas had led to a dramatic change for Janet. Yes, this really is a true story!

Because sibling competition frequently is a causal component of underachievement syndrome, changing the expectations of siblings is important. In the sibling rivalry that often exists, an achieving child may have assigned to an underachieving brother or sister the role of "loser," and the anticipated change of that sibling's role may feel threatening to the "winner." An individual and personal communication to the "winner" about the expected change is helpful. Parents should provide the assurance that the sibling's changed status will not displace the achiever's role. Genetically and environmentally, a "whole smart family" is not only possible, but more likely. This explanation may deter the achiever from subtly trying to sabotage the underachiever's improved status.

Self-expectations can also be modified by small-group or class discussion. Table 11.2 includes a list of sample topics. Source books for adolescent group discussion topics and projects are *Gifted Kids Have Feelings Too* (Rimm, 1990) and *Exploring Feelings* (Rimm & Priest, 1990).

**TABLE 11.2. Topics of Discussion for Small-Group or Class Sessions for Prevention and Reversal of Underachievement**

1. Competition—game playing
   Discussion of feelings

2. Competition—sports model

3. Peer relations—popularity versus friendship
   Reading and discussion—*It's Dumb to Be Smart,* in *Gifted Kids Have Feelings Too* by S. Rimm, 1990, Watertown, WI: Apple Publishing Co.

4. Siblings—Competition with sisters and brothers

5. Pressure—how to cope and how much is too much

6. Leadership versus "Bossyship"

7. Understanding parents

8. Responsibility

9. Perfectionism

10. Creative problem solving

From S. B. Rimm, 1990 Underachievement Institute, Oconomowoc, WI.

### Role Model Identification

A critical turning point for the underachieving child is the discovery of a role model for identification. All other treatments for underachievement dim in importance compared with strong identification with an achieving model. As noted, Bloom's (1981; Bloom & Sosniak, 1981) biographical research with highly talented students showed that parents modeled the values and the lifestyles of successful achievers in the talent area. Identification research indicates that the best family environment for a gifted boy is provided when a father is viewed as competent, is satisfied with his job, and permits his son to master tasks independently. Because this ideal situation may not be provided for the gifted underachiever, parents and teachers need to change the environment to encourage students to identify with good role models.

Research on parent identification (Mussen & Rutherford, 1963) indicates that the selected parent identification figure is nurturing, powerful, and shares common characteristics with the child. These same characteristics can be used to locate an appropriate achieving model for the underachieving gifted child. As a warning, however, an underachieving adolescent sometimes selects a powerful, nurturing model who shares the underachieving characteristics of the adolescent. This person may then become a strong model for underachievement.

Underachieving children should be matched with achieving persons who will serve as mentors for them. Persons selected can serve in model capacities for more than one child. The model's actual role may be tutor, mentor, companion, teacher, parent, sibling, counselor, psychologist, minister, scout leader, doctor, and so on. Persons who may serve as appropriate role models may be invited to schools to talk to students about their careers. Videotapes of these talks may provide a continuing role model for other students. One teacher may serve as a role model for many students. The following letter about a teacher model written by a gifted underachiever will provide an impressive example of how important teachers can be:

> After I finished sixth grade at Seven Oaks, I started seventh grade at Irmo Middle School, Campus R. Middle school was very different from elementary school. I got a lot more homework than I did at Seven Oaks, but I also got a lot more privileges.
>
> Eighth grade, so far, has been pretty good. Although my grades have dropped since I have been at Irmo, I have also learned a lot since I have been here. The things I am talking about are not physical, but mental. I have learned a lot about myself and others from a very important person. Believe it or not, this person is a teacher. His name is Mr. Talbert. He is not a regular teacher; he is more like a father or something.

There are about 24 of us in his class, and I feel that he has touched each and every one of us in a way I do not think anyone else on this earth could do. I know that he is my favorite teacher ever, and I am pretty sure he has some other great admirers. One of the reasons I enjoy him so much is because I think we are alike in many ways. In his class, we learn about the values of life and friendship. He has taught me more than social studies. He has taught me what life is all about.

(Written by a student from Irmo Middle School, Columbia, South Carolina. Reprinted with permission by Garry Talbert, Teacher at Irmo Middle School, Campus R.)

### Correcting Skill Deficiencies

The underachieving gifted child almost always has skill deficiencies as a result of inattention in class and poor work and study habits. However, because he or she is gifted, most skill deficiencies can be overcome reasonably fast. This is less of a problem for a very young child because the deficiencies are less likely to be extensive. Tutoring should be goal directed with movement to a higher reading or accelerated math group or acceptance into an accelerated class as the anticipated outcome. Rather than being ongoing, tutoring should be of specified duration—for example, weekly for 2 months until the child takes a proficiency test. Parents and siblings are usually not appropriate tutors because the personal relationships are likely to cause the child additional pressure and dependency. Children have often described the assistance given by an older sibling as helpful but as having a secondary effect of "making them feel dumb." The correction of skill deficiencies must be conducted carefully so that (a) the independent work of the underachieving child is reinforced by the tutor, (b) manipulation of the tutor by the child is avoided, and (c) the child senses the relationship between effort and the achievement outcomes. Charting progress during tutoring helps visually confirm the rapid progress to both child and tutor and encourages feelings of internal locus of control.

Sometimes, underachieving gifted students actually have learning disabilities. Other times, their dependent patterns look like learning disabilities. Table 11.3 compares dependencies to disabilities and can provide teachers with a diagnostic guide for actual disabilities.

### Modification of Reinforcements at Home and School

Parent and teacher discussions will certainly identify some of the manipulative rituals discussed previously in the home and school etiology sections. These behaviors need to be modified by setting important long-term goals and some short-term objectives that can ensure imme-

**TABLE 11.3.  Ways to Discriminate Between Dependence and Disability**

| Dependence | Disability |
| --- | --- |
| 1. Child asks for explanations regularly despite differences in subject matter. | Child asks for explanations in particular subjects that are difficult. |
| 2. Child asks for explanation of instructions regardless of style used, either auditory or visual. | Child asks for explanations of instructions only when given in one instruction style, either auditory or visual, but not both. |
| 3. Child's questions are not specific to material but appear to be mainly to gain adult attention. | Child's questions are specific to material and once process is explained child works efficiently. |
| 4. Child is disorganized or slow in assignments but becomes much more efficient when a meaningful reward is presented as motivation. | Child's disorganization or slow pace continues despite motivating rewards. |
| 5. Child works only when an adult is nearby at school and/or at home. | Child works independently once process is clearly explained. |
| 6. Individually administered measures of ability indicate that the child is capable of learning the material. Individual tests improve with tester encouragement and support. Group measures may not indicate good abilities or skills. | Both individual and group measures indicate lack of specific abilities or skills. Tester encouragement has no significant effect on scores. |
| 7. Child exhibits "poor me" body language (tears, helplessness, pouting, copying) regularly when new work is presented. Teacher or adult attention serves to ease the symptoms. | Child exhibits "poor me" body language only with instructions or assignments in specific disability areas and accepts challenges in areas of strength. |
| 8. Parents report whining, complaining, attention getting, temper tantrums, and poor sportsmanship at home. | Although parents may find similar symptoms at home, they tend to be more sporadic than regular, particularly the whining and complaining. |
| 9. Child's "poor me" behavior appears only with one parent and not with the other; only with some | Although the child's "poor me" behaviors may appear only with one parent or with solicitous |

*(continues)*

**TABLE 11.3.** *(Continued)*

| Dependence | Disability |
|---|---|
| teachers and not with others. With some teachers or with the other parent, the child functions fairly well independently. | teachers, performance is not adequate even when behavior is acceptable. |
| 10. Child learns only when given one-to-one instruction but will not learn in groups even when instructional mode is varied. | Although child may learn more quickly in a one-to-one setting, he or she will also learn efficiently in a group setting provided the child's disability is taken into consideration when instructions are given. |

*It is critical to realize that some children who are truly disabled have also become dependent. The key to distinguishing between disability and dependence is the child's response to adult support. If the child performs only with adult support when new material is presented, he or she is too dependent, whether or not there is also a disability.*

From *Underachievement Syndrome: Causes and Cures* (p. 219) by S. B. Rimm, 1986, Watertown, WI: Apple Publishing Co. Copyright 1986 by Apple Publishing Co. Reprinted by permission.

diate small successes for the child both at home and school. These successful experiences may be temporarily reinforced by extrinsic rewards. Rewards may be based on activities completed or on the quality of the activity. Rewarding the process rather than the actual grades earned seems to be more effective. Although stickers and money have been found to be effective, one-to-one attention by an adult is probably most effective. The student should find that the satisfaction of accomplishment is sufficiently reinforcing.

Modifying reinforcements for homework and study are an important component of reversing underachievement syndrome. However, this modification by itself will not be sufficient. Dozens of other recommendations for home and school changes are given in *Underachievement Syndrome: Causes and Cures* (Rimm, 1986b). The extrinsic reinforcers used during the underachievement cure are only temporary, and intrinsic reinforcement and real-world extrinsic motivations will become the only effective long-term motivators.

## Recommendations for Parents

The following general recommendations for parenting gifted children emerge from the comparison of gifted underachievers and achievers:

> *The preschool years*—Child-centered environments are typical for gifted children. However, conferring adult status on children carries the risk of later "depowerment." Too *much* praise and admiration and the use of frequent superlatives confer a "specialness" to which the child can rarely adjust in school. Dependence on too much positive reinforcement may reduce intrinsically motivating behaviors.

> *Parenting styles*—Styles of parenting seem to be much less important than consistency in parenting. Dissimilarities between parents, with one expecting too much and the other protecting too much, are a main source of problems for children.

> *Homework and learning*—Gifted children (or any children) do not need regular help with homework. Positive monitoring of homework and study habits is effective. Encouraging intrinsically interesting learning experiences and independence is important.

> *Modeling*—Parental interest in the value of personal careers and work provides an important model for children's achievement, depending on what they see and hear.

> *Organization*—Reasonable standards of organization provide a model for organization and leave more time for development of family interests and independence.

# CONCLUSION

Clinical experiences with underachievers indicate that school, home, and peer environments should be modified to cure underachievement syndrome in gifted children. Although the reversal is difficult, the satisfaction felt by the child and family and the achievement of potential contributions to society make the extraordinary efforts worthwhile.

STUDENT INTAKE INTERVIEW

Name _____ Grade _____ Date _____
School _____

1. Description of appearance _____

2. Let's talk about school first. How do you feel about school? _____

What's good about it? _____

What's bad about it? _____

How do you like your teachers? _____
_____

Subjects (favorite) _____

Subjects (least favorite) _____

Subjects (easiest) _____
Subjects (hardest) _____

3. How were your grades this last quarter? _____

4. If you ever get a grade that's bad, why do you think you get that grade? _____
_____

5. Compared to other kids in your class, how "smart" do you think you are? _____

How smart would you like to be? _____

6. If you like or don't like a subject, is it because of the teacher or the subject or the grades you get? _____

7. What years in school were best for you? Why? _____

Which were worst? Why? _____

8. How much time do you spend on homework on an average school night? _____
How hard do you think you are working now? _____
Where in your home do you do your homework? _____
Does anyone help you with your homework?
_____ Yes _____ No
Who and how much? _____

9. What would you like to do after high school? _____

10. What about friends? Who are they? What kinds of things do you like to do with them? _____
_____

11. Do you have any problems with friends now, or have you ever had any? _____

12. Do you think of yourself as a leader or follower? _____ Which would you rather be? _____

13. What kinds of interests do you have outside school? _____

Sports _____

Hobbies, collections, reading, other interests _____

14. How do you feel when you lose at games? What do you do? _____

15. Do you like to work? _____ Yes _____No
What kind of work do you like to do? _____

16. How many hours do you watch TV on a weeknight? _____

What shows do you like to watch? _____

17. Do you like computers? _____ Yes _____ No
_____ Programming _____ Games
_____ Word processing _____ Other

18. Who are you most the same as, your mom or your dad? _____
Other? _____ How are you the same? _____

19. Who is easier on you, your mom, dad, or stepparent? _____

How is that? _____

20. Do you think your mom was a good student?
_____ Yes _____ No _____ Don't Know
Your dad? _____ Yes _____ No _____ Don't Know

21. What kinds of grades do you think your mom expects of you? _____
Your dad? _____
What do you expect of yourself? _____

22. How do you get along with your mom (and/or stepmom)? _____
Do you argue very much? About what? _____

What kinds of things do you like to do together? _____

23. How do you get along with your dad (and/or stepdad)? _____
Do you argue very much? About what? _____

What kinds of things do you like to do together? _____

24. Do you have any grandparents? When do you see them? How do you get along with them? _____

25. What are your brothers' and sisters' names and ages? _____

26. How do you get along with each of them? _____

Do you argue very much? _____
Things you like to do together. _____

27. What kinds of things do you worry about? _____

28. Pretend I am your fairy godmother. What 3 wishes would you ask for? _____

29. Miscellaneous _____

30. Draw family picture for elementary children. GIFT or GIFFI and Sentence Completion. Review family notes and question any other concerns afterward. Leave students with statement about hoping to be able to help them with their problems.

From *Guidebook—Underachievement Syndrome: Causes and Cures* by S. Rimm, M. Cornale, R. Manos, and J. Behrend, 1989, Watertown, WI: Apple Publishing Co.

FAMILY INTAKE INTERVIEW: INITIAL ASSESSMENT

Name of Child _____ Date _____
Names of Parents _____
Grade _____ Age _____ School _____
Other Siblings _____

I'd like to begin by having you describe _____'s problem as you see it now. Then we'll go back to look at how the problem began and what we can do about it.

*Precipitating Events*

Description of the Problem At This Time

_____
_____
_____
_____
_____
_____
_____
_____

*Emotional Problems and Interests*

Temper _____

"Poor me" _____

Tension symptoms _____

Depression _____

Other _____

Identification _____ Mother _____ Father _____ Other _____

Sibling relationships _____

Peer relationships, recreational activities, hobbies, interests, reading, competition _____

TV — How much each night?/What kind of shows? _____
Does he/she like computers? _____ Yes _____ No
_____ Programming? _____ Games?
_____ Word Processing? _____ Other Programs?
Any other escapes? _____

*Origin of the Problem — Brief History*
Parent(s) backgrounds and relationships _____

_____

_____

_____

Manipulations and sabotage rituals _____

_____

Length of time married before birth _____
Parent(s) attitude about birth _____

Other adults in infancy _____

Pregnancy and birth _____
Adoption? _____ At what age? _____
Weight _____
Temperament at infancy _____

*Preschool Developmental Milestones*
Walking _____ Talking _____
Reading _____
Other _____
Early environmental experiences _____

_____

_____

_____

_____ Nursery school _____ Day-care _____ Babysitters
Describe _____

Responses to other siblings _____

Early illnesses _____

_____

_____

Elementary Grades
Beginning of underachievement _____

Kindergarten _____

1st Grade _____

2nd Grade _____

3rd Grade _____

4th Grade _____

5th Grade _____

6th Grade _____

Other Elementary _____

Middle School, Junior, or Senior High School _____

_____

_____

Other _____

_____

Preliminary Diagnosis _____

Estimated Length of Treatment _____

Probable Underachievement Pattern
Dependent _____  Dominant _____
Prototype _____
Treatment Plan _____
Goals _____

_____

_____ Testing        _____ Group Therapy
_____ Intake Interview  _____ Parent Therapy
_____ Individual Therapy
Prognosis _____
Therapist _____

From Guidebook—Underachievement Syndrome: Causes and Cures by S. Rimm, M. Cornale, R. Manos, and J. Behrend, 1989, Watertown, WI: Apple Publishing Co.

# APPENDIX C

## 1. ELEMENTARY
### DAILY EVALUATION FORM

Student Name _____ Date _____ Teacher Name _____

Assignments Complete:
____ All ____ Most ____ Half ____ Less than half

Quality of general class work:
____ Excellent ____ Satisfactory
____ Fair ____ Unsatisfactory

Behavior:
____ Excellent ____ Satisfactory ____ Fair ____ Unsatisfactory

Comments and missing assignments _____
_____
_____

Thank you very much for your help.

## 2. UPPER ELEMENTARY
### or
### SECONDARY
### WEEKLY EVALUATION FORM

Student Name _____ Date _____ Teacher Name _____

Subject _____
Approximate grade for week: _____

Assignments Complete:
____ All ____ Most ____ Half ____ Less than half

Effort:
____ Excellent ____ Satisfactory ____ Fair ____ Unsatisfactory

Behavior:
____ Excellent ____ Satisfactory ____ Fair ____ Unsatisfactory

Comments and missing assignments: _____
_____
_____

Thank you very much for your help.

From *Guidebook—Underachievement Syndrome: Causes and Cures* by S. Rimm, M. Cornale, R. Manos, and J. Behrend, 1989, Watertown, WI: Appleton Publishing Co.

# REFERENCES

Baldwin, A. Y. (1984). *The Baldwin Identification Matrix 2 for the identification of the gifted and talented: A handbook for its use.* New York: Trillium Press.

Bloom, B. S. (1981, November). *The limits of learning.* Paper presented at the meeting of Council for Exceptional Children–The Association for Gifted National Topical Conference on the Gifted and Talented Child, Orlando, FL.

Bloom B. S. (Ed.). (1985). *Developing talent in young people.* New York: Ballantine Books.

Bloom, B. S., & Sosniak, L. A. (1981). Talent development vs. schooling. *Educational Leadership, 39,* 86–94.

Brown, B. B., & Steinberg, L. (1990). Academic achievement and social acceptance: Skirting the "brain-nerd" connection. *Education Digest, 55,* 55–60.

Cornale, M. (1988). *Dependence and dominance in preadolescent academic underachievers.* Unpublished research paper, University of Wisconsin–Madison.

Davis, G. A., & Rimm, S. B. (1994). *Education of the gifted and talented* (3rd ed.). Needham Heights, MA: Allyn & Bacon.

Deci, E. L. (1986). Motivating children to learn: What you can do. *Learning 86, 14,* 42–44.

DeLeon, P. H. (1989, February). *Why we must attend to minority gifted: A national perspective.* Paper presented at the meeting of Johnson Foundation Wingspread Conference, Racine, WI.

Felton, G. S., & Biggs, B. E. (1977). *Up from underachievement.* Springfield, IL: Charles C. Thomas.

Frasier, M. M. (1991). Disadvantaged and culturally diverse gifted students. *Journal for the Education of the Gifted, 14*(3), 234–245.

Frazier, A., Passow, A. H., & Goldberg, M. L. (1958). Curriculum research: Study of underachieving gifted. *Educational Leadership, 16,* 121–125.

French, J. L. (1959). *Educating the gifted: A book of readings.* New York: Holt.

Hom, H. L., Jr., Gaskill, B., & Hutchins, M. (1988, April). *Motivational orientation of the gifted student, thread of evaluation and its impact on performance.* Paper presented at the American Education Research Association, New Orleans.

Jackson, R. M., Cleveland, J. C., & Mirenda, P. R. (1975). The longitudinal effects of early identification and counseling of underachievers. *Journal of School Psychology, 13,* 119–128.

Kulik, J. A. (1992). *An analysis of the research on ability grouping: Historical and contemporary perspectives* (No. 9203). Storrs: The University of Connecticut, The National Research Center on the Gifted and Talented.

Laffoon, K. S., Jenkins-Friedman, R., & Tollefson, N. (1989). Causal attributions of underachieving gifted, achieving gifted, and nongifted students. *Journal for the Education of the Gifted, 13*(1), 4–21.

Matthew, J. L., Colin, A. K. Moore, M. W., & Balter, U. (1992). Use of SOMPA in identification of gifted African-American children. *Journal for the Education of the Gifted, 15*(4), 344–356.

Mussen, P. H., & Rutherford, E. (1963). Parent–child relations and parental personality in relation to young children's sex-role preferences. *Child Development, 34*, 589–607.

National Commission on Excellence in Education. (1984). *A nation at risk: The imperative for educational reform.* Washington, DC: U.S. Government Printing Office.

Perkins, J. A., & Wicas, E. A. (1971). Group counseling bright underachievers and their mothers. *Journal of Counseling Psychology, 18*, 273–278.

Richert, E. (1987). Rampant problems and promising practices in the identification of disadvantaged gifted students. *Gifted Child Quarterly, 31*, 149–154.

Rimm, S. B. (1976). *GIFT: Group Inventory for Finding Creative Talent.* Watertown, WI: Educational Assessment Service.

Rimm, S. B. (1980, September/October). Congratulations Miss Smithersteen, you have proved that Amy isn't gifted. *Gifted Child Today*, pp. 23–24.

Rimm, S. B. (1985, November/December). Identifying underachievement: The characteristics approach. *Gifted Child Today*, pp. 2–5.

Rimm, S. B. (1986a). *AIM: Achievement identification measure.* Watertown, WI: Educational Assessment Service.

Rimm, S. B. (1986b). *Underachievement syndrome: Causes and cures.* Watertown, WI: Apple Publishing.

Rimm, S. B. (1987a). *GAIM: Group Achievement Identification Measure.* Watertown, WI: Educational Assessment Service.

Rimm, S. B. (1987b, November/December). Why do bright children underachieve? The pressures they feel. *Gifted Child Today, 10*, 30–36.

Rimm, S. B. (1988). *AIM-TO: Achievement Identification Measure–Teacher Observation.* Watertown, WI: Educational Assessment Service.

Rimm, S. B (1990). *Gifted kids have feelings too.* Watertown, WI: Apple Publishing.

Rimm, S. B. (1992). *Sylvia Rimm on raising kids.* Watertown, WI: Apple Publishing.

Rimm, S. B., Cornale, M., Manos, R., & Behrend, J. (1989). *Guidebook— Underachievement syndrome: Causes and cures.* Watertown, WI: Apple Publishing.

Rimm, S. B., & Davis, G. A. (1979). *GIFFI I: Group inventory for finding interests.* Watertown, WI: Educational Assessment Service.

Rimm, S. B., & Lovance, K. J. (1992a). How acceleration may prevent underachievement syndrome. *Gifted Child Today*, 9–14.

Rimm, S. B., & Lovance, K. J. (1992b). The use of subject and grade skipping for the prevention and reversal of underachievement. *Gifted Child Quarterly, 36*, 100–105.

Rimm, S. B., & Lowe, B. (1988). Family environments of underachieving gifted students. *Gifted Child Quarterly, 32*, 353–359.

Rimm, S. B., & Priest, C. (1990). *Exploring feelings.* Watertown, WI: Apple Publishing.

Rogers, K. B. (1990, November). *Using effect size to make good decisions about acceleration.* Paper presented at the meeting of the National Association for Gifted Children, Little Rock, AR.

Seligman, M. E. (1975). *Helplessness: On depression, development and death.* San Francisco: Freeman.

Silverman, L. K., & Kearney, K. (1992, September). The case for the Stanford–Binet, L-M as a supplemental test. *Roeper Review, 15*, 34–37.

Smith, J., LeRose, B., & Clasen, R. E. (1991). Underrepresentation of minority students in gifted programs: Yes! It matters. *Gifted Child Quarterly, 35*, 81–83.

Stanley, J. C. (1978). Identifying and nurturing the intellectually gifted. In R. E. Clasen & B. Robinson (Eds.), *Simple gifts* (Vol. 1, p. 181). Madison: University of Wisconsin–Extension.

Stanley, J. C., & Benbow, C. P. (1986). Extremely young college graduates: Evidence of their success. *College and University, 58*, 361–371.

Steinberg, L., Dornbusch, S. M., & Brown, B. B. (1992). Ethnic differences in adolescent achievement—An ecological perspective. *American Psychologist, 47*, 723–729.

Swiatek, M. A., & Benbow, C. P. (1991, November). *Acceleration: Does it cause academic or psychological harm?* Paper presented at the meeting of the National Association for Gifted Children, Little Rock, AR.

Terman, L. M., & Merrill, M. A. (1960). *Stanford–Binet Intelligence Scale.* Boston: Houghton-Mifflin.

Thorndike, R. L., Hagen, E. P., & Sattler, J. M. (1986). *Guide for administering and scoring the Stanford–Binet Intelligence Scale: Fourth Edition.* Chicago: Riverside.

Wechsler, D. (1974). *The Wechsler Intelligence Scale for Children–Revised.* San Antonio, TX: Psychological Corporation.

Wechsler, D. (1991). *The Wechsler Intelligence Scale for Children–Third edition.* San Antonio, TX: Psychological Corporation.

Weiner, B. (1974). *Achievement motivation and attribution theory.* Morristown, NJ: General Learning Press.

Weiner, B. (1980). *Human motivation.* New York: Holt.

Whitmore, J. R. (1980). *Giftedness, conflict, and underachievement.* Boston: Allyn & Bacon.

Zilli, M. G. (1971). Reasons why the gifted adolescent underachieves and some of the implications of guidance and counseling of this problem. *Gifted Child Quarterly, 15*, 279–292.

# Chapter 12

# *The Special Characteristics and Needs of Gifted Students with Disabilities*

**Marlene Bireley**

◆  ◆  ◆

THE FOLLOWING NAMES are identifiable from history books or today's headlines: Leonardo da Vinci, Thomas Edison, Helen Keller, Albert Einstein, Woodrow Wilson, Nelson Rockefeller, Cher, Tom Cruise, Danny Glover, Greg Louganis, and Bruce Jenner. But what do these individuals have in common other than fame? Under various accepted definitions, each could be identified as gifted. Additionally, under the guidelines of current law, each would have qualified for one or more programs for children with disabilities. One can only speculate at the outcome if da Vinci or Cruise had been placed in a program for the learning disabled, Einstein in one for the language delayed, or Edison in one for the hearing impaired or behaviorally disordered.

Historically, school support personnel have existed to serve children and youth with disabilities. They have served as conduits for identification and delivery of educational, medical, and other therapeutic services. Through a combination of legal mandates and accepted practice, the job emphasis has been to assess, remediate, and/or contain the effects of disabilities, and much less concern has been placed on recognizing and supporting the ability of persons with mental or physical difference.

In the last decade, however, a number of gifted educators (most of whom have background training in special education and/or school psychology) have turned their attention to the ramifications of being both gifted and disabled, the so-called dually labeled population. These educators have raised such questions as the appropriateness and capability of either special education or gifted education for serving the needs of this small, but important, subpopulation and the adequacy of our training programs for giving teachers and support personnel the skills to both recognize and serve students with both high cognitive ability and disabilities. One of the most positive outcomes of the current movement toward inclusion may be increased appropriate service to such children who need accommodation for their widely disparate abilities.

In spite of the obvious shortcomings of recent practice, several models exist for serving gifted children with disabilities. These models have several commonalities regardless of the type of exceptionality served (e.g., learning disabled, emotionally disabled, visually impaired). The curriculum of pilot programs reported in the literature has expanded beyond an emphasis on basic skills to include critical thinking, creative problem solving, decision making, and affective activities and/or counseling. Most programs ran for only a summer or a single academic year and were not always subjected to rigorous evaluation, but observation and informal feedback from parents, teachers, and participants were generally positive (Baldwin & Garguilo, 1983; Hackney, 1986; Whitmore, 1980). Like some programs for nondisabled gifted students, Hackney (1986) reported that a successful summer program for gifted students with visual disabilities at the Texas School for the Blind was criticized by unnamed persons as being "elitist."

Whether the delivery of services for a bright student with a disability occurs in a special education, gifted education, or general education setting, one outcome should be the development of skills that will allow the student who so chooses to participate in postsecondary education. The curriculum of elementary special education classes tends to be limited by the high incidence of children with average or below-average intelligence and the large amount of time spent on developing compensatory skills (e.g., Braille, speechreading, computer usage). It is critical to their long-term development, however, that gifted children with disabilities be exposed to content in social studies, science, and higher level language arts and mathematics to the same extent as children without disabilities and that they be given ample opportunity to develop higher level thinking skills. Early and sustained inclusion in regular and/or gifted education classes is necessary for this to occur. Including gifted program educators on the team for planning educational programs would help to develop appropriate opportunities for such children. If an inclusionary model is used for service, support personnel should include gifted program educators as well as the appropriate special education personnel. In-house training and support for regular educators who agree to accommodate students with physical or learning disabilities are equally important.

# GIFTED STUDENTS WITH PHYSICAL DISABILITIES

The literature is very sparse on cognitively able students with physical disabilities. Whitmore and Maker (1985) provided the most comprehensive look at the lives of ordinary people who have survived and excelled in extraordinary circumstances. They presented five case studies representing visual, hearing, physical, and learning disabilities. Each story is, of course, unique, but the authors identified 10 recurring themes across these case studies (and from a synthesis of other literature): exceptional persistence, flexible and creative coping strategies, recognition and use of personal strengths, a constant struggle to maintain healthy self-esteem, mixed messages from others concerning their ability and acceptability, a strong desire to be accepted by themselves and others, motivating but realistic parental support, ongoing struggles with embarrassment and shame, frustration and anger, and the need to release frustration through a rewarding activity.

To help teachers and parents facilitate growth in gifted students with disabilities, Whitmore and Maker (1985) recommended a number of guidelines:

1. Keep perceptions of the individual's limitation open-ended.

2. Convey positive, realistic expectations.

3. Encourage the development of increasing levels of independence.

4. Help the child to formulate a positive, attainable goal for the future.

5. Guide the child's development of self-understanding and constructive coping strategies.

6. Provide daily opportunities for the child to build inherent superior abilities and to enjoy feelings of success.

7. Advocate for appropriate educational opportunities.

8. Pursue positive social experiences for the child. (pp. 231–234)

Many of these guidelines could be facilitated by school psychologists and counselors. Indeed, they could serve as a model for interaction between the helping professions and the gifted population with disabilities.

# GIFTED STUDENTS WITH LEARNING DISABILITIES

Significant interest has focused on the learning disabled/gifted (LD/G) population. Most of the personalities cited at the beginning of this chapter exhibited the characteristics of specific learning disability. They are cited in both special education and gifted education as proof that this is an important area of concern. Within the last decade, identification procedures, programming models, and decision-making guidelines have come from many sources. When viewed together, they contain considerable support for anyone attempting to serve a gifted student with a specific learning disability.

## Cognitive Ability Characteristics

Most studies on identification of gifted students with learning disabilities have focused on a population with one or more IQs above 120. Those who research this population have recognized that the disabilities may interfere with certain subtest functioning which, in turn, lowers the overall IQ. Using 115 or 120 rather than 130 as the cutoff for defining this population is justified.

Subtest patterns rather than total IQ have been the focus of most of these studies. For example, Barton and Starnes (1989) compared 41 LD/G students with at least one IQ of 120 on the *Wechsler Intelligence Scale for Children–Revised* (WISC-R) and an ability–achievement discrepancy with 80 randomly chosen gifted children so identified by the WISC-R and the *California Achievement Test* and a previous superior LD sample reported by Schiff, Kaufman, and Kaufman (1981). In both learning disabled samples, similar patterns were found: The Verbal Comprehension scores were highest and the Sequencing or Freedom from Distractibility scores were lowest. Although Schiff et al.'s group had a large Verbal–Performance discrepancy (127.6 Verbal to 112.9 Performance), Barton and Starnes found only a 7.2-point difference in their LD/G group and a 9.7-point (Verbal > Performance) discrepancy in their gifted group. Similarly, Coding was the lowest and Similarities the highest in both groups, although the range was nearly 9 points in the LD/G group compared with 3.5 in the gifted population.

In contrast to the Verbal superiority found in these two studies, Bireley (1992) found a slight group Performance superiority (125.3 to 122.1 Verbal) in 47 Ohio LD/G children. When examined individually so that the Verbal > Performance and Performance > Verbal scores did not dilute each other, an individual mean discrepancy of 14.38 was found. Sattler (1988) listed the Verbal–Performance $p < .01$ difference at 15, but, because Silver and Clampit (1990) found that about half of

the gifted population has a discrepancy of 12 points or more, this difference should not be overinterpreted.

Just as factor patterns are more meaningful than Verbal–
Performance discrepancies as a meaningful way to identify LD/G children, Silverman (1989) recommended that discrepancies between the
high and low subtest scores can be used for this purpose. She reported
a "typical" discrepancy of 9 to 12 points between high and low subtests
in over 200 LD/G cases that she examined (7 points is significant at the
$p < .05$ level [Sattler, 1988]). In support of her observation, the mean
for the group that Bireley (1992) studied was 9.32. Typically, the high
score is one from the Verbal Comprehension factor and the low score is
from Freedom from Distractibility. Given the pervasiveness of this
pattern, Bireley, Languis, and Williamson (1993) recommended that
the Arithmetic and Coding subtest scores be dropped and an extrapo-
lated IQ be used to determine eligibility for gifted programming (and,
for that matter, for determining ability–achievement discrepancies).
To do otherwise may keep children whose scores are lowered by distractibility, but are in need of enrichment, from accessing gifted programs.

## Affective Characteristics

In addition to low Freedom from Distractibility subtest scores,
many LD/G students exhibit other characteristics associated with attention deficit hyperactivity disorder (ADHD). In addition to the usual
problems associated with hyperactivity, distractibility, and disorganization, several other factors have been identified and discussed as common in the LD/G population. From her review of the literature, Silverman (1989) added perfectionism, supersensitivity, social skills deficits,
unrealistic self-expectations or excessive self-criticism, and psychomotor inefficiency. Additionally, Frey (1991) cited the emotional vulnerabilities of nondisabled gifted students as perfectionism, a lack of
risk taking, uneven development, an inordinate desire to please, and a
feeling of isolation or difference from peers. Any or all of these might
apply to the LD/G student. One trait for which the LD/G student
appears to be particularly at risk is that of self-efficacy, or the belief
that one can be successful at some behavior (Baum & Owen, 1988).
They found that LD/G children were likely to perceive themselves less
frequently as self-efficacious than either students with learning disabilities and average ability or students who were gifted. They attributed this finding to a component of self-efficacy, namely the need to
believe that the task one is pursuing is meaningful. It is logical to
assume that LD/G students who are perceived as disabled, but not
gifted, and are required to perform only low-level, basic academic tasks

may neither perceive meaning in nor feel a sense of personal accomplishment about their schoolwork.

Coleman (1992) studied the coping strategies of the LD/G group. The literature on giftedness finds consistent superiority in selecting, using, and monitoring problem-solving strategies when compared with average students and, to an even greater extent, when compared with LD students of average ability. LD/G students may draw upon these skills when coping with stress, but may be inhibited by their disorganization, lack of order in their world, perfectionism, and oversensitivity. The frustration they feel may be exacerbated by a higher cognitive ability that allows them to be more aware of their problems than their more average peers. Coleman (1992) studied 42 middle school children by administering a Likert-scale coping resources inventory and by interviewing each student regarding his or her strategies for dealing with typical difficult school situations. Half of the children were of average ability and half had at least one WISC-R IQ above 125.

No differences were found in the average and LD/G groups in their perceptions of available resources, the number of coping strategies used, or the perceived effectiveness of the strategies used. However, the LD/G group was more likely to report use of the strategy of planful problem solving, whereas the average group was more likely to report distancing (detachment from the event), escape avoidance, and helplessness behaviors. Neither group reported the use of confrontation as a frequent strategy. Coleman (1992) recommended that positive coping strategies be directly taught to all LD children, that parent training be a component part of the training program, and that counseling concerning the frustrations of the school situation be made available to these children, many of whom expressed surprise in the interview that other students were experiencing the same problems that frustrated them.

## Academic Characteristics

Silverman (1989) accurately described the academic dilemma of the LD/G child when she stated that "the harder the task, the better they do; it's the easy work they can't master" (p. 39). The weaknesses of this group appear to be based on their ADHD characteristics, perceptual and/or motor problems, and difficulties with rote memorization of isolated information such as spelling words or basic math facts. Unlike their more average LD peers, these weaknesses may be counterbalanced by high abstract reasoning ability, ability to comprehend complex relations, good mathematical reasoning, and good creativity and/or imagination. When placed in a school setting where only the former skills are required, the giftedness of these students may be overlooked and never developed.

The group that Bireley (1992) studied fits Silverman's description very well. Achievement patterns revealed good skills in mathematics (although rote memory of facts was sometimes a problem), widely varied reading skills, and consistent deficits in written language. Work with adult LD individuals in college and vocational settings has led me to believe that educators are underestimating the prevalence, importance, and tenacity of the written language deficit in the entire LD population. If less vigilance is used in assessing written language than math and reading skills, and Individualized Education Programs (IEPs) fail to focus on comprehensive writing skills, the major deficit of most LD/G students may be underattended. Educators must help LD students develop compensatory, computer-based skills for this pervasive deficit.

## Neurocognitive Characteristics

Over the last decade, a new approach to understanding the cognitive functioning of the human brain has been developed and is being applied to the understanding of average, gifted, and learning disabled populations. A national network of more than 20 medical or psycho-educational research centers now exists to study this new approach, which relies on computer systems that translate brain activity patterns into topographic colored maps that depict both the sites and the intensity of brain activity when confronted with evoked potential or higher level cognitive tasks. Data are gathered through 20 sensors located at the usual electroencephalographic (EEG) sites that gather electrical activity readings at the rate of 256 times per second. These readings can be averaged for individual subjects or for groups (Languis & Miller, 1992). Languis and his associates have developed normative data for average, LD, gifted, and LD/G persons. These normative data are now being used to compare the functioning of individuals with students of similar ages and within the various categories. Findings of various studies that may have implications for the LD/G group include the following:

- LD subjects consistently exhibit slowing of EEG activity, particularly in the frontal and temporoparietal areas. This slowing is manifest by increases in theta and alpha wave activity that are associated with cortical inactivity (Duffy, Denckla, Bartels, & Sandini, 1980; Gibson, 1987).

- The patterns of brain activity in sixth-grade LD students resembled those of third-grade nondisabled students, suggesting a detectable developmental delay (Naour, Languis, & Martin, 1991).

• On visual and auditory evoked potential tasks (a reversing checkerboard pattern or intermittently flashing lights within goggles and intermittent tone bursts within headsets, respectively), the markers for selective attention have lower amplitudes, greater asymmetries, and longer latencies in LD subjects (Cobbs, 1986; Drake, Simmons, & Languis, 1989). More specifically, one waveform, the P300, is normally elicited for target, but not nontarget, stimuli in effective learners. The elicited event-related potential denotes that the subject has successfully discriminated and classified a cognitively relevant event from an irrelevant one. Students with attention deficits often lack this capacity and generate a P300 waveform in response to both target and nontarget tones. These differences are being used as a diagnostic indicator of distractibility (Languis, 1988; Languis & Miller, 1992; Languis & Wittrock, 1986). Studies concerning the efficacy of using various intervention strategies for changing these patterns have been promising and are of continued interest.

• Compared with average peers, gifted subjects exhibit higher peak amplitudes and shorter latencies, and they process cognitive tasks with lower amplitudes. These findings have been interpreted as enhanced brain activity and efficient brain functioning which, in turn, may allow gifted learners to process a greater amount of and more diverse cognitive information (Languis, 1988; Languis, Brigner, & Holland, 1990).

• In a study of 11 LD/G students, the same high cortical arousal associated with the gifted population was observed; visual processing patterns were dramatically higher than in any other group, exceeding normal peers threefold; delayed and asymmetrical auditory processing patterns were interpreted as a learning disorder in cognitive processing of auditory stimuli; and frontal lobe activity on a computerized version of the *Category Test* was less focused than that of a heterogeneous group. The LD/G group appeared to have the higher amplitude potential of the gifted group, but their brains were inefficient in using this potential, resulting in various manifestations of learning disability (Bireley et al., 1993).

The unusually high visual processing amplitudes of the LD/G group led to the inclusion of an educational vision specialist (Williamson) on our research team. He had been studying the incidence of two conditions, hyperacuity and contrast sensitivity, in LD populations.

Above-normal ability in these two functions leads to intolerance of busy patterns, fluorescent lights, bright sunlight, and high-contrast reading matter. Williamson's contention is that "moving" print, fatigue, and nausea (including motion sickness), as well as ADHD-like distractibility and inattentiveness, may result from these visual overload conditions. All 10 of the LD/G subjects assessed in Bireley et al.'s (1993) study exhibited these characteristics. Subsequent monitoring of the visual processing amplitudes of bright LD children now being seen in our clinical practice (Languis & Bireley, 1992) is resulting in high readings in about 60% of the cases. We are now gathering data on the effect of visual training and various colored lenses on the functioning of LD/G children.

This work, while of great personal interest, may not touch the lives of individual school support personnel at the present time because of the relative inaccessibility and high cost of the technology. At the clinic where we work (Languis and Bireley), the decision to assess children for individual rather than research purposes is done cautiously and for a minority of our clients. For many, the intervention needs are obvious through traditional psychoeducational assessment, and no purpose is served through gathering additional information. However, we do find that we can pinpoint and clarify problems in those cases where the psychometric and portfolio data are confusing or contradictory.

Our long-range goal is to document the efficacy and efficiency of some of the interventions and therapies that are the most controversial. We believe that there is no such thing as a bad intervention, but there is pervasive poor application of certain therapies to the wrong individuals. There is a need for more precise documentation of the interaction of an individual and a specific intervention strategy (e.g., medication, visual training, and/or the teaching of cognitive strategies). It is of particular importance to bright, disabled individuals that time that could be used for enhancing their gifts not be stolen by years of emphasis on ineffective interventions. We hope that the controversy surrounding many such approaches may be alleviated by a more proper selection of candidates for specific interventions, and that this line of research will lay to rest some of these long-standing debates.

# PROGRAMMING FOR THE DISABLED/GIFTED CHILD

In spite of several prototypic programs designed especially for gifted students with disabilities, it is safe to assume that the rarity of such individuals in most school districts will necessitate programming within existing resources. Should the student be served in the regular classroom with consultation services from appropriate special and gifted educators? Should he or she be placed in either a special education or a gifted resource room? Should "triple programming" be considered (e.g., an LD tutor, a gifted pull-out program, and the remainder of the week in a regular classroom)? Obviously, no one answer exists because individuals vary according to disability type, degree of involvement, and remediation/compensation needs, as well as types of giftedness. One set of guidelines has been developed to assist in the decision-making process (Bireley, 1993). Although based upon work with the LD/G population, these could be adapted for students with other disabilities.

1. If medical intervention is needed, it should be sought early and maintained as long as necessary. Medical input should be sought when programming is developed.

2. Structure, organization, and other coping strategies should be considered as the first basic skills to be taught and should receive primary emphasis in early IEPs or other programming plans.

3. Remediation should be considered until a functional reading and mathematics repertoire is in place. Because writing appears to be a long-range deficit in most LD/G children, alternatives to handwriting should be considered (word processors, buddy note takers, etc.) as ways to help the child access regular and gifted education. Nearly every LD/G child will benefit from training in and freedom to use computers and calculators. If the problem is physical, then technological aids, language or mobility training, or other support services should be given high priority.

4. If the decision is not to place the child in a gifted education setting, then support services that reinforce the child's giftedness should be instituted. These might include self-esteem counseling and enrollment in extracurricular activities that support the development of creativity, higher order thinking, and problem-solving skills, such as university summer or weekend enrichment programs, Future Problem Solving or Odyssey of the Mind programs that characteristically are open to students beyond those officially enrolled in gifted classes, or parent-provided enrichment opportunities.

5. Regardless of the placement chosen, the educational planning team for each child should include gifted as well as

special educators. Flexibility and the ability to overcome the "but we've never done it this way before" syndrome are critical team behaviors in these cases.

6. The team should assist the student and parents to understand the critical decision making that must take place in eighth grade if postsecondary education is to be considered. Career planning may not be seen as a priority in families that have been struggling with the early needs of a disabled child. School counselors will need to examine their own biases about encouraging disabled students to enter college preparatory programs. Children, if they are to be competitive in postsecondary settings, will need to have access to general content curriculum throughout their intermediate and junior high/middle school years and to college preparatory courses in high school.

7. The student should be involved in the decision-making process as soon as possible. Avoiding learned helplessness and taking responsibility for one's own life and learning are critical elements in educational, vocational, and adult success.

# RESOURCES FOR TEACHING COPING STRATEGIES

The guidelines listed above address both the delivery system that will be used to provide an educational program for the gifted child with a disability and the content of that education. Those recommendations reflect the shift in the focus of intervention for the learning disabled from a total emphasis on diagnostic–prescriptive teaching to include the teaching of specific cognitive strategies for solving educational and life-based problems (Reid, 1988). Most of these strategies not only apply to the LD/G population, but overlap remarkably with the emphasis on problem solving found in gifted curricula. Educators must place major emphasis on giving these tools of learning to children if the children are to be expected to deal adequately with general education content. Many resources or ideas exist that may be useful in achieving that objective. Among those that I consider to be most helpful are the following:

* *Think Aloud* (Camp & Bash, 1985) and *Stop and Think* (Kendall, 1988), which provide detailed exercises to enhance self-control of impulsive behavior.

- Memory enhancers, such as visualization (see Bagley & Hess, 1984; Eberle, 1982), multisensory materials, or applied situational learning.

- Programs that directly train social skills by utilizing behavioral and cognitive strategies, teacher-led discussions, role playing, and the use of videotape (as reviewed by Gesten, Weissberg, Amish, & Smith, 1987).

- Numerous specific activities for enhancing self-esteem, best illustrated by Canfield (1976) and Frey and Carlock (1989).

- Adderholdt-Elliott's (1987) outline of the steps needed for breaking the cycle of perfectionism.

- Reid's (1988) academically oriented *Teaching the Learning Disabled: A Cognitive Developmental Approach* and Pressley and Associates' (1990) *Cognitive Strategy Instruction that Really Improves Children's Academic Performance.*

- Various graphic organizers for those who find the traditional outline a difficult or inadequate means of organizing. Graphic organizers are ideal for enhancing limited writing skills by providing additional visual cues. Rico (1983) used this technique in the creative writing process, and the authors of *Breakthroughs: Strategies for Thinking* (1990) adapted it for social studies and science content.

- Neill and Neill's (1989, 1991) listing and evaluation of K–12 software in the areas of word processing, keyboarding, and typing.

- Several good resources for the teaching of thinking, including those that discuss integrating the teaching of thinking into other content, such as Baron and Sternberg (1987) and Beyer (1987), and those that provide separate courses on teaching thinking, such as de Bono's (1986) CoRT thinking materials and Lipman's (1978–1983) Philosophy for Children series.

- Mangrum and Strichart's (1984) comprehensive guide for developing the skills for and selecting a college that will serve the needs of a student who is learning disabled. They urged looking for institutions that provide counselors with specific knowledge about learning disabilities, taped textbooks, diagnostic assessment, remedial courses, test proctoring, and student support groups.

# CONCLUSION

Identifying and providing for the educational and social–emotional needs of a gifted student with a disability create an interesting challenge for any educational team. Careful plans must be made to attend to the needs of both the ability and the disability and to ensure the development of the self-concept of a person who is cognitively able as well as disabled. To accomplish these objectives, planning teams may need to be innovative, flexible, and willing to try new ways of placing and serving this small, but important, underserved group of the gifted.

# REFERENCES

Adderholdt-Elliott, M. (1987). *Perfectionism: What's bad about being too good?* Minneapolis: Free Spirit Press.

Bagley, M., & Hess, K. (1984). *200 ways of using imagery in the classroom.* New York: Trillium Press.

Baldwin, L., & Garguilo, D. (1983). A model program for elementary-age learning disabled/gifted youngsters. In L. Fox, L. Brody, & D. Tobin (Eds.), *Learning disabled/gifted children: Identification and programming* (pp. 207–222). Baltimore: University Park Press.

Baron, J., & Sternberg, R. (Eds.). (1987). *Teaching thinking skills: Theory and practice.* New York: W. H. Freeman.

Barton, J., & Starnes, W. (1989). Identifying distinguishing characteristics of gifted and talented/learning disabled students. *Roeper Review, 12,* 23–28.

Baum, S., & Owen, S. (1988). High ability/learning-disabled students. *Gifted Child Quarterly, 32,* 321–326.

Beyer, B. (1987). *Practical strategies for the teaching of thinking.* Boston: Allyn & Bacon.

Bireley, M. (1992). *Crossover children: A sourcebook for helping the learning disabled/gifted child.* Columbus, OH: Greyden Press.

Bireley, M. (1993). *Crossover children: A sourcebook for helping the learning disabled/gifted child.* Columbus, OH: Greyden Press.

Bireley, M., Languis, M., & Williamson, T. (1993). Physiological uniqueness: A new perspective on the learning disabled/gifted child. *Roeper Review, 15,* 101–107.

*Breakthroughs: Strategies for thinking.* (1990). Columbus, OH: Zaner-Bloser.

Camp, B., & Bash, M. A. (1985). *Think aloud: Increasing social and cognitive skills—A problem-solving program for children.* Champaign, IL: Research Press.

Canfield, J. (1976). *100 ways to enhance self-esteem in the classroom.* Englewood Cliffs, NJ: Prentice Hall.

Cobbs, G. (1986). *AEP300 differences in learning disabled and peer control college students*. Unpublished master's thesis, The Ohio State University, Columbus.

Coleman, M. R. (1992). A comparison of how gifted/LD and average/LD boys cope with school frustration. *Journal for the Education of the Gifted*, *15*, 239–265.

de Bono, E. (1986). *CoRT thinking program*. Elmsford, NY: Pergamon Press.

Drake, M., Simmons, G., & Languis, M. (1989). Event related potentials in dyslexia. *Clinical Electroencephalography, 20*, 75–76.

Duffy, F., Denckla, M., Bartels, P., & Sandini, G. (1980). Dyslexia: Regional differences in brain electrical activity by topographic mapping. *Annals of Neurology, 7*, 412–420.

Eberle, B. (1982). *Visual thinking*. Buffalo, NY: DOK.

Frey, D. (1991). Psychosocial needs of the gifted adolescent. In M. Bireley & J. Genshaft (Eds.), *Understanding the gifted adolescent: Educational, developmental, and multicultural issues*. New York: Teachers College Press.

Frey, D., & Carlock, J. (1989). *Enhancing self-esteem* (2nd ed.). Muncie, IN: Accelerated Development.

Gesten, E., Weissberg, R., Amish, P., & Smith, J. (1987). Social problem-solving training: A skills-based approach to prevention and treatment. In C. Maher & J. Zins (Eds.), *Psychoeducational intervention in the schools*. New York: Pergamon.

Gibson, N. (1987). *Analytical and synthetic cognitive style dimensions–academic task performance among learning disabled and non-learning disabled college students*. Unpublished doctoral dissertation, The Ohio State University, Columbus.

Hackney, P. (1986). Education of the visually handicapped-gifted: A program description. *Education of the Visually Handicapped, 18*, 85–95.

Kendall, P. (1988). *Stop and think workbook*. Merion Station, PA: Philip Kendall.

Languis, M. (1988). *Developmental and group differences in the auditory evoked potential (AEP300) task*. Paper presented at the meeting of the American Educational Research Association, New Orleans.

Languis, M., & Bireley, M. (1992). [Visual processing amplitudes of bright learning disabled children]. Unpublished raw data.

Languis, M., Brigner, L., & Holland, S. (1990). *Differences in brain electrical activity patterns among four groups of learners: Academically gifted, learning disabled, gifted/LD, and peer controls*. Paper presented at the meeting of the Ohio Consortium of Coordinators of the Gifted, Columbus.

Languis, M., & Miller, D. (1992). Luria's theory of brain functioning: A model for research in cognitive psychophysiology. *Educational Psychologist, 27*, 493–511.

Languis, M., & Wittrock, M. (1986). Integrating neuropsychological and cognitive research: A perspective for bridging brain behavior relationships. In J. Orbzut & G. Hynd (Eds.), *Child neuropsychology* (Vol. 1, pp. 209–239). New York: Academic Press.

Lipman, M. (1978). *Suki*. Upper Montclair, NJ: First Mountain Foundation.

Lipman, M. (1980). *Mark*. Upper Montclair, NJ: First Mountain Foundation.

Lipman, M. (1981). *Pixie*. Upper Montclair, NJ: First Mountain Foundation.

Lipman, M. (1982a). *Harry Stottlemeier's discovery*. Upper Montclair, NJ: First Mountain Foundation.

Lipman, M. (1982b). *Kio and Gus*. Upper Montclair, NJ: First Mountain Foundation.

Lipman, M. (1983). *Lisa*. Upper Montclair, NJ: First Mountain Foundation.

Mangrum, C., & Strichart, S. (1984). *College and the learning disabled student*. Orlando, FL: Grune & Stratton.

Naour, P., Languis, M., & Martin, D. (1991). Developmental component in brain electrical activity of normal and learning disabled boys. In M. Languis, J. Buffer, D. Martin, & P. Naour (Eds.), *Cognitive science: Contributions to educational practice* (pp. 148–163). Philadelphia: Gordon & Breach.

Neill, S., & Neill, G. (1989). *Only the best: The discriminating software for preschool–grade 12*. New York: Education News Service.

Neill, S., & Neill, G. (1991). *The annual guide to highest-rated educational software: Only the best. Preschool–Grade 12*. New York: R. R. Bowker.

Pressley, M., & Associates (1990). *Cognitive strategy instruction that really improves children's academic performance*. Cambridge, MA: Brookline Books.

Reid, D. K. (1988). *Teaching the learning disabled: A cognitive developmental approach*. Boston: Allyn & Bacon.

Rico, G. (1983). *Writing the natural way*. Los Angeles: J. P. Tarcher.

Sattler, J. (1988). *Assessment of children* (3rd ed.). San Diego: Author.

Schiff, M., Kaufman, A., & Kaufman, N. (1981). Scatter analysis of WISC-R profiles for learning disabled children with superior intelligence. *Journal of Learning Disabilities, 14*, 400–404.

Silver, S., & Clampit, M. (1990). WISC-R profiles of high ability children: Interpretation of Verbal–Performance discrepancies. *Gifted Child Quarterly, 34*, 76–79.

Silverman, L. (1989). Invisible gifts, invisible handicaps. *Roeper Review, 12*, 37–42.

Whitmore, J. (1980). *Giftedness, conflict, and underachievement*. Boston: Allyn & Bacon.

Whitmore, J., & Maker, C. J. (1985). *Intellectual giftedness in disabled persons*. Rockville, MD: Aspen.

# Chapter 13

# *Highly Gifted Children*

Linda Kreger Silverman

◆ ◆ ◆

HUMAN BEINGS DISPLAY a vast range of intellectual abilities. This unpopular fact has met strong resistance in the current wave of fierce egalitarianism. It seems almost un-American that some children are simply born smarter than others. Talent in a specific domain is more palatable than extraordinary general intellectual abilities because talent appears to be developed through hard work—an American value. The greater the degree of a person's intellectual difference, the greater the discomfort such an intellect seems to bring to his or her world, and that world responds by creating discomfort for the individual (Roeper, 1982). Highly gifted children are vulnerable in a society that cannot accept differences, and they are often physically or emotionally abused.

The problem seems to be rooted in the competitiveness of society, which is reflected in the schools. Perceived as having an "advantage" over others in the race toward power, status, and material goods, the highly gifted receive little empathy for their individual differences and needs. There are those who even feel justified holding back such children—handicapping them so that their age peers can "catch up." This leveling mentality limits the development of the most capable members of society. It is often the role of school support personnel (e.g., school psychologist, counselor), who understand most clearly the range of human abilities, to translate that understanding to the entire school community. When support personnel play an active role in communicating the special needs of children on both ends of the spectrum, school becomes a humane place where differences are accepted and children feel safe to express their individuality.

# WHO ARE THE HIGHLY GIFTED?

Giftedness is not a dichotomy between those who have it and those who do not. Rather, it is a matter of degree and type. The greater the degree of difference from the norm in either direction, the greater the needs of the child. Highly gifted children are those whose measured abilities are at least three standard deviations above the mean. They correspond in degree of exceptionality to those whose abilities are three standard deviations below the mean or lower. The understanding of developmentally delayed children, however, is much clearer than that of developmentally advanced children. Differentiation among mildly, moderately, severely, and profoundly delayed children is accepted practice, whereas gradations of difference in the opposite direction are rarely recognized.

In keeping with special education designations, it is possible to roughly categorize gifted children as mildly, moderately, highly, and extraordinarily gifted. The ranges of giftedness can be characterized as follows:

| | | |
|---|---|---|
| 115–129 IQ | Mildly gifted | (+1–2 *SD*) |
| 130–144 IQ | Moderately gifted | (+2–3 *SD*) |
| 145–159 IQ | Highly gifted | (+3–4 *SD*) |
| 160+ IQ | Extraordinarily gifted | (>+4 *SD*) |

This categorization is based upon a standard deviation (*SD*) of 15 points. (These scores need to be adjusted for the *Stanford–Binet Intelligence Scales*, which have a standard deviation of 16 points.) Most programs for the gifted use 2 *SD* or 130 as the cutoff range, although some choose 120 IQ—the superior range—which appears to be a threshold of psychological complexity necessary for creativity (Guilford, 1968). In addition, the means of gifted students in the normative samples of current tests cluster in the 120 range (Thorndike, Hagen, & Sattler, 1986; Wechsler, 1991). Still other gifted programs use the mildly gifted range, or 115 IQ, if they wish to serve children in lower socioeconomic circumstances, gifted children with learning disabilities, and bilingual or culturally diverse children for whom standardized tests may be culturally biased. Even lower cutoff scores may be found in school districts that embrace a broad, multitalent view of giftedness. However, the broader the net, the less value a program is likely to have for children in the highly (>3 *SD*) or extraordinarily (>4 *SD*) gifted ranges. These children require both unusual identification and programming procedures.

Highly gifted children can also be found through administration and analysis of *above-level* aptitude or achievement tests. The third standard deviation criterion can be applied to discriminate highly from moderately gifted students on these measures. This method would be ineffective on grade-level–based assessments because there is an attenuated range at the top of the scale. The instrument must provide sufficient ceiling to spread the scores to differentiate degrees of exceptionality (Robinson, 1992). Talent searches provide an excellent view of what happens when ceiling effects are removed. They are an effective method of locating the highly gifted in junior high school populations.

Students who achieve at the 95th (or 97th) percentile on grade-level achievement tests in reading and mathematics are eligible to take the *Scholastic Achievement Test* (SAT) or *American College Test* (ACT) in seventh and eighth grades. Extremely precocious students can qualify in fifth or sixth grades. When an examination designed for college entrants is given to 12- and 13-year-olds who appear on achievement tests to be quite similar in ability, their scores spread across the full gamut of the test, from 200 to 800. For many students, this is the first opportunity they have had to demonstrate the full strength of their capabilities.

According to the normal curve of distribution, approximately:

| | |
|---|---|
| 2 out of 100 | score above 130 IQ |
| 1 out of 1,000 | scores above 145 IQ |
| 1 out of 10,000 | scores above 160 IQ |
| 1 out of 1,000,000 | scores above 180 IQ |

However, reality does not match theory, and many more highly gifted children have been found than would be predicted. At the Gifted Child Development Center in Denver, we have located approximately 180 children with IQ scores above 160 out of 1,700 referred to the center. Thirty-five of these children attained IQ scores from 180 to 236+. Several other investigators have discovered unexpectedly frequent scores at the upper end of the IQ distribution that parallel the higher frequencies found at the lower end of the continuum (Jensen, 1980; McGuffog, Feiring, & Lewis, 1987; Robinson, 1981; Terman, 1925).

Unusually high frequencies in the upper ranges were actually noted from the very beginning of IQ testing (Terman, 1925). Terman's first sample of 643 gifted children contained 98 above 150 IQ (15%) and 32 above 160 IQ (5%). Terman was a major proponent of the proposition that intelligence is distributed along a continuum resembling the normal curve. Yet, from the results of his study, he was forced to conclude the following:

> The group contains an unexpectedly large proportion of cases in the upper IQ ranges. . . . There is an appreciable excess of 150 IQ cases, or better, over and above the theoretical expectation. Above

160 IQ the number of cases found increases out of all proportion to the theoretically expected number and by IQ 170 exceeds it several times. Unless this discrepancy can be explained as due to the imperfection of the IQ technique it would appear that the distribution of intelligence in the child population departs considerably from that described by the normal probability curve. (Terman, 1925, p. 633)

The actual distribution of intelligence is trimodal (Jensen, 1980), which means that all tests reporting standard deviations from the mean compress scores at both extremes. This distortion artificially lowers scores of highly gifted students to force-fit them into the curve. The highly gifted have lost approximately 31 IQ points over the last 31 years as opposed to the average population, which has lost approximately 8 or 9 IQ points during this same time period (Silverman & Kearney, 1992a, 1992b). As tests are "renormed," the greatest discrepancies between old and new norms are found in the highly gifted range: 11- to 14-point differences between the 1960 and the 1972 norms on the *Stanford–Binet L-M*, 13.5-point mean discrepancies between the 1972 L-M norms and the 1986 *Stanford–Binet IV* norms (which correlate highly with the norms from the 1974 *Wechsler Intelligence Scale for Children–Revised* [WISC-R]), and 6-point mean differences between the WISC-R and the 1991 *Wechsler Intelligence Scale for Children– Third Edition* (WISC-III) norms (Thorndike et al., 1986; Wechsler, 1991).

As intelligence testing is not conducted on a regular basis in the schools, it is likely that many undetected highly gifted children are languishing in the regular classroom, unable to focus their attention on material that was mastered long ago, is unbearably simplistic, and has been reiterated beyond their tolerance level.

# LEARNING AND PERSONALITY CHARACTERISTICS

Any plan for the highly gifted must take into account their unique attributes. The following characteristics personify the majority of highly gifted students:

- Intense intellectual curiosity
- Fascination with words and ideas
- Perfectionism
- Need for precision
- Argumentativeness

- Ability to perceive many sides of an issue
- Metaphoric thinking
- Ability to visualize models and systems
- Learning in great intuitive leaps
- Intense need for mental stimulation
- Difficulty conforming to the thinking of others
- Early moral and existential concern
- Tendency toward introversion

Intellectual and personality characteristics are intertwined. Extraordinary abstract reasoning ability leads to perfectionism, as perfection is an abstract concept (Silverman, 1993). The asynchrony (unevenness) of a child's development also feeds perfectionism: When the mind develops faster than the body, the reasoning and values of the child are more like those of his or her mental peers than like those of age-mates.

Highly gifted children have logical imperatives, very much like moral imperatives, that ensue from their complex thought processes (E. Maxwell, personal communication, June 5, 1991). They expect the world to make sense and they react very strongly when it does not. The need for precision particularly characterizes the highly gifted (Kline & Meckstroth, 1985).

> *Exactness* in all mental performances is characteristic, and keen love of precise facts. Allied to this is the perception of things in their multitudinous relationships, with frequent use of the phrase, "Well, that depends." A young child who spontaneously utters the phrase, "That depends," is sure to catch the attention of one who thoroughly knows gifted children. (Hollingworth, 1927, p. 4)

The necessity for the world and the people in it to be logical often results in argumentativeness. These children feel compelled to correct errors and to call attention to cases that disprove a particular statement. This demand for accuracy, exactness, and precision of thought and expression often alienates highly gifted children from their classmates.

An intense need for mental stimulation differentiates the exceptionally gifted from their more moderately gifted peers (Lovecky, 1992a). This trait shows up very early in life (Tannenbaum, 1992), catalyzed by high levels of curiosity and rapid learning rate. They cannot concentrate on schoolwork that is dull; their minds take off on journeys that are beyond their control (Tolan, 1985).

Jim very much wanted to please the teacher. Yet, every time he started a page of problems, he would find himself in trouble for not working. Jim's brain could not work with the material offered, and his mind would not focus on the task. Given material at his level, Jim had no trouble with concentration or completing tasks. (Lovecky, 1992a, p. 4)

A keen sense of justice and early concern with moral issues has been observed frequently in the gifted (Hollingworth, 1942; Passow, 1988). These traits intensify in the highly gifted and appear at earlier stages of development.

> The highly gifted also deal with complex moral issues at a very tender age. A 5-year-old said to her mother, "Mommy, did you kill that chicken? If you did, I'm not going to eat it." One 9-year-old refused to eat any living thing that had to die for him, which left him very little to eat. More than one highly gifted child has become a vegetarian in a meat-eating family. They tend to ask difficult questions: "What is evil?" "Why is there violence?" "Is there a God?" "What happens when you die?" "How do we know we aren't part of someone else's dream?" (Silverman, 1989, p. 76)

The capacity for both introspection and reflection—intellectual characteristics of the highly gifted—is derived from a predominantly introverted personality structure. Introverts gain their energy from inside themselves, whereas extroverts gain energy from the people and environment that surround them. In the general population, about 75% are extroverted, whereas among the highly gifted, approximately 75% are introverted (Silverman, 1986). Introversion appears to increase with IQ.

## ASYNCHRONOUS DEVELOPMENT

A new definition of giftedness provides greater insight into the atypical issues of the highly gifted. It focuses on the phenomenological experience of the child, rather than on potential for achievement:

> Giftedness is *asynchronous development* in which advanced cognitive abilities and heightened intensity combine to create inner experiences and awareness that are qualitatively different from the norm. This asynchrony increases with higher intellectual capacity. The uniqueness of the gifted renders them particularly vulnerable and requires modifications in parenting, teaching and counseling in order for them to develop optimally. (Columbus Group, 1991)

As described in Chapter 2, asynchronous development means that mental, physical, emotional, and social development all are occurring at dramatically different rates. Therefore, the child may not be emotionally ready to cope with the heightened awareness that ensues from advanced cognition (Hollingworth, 1931; Morelock, 1992). The child is also out-of-sync socially with others of the same age and with the cultural and scholastic expectations for his or her age group (Terrassier, 1985).

The intelligence quotient provides a minimal estimate of the *degree* of asynchrony. Therefore, the higher the child's IQ, the more asynchronous the development. The difficulties highly gifted children experience trying to fit in with age peers and a curriculum designed for average students can be understood once their degree of exceptionality is identified. Without assessment, their inability to fit in or to enthusiastically complete inappropriate schoolwork may be attributed to various emotional disturbances or family dysfunction. The school then takes a punitive stance toward these children instead of adjusting the curriculum and the peer group to meet the children's needs.

From the vantage point of this new definition, it can be seen that highly gifted children have unique needs—emotionally, socially, and cognitively. As IQ increases, so does the vulnerability of the child (Roedell, 1984). Modifications of parenting, teaching, and counseling are as necessary for highly gifted children to develop optimally as they are for severely disabled children. (See Chapter 2 for more information about asynchrony.)

## ISSUES IN IDENTIFICATION AND ASSESSMENT

Assessment of highly gifted students is complex. Differences in scores on various instruments are much greater for this group than for any other population. Discrepancies have been found in excess of 100 points (Silverman & Kearney, 1992b)! By comparison, relatively little variation in scores occurs from test to test for children who are average or developmentally disabled. The culprit is *ceiling effects*, which occur when the child's knowledge goes beyond the limits of the test. None of the modern individual and group tests have items of sufficient difficulty to assess the full strength of the abilities of highly gifted students (Silverman & Kearney, 1989, 1992a).

A recent study compared IQ scores of 20 highly gifted children derived from both the *Stanford–Binet L-M* and the WISC-III (Silverman & Atkinson, in preparation). These children attained scores in the 151 to 191 range on the L-M, with a mean of 173. On the WISC-III, they scored in the 116 to 150 range, with the following means: 134 Full

Scale IQ, 141 Verbal IQ, and 120 Performance IQ. The highest score on the WISC-III was below the lowest score on the L-M; only three of the children scored in the highly gifted range on the WISC-III, attaining Full Scale IQ scores of 146, 148, and 150. Discrepancies ranged from 14 to 60 points (mean difference 37 IQ points). One child obtained an IQ score of 124 on the *Kaufman Assessment Battery for Children* (K-ABC), 137 on the WISC-R, and a year later 229+ on the *Stanford–Binet L-M* (Silverman & Kearney, 1992b).

The resolution to the problem is a two-stage process that may be costly, but appears justified. Originally, it was recommended that "when a child obtains *three* subtest scores at or near the ceiling of any current instrument, he or she should be retested on the Stanford–Binet Form L-M" (Silverman & Kearney, 1989, p. 48). In the last few years, this recommendation has been adopted by several psychologists who assess highly gifted children. However, when the three-subtest criterion was applied to the data on the WISC-III, less than half of the highly gifted children in the sample were located (Silverman et al., in preparation). Rimm and Lovance (1992) suggested that children be retested on the L-M when they attained ceiling level scores on only *two* subtests.

> The Wechsler IQ tests are used for initial testing because the subtest scores are viewed as important for curriculum-related decisions. When students are at or near the ceiling score on at least two subtests, the Clinic recommends further testing using the Stanford–Binet, Form L-M. (Rimm & Lovance, 1992, p. 101)

Using this criterion, 90% of the highly gifted sample was located. Although the three-subtest rule appeared to be adequate for the WISC-R, it is recommended that two subtests of the WISC-III be used as the criterion for retesting.

The *Stanford–Binet L-M* is also recommended if the child has a known eye–hand coordination problem, is highly reflective and a slow processor, or has difficulty with timed tests. The newer tests have substantially increased the bonus points for speed as a method of increasing reliability. If a 12-year-old solved every Performance item correctly on the WISC-III, but received no bonus points for speed, he or she would score below average on every subtest (Kaufman, 1992).

> The biggest negatives for gifted assessment are the new emphasis on problem-solving speed on the WPPSI-R [*Wechsler Preschool and Primary Scale of Intelligence–Revised* and] the substantially increased stress on performance time in the WISC-III compared to the WISC-R. . . . The speed factor will penalize gifted children who are as reflective as they are bright, or who tend to go slow for other non-cognitive reasons such as a mild coordination problem. (Kaufman, 1992, p. 158)

The L-M is essentially untimed, and has few motor demands. Therefore, it is a better instrument for children whose Verbal IQ scores are significantly higher (15 points) than their Performance IQ scores. Thirteen of the 20 children in our sample had Verbal–Performance discrepancies of 15 points or greater (15 to 44 points). One child who scored 164 on the L-M obtained only a 99 on the Performance section of the WISC-III (Silverman et al., in preparation).

Reservations psychologists might have about using the *Stanford–Binet L-M* are addressed elsewhere (Silverman & Kearney, 1992a, 1992b). However, it is important to note that it is *not* "unethical" to use a dated test. Stanley E. Jones, director of the Office of Ethics for the American Psychological Association, wrote,

> It would not be my reading that Principle 2.9 would prohibit the use of any test for a purpose that can be defended. It does make it the responsibility of the psychologist to provide such a defense when using tests which are not obviously current. (personal communication to Sylvia Rimm, November 25, 1991)

# PROVISIONS FOR HIGHLY GIFTED STUDENTS

Underachievement is a major problem for the highly gifted—even among straight "A," "high" achievers. Schools rarely provide the kind of curriculum that truly challenges these youngsters. Experiments undertaken at Johns Hopkins, Purdue, Duke, Northwestern, University of Denver, and other academic institutions have demonstrated that highly gifted junior high students can master algebra, geometry, trigonometry, college-level physics, and courses in many other subject areas in 3-week summer programs (Feldhusen, 1983). It is evident that the rate at which these students are capable of learning far exceeds the pace at which they are offered instruction.

With appropriate guidance, exceptionally gifted high school students have had remarkable achievements, as demonstrated at the Bronx High School of Science and at Calasanctius, a private school for the gifted in Buffalo, New York. From seventh grade on, students at Calasanctius learn how to conduct research. During a 6-month period, they are expected to produce a comprehensive research paper, including a main thesis, counterarguments, information in support of their thesis, implications, and conclusions. Upon completion of their projects, the students face an oral defense by five of their teachers, who cross-examine their arguments, methodology, and conclusions. Students experience three or four of these oral defenses before they graduate from high school. During senior high school, they investigate real problems with community mentors, and often write publishable papers. Here are some examples of seminar papers completed by high school juniors at Calasanctius:

- Patient Specificity of Tumor Cell Antigen in the Leukocyte Migration Inhibition Test
- The Dual Linear Programming Problem as Complementary to the Primal Problem in the Use of Simplex Algorithm as an Optimal Solution Technique for Systems of Linear Inequality
- The Hassidic Foundation of Martin Buber's Theology (Calasanctius School, 1974)

It is apparent from these titles that gifted students are capable of a great deal more than they are asked to do in public school programs. The waste of time and forced underachievement of this population is contributing to the international loss of standing of the United States. It is essential that the curriculum for gifted and highly gifted students be upgraded.

## A Continuum of Services

The normal curve of distribution of intelligence can serve as a guide for determining provisions for the highly gifted beyond those available for modestly gifted children. The basic curriculum, the pace of instruction, the amount of drill and repetition in the textbooks, and typical instructional strategies were all designed for average learners. As one moves down the continuum, the amount of drill and repetition needed increases exponentially, while the level of abstraction and complexity that is comprehended markedly decreases. As shown in Table 13.1, modifications of regular classroom work are required for students who are either below or above the norm to be successful.

Each standard deviation of ability is met with a different type of provision at the lower end of the continuum, as well as at the upper end. Increased intelligence means greater ability to deal with complexity, abstraction, and advanced concepts, and less need for repetition. An advanced pace of instruction is required to match the rapid learning rate of the child. At approximately 115 IQ, children are fast learners in the regular classroom and profit from general enrichment activities. At approximately 130 IQ, individual diagnosis, certified teachers, resource rooms, special classes, and individualized programs are needed. At approximately 145 IQ, full-day placements with specially trained teachers and a specially tailored curriculum provide the

**TABLE 13.1.   Provisions for Exceptional Learners**

| Difference | Below the Norm | Above the Norm |
|---|---|---|
| 1 *SD* (85 IQ vs. 115 IQ) | Remedial instruction in the regular classroom<br>Modified curriculum<br>Consultants to teachers | Enrichment in the regular classroom<br>Modified curriculum<br>Consultants to teachers |
| 2 *SD* (70 IQ vs. 130 IQ) | Resource room for academic subjects<br>Individualized Educational Programs (IEPs)<br>Special curriculum<br>Certified teachers<br>Adapted teaching strategies<br>Decreased pace of instruction | Special classes for academic subjects<br>IEPs<br>Special curriculum<br>Certified teachers<br>Adapted teaching strategies<br>Increased pace of instruction |
| 3 *SD* (55 IQ vs. 145 IQ) | Instruction in self-contained classes<br>Radical adaptation of curriculum<br>Socialization with peers of similar abilities | Instruction in self-contained classes<br>Radical acceleration of curriculum<br>Socialization with peers of similar abilities |
| 4 *SD* (40 IQ vs. 160 IQ) | Special facilities<br>Individual instruction | Special facilities<br>Individual instruction |

*Note: SD* = standard deviation.

least restrictive environment for these children (Silverman, 1989). At approximately 160 IQ, special facilities would be helpful. It is obvious that a model of the type shown in Table 13.1 would not fit with current political ideologies, but the pendulum will likely swing again toward considering individual needs of children, and a parallel continuum of services for both ends of the spectrum could guide future practice.

## Appropriate Provisions

A combination of the following provisions would be suitable for highly gifted children and, to some extent, moderately gifted children. Moderately gifted and highly gifted students can be grouped together, as long as the pace of instruction is sufficient to challenge the highly gifted students in the group.

- Individualized Education Programs
- Fast-paced, challenging courses that offer advanced material
- Acceleration
- Mentors
- University-based programs
- Self-contained classes
- Special schools or programs
- Private education
- Community enrichment opportunities
- Homeschooling
- Counseling

Individualization is a fundamental principle for serving this population:

> The higher the deviation above the mean, the greater the number of possible combinations and recombinations of abilities. No one highly gifted child can be expected to be like any other child with the same score. Therefore, no single-focus program . . . can hope to adequately serve a population with such potentially complex profiles. (Lewis, 1984, p. 134)

It is important to have an Individualized Education Program (IEP) for every highly gifted student in the school district. The diagnostic component provides an assessment of the student's strengths and needs, and the staffing component assures that staff members work collaboratively to meet those needs. The school psychologist should conduct a comprehensive individual assessment, including an examination of intellectual capability, academic strengths, self-concept, social development, and student interests. The student should be interviewed prior to the staffing, because highly gifted students are often in the best position to tell what they need for their optimal development. Ideally, administrators, parents, teachers, the counselor, the school psychologist, support personnel, and the student should all be involved in collaboratively planning the IEP.

In Boulder, Colorado, an effective plan was designed by the principals of an elementary, junior, and senior high school who met to determine how to provide for the continuous progress of an extraordinarily gifted child. They allowed the student to be dually enrolled in elementary and junior high school, and to take chemistry classes at the high school. They arranged with a local university to enable the student to take college chemistry courses when he had exhausted the high school offerings. The parents were responsible for transportation. These administrators were able to circumvent red tape, which is the major obstacle to appropriate programming for the highly gifted.

Part of any plan for the highly gifted must involve exposure to a challenging, conceptually rich curriculum. This may take a variety of forms: fast-paced course work, such as enrolling in advanced placement physics in seventh grade; innovative programs that allow for continuous progress; independent study opportunities with proper guidance in developing research skills; and self-contained enrichment classes in which the students help design the curriculum. High-powered instructors may be brought in from local colleges, and study groups can be formed with students who have similar interests. The question of acceleration versus enrichment is irrelevant, because this group of students needs both. They learn at a very accelerated pace and they need high-level conceptual material outside the regular curriculum.

Acceleration is a necessary response to a highly gifted student's faster pace of learning. Acceleration has a long, positive history in American education and it is once again gaining popularity (Wernick, 1992). Until the last few decades, it was common for gifted children to be placed with children 1 or 2 years older than themselves. The term acceleration was applied only to 3 years of advancement or more—what is called "radical acceleration" today. A considerable amount of research conducted on the effects of acceleration (Daurio, 1979; Robinson & Noble, 1991; Southern & Jones, 1991) supports it as a viable option, socially as well as academically. To determine if this is the right option for a particular student, it is important to *ask the student*. Children who want to be accelerated have no difficulty with social adjustment. However, it is never appropriate to accelerate a child against his or her wishes.

Many forms of acceleration can be considered: early entrance into kindergarten; grade skipping; content acceleration in one or two subject areas while remaining with age peers; continuous progress classes in which students can complete 3 years of curriculum in 2 years; telescoping, which is the compacting of course work so that it can be covered in less time; testing out of courses or partial course requirements; taking advanced courses for credit in summers or after school; correspondence courses for credit; advanced placement courses that offer college credit during high school; dual enrollment in high school and college; early graduation; early enrollment in college; and radical acceleration (e.g., skipping junior high school, going directly from elementary to high school).

Exceptionally gifted students often indicate that the ideal situation would be the opportunity to accelerate with a group of highly gifted peers, as is being done at the University of Washington. Each year since 1977, approximately 15 highly selected 13- and 14-year-olds have successfully enrolled as full-time students on the Seattle campus.

The early entrants have a full year in a transition program that prepares them for college and enables social bonding to occur. Psychological support is available to the students throughout their matriculation. Students live at home with their families, because no residential program is available. These students have been carefully followed to determine the effects of early entrance, and by all reports the program has been extremely successful (Janos, Robinson, et al., 1988; Robinson & Noble, 1991).

A mentor is a guide, adviser, role model, counselor, and friend (Beck, 1989) who works with a student individually in his or her areas of interest. Mentors have been found to play critical roles in shaping gifted students' career aspirations (Hamilton & Hamilton, 1992; Hollinger, 1991; Swassing & Fichter, 1991). They appear to be particularly important for girls and students from economically disadvantaged backgrounds. Community members, university professors, college students, and older gifted students can serve as mentors for highly gifted students. Meetings between the student and the mentor usually take place after school hours, at the mutual convenience of both. Sometimes the mentorship is like an apprenticeship and takes place at the mentor's workplace. A dedicated, full-time coordinator is usually needed to find and train mentors, select students, match the students to the mentors, and monitor the program. Student maturity, depth of interest, and task commitment should be taken into account in selecting protégés in order to prevent mentor burnout.

The university has become a haven for highly gifted students. The number of precollegiate programs housed on university campuses is burgeoning. A network of university personnel involved in providing services for gifted students has been recently established. Thirteen colleges and universities were represented at the inaugural meeting in 1992 of the Association for Precollegiate Talent. All but one offer summer programs, 10 provide Saturday or after-school programs, 7 sponsor talent searches using the SAT or ACT, 5 provide mentorships, 7 have counseling and assessment services, and several other services were mentioned. Early entrance to college apparently has become standard at most institutions of higher education, and concurrent enrollment in high school and college is encouraged at 6 of the institutions represented by this group.

Self-contained classes enable the highly gifted to develop social relationships as well as to learn at an advanced pace. Several school districts have almost apologetically resorted to self-contained classes for the gifted instead of pull-out programs, because they are less expensive. They simply require reorchestration of existing students, teachers, and resources, instead of hiring new personnel. However, teachers within the system who volunteer to teach the gifted classes need special training and the support of the rest of the faculty. Teaching the gifted is a difficult task that may not be fully appreciated by one's colleagues.

Special schools for the highly gifted are becoming more popular in urban areas. The Bronx High School of Science and the High School for the Performing Arts have given birth to high achievements. The High School for Math and Science in Durham, North Carolina, and the Illinois Mathematics and Science Academy are among the publicly supported residential high schools for exceptionally talented students. The concern that segregating students of high ability leads to elitism appears to be unfounded (Newland, 1976). People have no objections to postsecondary institutions such as The Julliard School of Music and the Massachusetts Institute of Technology, because they know that the most capable young people need high-powered institutions at which to perfect their talents. Eliminating all such centers of talent would lead to mediocrity rather than foster democratic ideals.

Other types of public school programs for the gifted include magnet schools, which sometimes focus on specific subject areas, such as the sciences, the humanities, or the arts; governor's schools—usually summer camps or residential programs; the International Baccalaureate program, a demanding internationally standardized curriculum and testing program for high school students that leads to an international diploma; special study centers, such as Talcott Mountain Science Center in Avon, Connecticut; alternative schools that offer opportunities for independent study; or school-within-a-school programs, in which a portion of the school is reserved for gifted students in special classes. Some urban districts have turned schools with declining enrollments into magnet schools or school-within-a-school programs, making better use of the facilities (Silverman, 1981).

Private education needs to be considered as an option for highly gifted students. There are a limited number of highly gifted children in the population and they are more likely to find each other in private schools set up specifically to serve them. The cost of private education makes it prohibitive to many families. However, voucher systems are being attempted in several communities, in which the state or district at least partially supports the child's education in a private institution. Scholarships and trading of services also should be explored as means of funding private education.

Some private organizations, such as MENSA, provide classes or interest groups for gifted students. Parent groups can be encouraged to develop their own activities for these children to meet their social needs. Community agencies, such as museums, galleries, planetariums, zoos, community schools, parks, and camps have enrichment opportunities for gifted students. Private agencies can also be found that offer special programs for gifted students: computer camps or networks, science schools or clubs, arts programs, archaeology explorations, music studios, centers for theater arts, and self-concept seminars.

Homeschooling is gaining in popularity as an alternative method of educating highly gifted children (Linehan, 1992). Many eminent individuals were homeschooled, including Thomas Edison, Laura Ingalls Wilder, Pearl Buck, John Stuart Mill, Franklin Delano Roosevelt, and Andrew Wyeth (Kearney, 1989). This option is particularly inviting in rural areas, where exceptionally gifted children are few in number and services are limited. This alternative demands a serious commitment of time and energy on the part of the parents, and considerable skill in educating as well as parenting. It enhances the closeness of families and allows the children to have a totally individualized curriculum taught at their own pace. Although the major concern is that homeschoolers will miss opportunities for socialization, many report that social development actually blossomed outside the school context (Alexander, 1992).

> Most public schools provide an unrealistic and frequently a harmful social environment for their students. The familiar specter of peer pressure is difficult to exorcise and dangerous to ignore—assaults on a student's integrity and self-respect occur with alarming regularity. Many of the friendships and relationships that develop among public school students are associations of convenience only, and rapidly fail when graduation renders them unnecessary. Furthermore, the world at large is simply not composed entirely of anyone's age peers. If a child learns to relate only to others of the same age from the same town, he or she is likely to encounter difficulties when adulthood and its challenges approach. . . . I can say with confidence that I did not miss public school socialization . . . and I was certainly happy not to be forced to spend half of each day with a group selected for age and not compatibility. (Alexander, 1992, p. 13)

Most homeschooling parents supplement their children's program with extracurricular activities to provide opportunities for social development. It is also possible to enroll homeschooled children in some public or private schools for part of the day or week.

Counseling is an essential component of programming for the highly gifted. Their asynchronous development makes life especially difficult at times. They may have bouts of despair at the violence in the world, and feel helpless to change the injustices they see in the television newscasts. Heightened awareness and emotional intensity increase the amount of internal stress with which they must deal on a daily basis. In addition to these internal stresses, highly gifted children are continually pressured to fit in with others, an extremely complex task when one's thought processes are so very different from others'. In counseling, much more emphasis is placed on a child's socialization than on his or her academic progress. Unfortunately, socialization and social development have become confused in people's minds. Socialization is merely adapting to the needs of the group, whereas social development is the ability to develop and sustain long-term intimate friendships and to have positive, humanitarian attitudes toward others (Silverman, 1992). The press toward socialization may actually interfere with a highly gifted child's social development. Although all provisions for gifted children are attacked on the grounds that they may impede socialization, the research indicates that these provisions enhance both socialization and social development (Robinson & Noble, 1991; Silverman, 1992, 1993).

Counselors are needed to help the student and the family determine which of the available options to pursue. Several of the above provisions may have to be explored simultaneously until a program is developed that supports both cognitive and emotional development. Also, all provisions should be evaluated on a regular basis, as these children's needs change rapidly. What works at the beginning of the year may not work mid-year, and a new plan may have to be formulated (Kearney, 1992b).

# MEETING THE NEEDS OF HIGHLY GIFTED CHILDREN IN THE CLASSROOM

Given the current trend in education, most highly gifted students are found in the regular classroom, and many classroom teachers are at a loss as to how to meet their needs. The following 12 guidelines will help teachers to differentiate instruction for this population:

1. *Find out what they know before teaching them.* It is untenable to reteach a child what he or she has already mastered. Therefore, the most essential task in teaching the highly gifted is *assessment*, which can be done through standardized tests, interviews, discussions with parents, work samples, end of the year tests, end of chapter tests, and so on.

2. *Omit drill from their diets.* Highly gifted children learn the first time a concept is presented and retain it permanently. Drill is insufferable for them and takes all the joy out of learning. The amount of drill needed for concept formation is inversely proportional to a child's intelligence.

3. *Be flexible in determining their program.* They need advocates to help them bypass requirements that are merely "hoops" they have to jump through. All kinds of alternatives can be considered, such as those listed in the provisions section.

4. *Design an Individualized Education Program.* Exceptionally advanced children need IEPs as much as profoundly delayed children do. Disabled children are protected by federal and state law, but the gifted can be protected only by moral law. Nothing is gained in the name of democracy by having a third grader who reads at the eighth-grade level repeat the third-grade reader. Because children progress at different rates, their educational programming must be differentiated to match their learning rates.

5. *Help them find "like-minded" friends.* A great depth of loneliness can accompany giftedness unless these children find their own kind. This is actually the most compelling reason for special classes, enrichment programs, or ability grouping. If these are not feasible, gifted peers with similar interests can be located through local parent advocacy groups.

6. *Pace instruction to the rate of the learner.* Highly gifted children learn at an amazing pace, absorbing a month's curriculum in a few days. Special classes are ideal for accelerating the pace of learning. When this is not possible, highly gifted learners should be allowed to learn the material on their own. At no time is it justifiable to hold back their learning to the norm of the class.

7. *Use discovery learning techniques.* The minds of highly gifted children are uniquely designed for pattern recognition, and this is the type of learning they like best. This enables them to take great intuitive leaps in their learning. Inductive learning strategies are available in every subject area.

8. *Focus on abstract ideas.* The more abstract and complex the concept, the more interesting it is for highly gifted students to learn. The easier the concept and the more repetitious the instruction, the more likely their minds are to wander out of the classroom.

9. *Allow them to arrive at answers in their own way.* Exceptionally gifted students should not be forced to show the steps they take in solving a problem because they do not

learn in the same step-by-step fashion as the textbook describes. They can devise their own problem-solving techniques, make great intuitive leaps, and skip many of the routine steps in learning.

10. *Allow them to form their own cooperative learning groups.*
A common practice in today's schools is assigning children to cooperative learning groups of mixed ability and making the brightest child in the group responsible for everyone else's learning. Despite claims to the contrary, there is no research evidence indicating that this type of learning is good for highly gifted children (Slavin, 1990). Obviously, profoundly retarded children do not benefit from it either. Cooperative learning works best for the gifted when they choose their own groups and work with other bright, motivated students.

11. *Allow students to observe.* Highly gifted children are often introverted, and introverts learn best by observation rather than by trial and error. Instant answers should not be demanded; they need time to think. Introverts also are more comfortable working alone or in groups of two or three than in large groups.

12. *Teach the fine art of argumentation* (Hollingworth, 1939). Because they argue anyway, help them learn (a) techniques for arguing fairly; (b) skills in determining when arguing is appropriate; and (c) reactions of others to their argumentativeness.

These 12 guidelines can be used in various settings, from regular classrooms to special schools. Differentiated instruction is a requirement for meeting the needs of exceptionally gifted children.

# ROLES OF SCHOOL PERSONNEL AND PARENTS

The *school psychologist* is the key individual in the identification of highly gifted children because these children are best identified through psychometric techniques. A school psychologist who recognizes the child's degree of exceptionality is in an excellent position to translate psychometric information into programmatic adaptations. VanTassel-Baska and Baska (1993) described this process in detail and provided examples.

*School counselors* play a critical role in the lives of exceptionally gifted children. They assist these children and youth in dealing with the difficulties attendant to their extreme differences from the norm. Counseling groups, individual counseling, and simply being a friend, mentor, and advocate to whom the child can turn are all highly recommended. School counselors can also help teachers understand the cognitive and emotional needs of these children. They may be called upon to act as mediators between the home and the school. Finally, counselors will need to provide support and guidance to families of gifted children in dealing with the complexities of raising an exceptional child. Information on preventive counseling, group counseling, individual counseling, career counseling, academic counseling, and family counseling is presented in Silverman (1993).

In most school settings, highly gifted children are placed in the regular classroom, and they are the full responsibility of the *regular classroom teacher*. Flexibility and individualization are the two most important factors to keep in mind in teaching this population. Programs may have to be modified often. Parents and teachers need to work together to explore options for a given child. Sometimes a combination of acceleration, mentorship, and partial homeschooling is useful in meeting the child's needs.

*Parents* are the most important ingredient in the healthy development of highly gifted children. Families with exceptionally gifted children are often close knit, with family members becoming the child's closest companions (Kearney, 1992a). These children apparently crave a great deal of attention from infancy on. In addition, parents are usually called upon to play strong advocacy roles for their children. This makes parenting one of these exceptional children a full-time job. Mothers often have difficulty finding time to meet their own needs. As gifted children usually have gifted parents (Kline & Meckstroth, 1985; Meckstroth, 1991; Tolan, 1992), it is important for parents to receive guidance about the full development of their own abilities.

# CONCLUSION

Although highly gifted children are one of society's greatest assets, they are often made to feel as if they were a detriment. They are particularly vulnerable in the current era in which giftedness is being equated with racial and socioeconomic privilege. Gifted children come from all socioeconomic levels of society, and they come in all colors. If allowed to progress at their own paces, these young people have enormous contributions to make in adult life. Their contributions may lead to eminence. In most cases they will not, because there is room for very few giant figures in each era (Lovecky, 1992b). However, the contributions that highly gifted individuals make to teaching, counseling, parenting, volunteer work, and nurturing others are just as important. Educators need to value and nurture these children regardless of their potential for eminence.

If school is to meet the needs of *all* children, school personnel must remember that these children are part of that "all." They cannot be sacrificed to political ideologies. They have a right to an education that optimizes their abilities and protects them from scapegoating. They need an education that is sensitive to their individual differences and that does not pit them against other children. A truly humanitarian framework honors the unique learning styles and learning rates of all students. Natural collaborations are formed of students with similar interests and abilities. The school becomes a community of learners, each pursuing his or her own passions as well as absorbing a specific body of knowledge. Emotional development is considered equally as important as cognitive development. In this kind of environment, highly gifted children can flourish and become all that they were meant to be.

# REFERENCES

Alexander, E. (1992). Learning to fly: A homeschooling retrospective. *Understanding Our Gifted, 5*(1), 1, 11–14.

Beck, L. (1989). Mentorships: Benefits and effects on career development. *Gifted Child Quarterly, 33*, 22–28.

Calasanctius School. (1974). *Selected seminar papers* (Vol. 3). Buffalo, NY: Author.

Columbus Group. (1991, July). Unpublished transcript of the meeting of the Columbus Group, Columbus, OH.

Daurio, S. P. (1979). Educational enrichment versus acceleration: A review of the literature. In W. C. George, S. J. Cohn, & J. C. Stanley (Eds.), *Educating the gifted: Acceleration and enrichment* (pp. 13–63). Baltimore: Johns Hopkins University Press.

Feldhusen, J. F. (1983). Eclecticism: A comprehensive approach to education of the gifted. In C. P. Benbow & J. C. Stanley (Eds.), *Academic precocity: Aspects of its development* (pp. 192–204). Baltimore: Johns Hopkins University Press.

Guilford, J. P. (1968). *Intelligence, creativity, and their educational implications*. San Diego: Robert R. Knapp.

Hamilton, S. F., & Hamilton, M. A. (1992). Mentoring programs: Promise and paradox. *Phi Delta Kappan, 73*, 546–550.

Hollinger, C. L. (1991). Career choices for gifted adolescents: Overcoming stereotypes. In M. Bireley & J. Genshaft (Eds.), *Understanding the gifted adolescent: Educational, developmental, and multicultural issues* (pp. 201–214). New York: Teachers College Press.

Hollingworth, L. S. (1927). Who are gifted children? *Child Study, 5,* 3–5.

Hollingworth, L. S. (1931). The child of very superior intelligence as a special problem in social adjustment. *Mental Hygiene, 15,* 3–16.

Hollingworth, L. S. (1939). What we know about the early selection and training of leaders. *Teachers College Record, 40,* 575–592.

Hollingworth, L. S. (1942). *Children above 180 IQ Stanford–Binet: Origin and development.* Yonkers-on-Hudson, NY: World Book.

Janos, P. M., Robinson, N. M., Carter, C., Chapel, A., Cuffey, R., Curland, M., Daily, M., Guilland, M., Heinzig, M., Kehl, H., Lu, S., Sherry, D., Stoloff, J., & Wise, A. (1988). A cross-sectional developmental study of the social relations of students who enter college early. *Gifted Child Quarterly, 32,* 210–215.

Jensen, A. R. (1980). *Bias in mental testing.* New York: Free Press.

Kaufman, A. S. (1992). Evaluation of the WISC-III and WPPSI-R for gifted children. *Roeper Review, 14,* 154–158.

Kearney, K. (1989). Homeschooling gifted children. *Understanding Our Gifted, 1*(3), 1, 12–13, 15–16.

Kearney, K. (1992a). Life in the asynchronous family. *Understanding Our Gifted, 4*(6), 1, 8–12.

Kearney, K. (1992b). When promising practices go wrong. *Understanding Our Gifted, 5*(2), 16.

Kline, B. E., & Meckstroth, E. A. (1985). Understanding and encouraging the exceptionally gifted. *Roeper Review, 8,* 24–30.

Lewis, G. (1984). Alternatives to acceleration for the highly gifted child. *Roeper Review, 6,* 133–136.

Linehan, P. (1992). Homeschooling for gifted primary students. *Understanding Our Gifted, 5*(1), 1, 8–10.

Lovecky, D. V. (1992a). The exceptionally gifted child. *Understanding Our Gifted, 4*(4), 3–4.

Lovecky, D. V. (1992b). Standing on the shoulders of giants—Part II. *Understanding Our Gifted, 5*(1), 3.

McGuffog, C., Feiring, C., & Lewis, M. (1987). The diverse profile of the extremely gifted child. *Roeper Review, 10,* 82–88.

Meckstroth, E. (1991). Guiding the parents of gifted children: The role of counselors and teachers. In R. M. Milgram (Ed.), *Counseling gifted and talented children: A guide for teachers, counselors, and parents* (pp. 95–120). Norwood, NJ: Ablex.

Morelock, M. J. (1992). Giftedness: The view from within. *Understanding Our Gifted, 4*(3), 1, 11–15.

Newland, T. E. (1976). *The gifted in socio-educational perspective.* Englewood Cliffs, NJ: Prentice-Hall.

Passow, A. H. (1988). Educating gifted persons who are caring and concerned. *Roeper Review, 11,* 13–15.

Rimm, S. B., & Lovance, K. J. (1992). The use of subject and grade skipping for the prevention and reversal of underachievement. *Gifted Child Quarterly, 36,* 100–105.

Robinson, A. (1992). Promising practices for talented children. *Understanding Our Gifted, 5*(2), 1, 8–11.

Robinson, H. B. (1981). The uncommonly bright child. In M. Lewis & L. A. Rosenblum (Eds.), *The uncommon child* (pp. 57–81). New York: Plenum Press.

Robinson, N. M., & Noble, K. D. (1991). Social-emotional development and adjustment of gifted children. In M. C. Wang, M. C. Reynolds, & H. J. Walberg (Eds.), *Handbook of special education: Research and practice. Volume 4: Emerging programs* (pp. 57–76). New York: Pergamon Press.

Roedell, W. C. (1984). Vulnerabilities of highly gifted children. *Roeper Review, 6*, 127–130.

Roeper, A. (1982, October). *Stress can be a positive force in gifted children.* Paper presented at the First Annual Conference of the Atlantic Association for Gifted and Talented Children, Fredericton, NB.

Silverman, L. K. (1981). Secondary provisions for the gifted. *Journal for the Education of the Gifted, 4*, 30–42.

Silverman, L. K. (1986). Parenting young gifted children. *Journal of Children in Contemporary Society, 18*, 73–87.

Silverman, L. K. (1989). The highly gifted. In J. F. Feldhusen, J. VanTassel-Baska, & K. Seeley (Eds.), *Excellence in educating the gifted* (pp. 71–83). Denver, CO: Love.

Silverman, L. K. (1992). Social development or socialization? *Understanding Our Gifted, 5*(1), 15.

Silverman, L. K. (Ed.). (1993). *Counseling the gifted and talented.* Denver, CO: Love.

Silverman, L. K., & Atkinson, D. R. (in preparation). *Comparisons of the highly gifted on the WISC-III and the Stanford–Binet Form L-M.*

Silverman, L. K., & Kearney, K. (1989). Parents of the extraordinarily gifted. *Advanced Development, 1*, 41–56.

Silverman, L. K., & Kearney, K. (1992a). The case for the Stanford–Binet L-M as a supplemental test. *Roeper Review, 15*, 34–37.

Silverman, L. K., & Kearney, K. (1992b, November). *Don't throw away the old Binet.* Presented at the 39th annual convention of the National Association for Gifted Children, Los Angeles. (Appeared in part in *Understanding Our Gifted*, 1992, *4*(4), 1, 8–10.)

Slavin, R. E. (1990). Cooperative learning and the gifted: Who benefits? *Journal for the Education of the Gifted, 14*, 28–30.

Southern, W. T., & Jones, E. D. (Ed.). (1991). *The academic acceleration of gifted children.* New York: Teachers College Press.

Swassing, R. H., & Fichter, G. R. (1991). University and community-based programs for the gifted adolescent. In M. Bireley & J. Genshaft (Eds.), *Understanding the gifted adolescent: Educational, developmental, and multicultural issues* (pp. 176–185). New York: Teachers College Press.

Tannenbaum, A. J. (1992). Early signs of giftedness: Research and commentary. *Journal for the Education of the Gifted, 15*, 104–133.

Terman, L. M. (1925). *Genetic studies of genius: Vol. 1. Mental and physical traits of a thousand gifted children.* Stanford, CA: Stanford University Press.

Terrassier, J.-C. (1985). Dyssynchrony—Uneven development. In J. Freeman (Ed.). *The psychology of gifted children* (pp. 265–274). New York: Wiley.

Thorndike, R. L., Hagen, E. P., & Sattler, J. M. (1986). *Guide for administering and scoring the Stanford–Binet Intelligence Scale: Fourth edition.* Chicago: Riverside.

Tolan, S. S. (1985, November/December). Stuck in another dimension: The exceptionally gifted child at school. *G / C / T*, pp. 22–26.

Tolan, S. S. (1992). Only a parent: Three true stories. *Understanding Our Gifted, 4*(3), 1, 8–10.

VanTassel-Baska, J., & Baska, L. (1993). The roles of educational personnel in counseling the gifted. In L. K. Silverman (Ed.), *Counseling the gifted and talented* (pp. 181–200). Denver, CO: Love.

Wechsler, D. (1974). *Wechsler Intelligence Scale for Children–Revised.* San Antonio, TX: Psychological Corporation.

Wechsler, D. (1991). *Wechsler Intelligence Scale for Children–Third Edition technical manual.* San Antonio, TX: Psychological Corporation.

Wernick, S. (1992, July 8). Interest renewed in grade skipping as inexpensive way to aid the gifted. *The New York Times*, p. B7.

# Part IV

# Personal, Interpersonal, and Cultural Issues

# Chapter 14

# Impact of Family Patterns Upon the Development of Giftedness

### Sylvia B. Rimm

◆ ◆ ◆

PARENTS MAKE AN IMPORTANT CONTRIBUTION to their children's giftedness, and, although these children require mainly the same "good parenting" required by all children, gifted families have special needs and problems. For example, parents of gifted children are often accused of putting pressure on their children, whether or not they really do. A spouse, grandparents, teachers, and even children themselves may blame a parent or parents for that pressure when the giftedness itself may be causing children to feel pressured (Rimm, 1987). Gifted children, because of their large vocabulary and adult-sounding reasoning, are often given power too early in their lives and are treated almost as adults. Sibling rivalry can be more intense, depending upon how equally or differentially gifted other family members are. Large commitments of parent time required by some gifted children can rob siblings of attention from busy parents. Contrary to the popular belief that all parents believe their children are gifted, some parents actually deny their children's special giftedness because they view giftedness as socially unacceptable and prefer that their children be "well adjusted" and "normal."

This chapter describes the impact of family characteristics on gifted children, including structures, relationships, parenting styles, sibling issues, and peer issues. Communication between family and school is also included as it affects these children.

## FAMILY STRUCTURAL CHARACTERISTICS

Analyses of the family structures of eminent, achieving, and even underachieving gifted children (Bloom, 1985; Groth, 1975; Olszewski,

Kulieke, & Buescher, 1987; Rimm & Lowe, 1988) seem to show re-markable similarities. In those studies, small families were more com-mon, with more than half of the gifted children being oldest and ap-proximately a quarter of them being only children. Adopted children were rarely mentioned in research on eminence (Albert, 1980; Barbe, 1981; Goertzel & Goertzel, 1962; Walberg et al., 1981), except in one study of gifted underachievers in which 4 of the 22 sampled were adopted (Rimm & Lowe, 1988).

Most biographical analyses of eminence and achievement included all males, although Bloom's (1985) and Goertzel and Goertzel's (1962) studies included a few females. One must assume that this has much to do with the fewer opportunities available to females during the periods studied.

Higher education of parents was typical for all studies (Barbe, 1981; Benbow & Stanley, 1980; Groth, 1975; Rimm & Lowe, 1988; Roe, 1953; VanTassel-Baska, 1983), and the average age of the parents was older than typical at the time of their children's births. Although there was some evidence of family loss by illness and death, families seemed to be stable, for the most part, and there were few divorces. These statistics, however, may be time constrained. Nonconventional family lifestyles are more common to the current generation, and may thus cause fewer problems (Weisner & Garnier, 1992) than they would have in the periods of most biographical studies.

# FAMILY RELATIONSHIPS

## Parenting Styles

Studies of giftedness and eminence (Bloom, 1985; MacKinnon, 1965; Walberg et al., 1981) always found themes of family organization and consistent and predictable expectations for conduct. Considerable re-search also documents that authoritative, rather than authoritarian or permissive, families foster high achievement in children (Baumrind, 1989). This finding seems to be reflected in the biographical material on eminence, except in the early childhoods of creative artists and writers (Goertzel & Goertzel, 1962). Even into adolescence, family rela-tionships stayed mainly positive. Goertzel and Goertzel (1962) found only 25 of the 400 eminent persons to have been rebellious during adolescence.

Early enrichment by families was found in almost all biographical studies of giftedness. Even in the study of family environments of gifted underachievers, the informal learning during preschool years was dedicated and enhancing. High energy and achievement orientation were characteristic of all parents in Bloom's (1985) studies. Goertzel and Goertzel's (1962) study emphasized this dramatically by indicating that all parents but one of the 400 eminent persons whose lives they examined exhibited very high energy.

Bloom (1985) found family-shared work, learning, and play in the early childhoods of mathematicians, research neurologists, pianists, and sculptors, and Goertzel and Goertzel (1962) found the joy of work and love of learning modeled in 90% of the 400 families they described. In the studies of underachievers (Rimm & Lowe, 1988), parents modeled more of the frustrations than the satisfactions of achievement and often voiced a dislike of their work. Although most mothers in the family studies of eminence were full-time homemakers and involved in volunteer activities, they viewed their roles positively. The changing role of women will undoubtedly alter these findings when biographies of gifted young people of today are studied.

Parents' perceptions of children's giftedness does not appear to be harmful to their achievement. Cornell and Grossberg (1989) found that all of the 83 families of children in gifted programs thought of their children as gifted. There were no significant differences among children for either achievement or adjustment problems, regardless of how parents defined gifted or if they thought of their children as "usually" or "sometimes" gifted. However, the 25% of the children who were actually referred to as gifted by their parents were more likely to have adjustment problems that included discipline and/or poor self-control and internalized problems, such as anxiety and guilt. The authors pointed out the correlational nature of the study and do not assume causation, but do suggest that direct reference to the child as gifted may place excessive pressure on the child. Perhaps the direct reference to the child as gifted operates in the same way as does extreme praise, described by Rimm (1987). The analyses of biographies of eminent persons provide no information on the actual labeling of talented children, because gifted programs did not exist in schools during the childhoods of most of these persons. Despite lack of documentation of school programs, many students were accelerated or had special school opportunities (Goertzel & Goertzel, 1962), and parents had recognized their children's giftedness (Bloom, 1985).

## Sibling Relations

The typically small size of families of gifted children does not detract from the intensity of sibling rivalry. Gifted children are often highly competitive, which may be reflected in sibling relationships. Although no evidence exists indicating more rivalry in the families of gifted children, some sibling configurations related to giftedness seem to cause more stress (Davis & Rimm, 1994).

### The Gifted Child with Less Talented Siblings

The gifted child with very high intelligence or an extraordinary special talent provides impossible competition in his or her area of giftedness for other children in the family. The unique ability often requires an investment of an inordinate amount of time and resources to provide the special educational opportunities to develop the talents and meet this child's unconventional needs. In the process, the gifted child naturally receives a large amount of attention and recognition. His or her brothers and sisters need to be able both to admire the gifted sibling's success and to recognize that a similar level of success probably is not attainable for them. They are required to use a different measuring stick to evaluate their own abilities, or they may fall into the trap of viewing their own real successes (and themselves) as failures. In the words of one successful and gifted "second sibling,"

> Once I realized that there was nothing I could do to achieve as well as my sister, I decided to stop competing with her, to do the best I could, and to realize that what I was doing was really good too.

Although this youngster came to realize that he could be successful despite his being a "second-place" student, that realization was not automatic. In addition to rewarding the victories of their most gifted child, parents also must recognize and reward the success of other siblings, basing those successes on each child's abilities, efforts, and improvements.

Research on families in which one child is identified as gifted and others are not indicates that this may cause some problems for the nonlabeled child. Fisher (1981) found that parents recognized a "disruptive" and negative effect on the nongifted siblings, which disturbed the status quo of the family. Cornell (1983) also found the "nongifted" siblings of the gifted children to be less well adjusted than a control group of other nongifted children. In another study by Cornell and Grossberg (1986), children who had been rated as "less gifted" than their siblings had higher anxiety and lower self-esteem than their sisters and brothers in gifted programs. Grenier (1985) also found improved self-esteem of the labeled children and negative effects for their unlabeled siblings. Friction was increased when the age difference between siblings was less than 3 years. Pfouts (1980) found similarly that the closer the age spacing, the more the siblings were affected negatively in family relationships and personal adjustment, and younger siblings were also affected negatively in academic performance. Strangely enough, Ballering and Koch (1984) found that the gifted children actually perceived the sibling relationships as more negative than did their nongifted siblings.

Although all of the above studies included labeled gifted children and their nonlabeled siblings, Pfouts's (1980) study was based on siblings of all intelligence levels, thus suggesting that gifted versus nongifted studies may reflect only normal sibling rivalry, and the findings may be less related to the labeling than to sibling rivalry in general. Furthermore, Colangelo and Brower (1987) concluded that no long-term effects (5 years or more) resulted from the differential labeling within the family, and that nongifted siblings eventually "came to terms" with the gifted labeling of their siblings.

### The Gifted Child in a Family of Other Achieving Gifted Children

It is not unusual to find that all of the children in a family are gifted. This could be due to genetics, a favorable environment, positive parent and teacher expectations, or, most likely, to all of the above. It is important to recognize that each child in the family will feel increased pressure to fulfill the expectations set by preceding siblings. The first day of school for "child two," "child three," or "child four" inevitably begins with, "Oh yes, I know your sister. She was such a good student!" If the child is gifted and confident, this identification may be pleasing because he or she recognizes that the teacher has expectations that can be fulfilled. Moreover, this early recognition may quickly produce privileges and trust that otherwise would take longer to earn.

On the other hand, a less confident child may see the early identification by the teacher as a threat, because the child may worry that his or her performance may be less adequate than that of the older sibling. A sensitive teacher will quickly learn to recognize the individuality of each child. Nonetheless, parents may still need to explain that "Mr. Arnez had Sara too, but he'll soon get to know that you're a good worker and that you are also a separate individual."

Perhaps most important, parents of several gifted children may need to make a specific effort to ease the grade pressure for younger children. Parents should let their children know that they understand the special pressures the children feel due to the inevitable comparison with their siblings. Even when parents make no overt comparisons, children tend to assume that they are being compared. The parents' message should be that each child is expected to do the very best he or she can, and that the child's performance will be individually evaluated, not compared with the records of the older brothers or sisters. This noncomparative message needs explicit pronouncement to avoid children's internalized feelings of comparative pressure.

### The Gifted Child with a Close Age Older Sibling of Lesser Ability

Undoubtedly, one of the most difficult relationships is that of a younger gifted child and a brother or sister of average ability who is only 1 or 2 years older. The most typical tendency is for parents to refrain from providing appropriate enriched opportunities, and particularly acceleration, for the gifted child for fear of embarrassing the inevitably insecure older child. For the gifted child, this strategy produces both frustration, from the reduced opportunities for skill development, and pressure to underachieve and hide the high ability. The older child, of course, feels the sibling pressure anyway. In many cases, the older child also acquires lower achievement motivation related to the parental anxiety about the younger child's outperforming the older child.

A better approach is to reinforce the gifted child's achievements, even if it means acceleration to the same grade as the older child. (Needless to say, it is best if the siblings are not in the same classroom.) Also, parents absolutely must reinforce the older child's achievements according to that child's efforts and abilities. As the children become mature enough to discuss their differing abilities and the sense of competition they feel, open discussions of their feelings will help them deal with their sense of personal worth, despite obvious differences in talent, school grades, and academic recognition.

Some parents feel an altruistic commitment to "root for the underdog." Although culturally this may be very American, this attitude can put unpleasant pressure on all children. The younger high achiever, especially, will not receive recognition at home for his or her superior achievements. In some cases, he or she may exhibit symptoms of pressure but will continue to achieve, and the less talented older child may become even less motivated to achieve. In other cases, the younger child will underachieve because he or she can earn more parent attention by not achieving. The child thus may learn to unconsciously use the nonachieving behavior to manipulate and control the parents' attention.

Regardless of differences in sibling ability, it is usually better to acknowledge achievements and to reward them, relative to each child's capabilities. Democratically pretending that differences do not exist, withholding important opportunities from the gifted child, or accepting less than the best efforts from less capable children are common but unproductive responses of parents of gifted and talented children.

Children within a family have different abilities and different needs, and the most productive (and most fair) approach is to accommodate those differences. Treating siblings the same actually exacerbates competition as children vie for recognition of their own individuality.

## Family Problems

Colangelo and Dettmann (1983) emphasized that it would be a misinterpretation of the research to assume that families of gifted children have greater problems than others. However, Goertzel and Goertzel (1962), in their study of 400 eminent men and women (many more men than women), found troubled homes, especially among many of the actors, authoritarian politicians, novelists, playwrights, composers, and musicians. The types of problems found included rejecting or dominating parents, broken homes, death of one or both parents, anxiety about money, and parental dissatisfaction with the children's school programs or choice of profession.

Families of gifted underachievers (Rimm & Lowe, 1988) were also found to be different from those of most types of achievers. Although early child-centeredness and liberal parenting encouraged independence and often too much power, later parenting became inconsistent. Family organization was much less predictable. Parents appeared to be on "overload," and there were great differences in parenting styles between mothers and fathers. One parent became the "mean" parent, while the other parent took the role of "protector." Expectations and organization were not clear. Husbands and wives often opposed each other in their parenting roles. In some cases, one sibling allied himself or herself with the mother while the other sibling formed an alliance with the father. In other cases, all the children in the family united with one parent against the other. In an effort to be reasonable and flexible, parents were often viewed by children as inconsistent, weak, and easy to manipulate. Rimm (1986) referred to these cross-generational, oppositional alliances as "ogre and dummy" games, and verified by case studies their path to underachievement problems.

## FAMILY AND PEER ISSUES

Gifted youth, like all adolescents, may have a difficult time during the "identity crisis" period (Erikson, 1968). Close family relationships and good parent models will help to diffuse some of the ambiguity, but the necessary task of establishing an identity separate from family often reduces parental influence during this period and strengthens peer influence. This adolescent period may be especially difficult for gifted youth, who may struggle with an independence–conformity conflict.

Although positive relationships with parents typically are not harmful to peer relationships (Montemayer, 1984), reliance on peers for advice and acceptance can have negative effects on closeness to parents (Kandel & Lesser, 1972). Hill (1980) suggested that continuous bickering with parents seems to propel adolescents to more dependence on and acceptance of peer norms, along with rejection of parent norms. Unfortunately, in many schools, the peer norm may be strongly antilearning. The gifted child who previously had taken pride in earning high grades now faces a difficult personal contradiction: whether to be true to his or her personal academic motivation or to underperform to fit in with peers. The greatest tragedy occurs when the gifted young person mentally drops out of school, literally accepting the peer mandate that "studying is not cool." Maintaining a positive family environment helps gifted children deal with the "antigifted" peer pressure they may feel during adolescence. The book *Gifted Kids Have Feelings Too* (Rimm, 1990a) and its discussion guide, *Exploring Feelings* (Rimm & Priest, 1990), describe, in story form, teenagers who are faced with conflicting peer and academic pressures. The book and guide help adolescents share and discuss solutions to these problems.

Coleman (1961) pointed out that uncomfortable peer pressures are reduced for scholarly adolescent boys if they can dissipate their brainy image with excellence in sports, and for girls if they have the good fortune to be pretty. Unfortunately, the pressure to be pretty may also emphasize the need to be thin, which, in part, explains the increasing numbers of eating disorders among high school and college females (Rimm, 1987). Another important qualification for peer acceptance is skill in playing down one's academic ability and excellence—for example, by not using a sophisticated vocabulary, not showing great enthusiasm for high achievement, not carrying too many books, and not mentioning one's large quantity of reading and studying or one's enjoyment of intellectual interests. One high school student described himself as a "closet" gifted student. He was not willing to risk the image of being gifted. Nevertheless, he continued to achieve as covertly as possible. His need to "cover up" his intelligence is a sad commentary on the adolescent value system.

A survey conducted by Brown and Steinberg (1990) of 8,000 high school students in California and Wisconsin confirmed the existence of peer pressure. It found that less than 10% of the high achievers were willing to be identified as part of the "brain" crowd, and students often withdrew from debate, computer clubs, and honors classes to avoid being labeled as "geeks" or "nerds." The percentage was lower for females than for males, higher for Asians (14%), and lower for African-Americans. Actually, none of the high-achieving African-Americans acknowledged willingness to be considered part of the brain crowd. Luftig and Nichols (1989) also found evidence that gifted boys hide or mask their giftedness by being funny and highly verbal. A sense of humor has actually been found to be helpful to adolescents who struggle with peer pressures.

In contrast, a later study by Luftig and Nichols (1990) of social acceptance of gifted and nongifted girls and boys found that gifted boys ranked as most popular, nongifted boys and nongifted girls as second most popular, and gifted girls as significantly least popular of the four groups. There are probably differences among varying school environments. Rachel Seligman (1990), who described experiences with her giftedness in *Gifted Child Today*, was temporarily coping with peer pressure at the beginning of the ninth grade and explained it in her own words:

> The most foolish thing I have done this year is to compromise my intelligence. You may ask why, and the answer is simple: Love. I was dating a sophomore who has also been identified as gifted. At the beginning of the relationship I let him do all the talking. It finally got to the point where I would say nothing even though I knew I was right or I knew I was comprehending something a lot better than he was. He grew so accustomed to my saying inane things that I continued to act silly around him. Once in a while I would pop out with something intelligent, but he'd just look at me as if I were crazy. Isn't it awful what love can do to a person? (p. 11)

Research by Steinberg, Dornbusch, and Brown (1992) found that peer groups actually had a mediating effect on achievement. When parenting was appropriate, peer influence could lower student achievement, and when parenting was inadequate, peer influence could improve it. The effects of peer pressure on achievement can be dramatic. Multiple studies that have compared peer pressures of moderately gifted students to students with extremely high IQs have found that popularity is a much greater problem for students with unusually high intelligence (Austin & Draper, 1981; Feldman, 1986; Freeman, 1979; Gallagher, 1958; Ross & Parker, 1980).

Families should be alerted to the pressures for gifted students demonstrated by this research. Brown and Steinberg (1990) asked a critical question: "Are we supporting a peer system that trains students to harbor diminished aspirations so that, as adults, gifted individuals continue to underachieve in order to be socially acceptable?" Surely, in schools, programming for gifted adolescents should incorporate the important effect of peer influence, and further research that explains family and peer interaction needs to be conducted.

## FAMILY AND SCHOOL ISSUES

Family advocacy and support for educational opportunities for gifted children are surely important to the adjustment of appropriate curriculum for gifted children. Because gifted children are a minority group, they may fall victim to a curriculum that is too shallow, too easy, or too slow unless particular teachers initiate programs. Furthermore, evidence (Gogel, McCumsey, & Hewett, 1985; Hanson, 1984) indicates that parents are able to identify their children's giftedness as early as the preschool level. In a national survey of 1,039 parents of gifted children, 70% of these children were identified accurately by parents by age 3.

Gina Ginsberg Riggs (1984), executive director of the 3,000-member Gifted Child Society of New Jersey, recommended that, if parents "want to earn partner status (in education), they should leave negative attitudes at home and concentrate on making their education partners (schools) look good at every opportunity" (p. 111). An important precaution about parent advocacy that supports Riggs's conclusions is based in the research on families and school relationships for underachieving gifted children. Parents were adversarial for 90% of the families (Rimm & Lowe, 1988) in this study. Negative and oppositional advocacy can backfire and can be viewed by children and adolescents as a message of disrespect and disdain for teachers and school and can encourage their taking "the easy way out." The research on eminence and achievement by Bloom (1985) found positive relationships between home and school, as did most of the literature on eminence and achievement.

The following three national support organizations for the gifted can direct parents and teachers to state and local groups. They are also a source of information and publications on giftedness and gifted education. School psychologists and counselors may wish to refer parents to these organizations for further information and support in parenting their gifted children.

Council for Exceptional Children—Talented and Gifted (CEC-TAG)
1920 Association Drive
Reston, VA 22091

Gifted Advocacy Information Network, Inc. (GAIN)
225 West Orchid Lane
Phoenix, AZ 85021

National Association for Gifted Children (NAGC)
4175 Lovell Road, Suite 140
Circle Pines, MN 55014

# THE SENSE OF SPECIALNESS

A subtle characteristic within the family relates to the "special" role of gifted children. The concept of specialness was discussed by Albert (1980) and Bloom (1985) in their analyses of eminence. In Albert's study of leaders in politics and science, which included 39 presidents and vice presidents, 48 prime ministers, and 39 Nobel Prize winners, he classified 90% of the political leaders and 74% of Nobel winners as "special children" either by birth position, death of a sibling, or death of a parent. Bloom (1985), in his studies of talent development, also described a "special" family position. Bloom's subjects described themselves as having arrived at a sense of specialness over time based on effort and accomplishment in their talent areas. The specialness was never an explicit pronouncement but was built on what Bloom called a "long-term commitment to learning."

The sample of underachieving gifted children described by Rimm and Lowe (1988) can also be viewed from a specialness perspective. Their specialness was either attached to the parents' early discovery of their gifted abilities or based on a long-awaited birth or unusual circumstance. Later, that specialness was withdrawn, and the special attribution was given to another family member. Sometimes the sense of specialness was lost as part of school adjustment. Rimm (1990b) referred to the withdrawal of specialness as a dethronement. In her clinical work, she found that these gifted children protect themselves by behavior problems, withdrawal, school phobia, and resulting underachievement. Families often change their formerly positive perceptions of these gifted children, and the problems are magnified while the characteristics of giftedness are diminished. Family therapeutic approaches can restore a positive sense of specialness, and academic acceleration, and even grade or subject skipping, have been found as useful adjuncts to restoring confidence while also providing more appropriate and challenging curriculum (Rimm & Lovance, 1992a, 1992b).

School support personnel are in an ideal position to evaluate needs for acceleration and to help parents and students prepare for it. However, they are often faced with so many prejudices against acceleration in the name of social adjustment that they may feel hesitant about advocating for grade or subject skipping. When communicating the gifted child's need for "earned specialness," it is easy for that to be interpreted by school authorities as elitism. Nevertheless, the opportunity for the gifted child to again feel unique by working harder on more challenging schoolwork often rebuilds the lost personal confidence, and when that sense of specialness is attached to achievement, it increases the probability that the child will adjust at school and within the family and, of course, will also make a contribution to society.

## CONCLUSION

A gifted child's family pattern impacts greatly upon his or her achievement and self-perception. The relationship between a gifted child and his or her parents influences how giftedness is handled within the family. This is manifested in the parental role of early enrichment for the gifted and also to the extent that parents share their perceptions of giftedness with the child.

The competitive nature of many gifted children sets a sometimes problematic tone for some sibling relationships. Normal sibling rivalry may be exacerbated by the presence of a gifted child, whether or not giftedness is present in the other children. Birth order and closeness in age also contribute to the manner in which a family deals with a combination of gifted and nongifted siblings, or even with multiple gifted siblings.

Peers also play a role in how the gifted child and the family interact, particularly in adolescence. Pressure to conform is heightened during the teen years, and some gifted teenagers may suppress their gifted tendencies so they do not appear to be different.

# REFERENCES

Albert, R. S. (1980). Family positions and the attainment of eminence: A study of special family positions and special family experiences. *Gifted Child Quarterly, 24*, 87–95.

Austin, A. B., & Draper, C. C. (1981). Peer relationships of the academically gifted: A review. *Gifted Child Quarterly, 25*, 129–133.

Ballering, L. D., & Koch, A. (1984). Family relations when a child is gifted. *Gifted Child Quarterly, 28*, 140–143.

Barbe, W. (1981). A study of the family background of the gifted. In W. Barbe & J. Renzulli (Eds.), *Psychology and education of the gifted* (3rd ed., pp. 302–309). New York: Irvington.

Baumrind, D. (1989). Rearing competent children. In W. Damon (Ed.), *Child development today and tomorrow* (pp. 349–378). San Francisco: Jossey-Bass.

Benbow, C. P., & Stanley, J. C. (1980). Sex differences in mathematical ability: Fact or artifact? *Science, 210*, 1262–1264.

Bloom, B. S. (Ed.). (1985). *Developing talent in young people*. New York: Ballantine Books.

Brown, B. B., & Steinberg, L. (1990). Academic achievement and social acceptance: Skirting the "brain–nerd" connection. *Education Digest, 55*, 55–60.

Colangelo, N., & Brower, P. (1987). Labeling gifted youngsters: Long-term impact on families. *Gifted Child Quarterly, 31*, 75–78.

Colangelo, N., & Dettmann, D. F. (1983). A review of research on parents and families of gifted children. *Exceptional Children, 50*, 20–27.

Coleman, J. S. (1961). *The adolescent society*. New York: Free Press.

Cornell, D. G. (1983). The impact of positive labeling on the family system. *American Journal of Orthopsychiatry, 53*, 322–355.

Cornell, D. G., & Grossberg, I. N. (1986). Siblings of children in gifted programs. *Journal for the Education of the Gifted, 9*(4), 253–264.

Cornell, D. G., & Grossberg, I. N. (1989). Parent use of the term "gifted": Correlates with family environment and child adjustment. *Journal for the Education of the Gifted, 12*(3), 218–230.

Davis, G. A., & Rimm, S. B. (1994). *Education of the gifted and talented* (3rd ed.). Needham Heights, MA: Allyn & Bacon.

Erikson, E. H. (1968). *Identity: Youth and crisis.* New York: Norton.

Feldman, D. H. (1986). Giftedness as a developmentalist sees it. In R. J. Sternberg & J. E. Davidson (Eds.), *Conceptions of giftedness.* Cambridge, England: Cambridge University Press.

Fisher, E. (1981). The effect of labeling on gifted children and their families. *Roeper Review, 3*(2), 49–51.

Freeman, J. (1979). *Gifted children.* Baltimore: University Park Press.

Gallagher, J. J. (1958). Peer acceptance of highly gifted children in elementary school. *Elementary School Journal,* 465–470.

Goertzel, V., & Goertzel, M. G. (1962). *Cradles of eminence.* Boston: Little Brown.

Gogel, E. M., McCumsey, J., & Hewett, G. (1985, November/December). What parents are saying. *Gifted Child Today,* pp. 7–9.

Grenier, M. E. (1985). Gifted children and other siblings. *Gifted Child Quarterly, 29,* 164–167.

Groth, N. (1975). Mothers of gifted. *Gifted Child Quarterly, 19,* 217–226.

Hanson, I. (1984). A comparison between parent identification of young bright children and subsequent testing. *Roeper Review, 7,* 44–45.

Hill, J. P. (1980). The family. In M. Johnson (Ed.), *Toward adolescence: The middle school years* (Seventy-ninth Yearbook of the National Society for the Study of Education). Chicago: University of Chicago Press.

Kandel, D. B., & Lasser, G. S. (1972). *Youth in two worlds.* San Francisco: Jossey-Bass.

Luftig, R. L., & Nichols, M. L. (1989). *Assessing the perceived loneliness and self-concept functioning of gifted students in self-contained and integrated settings.* Unpublished manuscript.

Luftig, R. L., & Nichols, M. L. (1990). Assessing the social status of gifted students by their age peers. *Gifted Child Quarterly, 34,* 111–115.

MacKinnon, D. (1965). Personality and the realization of creative potential. *American Psychologist, 20,* 273–281.

Montemayer, R. (1984). Changes in parent and peer relationships between childhood and adolescence: A research agenda for gifted adolescents. *Journal for the Education of the Gifted, 8,* 9–23.

Olszewski, P., Kulieke, M., & Buescher, T. (1987). The influence of the family environment on the development of talent: A literature review. *Journal for the Education of the Gifted, 2*(1), 6–28.

Pfouts, J. H. (1980). Birth order, age spacing, I.Q. differences and family relations. *Journal of Marriage and the Family, 42,* 517–521.

Riggs, G. G. (1984). Parent power: Wanted for organization. *Gifted Child Quarterly, 28,* 111–114.

Rimm, S. B. (1986). *Underachievement syndrome: Causes and cures.* Watertown, WI: Apple Publishing.

Rimm, S. B. (1987). Why do bright children underachieve? The pressures they feel. *Gifted Child Today, 10,* 30–36.

Rimm, S. B. (1990a). *Gifted kids have feelings too.* Watertown, WI: Apple Publishing.

Rimm, S. B. (1990b). A theory of relativity. *Gifted Child Today, 13,* 32–36.

Rimm, S. B., & Lovance, K. J. (1992a). How acceleration may prevent underachievement syndrome. *Gifted Child Today, 15,* 9–14.

Rimm, S. B., & Lovance, K. J. (1992b). The use of subject and grade skipping for the prevention and reversal of underachievement. *Gifted Child Quarterly, 36,* 100–105.

Rimm, S. B., & Lowe, B. (1988). Family environments of underachieving gifted students. *Gifted Child Quarterly, 32,* 353–359.

Rimm, S. B., & Priest, C. (1990). *Exploring feelings.* Watertown, WI: Apple Publishing.

Roe, A. (1953). *The making of a scientist.* New York: Dodd, Mead.

Ross, A., & Parker, H. (1980). Academic and social self-concepts of the academically gifted. *Exceptional Children, 47,* 6–10.

Seligman, R. (1990). A gifted ninth grader tells it like it is. *Gifted Child Today, 13,* 9–11.

Steinberg, L., Dornbusch, S. M., & Brown, B. B. (1992). Ethnic differences in adolescent achievement: An ecological perspective. *American Psychologist, 47,* 723–729.

VanTassel-Baska, J. (1983). Profiles of precocity. The 1982 midwest talent search finalists. *Gifted Child Quarterly, 27,* 139–144.

Walberg, H. J., Tsai, S.-L., Weinstein, T., Gabriel, C. L., Rasher, S. P., Rosecrans, T., Rovai, E., Ide, J., Trujillo, M., & Vukosavich, P. (1981). Childhood traits and environmental conditions of highly eminent adults. *Gifted Child Quarterly, 25,* 103–107.

Weisner, T. S., & Garnier, H. (1992). Nonconventional family lifestyles and school achievement: A 12-year longitudinal study. *American Educational Research Journal, 29,* 605–632.

# Chapter 15

# *Stress and the Gifted*

Judy L. Genshaft
Steven Greenbaum
Susan Borovsky

◆ ◆ ◆

JASON, A 7-YEAR-OLD, arrived home one day from school with tears in his eyes. "What's the matter?" his parents asked. "Today we learned that the ozone hole is getting bigger and could hurt all of us, so we have to stop using the refrigerator!" he responded.

Gifted children experience stress differently from their peers because of the uniqueness of their developmental growth. Both peers and adults often misunderstand the intensity of feeling that gifted children demonstrate. This intensity may be directed toward both global concepts and personal concerns (Maxwell, 1994). As the example above illustrates, the need of gifted children to make changes for a better tomorrow, as they see it, may alienate those around them. Additionally, gifted children's drive to succeed academically, often at all costs, casts them in a role that may conflict with the values of the peer group. Their need to create something unique, whether it is with their hands, voices, or instruments, may come at the expense of developing peer relations. Such factors can weigh heavily on gifted children and lead to intense and even debilitating stress.

As first defined by Hans Selye (1956), stress is "the nonspecific response of the body to any demand made upon it. An external stimulus that evokes a stress response is a stressor" (p. 84). Although current theorists generally base their work upon that of Selye, they allow individuals more cognitive roles in their reactions to the outside stressors. Lazarus (1981) regarded stress as having three distinct elements—social, psychological, and physiological—which function both interdependently and independently. The degree to which individuals integrate these three elements is a function of the stress they perceive.

Copeland (1987) identified several characteristics of stress, and some are particularly appropriate for the gifted. One characteristic involves how gender and related constitutional factors play a significant role as to how stress is handled. Also, because stress is cumulative and progressive, improved resources and coping patterns are necessary to reduce adverse effects. Stress may even be more debilitating in the gifted because the heightened intellectual capacity of the gifted may allow stress to become progressively worse faster. Stress appraisal and coping capabilities increase with age and cognitive development. The gifted advance in cognitive development at an unequal pace to their chronological development, thereby putting a possible strain on their ability to cope.

In the gifted child, these characteristics of stress are magnified because of the accelerated cognitive development present without the associated maturity to understand the constituent pieces that contribute to stress. Gifted children may experience stress without necessarily having learned the mechanisms to deal with it.

## CAUSES OF STRESS

Researchers are now beginning to examine stress to a greater degree and, in particular, are turning their attention to stress and gifted children. Kuczen (1987, p. 15) cited several contributing sources of stress, including social issues, shyness, opposite sex, competition, burnout from too many activities, self-concept, fair play, peer pressure, and self-criticism. Although these general sources may impact on all children, the gifted have these and others that are generated and/or complicated by their giftedness. Leaverton and Herzog (1979) maintained that the additional stressors with which gifted children must deal may lead to emotional and/or disciplinary problems. Some of these additional sources of stress are specific to gifted children (Clemens & Mullins, 1981).

The gifted are qualitatively different from the average child. The term *asynchronous* is often used when describing the gifted (Columbus Group, 1991). It implies a lack of moving or occurring at the same time, or growth that does not have identical periods or phases. This term refers to the different aspects of the gifted, in that their intellectual, physical, and emotional selves are not developing at the same rate as those of the average child their age.

As Maxwell noted in Chapter 2 of this book, gifted children can be many ages at the same time. The educational system expects children to progress at the same rate based solely upon their chronological age.

For example, all children are expected to attend kindergarten at 5 years of age. For the gifted, however, their interests and accomplishments can be age independent. This puts them out of step with their age-mates.

One source of stress for the gifted child comes from the knowledge of giftedness on the part of others (usually parents and teachers). This knowledge, if not handled properly, can be dangerous because of heightened expectations by those around the gifted child. There is a chance that the child may fall below those expectations, often because the expectations are either unrealistic or uninformed. Because a gifted child is often also a sensitive child, stress can result from failing to meet others' expectations, especially if these people are significant players in the child's life.

In a like manner, gifted children often impose perfectionistic goals upon themselves. Any inability to attain these goals—whether a drawing falls short of what they have held in their mind's eye or they achieve less than a perfect score on a routine spelling test—could lead to stress.

Another potential source of stress occurs when the gifted child reaches school. Any mismatch between the child's capabilities and intellectual and/or emotional needs will result in stress, particularly in the classroom. A repetitive and boring school experience can hold little or no challenge to the student, resulting in stress. A report from the U.S. Department of Education (1993) stated that the "most academically talented students have already mastered up to one-half of the required curriculum offered to them in elementary school" (p. 19). The gifted student may spend up to three-quarters of the day waiting for other students to complete work that he or she has already finished. For example, Jamie, 11, gets bored in her sixth-grade classes. She already knows what is being taught. "The book I'm reading now [in English class] I read in second grade," Jamie said. "I understood it all then" (Nelis, 1993).

Another potential source of stress for the gifted is poor peer relationships, which may result from an inability of gifted students to effectively communicate with peers at their level. Gifted students maintain high levels of intensity about causes that are important to them. This intensity is extremely difficult for the nongifted to comprehend and may alienate the gifted from a prospective peer group. A lack of appropriate social skills can also compound this, as many gifted students operate at an intellectually higher level than their peers. Sometimes the gifted will try to socialize with their intellectual peers, who may often be years older than they, but because of a mismatch in social skills the possibility of rejection looms large.

Blackburn and Erickson (1986) discussed several predictable crises and sources of stress for gifted students: developmental immaturity, underachievement, fear of success, multipotentiality or "overchoice," and nonsuccess.

*Developmental immaturity* is often found in very young boys and manifests itself when they do not have the physical or social attributes necessary to make teachers aware of their advanced intellectual abilities. The student's inability to sit still or wait to take one's turn can cloud a teacher's ability to assess the child properly. The child will sometimes be labeled as immature, suffering from attention deficit disorder, or hyperactive—all of which are frequently inaccurate diagnoses. There are also serious consequences if a misdiagnosis sticks with the child, hindering intellectual and emotional development.

*Underachievement* can become a factor when students are constantly compared with a set of test scores. If gifted students do not score well, they are often chided by parents and/or teachers for not maintaining consistent academic excellence. If they score poorly in achievement when their potential has clearly been determined, they are considered less capable than their potential shows. This label of underachievement can echo in a gifted child's ears and cause him or her to withdraw. Likewise, because most gifted children resent routine busywork, which they usually find boring and understimulating, they may complete their required assignments in a sloppy and careless manner or slow down their performance. In such circumstances, gifted students find themselves in a lose–lose situation.

*Fear of success* is generally considered a concern with girls. Gifted girls have been shown to withdraw from competition, especially with boys. By repressing their desire to excel, they also repress their intellectual potential (Horner, 1972).

*Multipotentiality* or over-choice is a problem with its root cause in the intellectual abilities many gifted students display. The vast choices gifted children perceive among areas of interest, career aspirations, and goals may overwhelm them so that they are unable to make and stick to their decisions.

*Nonsuccess*, to many gifted, is a new and potentially devastating experience. Academically gifted students rarely experience academic failure in their younger years. Therefore, they have little or no experience in coping with feelings of inadequacy. Because they often possess the skills needed to complete their schoolwork and rarely must study, they have not developed the study skills or work habits necessary for academic success. Thus, when faced with an academic challenge they cannot overcome, do not know, or have not been taught, they do not command the strategies necessary to compensate for such a challenge.

In a survey of gifted adolescents, Karnes and Oehler-Sinnett (1986) found that gifted students perceive as particularly stressful events related to achievement, social status, and career aspirations. Moreover, they find events related to academic achievement as most stressful, yet schools do not generally provide them with a stimulating, productive environment or support mechanisms responsive to their needs. In general, these students did not regard being labeled as gifted as stressful; however, they regarded as moderately stressful the pressures and expectations related to being gifted. Interestingly, they rated events that they anticipated but had not yet experienced (e.g., the death of a loved one) as major stressors.

Gifted children may experience stress from feeling out of step with their peers and environment. Because of their intelligence, gifted children are aware of societal problems at a very young age and experience stress at their inability to personally make changes that will solve the entire problem (e.g., fixing the ozone hole). The gifted child tends to hold moral and intellectual views that differ from those of peers or significant others, and these discrepancies most often lead to stress. Finally, there are the unrealistic expectations of others, such as parents and teachers, and their own high expectations, that the gifted children will always have the correct answer or do the correct thing. These are major sources of stress for many gifted students.

# MEASURING STRESS

To date, no consistently reliable measures of stress have been developed for "typical" children, let alone the gifted. Stress in gifted children has traditionally been measured by using information either from outside reports of parents and/or teachers or from standardized inventories. One of the first inventories developed for children was the *Adolescent Life Change Event Scale* (ALCES) (Yeaworth, York, Hussey, Ingle, & Goodwin, 1980). The *Life Events Scale for Adolescents* (LES-A) (Coddington, 1972) was developed by modifying an adult stress scale using input from parents and pediatricians. Sadly, although most gifted children report school problems as their primary stress producer, only one questionnaire, a 50-item survey (Dobson, 1980), is devoted to school stressors; however, this instrument lacks basic psychometric properties (Copeland, 1987). Thus, although many questionnaires and inventories have been developed to assess stress in gifted, none is complete.

# SIGNS OF STRESS

Each child exhibits stress uniquely. Moreover, reactions to stress vary, depending on whether the child is identified as gifted, is not identified but is gifted, or is not gifted.

A child's physical symptoms that have no apparent medical basis offer one primary way to note stress. In many cases, in fact, the child is not a hypochondriac, but his or her body prepares for a "fight-or-flight" reaction to stressful conditions, and the additional hormones pumping lead to bodily changes. Once the feeling of being out of control becomes too much for the child, he or she may manifest such physical symptoms as a faster heart beat, perspiration, and a flushed complexion, and he may complain of stomach, head, or back pains and even shortness of breath. As the child's physical symptoms develop, he or she will look for some way to be extricated from the stress-producing situation (Kuczen, 1987).

In addition to physical manifestations, many children exhibit a range of antisocial behavior in response to undue stress. Kuczen (1987) noted that such responses may appear as the following antisocial behaviors:

> acts of violence or vandalism; aggression or hostility; boasts of superiority; criminal activity; daredevil stunts; firestarting; impatience; negativism; rudeness; self-harm or self-abuse; stealing; testing or defying authority; use of bad language; unusual difficulty getting along with friends; unusual jealousy of close friends and siblings; vicious acts against animals or other people; clinging dependency; dislike of school; downgrading of self; escapism; excessive daydreaming; excessive sleeping; regressive behavior; lying; overeating; procrastination; solitary behavior; rigid conformity to rules and regulations; scapegoating; sexual behavior; shyness; smoking; use of alcohol; use of drugs; withdrawal from school or social activities. (pp. 337–338)

In addition to the ways normal children manifest stress, gifted children may exhibit other reactions. Burdensome stress (Webb, Meckstroth, & Tolan, 1982) occurs when gifted children become overly concerned with problems beyond the realm of their influence. "They are keenly aware of problems at a young age, yet may feel overwhelmed by a sense of helplessness since they are also sensitively aware that they are 'just children'" (p. 109).

Because gifted children tend to seek perfection, especially in their schoolwork, they tend to be overly critical of themselves. As such, they maintain unrealistic self-expectations, and they often suffer from feelings of inadequacy. According to Webb et al. (1982), gifted children engage in negative "self-talk" (p. 111) from an early age, and this negativism creates more stress.

# STRESS MANAGEMENT FOR THE GIFTED

Although little has been written about specific ways to reduce stress in gifted children, it is essential that these children receive assistance. Unless the child is able to find positive ways to vent stress, "undue stress, lack of self-acceptance and feelings of anger, frustration and even rage toward the world may result" (Webb et al., 1982, p. 113).

Webb et al. (1982) discussed specific and useful approaches to dealing with stress management and the gifted child. These approaches are helpful to parents and support personnel.

1. Talk with the child about his or her problems. The child needs to discuss, not debate, the sources of stress. By rewording the gifted child's concerns, it is possible to illuminate the demands with which the student may be wrestling. Whether or not these demands are rational, getting the problems out into the open can be very helpful to both the child and the adult.

2. Teach the child tools for making decisions. These can be invaluable in eliminating or at least alleviating stress. Such problem-solving techniques include "(a) defining the situation and the priorities, (b) defining the problem in terms of what needs to be done, (c) listing all of the possible solutions to the problem, (d) gathering information about the possible solutions, (e) evaluating the feasibility of those possibilities, and (f) making the decision" (p. 116).

3. Help the child reward himself or herself both for attempts at success and for achieving success. In the words of the old sports axiom, "It is not whether you win or lose, but how you play the game." The gifted child should learn that winning is not everything.

4. Teach the child that blaming others is not helpful for reducing stress. The child must also learn to take responsibility for his or her own actions.

5. Teach the child that a problem situation often can work for, rather than against, him or her. The adage that every problem is an opportunity can hold true for the gifted.

6. Help the child develop compartmentalized thinking. The child needs to understand that a stressful situation in one part of his or her life does not necessarily have to impact upon the rest of life.

7. Instruct the child in use of immediate calming techniques; these can be helpful in reducing stress reactions. Such techniques as deep breathing can be immensely helpful in diffusing a potentially stressful situation.

8. Show the child that tense situations can be handled with humor.

9. Show the child that he or she can control tense situations by expressing appreciation and understanding of others who are upset or critical of the child.

10. Help the child cope with stressful situations through "active ignoring." This technique enables the child to focus energies apart from a stressor and enables him or her to be able to deal with this situation in his or her own terms. For example, a classmate who constantly acts out may upset a gifted child who sits nearby. By intellectually removing himself or herself from the situation, the gifted child may well benefit.

11. Teach the child to question "whose problem is it?" A gifted child sometimes assumes responsibility needlessly, and must learn that he or she does not have to shoulder the entire burden. Often a stressful situation is the result of someone else's doing, so the gifted child must learn that others must take responsibility for their actions.

Webb et al. (1982) emphasized that the approach used with gifted students must focus on each child's priorities and values. The authors placed the burden of stress management upon the gifted child in accordance with the techniques the child has been taught and the child's level of sophistication. The duty of the helping professional is to equip the gifted child with the tools necessary to maintain a healthy grasp of how to handle stress. In addition, the helping professional must be regularly available to help the gifted child work through particularly stressful situations and events.

Gifted students themselves can learn to manage stressful situations; many have found relaxation techniques beneficial. Such techniques, when applied correctly, can lead to released muscle tension and quieter behavior (Genshaft & Broyles, 1991). To benefit from such techniques, the child needs to recognize the physical signs of stress, assume a comfortable position, systematically relax body parts while breathing deeply, and then remain calm and quiet for a short time. Learning how to use relaxation techniques in stressful situations helps gifted children to gain control of themselves in such circumstances.

# THE HELPING PROFESSIONAL
# AND THE GIFTED

In reviewing educators' responses to the needs of gifted students, De-lisle (1983) stated that educators must know how to stimulate gifted students so that they will want to learn. Support personnel also figure prominently in the needs of the gifted student, and they must have a variety of methods to draw upon while working with such students. It is especially important that gifted students should be able to look to teachers, school psychologists, counselors, and other educational personnel for assistance in making choices about their career paths.

Among other duties, the helping professionals should make the school system, as well as the parents of the gifted child, aware of academic or curricular choices that could alleviate stress on both the child and the school system. Such choices might take the form of academic placement in the manner of acceleration, special gifted classes, inter-age classes, or other alternatives. The education professional might also make available for certain gifted children such alternatives as individualization and departmentalization to enable them to move from one grade placement to another for specific subjects. In short, the helping professional must be the advocate for proper academic and social placement for gifted children.

Zaffrann and Colangelo (1977) proposed that counseling for gifted students be structured around a developmental base. The professional, however, needs to be aware that the developmental level of each gifted child differs not only from every other gifted child, but also from all children. Therefore, gifted individualization becomes a necessity.

The need for individualization can, however, be seen in terms of developmental goals. Blackburn and Erickson (1986) enumerated 11 developmental goals for the gifted:

1. Healthy, realistic self-esteem based on a clear understanding of strengths and weaknesses.
2. A healthy sense of responsibility for development not contingent on fate or others' actions.
3. Internal motivation and evaluation through de-emphasis on competition with others and encouragement of personal goal setting and self-evaluation.
4. A concept of self as a continual process rather than as a finished product.
5. Understanding of gifted individuals' own needs and motivations as well as those of others, and the use of skills of identification and empathy to develop cooperative, rather than competitive, behavior.

6. A willingness to accept mistakes, resulting in pride in learning from errors and reduced fear of failure.

7. Use of brainstorming and problem-solving skills to enhance naturally divergent creative thinking.

8. Assertive behavior in communicating with others about differences and concerns without being aggressive and obnoxious.

9. Methods of using frustration and stress in creative ways to avoid burnout.

10. Ability to accept help as well as give it and to learn something from all people, regardless of their level of intelligence, talent, or skill.

11. A sense of humor about themselves and the events outside their control, allowing them not to take everything so seriously as to be debilitating and self-defeating. (p. 554)

Incorporation of these goals into a comprehensive stress management and reduction program should form the basis of any intervention that is prescribed for the gifted student.

The helping professional's responsibility to the gifted child is only half completed, however, when the professional focuses on the gifted child; the other half of the support personnel's responsibility is to work with the educator with whom the gifted child interacts daily. To address that responsibility, the professional must begin training of inservice staff to make teachers, principals, and other helping individuals aware of the diverse and special needs of the gifted student population.

One academic placement solution often advocated for the highly gifted adolescent is acceleration, which may, in itself, be stress producing. Gregory and Stevens-Long (1986) suggested that counselors and school psychologists, for example, spend time counseling the parents of students about to accelerate through school.

The stereotypical view of a gifted child who is accelerated through school to his or her intellectual benefit and social detriment is both dated and wrong. Although advanced placement can create problems, lack of intervention for gifted children can be just as damaging. Webb et al. (1982) contended that unidentified gifted children will likely exhibit increased signs of depression and stress as they progress through school without receiving any academic or social interventions. A laissez-faire attitude toward these children can be more harmful than accelerating them appropriately. "The misapprehension that a gifted child is socially or emotionally deviant, and the assumption that forcing the child to remain in the mainstream will somehow correct the problem is seldom justified" (Gregory & Stevens-Long, 1986, p. 154). It is often necessary to acknowledge the stress caused in both the parents and the students even when the placement is totally appropriate.

The professional population should be made aware of two issues: First, gifted students will not make it on their own because they are so bright. Second, they have needs as pressing, immediate, and unique as students of average ability.

# CONCLUSION

Although everyone experiences stress at certain times, the gifted child's stress differs from that of others in significant ways. Gifted students grow up with twin burdens: unequal development compared with their peers and living up to the expectations of their parents, schools, and themselves. When they enter school, they may be faced with a boring and repetitive curriculum. If or when there is gifted programming, it is seldom coordinated with the regular program, leaving the gifted with confusing tasks. In addition, when the gifted have difficulty communicating with other students, this leads to poor peer relations and a burdensome sense of having inappropriate social skills.

It is understandable, then, that gifted students' stress manifests itself in underachievement, fear of success, inability to choose wisely, evidence of and thoughts about nonsuccess, and lowering of achievement and accomplishments so that they do not appear gifted. The duty of educational professionals, whether they use a counseling curriculum as recommended by Buescher (1987; Buescher & Higham, 1989), group counseling based upon developmental goals, or other means, is to enable gifted students to come to terms with the unique stress they face each day. Helping the best and brightest is perhaps the most challenging and rewarding accomplishment of all.

# REFERENCES

Blackburn, A. C., & Erickson, D. B. (1986). Predictable crises of the gifted student. *Journal of Counseling and Development, 64*, 552–555.

Buescher, T. (1987). Counseling gifted adolescents: A curriculum model for students, parents, and professionals. *Gifted Child Quarterly, 31*, 90–94.

Buescher, T. M., & Higham, S. J. (1989). A developmental study of adjustment among gifted adolescents. In J. L. VanTassel-Baska & P. Olszewski-Kubilius (Eds.), *Patterns of influence on gifted learners* (pp. 102–124). New York: Teachers College Press.

Clemens, F. W., & Mullins, H. T. (1981). *Helping the gifted child cope with stress.* (ERIC Document Reproductions Service No. ED 212 126)

Coddington, R. D. (1972). The significance of life events as etiologic factors in the diseases of children. *Journal of Psychosomatic Research, 16,* 205–213.

Columbus Group. (1991, July). Unpublished transcript of the meeting of the Columbus Group, Columbus, OH.

Copeland, E. P. (1987). Children and stress. In A. Thomas & J. Grimes (Eds.), *Children's needs: Psychological perspectives* (pp. 586–594). Washington, DC: National Association of School Psychologists.

Delisle, J. R. (1983). Counseling the gifted: What we know, and how it can help. *Gifted Education International, 2,* 19–21.

Dobson, C. B. (1980). Sources of sixth form stress. *Journal of Adolescence, 3,* 65–75.

Genshaft, J., & Broyles, J. (1991). Stress management with the gifted adolescent. In M. Bireley & J. Genshaft (Eds.), *Understanding the gifted adolescent* (pp. 76–87). New York: Teachers College Press.

Gregory, E. H., & Stevens-Long, J. (1986). Coping skills among highly gifted adolescents. *Journal for the Education of the Gifted, 9,* 147–155.

Horner, M. S. (1972). Toward an understanding of achievement related conflicts in women. *Journal of Social Issues, 28,* 157–175.

Karnes, F. A., & Oehler-Sinnett, J. J. (1986). Life events as stressors with gifted adolescents. *Psychology in the Schools, 23,* 406–414.

Kuczen, B. (1987). *Childhood stress* (2nd ed.). New York: Delta.

Lazarus, R. S. (1981). The stress and coping paradigm. In C. Eisdorder, D. Cohen, A. Kleinman, & P. Maxim (Eds.), *Models for clinical psychopathology* (pp. 177–214). New York: Spectrum.

Leaverton, L., & Herzog, S. (1979). Adjustment of the gifted child. *Journal for the Education of the Gifted, 2,* 149–152.

Nelis, K. (1993, November 14). Program challenges children. *Times–Union,* Albany, NY, p. C-12.

Selye, H. (1956). *The stress of life.* New York: McGraw-Hill.

U.S. Department of Education, Office of Educational Research and Improvement. (1993). *National excellence: A case for developing America's talented.* Washington, DC: U.S. Government Printing Office.

Webb, J. T., Meckstroth, E. A., & Tolan, S. S. (1982). *Guiding the gifted child.* Columbus: Ohio Psychology Publishing.

Yeaworth, R., York, J., Hussey, M., Ingle, M., & Goodwin, A. (1980). The development of an adolescent life change event scale. *Adolescence, 15,* 91–97.

Zaffrann, R. T., & Colangelo, N. (1977). Counseling with gifted and talented students. *Gifted Child Quarterly, 21,* 305–319.

# Chapter 16

# Stress as a Function of Gender: Special Needs of Gifted Girls and Women

Constance L. Hollinger

◆  ◆  ◆

AS DESCRIBED IN CHAPTER 15, the gifted and talented may be more likely than their peers to experience stress due to a number of unique personality attributes. As a function of sex-role socialization and societal expectations, gifted girls and women may be even more vulnerable to the experience of stress and in greater need of support and intervention than their gifted male counterparts.

Understanding a gifted female's experience of stress requires an examination of (a) the potential stressors in her environment, (b) the ways in which her environment has contributed to her perception of and response to stress, and (c) the cognitive processes that mediate her experience of stress. Two particularly salient mediators are her perceptions of her own abilities or sense of competence and her perceptions of her ability to cope with the stressors in her environment. Such perceptions determine what she will actually perceive as stressful, as well as her confidence in her ability to cope with those stressors (Rosenbaum, 1990; Sternberg & Kolligian, 1990).

## THE ENVIRONMENT'S CONFLICTING MESSAGES TO GIFTED GIRLS

The issue central to understanding the stressors inherent in the gifted female's environment is summarized by Mulqueen's (1992) observation that

> One of the inherent contradictions facing American women today is the conflict between an innate motivation to be competent and the

existing pattern of sex-role socialization which relegates women's expression of competence to spheres devalued by society. Women face the "choice" of being perceived as either competent or feminine, since being competent and feminine is contradictory in contemporary American society. (p. 1)

The distinction between the concepts of "instrumentality" and "expressiveness" (Parsons & Bales, 1955) or between "agency" and "communion" (Bakan, 1966) provides the theoretical basis of differential sex-role socialization. Men are socialized to be instrumental or agentic in order to interface and compete successfully with the environment. Women, in contrast, are socialized to be expressive or communal in order to meet and attend to the needs of the family unit. To achieve these distinct adult roles, males are socialized to become independent, confident, logical, and competitive, whereas women are socialized to become gentle, kind, and sensitive to the feelings of others (see Hollinger, 1991, for further discussion of gender stereotypes and sex-role socialization). The societal messages inherent in the culture of the 1990s clearly indicate that the socialization of children continues to perpetuate the culture's messages along these same stereotypic lines (Unger & Crawford, 1992).

Constructs such as learned resourcefulness (Meichenbaum, 1977), hardiness (Orr & Westman, 1990), and self-efficacy (Bandura, 1977) provide profiles of personal attributes that signal not only physical and emotional health, but also preparedness for dealing with the perceived stressors in one's life. Unfortunately, the majority of such attributes (e.g., self-esteem, self-confidence, sense of competence and control) are those characteristic of male, not female, sex-role socialization.

Although many positive characteristics are associated with the feminine stereotype (e.g., cooperative, concerned about the feelings of others) (see Gilligan, 1982; Gilligan, Ward, & Taylor, 1988; Jordan, Kaplan, Miller, Stiver, & Surrey, 1991), expressive or communal attributes better predict experiencing stress than successfully managing it. As a function of sex-role socialization, women may experience low self-esteem, an externalized locus of control, and high state and trait anxiety. Similarly, women are socialized to disparage and underestimate their own abilities, which leads them to underestimate their true abilities (Eccles, 1983; Phillips & Zimmerman, 1990). Some of these personal characteristics have specifically been identified as significant predictors of stress and burnout among gifted populations (Fimian, 1988). Indeed, a composite of stereotypically feminine attributes is quite characteristic of Seligman's (1975) concept of learned helplessness, rather than self-efficacy (Bandura, 1977), hardiness (Orr & Westman, 1990), learned resourcefulness (Meichenbaum, 1977), or agency

(Hollinger, 1988), which are predictive of successful coping with life events and general life satisfaction.

In addition, sex-role socialization teaches women how they should be in relationship to others. For example, women should not outperform men, nor should they separate or "individuate," but rather grow and develop while remaining closely connected with others. Such emphasis on the importance of relationships and connectedness to others may lead to the belief that "I am obligated to you," a personal belief identified by Kuczen (1987) as contributing to stressful reactions. Socialized to "grow in connection," women frequently experience guilt and stress when they choose options in their own best interest rather than the interests of others (Jordan et al., 1991).

The most critical aspect of sex-role socialization for gifted women, however, is not what and how they are taught to be, but rather what they are taught not to be. In order to be "feminine," one must not be "masculine" (e.g., independent, confident, competent). This prohibition against the acquisition of the so-called masculine characteristics associated with successful stress management is more detrimental than the acquisition of stereotypic feminine attributes, per se.

For the gifted female, the conflict described by Mulqueen (1992) is exacerbated by the expectations that the significant others in her life have for her as a gifted individual. As a *gifted* child, she is expected to use her talents and abilities so as to do well in school, achieve, and strive to realize her full potential through educational accomplishments and career successes. As a *female* child, she is also expected to be feminine.

## Parents

The gifted girl will receive messages from many sectors of her environment that are either contradictory, as described above, or simply sex-role stereotypic. As products of the culture themselves, parents communicate different expectations to their gifted daughters than to their sons. From infancy, parents tend to help or assist daughters more than sons (Burns, Mitchell, & Obradovich, 1989; Snow, Jacklin, & Maccoby, 1983). Parents of high-ability daughters attribute good grades in math to their daughters' effort rather than their abilities, a pattern associated with a child's lower sense of confidence in her ability. As Eccles (1985) concluded, "although parents have a generally positive attitude toward their daughters' intellectual talents, they do not appear to be encouraging their daughters to develop these talents in occupational pursuits. And, in many cases they appear to underestimate their daughters' talents" (p. 283). Providing assistance, attributing success to effort rather than ability, and communicating lower expectations for achievement are but a few ways in which parents contribute to their daughters' lowered sense of self-confidence and competence.

## Educators

Teachers, school psychologists, and other professionals are no less immune to sex-role stereotyping than are parents. For example, extensive documentation exists regarding gender inequities in the classroom (Sadker, Sadker, & Klein, 1991; Streitmatter, 1994). The inequities in teacher–student interaction, classroom participation, and curricular materials all encourage and reinforce girls to be passive and "good," rather than active, inquisitive learners. Unfortunately, perceiving oneself as passive is incongruous with perceiving oneself as competent!

## Peers

In adolescence, peers become powerful socializing agents. Unfortunately for the achieving, gifted female adolescent, her male peers' views of sex-role appropriate behavior are quite traditional (Dolny, 1985; Fox, Brody, & Tobin, 1980). Views and opinions of her peers in general tend to be sex-role stereotyped (Frieze & Hanusa, 1984). Fear of peer disapproval for not conforming to gender-appropriate stereotypes can be quite stressful.

## THE PERSON: GIFTED AND FEMALE

According to White (1959), competence motivation is an innate human characteristic, regardless of gender. An individual strives to achieve competence through mastery of his or her environment. White's theory also recognizes the critical role of the environment and its response to the individual's efforts to establish a sense of competence. As a function of that response, an individual's efforts may be reinforced or extinguished.

The gifted girl, possessing motivation toward competence comparable to that of her male counterpart, nonetheless encounters, from the day of birth, an environment in which mastery, requiring agentic or instrumental attributes, is appropriate for men, not women. To the extent that she internalizes societal messages, the gifted girl may perceive and incorporate into her self-belief system only that information from the environment that is congruent with the feminine stereotype.

Conversely, feedback regarding her ability to cope with a crisis, her competence, or her leadership skills would not be "heard" because they simply do not fit with her internalized stereotype (Bem, 1981). Through this selective filtering process, the gifted girl herself may perpetuate the gender bias inherent in her environment. Evidence of her ability to cope with challenges, her mastery of her environment, and her talents and abilities simply are not perceived.

As a function of individual differences and/or differences in individual environments, some gifted girls will not assimilate sex-typed messages and expectations. They are open to and capable of incorporating feedback regarding coping capabilities, competencies, and other attributes stereotypically associated with masculinity. However, as they become aware of social realities, they recognize that they are different. The "differentness" of being gifted is exacerbated by their recognition that they are also different from the feminine stereotype.

In either instance, the gifted girl cannot meet both sets of societal expectations. If she processes feedback from her environment through a sex-typed cognitive schematic filter, she will perceive herself as an "imposter" (Clance & O'Toole, 1987). If she perceives herself as highly competent and capable of coping with the challenges of her environment, she will feel as though she is not feminine. The two options constitute a lose–lose situation.

# THE PERSON, THE ENVIRONMENT, AND THE EXPERIENCE OF STRESS

As is apparent from the above descriptions of both the environment and the consequences of environmental socialization, the gifted female may be at a significant disadvantage with respect to the likelihood that she (a) will perceive an external stimulus as stressful and (b) be less confident in her own abilities to cope with the perceived stressor. Discrepancies between one's self-perceptions and the perceived expectations of others, which play a central role in both achievement behavior and self-esteem (Moretti & Higgins, 1990; Wiley, 1979), is compounded for the gifted female. Even if she succeeds in achieving congruence between her self-perceptions of competence and her perception of others' expectations for competence, she will, by definition, fail to meet expectations for her to be feminine. Conversely, if she incorporates the feminine stereotype into her self-belief system, she will perceive herself as lacking the competence and the coping capabilities essential for managing stress. Put quite simply, the gifted girl "loses," whether or not she perceives herself as being able to deal with stress.

Young women have clearly indicated a desire to "have it all" (Fleming & Hollinger, 1979b; Smith & Ludec, 1992). Looking to the future, gifted young women express a desire to combine home, family, and career. Many, however, find few adult role models who have themselves succeeded in achieving it all. Instead, as Rubenstein (1992) noted, many of these young women may see their mothers, aunts, or other adult women in their lives struggling to define their own roles in contemporary society. The interaction of gifted girls with an environment in which adult roles for women are ambiguous may be stress producing in and of itself.

# COPING WITH STRESS

According to Frey (1991), gifted adolescents tend to cope with stress by seeking solitude, working to find a solution, and/or trying to relax. Consistent with Casserly's (1980) findings, Frey added that gifted female adolescents, unlike their male counterparts, also cope with stress by talking with friends. Indeed, through young adulthood, gifted young women cite talking with one's spouse or significant other as a primary strategy for coping with stress (Fleming & Hollinger, 1990).

Although many gifted girls and women employ such constructive strategies to cope successfully with stress, others do not. As Kate Noble (1987) observed,

> The result of struggling with cultural confusion about what is and is not appropriate for gifted women can be underachievement, underemployment, chronic dissatisfaction with one's life, depression, anxiety, illness, eating disorders, perfectionism, isolation and the exhaustion of the superwoman syndrome. (p. 373)

Whether gifted women choose to pursue competence, achieve the feminine ideal, or attempt to accomplish both, the stress inherent in conflicting role expectations may well exceed the coping capabilities of the individual. Among gifted female adolescents, particularly those in highly competitive situations, eating disorders are common, a finding that Steiner-Adair (1989) suggested may directly reflect conflicting role expectations. The emphasis here is not on the ability or inability to cope with the stressors inherent in role expectations, per se, but rather on the conflict resulting from contradictory role expectations. Hence, studies report higher suicide rates and chemical dependencies among women physicians and scientists than among the population of women in general (Noble, 1989), higher rates of depression among women who choose not to work outside the home (Unger & Crawford, 1992), and the burnout thought to be characteristic of the superwoman who strives to fulfill both sets of role expectations.

Although the potential stressors confronting the gifted woman should not be minimized, certain cautions are in order. First, studies finding statistically significant differences (e.g., between superwomen and women pursuing traditional roles) are more likely to be published than those reporting nonsignificant differences, which might contribute to a distortion of findings in the published research literature. Second, although significant differences may be found, the magnitude of those differences and the percentage of variance accounted for need to be considered. Finally, selected studies that "confirm" current sociopolitical trends may receive disproportionate media coverage (Faludi, 1991). To date, little is known about superwomen, full-time homemakers, and career women who do not manifest the symptoms of stress but instead experience complete satisfaction and fulfillment within the context of their individual lifestyle choices. For example, Project CHOICE participants, the majority of whom combine high-level careers with marriage, report high levels of life satisfaction while only a few report, in retrospect, a desire to have done anything differently with their lives (Fleming & Hollinger, 1990).

# HELPING THE GIFTED FEMALE COPE WITH STRESS

Although interventions have been implemented to help gifted young women cope with the stress of conflicting role expectations, such interventions do not address the crux of the problem. The dilemma of conflicting role expectations resides within the culture and the significant others who serve as agents for cultural transmission. The problem does not reside within the gifted girl who nonetheless is forced, with or without assistance, to cope with the stressors inherent in conflicting expectations. Therefore, ultimate resolution resides with altering the messages and expectations of significant others, rather than continuous intervention to enable the gifted female to cope with the status quo.

Before working with parents, teachers, significant others, and gifted girls themselves, school support personnel (e.g., school psychologists, counselors, school social workers) committed to intervening on behalf of gifted girls must critically examine their own beliefs for cultural biases regarding (a) the gifted, (b) women, and (c) gifted girls and women in particular. Transcending one's own cultural stereotypes and biases is a difficult and challenging prerequisite.

Common to all interventions is the need to break the stereotypic association of skills, abilities, talents, and attributes with the concept of gender. Gifted girls and young women experience a disproportionate amount of stress because their identities as women erroneously define the parameters of their abilities, talents, and attributes as being a function of their genetic "XX" inheritance. Gifted women and the significant others in their lives must recognize that competence, mastery, and other gender-stereotyped attributes are societally assigned to, not inherent in, one gender or the other.

## Working with Agents of Socialization

In working with parents, support personnel should begin as early as possible, given the pervasive nature of gender stereotypes. Parent groups need to examine not only the nature of their expectations for their daughters, but also the very subtle, and not so subtle, ways in which those expectations are communicated. If a daughter encounters a challenge, does the parent intervene rather than assist her in finding her own solution? Does her interest in a summer computer camp or a science fair project receive unconditional parental support? In general, is she encouraged to interact with and master her environment?

Support personnel must direct equal attention to classroom teachers and the classroom as other sources of powerful and conflicting messages. Staff development activities are essential for raising a basically subliminal experience into full conscious awareness. Videotapes such as *Breaking the Silence* produced by Sadker and Sadker (1989) highlight the inability of people to see what they have been socialized "not to see." Following sensitization to gender issues, support personnel can work with teachers in the examination of classroom practices that may inadvertently, though powerfully, convey the "gender-inequity" message to gifted girls. One of many helpful resources is Streitmatter's (1994) *Toward Gender Equity in Teaching*, which provides specific, concrete strategies adopted by teachers as they strive to implement their own individual definitions of equity and equality within the classroom.

A more ambitious consultation project would involve working with one or more teachers interested in moving from traditional instructional strategies to instruction more congruent with "women's ways of knowing." For example, cooperative learning (Slavin, 1983) and "connected teaching" (Belenky, Clinchy, Goldberger, & Tarule, 1986) are two approaches that emphasize collaboration and connectedness over competition. To the extent that she is a product of traditional sex-role socialization, the gifted girl or young woman will find the cooperative, noncompetitive learning environment more compatible with her own learning style. Still others would argue for single-sex classrooms, particularly for course work perceived as being in the male domain, such as math and the sciences (MacDonald, 1980). Such classrooms remove the stress of demonstrating one's "sex-role inappropriate" achievement before a jury of one's male peers.

Of less immediate but perhaps of greater ultimate consequence are interventions directed toward gifted boys and young men. Kerr's (1986) work is unique in its focus on lifework planning with gifted boys as an approach that concomitantly assists gifted girls. The boys' expectations, during adolescence and for adulthood, can create a dilemma for the gifted female if the boys expect her to deny her own competence. Regardless of intervention effectiveness in raising the aspirations, coping strategies, and so forth of gifted women, failure to educate gifted young men in the process will result in continued inequity, conflict, and stress. As McWilliams (1992) noted, a primary determinant of stress experienced by women working outside the home is the lack of active support from their spouses in the domestic sphere.

## Working with the Gifted Female

As cautioned earlier, to assume that a gifted girl is a victim of gender role socialization is to participate yet again in the process of stereotyping. Not all gifted girls and young women perceive stress in their environment, not even those potential stressors resulting from conflicting role expectations. Just as the much-publicized "stress and burnout" of working women is unjustified when the complete research literature is reviewed (see Faludi, 1991), assuming that all gifted girls and young women experience overwhelming stress in their lives may well be a perpetuation, however inadvertent, of sex-role stereotypes. Therefore, Fimian's (1989) scale or others used for identifying those vulnerable to the stressors of giftedness might be combined with Bem's (1974) *Sex Role Inventory* or Spence, Helmreich, and Stapp's (1974) *Personal Attributes Questionnaire*, both measures that assess the extent of sex-role stereotypic self-perceptions, to identify those gifted young women most likely to succumb to the pressures of conflicting role expectations.

As noted in Chapter 15, the gifted need individual attention in coping with stress. This is especially true for gifted girls. Special attention must be paid to modifications required by the fact that the goals and objectives of some stress intervention programs may directly conflict with the gifted girl's concept of femininity and sex-role appropriateness.

To the extent that gifted females experience stress as do other groups of children, in general, and their gifted male counterparts, in particular, generic stress reduction interventions will be helpful. School psychologists and counselors should consult work focused on specific relaxation techniques (Benson, 1975; Kuczen, 1987; Richter, 1984), Meichenbaum's (1985) *Stress Inoculation Training*, Strayhorn's (1988) model of intervention designed to foster the development of a sense of competence, and Bandura's (1990) recommendations for enhancing self-perceptions of efficacy.

Close examination of these general approaches, however, is necessary, because some components particularly salient for gifted girls and women require social change in the "structures of opportunity" (Astin, 1985) available to gifted girls. For example, Bandura emphasized the importance of mastery experiences—performance successes that promote a sense of personal efficacy. As long as gender inequity characterizes classrooms and girls are rewarded for passivity over active involvement in the learning process, the opportunities for gifted girls to experience such performance successes will be restricted. Likewise, the need for modeling of successes by "similar others" as well as social persuasion and encouragement of success (Bandura, 1990) highlights the importance of equitable gender representation in careers and socialization by significant others free of gender stereotypes.

Until gender equity becomes the social norm, interventions specifically designed to meet the unique needs of gifted girls are required. In general, such interventions focus on providing social support, examining sex-role stereotypes and societal inequities, and addressing directly those consequences of sex-role socialization that undermine the gifted girl's development of self-perceptions of ability and coping competence essential for successful stress management.

Peer support groups play a critical role for the gifted in general (Janos, 1990) and for gifted girls and women in particular who, as noted earlier, tend to "talk with friends" as a strategy for coping with stress (Casserly, 1980; Frey, 1991). Such groups provide the opportunity to (a) discover that others also experience the stressors of conflicting expectations, (b) learn coping strategies employed by others, and (c) receive and provide social support and encouragement.

Groups focused on self-exploration in general or on the development of specific skills, such as assertiveness or realistic self-perceptions of competence, have proven effective in undoing some, if not all, of the detrimental effects of sex-role socialization. Several group sessions of Project CHOICE (Fleming & Hollinger, 1979a) were designed to assist gifted female adolescents explore issues of sex-role socialization and develop improved self-esteem, assertiveness, achievement motivation, and comfort with success—all correlates or precursors of the sense of self-confidence and competence essential for coping successfully with stress. Longitudinal follow-up of participants reveals that they certainly still perceive stressors in their lives but that they have also developed strategies for coping with those stressors.

Rand and Gibb's (1989) Action Science was a model program designed to enhance gifted girls' self-confidence through the experiencing of success. Using female scientists as instructors, participants in girl-only classes were actively involved in conducting a variety of hands-on science activities. The project succeeded not only in improving the girls' level of confidence, but also in increasing their interest in and enthusiasm for careers in the sciences. Although the project focused specifically on enhancing self-confidence and interest in scientific pursuits, such building of confidence in self may well generalize to a confidence in coping with all stressors.

In contrast to the programs discussed above, Bell's (1989) program drew attention to the equally, if not more, important notion that "the problem does not reside within." In this project, gifted girls examined and learned to externalize sex-role stereotypic beliefs. Through discussion, gifted girls began to realize that many of the beliefs they had internalized were merely societal messages as to the residence of "the problem." Although women may be characterized as being "external" with respect to control, they are quite competent, but frequently inaccurate, in "internalizing" the locus of responsibility. Bell's program succeeded in reversing this stereotypic trend, a trend that exacerbates the experience of stress by perceiving oneself as having caused it.

Finally, for information on additional programs, professionals are encouraged to contact the Educational Design Corporation in Boston, publishers of many projects developed under the auspices of the Women's Educational Equity Act. In addition, the National Research Center on the Gifted and Talented, at the University of Connecticut, can provide not only the latest in research and programming, but also the names of consultant bank members specializing in gifted females. Both resources can provide critical assistance in a challenging and rewarding undertaking.

# CONCLUSION

In addition to the stressors typically associated with giftedness in general, gifted females confront conflicting cultural messages and expectations regarding competence and femininity. The "lose–lose" situation created by these conflicting messages is, in and of itself, stressful. To the extent that she has internalized cultural stereotypes through the process of gender socialization, the gifted female may be further disadvantaged by perceiving herself as less able to cope with this and other stressors in her environment. Although immediate intervention efforts to assist gifted young women are essential, the ultimate goal must be achieving a society in which being competent and feminine is no longer contradictory.

# REFERENCES

Astin, H. S. (1985). The meaning of work in women's lives: A sociopsychological model of career choice and work behavior. *Counseling Psychology, 12*(4), 117–126.

Bakan, D. (1966). *The duality of human existence*. Chicago: Rand McNally.

Bandura, A. (1977). Self-efficacy: Toward a unifying theory of behavior change. *Psychological Review, 84*, 191–215.

Bandura, A. (1990). Reflections on nonability determinants of competence. In R. J. Sternberg & J. Kolligian, Jr. (Eds.), *Competence considered* (pp. 315–362). New Haven, CT: Yale University Press.

Belenky, M. F., Clinchy, B., Goldberger, N. R., & Tarule, J. M. (1986). *Women's ways of knowing: The development of self voice and mind*. New York: Basic Books.

Bell, L. A. (1989). Something's wrong here and it's not me: Challenging the dilemmas that block girls' success. *Journal for the Education of the Gifted, 12*(2), 118–130.

Bem, S. L. (1974). The measurement of psychological androgyny. *Journal of Consulting and Clinical Psychology, 42*, 155–162.

Bem, S. L. (1981). Gender schema theory: A cognitive account of sex typing. *Psychological Review, 88*, 354–364.

Benson, H. (1975). *The relaxation response*. New York: Morrow.

Burns, A. L., Mitchell, G., & Obradovich, S. (1989). Of sex-roles and strollers: Female and male attention to toddlers at the zoo. *Sex Roles, 20*, 309–315.

Casserly, P. (1980). An assessment of factors affecting female participation in advanced placement programs in mathematics, chemistry, and physics. In L. H. Fox, L. Brody, & D. Tobin (Eds.), *Women and the mathematical mystique* (pp. 138–163). Baltimore: Johns Hopkins University Press.

Clance, P., & O'Toole, M. (1987). The imposter phenomenon: An internal barrier to empowerment and achievement. *Women & Therapy, 6*(3), 51–64.

Dolny, C. (1985). University of Toronto Schools' gifted students career and family plans. *Roeper Review, 7*(3), 160–162.

Eccles, J. (1983). Expectancies, values and academic behaviors. In J. T. Spence (Ed.), *Achievement and achievement motives* (pp. 75–146). San Francisco: W. H. Freeman.

Eccles, J. (1985). Why doesn't Jane run? Sex differences in educational and occupational patterns. In F. D. Horowitz & M. O'Brien (Eds.), *The gifted and talented: Developmental perspectives* (pp. 251–295). Washington, DC: American Psychological Association.

Faludi, S. (1991). *Backlash: The undeclared war against American women.* New York: Crown.

Fimian, M. J. (1988). Predictions of classroom stress and burnout experienced by gifted and talented students. *Psychology in the Schools, 25*(4), 392–405.

Fimian, M. J. (1989). The measure of classroom stress and burnout among gifted and talented students. *Psychology in the Schools, 26*(2), 139–153.

Fleming, E. S., & Hollinger, C. L. (1979a). *Project CHOICE: Creating her options in career exploration.* Boston: Educational Design Corporation.

Fleming, E. S., & Hollinger, C. L. (1979b). *Realizing the promise of female adolescents: A diagnostic–prescriptive model.* (ERIC Document Reproduction Service No. ED 179 902)

Fleming, E. S., & Hollinger, C. L. (1990, November). *Project CHOICE: Gifted young women ten years later.* Paper presented at the annual conference of the National Association for Gifted Children, Little Rock, AR.

Fox, L. H., Brody, L., & Tobin, D. (1980). *Women and the mathematical mystique.* Baltimore: Johns Hopkins University Press.

Frey, D. E. (1991). Psychosocial needs of the gifted adolescent. In M. Bireley & J. Genshaft (Eds.), *The gifted adolescent: Educational, developmental, and multicultural issues* (pp. 35–49). New York: Teachers College Press.

Frieze, I. H., & Hanusa, B. H. (1984). Women scientists: Overcoming barriers. In M. W. Steinkamp & M. L. Maehr (Eds.), *Women in science* (pp. 139–164). Greenwich, CT: JAI Press.

Gilligan, C. (1982). *In a different voice: Psychological theory and women's development.* Cambridge, MA: Harvard University Press.

Gilligan, C., Ward, J. V., & Taylor, J. M. (Eds.). (1988). *Mapping the moral domain.* Cambridge, MA: Harvard University Press.

Hollinger, C. L. (1988). Toward an understanding of career development among gifted and talented female adolescents. *Journal for the Education of the Gifted, 12*(1), 62–79.

Hollinger, C. L. (1991). Career choices for gifted adolescents: Overcoming stereotypes. In M. Bireley & J. Genshaft (Eds.), *The gifted adolescent: Educational, developmental, and multicultural issues* (pp. 201–214). New York: Teachers College Press.

Janos, P. M. (1990). The self-perceptions of uncommonly bright youngsters. In R. J. Sternberg & J. Kolligian, Jr. (Eds.), *Competence considered* (pp. 98–116). New Haven, CT: Yale University Press.

Jordan, J. V., Kaplan, A. G., Miller, J. B., Stiver, I. B., & Surrey, J. L. (1991). *Women's growth in connection: Writings from the Stone Center.* New York: Guilford.

Kerr, B. A. (1986). Career counseling for the gifted: Assessment and interventions. *Journal of Counseling and Development, 64*, 602–604.

Kuczen, B. (1987). *Childhood stress.* New York: Delta.

MacDonald, C. T. (1980). An experiment in mathematics education. In L. H. Fox, L. Brody, & D. Tobin (Eds.), *Women and the mathematical mystique* (pp. 115–137). Baltimore: Johns Hopkins University Press.

McWilliams, N. (1992). The worst of both worlds: Dilemmas of contemporary young women. In B. Wainrib (Ed.), *Gender issues across the life cycle* (pp. 27–36). New York: Springer.

Meichenbaum, D. (1977). *Cognitive-behavior modification: An integrative approach*. New York: Plenum Press.

Meichenbaum, D. (1985). *Stress inoculation training*. New York: Pergamon Press.

Moretti, M. M., & Higgins, E. T. (1990). The development of self-system vulnerabilities: Social and cognitive factors in developmental psychopathology. In R. J. Sternberg & J. Kolligian, Jr. (Eds.), *Competence considered* (pp. 286–314). New Haven, CT: Yale University Press.

Mulqueen, M. (1992). *On our own terms: Redefining competence and femininity*. Albany, NY: SUNY Press.

Noble, K. (1987). The dilemma of the gifted woman. *Psychology of Women Quarterly, 11*, 367–378.

Noble, K. (1989). Counseling gifted women: Becoming the heroes of our own stories. *Journal for the Education of the Gifted, 12*(2), 131–141.

Orr, E., & Westman, M. (1990). Does hardiness moderate stress, and how? A review. In M. Rosenbaum (Ed.), *Learned resourcefulness: On coping skills, self-control, and adaptive behavior* (pp. 64–94). New York: Springer.

Parsons, T., & Bales, R. F. (1955). *Family, socialization and interaction process*. Glencoe, IL: Free Press.

Phillips, D. A., & Zimmerman, M. (1990). The developmental course of perceived competence and incompetence among competent children. In R. J. Sternberg & J. Kolligian, Jr. (Eds.), *Competence considered* (pp. 41–66). New Haven, CT: Yale University Press.

Rand, D., & Gibb, L. H. (1989). A model program for gifted girls in science. *Journal for the Education of the Gifted, 12*(2), 142–155.

Richter, N. C. (1984). The efficacy of relaxation training with children. *Journal of Abnormal Child Psychology, 12*, 319–344.

Rosenbaum, M. (1990). From helplessness to resourcefulness. In M. Rosenbaum (Ed.), *Learned resourcefulness: On coping skills, self-control, and adaptive behavior* (pp. xxv–xxxv). New York: Springer.

Rubenstein, A. (1992). Clinical issues in the treatment of adolescent girls. In B. R. Weinrib (Ed.), *Gender issues across the life cycle* (pp. 17–21). New York: Springer.

Sadker, D., & Sadker, M. (Producers). (1989). *Breaking the silence* [videotape]. Silver Springs, MD: N.A.K. Production Associates.

Sadker, M., Sadker, D., & Klein, S. (1991). The issue of gender in elementary education. In G. Grant (Ed.), *Review of research in education* (vol. 17, pp. 269–334). Washington, DC: American Educational Research Association.

Seligman, M. E. P. (1975). *Helplessness: On depression, development, and death*. San Francisco: Freeman.

Slavin, R. E. (1983). *Cooperative learning*. New York: Longman.

Smith, N. J., & Ludec, S. K. (1992). *Women's work*. Calgary, Alberta: Detselig Enterprises.

Snow, M. E., Jacklin, C. N., & Maccoby, E. E. (1983). Sex-of-child differences in father–child interaction at one year of age. *Child Development, 54,* 227–232.

Spence, J. T., Helmreich, R. L., & Stapp, J. (1974). The Personal Attributes Questionnaire: A measure of sex-role stereotypes and masculinity–femininity. *Journal Supplement Abstract Service Catalog of Selected Documents in Psychology, 4,* 43, (Abstract No. 617).

Steiner-Adair, C. (1989). Developing the voices of the wise woman: College students and bulimia. *Journal of College Student Psychotherapy, 3,* 151–165.

Sternberg, R. J., & Kolligian, J. (1990). *Competence considered.* New Haven, CT: Yale University Press.

Strayhorn, J. M. (1988). *The competent child: An approach to psychotherapy and preventive mental health.* New York: Guilford.

Streitmatter, J. (1994). *Toward gender equity in teaching.* Albany, NY: SUNY Press.

Unger, R., & Crawford, M. (1992). *Women and gender: A feminist psychology.* New York: McGraw-Hill.

White, R. W. (1959). Motivation reconsidered: The concept of competence. *Psychological Review, 66*(5), 297–333.

Wiley, R. C. (1979). *The self concept: Theory and research on selected topics.* Lincoln: University of Nebraska Press.

# Chapter 17

# Serving the Needs of Gifted Children from a Multicultural Perspective

### Deborah L. Plummer

◆　　◆　　◆

AS THE NEXT MILLENNIUM APPROACHES, institutions across the United States are preparing to meet the challenges and demands of a more culturally diverse America. For example, attention to identification and education of ethnic/minority gifted children has increased at an unprecedented rate since the early 1990s. Responding to the inequities of participation by ethnic/minority children has been and remains a critical issue in gifted education (Frasier, 1992). Nevertheless, what educators actually know about the needs of minority gifted children and ways to address their needs is limited.

Shore, Cornell, Robinson, and Ward (1991) purported that the research base in the area of gifted minority/ethnic children is small and uneven. They cited as an example the larger number of empirical studies of blacks than of American Indians, as well as the tendency to report the successes of Asian and Jewish students. Many studies also fail to take into account within-group variability and often reduce educational achievement differences to simplistic cultural variables (Kitano, 1991). Still, these studies do increase awareness of the values contributed by culturally diverse populations.

Other researchers have examined the issue and lend their perspective to the speculation of causes that contribute to the disproportionately small numbers of minority children in gifted programs. What has emerged from this critical analysis are issues concerning identification practices, program applications, and evaluation procedures (Baldwin, 1985; Frasier, 1989, 1992; Maker & Schiever, 1989; Torrance, 1980). These issues are rooted in a provincial philosophical framework for understanding and educating gifted children in a multicultural society. Kitano (1991) asserted that cultural assimilation and cultural pluralism constitute two philosophical views affecting educational practices for culturally diverse students. She described an assimilationist as one who favors the ethnic/racial group's relinquishing its culture in order to be absorbed into the dominant culture. Pluralists support racial/ethnic groups retaining their culture, but doing so in a way that maintains and advances society as a whole. Although Kitano asserted that the multicultural perspective is a means to lend clarification to issues in educating underrepresented gifted learners, she failed to define what adhering to a multicultural perspective really means. Often, educators assume that multiculturalism is synonymous with pluralism or that embracing a multicultural perspective simply means recognizing and accepting cultural differences and practicing cultural-specific interventions in the schools. However, multiculturalism as a philosophical framework is far more complex than these assumptions.

A multicultural perspective is described as the viewing of self in relation to others and to social and cultural context (Ivey, Ivey, & Simek-Morgan, 1993). By definition, a multicultural perspective includes all groups, regardless of race, creed, gender, or socioeconomic status. It cuts across primary characteristics (race, age, gender) to secondary characteristics (religion, personality, emotional make-up). From a multicultural perspective, cultural differences are honored and valued as a necessary step for growth. Thus, this perspective differs from pluralism in that it does not require the minority culture to relinquish those characteristics that do not maintain society's status quo. Rather, it views society as being enhanced and enriched by these characteristics and, as a result, becoming a new and better society.

Multicultural training begins with one's own cultural awareness and acceptance of one's cultural identity. Once this is achieved, developing a multicultural perspective requires gaining a knowledge base about other cultures and using this knowledge to establish skills and interventions that embrace diversity and movement away from cultural encapsulation.

Applying this perspective to gifted education assumes that diversity is the framework (and not a special issue) from which one views the construct of giftedness and talent. It further assumes that one has a repertoire of culturally appropriate skills and operates by using a variety of culturally appropriate interventions in servicing the needs of all gifted and talented children. To date, application of this perspective to gifted education would mean a paradigm shift. Frasier (1990) listed adopting a multicultural perspective among many new initiatives in gifted education that appear to be moving the field toward new paradigms. Indeed, there has been continued concern over the years for improving services to culturally diverse gifted children, and many educators have challenged the field to go further than improving services

(Frasier, 1991b; Kitano, 1991; Tannenbaum, 1990). I believe that adoption of a multicultural perspective in gifted education would not only improve services to culturally diverse gifted children, but also would break through some of the limitations in servicing all gifted children.

School personnel are already expending much energy examining and solving the problem of servicing the needs of culturally diverse gifted students. These efforts are certainly commendable. However, a missing component that would serve as the foundation for this effort is a movement toward introspection by educators, school psychologists, and counselors to examine the institution's structures and attitudes toward multiculturalism and each individual's own development of a multicultural identity. This is the first of several steps in attempting to service the needs of multicultural gifted children.

Thus, this chapter aims first to address the issue of developing a multicultural identity as a necessary but not sufficient step in servicing the needs of multicultural gifted children. Second, it discusses the identification practices that are based on a multicultural perspective and that have been successful in promoting greater numbers of culturally diverse children in gifted programs. Third, it examines the characteristics of gifted programs that offer more opportunity for inclusion of minority children. Finally, it raises issues in establishing evaluation procedures from a multicultural perspective.

# DEVELOPING A MULTICULTURAL IDENTITY

The melting pot concept is the model of integration in American society and, therefore, in America's educational system. However, the concept has been challenged over the past decade. On both a societal and an educational level, Americans are more aware than ever that cultural differences do not easily melt. The assimilation practices of the past and present place considerable focus on the minority group to adapt, change, and in many cases shed its culture in order to matriculate through the system. The degree of assimilation is less for an individual depending on how closely his or her cultural make-up fits the dominant culture. For many culturally diverse children, this requirement of assimilation presents an overwhelming challenge as they struggle to develop a sense of self based on society, home, and school values. Often, these sources give them conflicting messages. Current knowledge about culturally diverse children and their developmental needs is limited. Eurocentric norms and guidelines have been traditionally used for measuring achievement of developmental tasks. More effort is generally spent on building the competence level of minority children to the dominant culture's standards than on building the cultural competence of the professionals who work with culturally diverse gifted children.

Professionals who serve culturally diverse gifted children must have an acceptable level of cultural competence. Cultural competence refers to possessing a knowledge base of the background of various cultures, including historical influences, demographics, family characteristics, educational issues, and cultural values that shape that particular culture. Cultural competence further implies that the professional has the skills necessary to apply this information in serving multicultural groups. Specifically, this means that those who serve culturally diverse gifted children incorporate factual knowledge of various cultures into their training and inservice programs and apply this information to the identification practices, program development, and evaluation procedures. Ideally, it calls for a paradigm shift from addressing the needs of gifted multicultural children as special needs to using a multicultural perspective as a universal approach to servicing the needs of the entire gifted child population. Realistically, this ideal may be years away, but the first steps toward this paradigm shift can already be achieved by professionals who are willing to establish a multicultural identity for themselves and by educational leaders who are willing to adopt diversity-affirming practices and incorporate these policies into their systems.

What, if any, are the benefits of establishing a multicultural identity? By achieving cultural competence, one's world view is expanded, allowing the professional to view the gifted child with a wider lens. Identification of potential strengths and possibilities for growth for the child become more apparent to the evaluator. Productivity and creativity for both the professional and the child are increased, and self-esteem is enhanced. These are clearly worthwhile benefits in an age when self-esteem is viewed as waning and commitment to excellence is often being challenged.

How does one establish a multicultural identity? For the professional working with gifted students, establishing a multicultural identity begins with heightening awareness of one's own culture and recognizing how one operates out of those cultural norms and values. This includes exploring one's own "isms," or destructive attitudes and beliefs, and examining stereotypes and biases about cultural differences. On an individual level, professionals can gain knowledge about other cultures by reading books and articles about the specific cultures and participating in multicultural activities. Reading *A Race Is a Nice Thing to Have: A Guide to Being a White Person or Understanding the White Persons in Your Life* by Janet E. Helms (1992) is a good start in this process. (This thought-provoking book can be obtained from Content Communications, P.O. Box 4763, Topeka, KS 66604.) On a group level, this goal is best addressed by diversity training or multicultural education workshops or inservices that are both experiential and didactic and use multicultural presenters as models. Professionals might begin by getting together for an informal discussion of Spike Lee's *Do the Right Thing* or John Singleton's *Boyz N the Hood*. Both of these films are rich with data on multicultural issues.

By first educating themselves, educators hopefully can understand their own and others' discriminatory behaviors, learn how to handle cultural clashes, and express differences in productive, healthy ways. The process is one of learning and practicing cross-cultural communication skills to become culturally competent and embrace a multicultural identity.

What would it mean for culturally diverse gifted children to have educators and professionals who are culturally competent and who embrace a multicultural identity? Kitano (1991) suggested that this perspective will cause educators of gifted children to reflect on and perhaps modify their values with regard to cultural diversity. Kitano contended that inherent to a multicultural perspective are diversity-affirming values and attitudes that can be applied to everyone. Thus, establishing such a perspective will not only improve the way culturally diverse gifted children are serviced, but also improve the way gifted children are served in general. Inevitably, educators who embrace a multicultural perspective will be able to identify more readily culturally diverse gifted children because of their ability to value a variety of culture-specific behaviors.

# IDENTIFICATION OF GIFTED CHILDREN FROM A MULTICULTURAL PERSPECTIVE

Culturally different gifted children have been identified among the underrepresented population in gifted programs. Richert (1987) reported figures from the U.S. Department of Education Office of Civil Rights estimating the underrepresentation of minority groups in gifted programs. Minority groups such as African-Americans, Latinos, and Native Americans are underrepresented by 30% to 70% in national gifted programs and overrepresented by 40% to 50% in special education programs. The difficulties inherent in the identification process are the most salient issue cited as a cause for this underrepresentation.

Underlying this issue of identification is the controversy around who exactly can be considered gifted or talented. Educators have been left a legacy by Terman and his associates of conceptualizing giftedness as an IQ score at least two standard deviations above average (Terman & Oden, 1925, 1947, 1959). Although the conceptualization of intelligence has broadened since Terman's time from a fixed score based on a single facet of intelligence to a multifaceted approach (e.g., Sternberg's "triarchic" or three-part concept of intelligence and Gardner's multiple intelligences [Craig, 1992]), educators still depend on intelligence and achievement scores for entry into many gifted programs (Frasier, 1992). Whitmore (1987) asserted that the general concept of giftedness undergirding this practice of measuring giftedness by test scores has been the belief that there is a reliable, direct tie between innate intellectual ability, ease of learning, and achievement in school—that is, "truly gifted" students excel academically in schools and on tests. This assumption is put into practice in the schools and largely goes unquestioned. Baldwin (1991) commented that the stumbling block of a test score to inclusion of minority gifted children in programs is largely the result of a federal, state, or city government requirement to allocate funds for programs based on certain scores on intelligence and achievement tests. This fact is an example of a discrepancy that Frasier (1991a) pointed out: Educators believe in the principle of using multiple criteria for entry into gifted programs yet rely, in practice, on a test as a sole measure of exceptional ability.

Relying on a test score for minority student eligibility for gifted programs raises the issue of acculturation. Minority students who are most acculturated are best identified through standardized test scores (Woliver & Woliver, 1991). If educators accept this assumption, then they must ask whether the tests are measuring these students' intelligence and giftedness or their degree of acculturation. In most cases, the tests are doing both.

The general consensus seems to be that culturally diverse children have much talent, creativity, and intelligence. Manifestations of these characteristics may be different and thus require not only different tools for measuring these strengths, but also different eyes from which to see them. Torrance (1977) compiled, from his personal experiences, readings, and research of culturally diverse children, an observational checklist for identifying strengths of gifted, culturally diverse children. This checklist is provided in Table 17.1.

Gay (1978) asserted that signs of giftedness may be reflected differently in black children to such an extent that special identification procedures should be employed to guarantee their inclusion in gifted programs in adequate proportions. She proposed a plan for identifying black gifted children which includes commitment from the administration for diversity-affirming policies and practices, nomination by teachers for candidates, setting up of a file for each candidate, discus-

**TABLE 17.1.  Observational Checklist for Identifying Strengths of Culturally Diverse Children**

1. Ability to express feeling and emotions.
2. Ability to improvise with commonplace materials and objects.
3. Articulateness in role playing, socio-drama, and storytelling.
4. Enjoyment of and ability in visual arts, such as drawing, painting, and sculpture.
5. Enjoyment of and ability in creative movement, dance, dramatics, etc.
6. Enjoyment of and ability in music and rhythm.
7. Use of expressive speech.
8. Fluency and flexibility in figural media.
9. Enjoyment of and skills in group or team activities.
10. Responsiveness to the concrete.
11. Responsiveness to the kinesthetic.
12. Expressive of gestures, body language, etc., and ability to interpret body language.
13. Humor.
14. Richness of imagery in informal language.
15. Originality of ideas in problem solving.
16. Problem centeredness or persistence in problem solving.
17. Emotional responsiveness.
18. Quickness of warmup.

From "Identifying and Capitalizing on the Strengths of Culturally Different Children" by E. P. Torrance, in *The Handbook of School Psychology* (pp. 481–500) by C. R. Reynolds and J. B. Gutkin, 1982, New York: Wiley. Copyright 1982 by John Wiley & Sons. Reprinted by permission.

sion with parents about the program and identification by parents of gifted behavior, individual conference and testing with each candidate, and performance on a group problem-solving task.

Ortiz and Gonzalez (1991) cited social and political factors as barriers to full participation of Hispanic students in gifted programs. They suggested that often school personnel are reluctant to try new approaches and methodologies for identification and resort to prescribed sets of identification methods in which they have been trained. These methods are often inappropriate for identifying Hispanic gifted students. Instead, the authors recommend a combination of informal and formal procedures for increasing Hispanic student participation in gifted programs, which include information provided by the teachers, performance on the *Wechsler Intelligence Scale for Children–Revised* (Wechsler, 1974) (or now presumably the *Wechsler Intelligence Scale for Children–Third Edition* [Wechsler, 1991]), achievement test records, and motivation and behavior factors as criteria.

Woliver and Woliver (1991) discussed the difficulty of assessing Asian-American and Pacific Islander gifted children. Often being set up as the "model minority," these students face racism and stereotypes that are difficult to combat. Identifying gifted Asian-American students must include issues of acculturation and home versus school values.

Native Americans are a visible ethnic minority group that has received little attention in the gifted literature. Their issues with identification in gifted programs are reflected in the fact that they are often an "invisible" or ignored population. Native American children are reported to do well in school until they are exposed to negative stereotypes about themselves as Indians (Red Horse, 1982). These negative views produce self-defeating behaviors that perpetuate the cycle of poverty and lack of opportunity. Thus, early identification practices are particularly crucial when working with Native American children. Tonemah (1987) stressed a multidimensional assessment for identifying gifted Native American children. Emphasis should be placed on the aesthetics, particularly such areas as creative writing, dance, music, and art.

As stated previously, a greater understanding of the specific racial/ethnic culture enables one to identify gifted and talented characteristics from a multicultural perspective. Because identification practices are directly linked to enrollment in gifted programs, identifying gifted children from a multicultural perspective should result in increased numbers among culturally diverse children. Frasier (1987) delineated identification principles that support a multicultural perspective. These "best practices" are listed in Table 17.2. Adherence to these principles does not limit the educator to specific interventions, but permits one to use a variety of practices that promote inclusion of minority children.

Identification practices that are based on a multicultural perspective and have been successful in promoting greater numbers of culturally diverse children in gifted programs include checklist and rating scales (Gay, 1978; Hillard, 1976; Torrance, 1977); the Baldwin (1984) matrix model; and culture-specific systems, such as the *System of Multicultural Pluralistic Assessment* (SOMPA) (Matthew, Golin, Moore, & Baker, 1992; Mercer, 1981; Mercer & Lewis, 1978). Even some stan-

## TABLE 17.2. Best Identification Practices

1. The focus should be on the diversity within gifted populations. The gifted are not a homogeneous group nor do they express their talents in the same way.

2. The goal should be inclusion rather than exclusion of students.

3. Data should be gathered from multiple sources; a single criterion of giftedness should be avoided.

4. Both objective and subjective data should be collected.

5. Professionals and nonprofessionals who represent various areas of expertise and who are knowledgeable about behavioral indicators of giftedness should be involved.

6. Identification for giftedness should occur as early as possible, should consist of a series of steps, and should be continuous.

7. Special attention should be given to the different ways in which children from different cultures manifest behavioral indicators of giftedness.

8. Decision making should be delayed until *all* pertinent data on a student have been reviewed.

9. Data collection during the identification process should be used to help determine the curriculum.

From "The Identification of Gifted Black Students: Developing New Perspectives" by M. Frasier, 1987, *Journal for the Education of the Gifted 10*(3), pp. 155–180. Copyright 1987 by *Journal for the Education of the Gifted*. Reprinted by permission.

dardized instruments, such as the *Kaufman Assessment Battery for Children* (K-ABC) (Kaufman & Kaufman, 1983), the *Raven Advanced Progressive Matrices* (Raven, 1956, 1962), and the *Torrance Tests of Creative Thinking* (TTCT) (Torrance, 1977), report empirical support for their effective use with culturally diverse populations.

Nominations by teachers are widely used as a screening tool for identifying gifted children. This is clearly an excellent source, provided the teacher is culturally competent. When teachers lack this competence, culturally diverse children are at a great disadvantage in being selected. When engulfed in dominant culture, culturally diverse children often display low risk-taking behaviors. As a result, the spark that educators often look for and the risk-taking behaviors, particularly in responding to questions, often are not exhibited in culturally diverse children. Thus, these children are not easily identified as gifted. Likewise, when there is not a strong commitment on the school's part to embracing culturally affirming values, minority children remain underrepresented in gifted programs.

# THE MULTICULTURAL GIFTED PROGRAM

Few programs are geared to the needs of culturally diverse gifted children. Most lack the human and material resources to develop the interests and strengths of such children. Often, gifted programs promote skills and attitudes that increase minority children's success in mainstream culture, but often at the detriment of their cultural identification. Torrance (1980) stated that it is important to attend to those kinds of excellences that are encouraged and valued by that particular culture. Ideally, a gifted program should have those components that embrace multicultural values.

Most educators and parents would agree that the needs of culturally diverse gifted children should be equally served in gifted programs. In principle, espousing multicultural values on paper is generally acceptable to most everyone. In practice, providing equal service and adhering to multicultural values become controversial.

VanTassel-Baska (1989) reported from a national survey that, although there is philosophical support of racial and ethnic diversity in gifted programs, this support does not translate into policies and procedures. This discrepancy is often explained from the perspective of "equality of treatment." Following an assimilationist philosophy, equality of treatment is most often translated as "same treatment." Unfortunately, same treatment for culturally diverse children can mean unfair treatment. Treatment is assessed, diagnosed, and planned from the behaviors and values of the dominant culture. Therefore, that treatment may have little or no relevance for the needs of culturally diverse gifted children.

Again in this regard, the issue of acculturation and its relationship to success is relevant. The closer the child's cultural group is to the dominant culture in behaviors and values, the better the child's needs are served in gifted programs. For a large number of children who are culturally embedded, their gifts and talents go largely ignored or missed. Even when identified as gifted or talented, they often cannot compete in gifted programs designed to meet the needs of majority children. Their failure is then evaluated from each child's inadequacies rather than the program's limitations.

Educators and parents are also concerned that adapting programs to meet the needs of culturally diverse children in some way "waters down" the program. These advocates believe that a program suffers if all children do not meet clearly defined criteria for programs and these programs are not rigorous. To change this belief, school personnel and parents must reframe their view of the programs as being "watered down," and instead think of the changes as creating new and different programs. "Different" is not necessarily better or worse; it is often merely different.

The challenge for educators is to develop programs that not only respect racial and cultural differences, but infuse diverse cultural values into the curriculum. Maker and Schiever (1989) summarized in their edited book recommendations for programs both within and across cultural groups. The following paragraph summarizes these findings.

For gifted American Indians, inclusion of opportunities for developing excellence in visual arts, singing, dancing, and chanting is recommended (Tonemah, 1985). Sharing program activities with the tribal community is further recommended (George, 1989). Asian-American student programs should move beyond mathematics and science to also developing and strengthening their writing, artistic, and musical abilities (Hasegawa, 1989; Wong & Wong, 1989). Bilingualism should be an added component for Hispanic students (Udall, 1989). For gifted American Indian, Asian, and Hispanic students, cooperative learning situations are recommended (Garrison, 1989; Kitano, 1989; Tanaka, 1989; Wong & Wong, 1989).

For gifted African-American students, a major area of development is self-esteem. Steele (1992) wrote that lack of treatment as a valued person is the root of the depression of black achievement. Students display "academic demotivation" and think less of their abilities. Their identity as authentic African-Americans is held hostage and made incompatible with school identification. Until gifted programs include African-American history and culture in their programs (outside of Black History Month), this academic demotivation will remain.

As an underrepresented population in gifted programs, culturally diverse gifted children are also underserved. The link between underrepresented and underserved is strong. The first step is to strengthen the capacity of educators, school psychologists, and counselors to more readily identify minority gifted children. Once these students are identified and enrolled in gifted programs in significant numbers, program models no doubt will change to meet their diverse needs.

# MULTICULTURAL ISSUES IN EVALUATING EFFECTIVENESS OF GIFTED PROGRAMS

Evaluating the effectiveness of gifted education is a healthy trend. However, educators must avoid conducting evaluations that ask the wrong questions, oversimplify results, or are too tightly constrained in specific information (Southern, 1992). Avoiding these pitfalls is imperative.

Valuing diversity is primarily an inner process requiring a continuous, lifelong commitment. If cultural differences are not honored by the evaluator, the results of the evaluation will always be poor or deficient because it is very easy to ask the wrong questions, simplify results, and view the program and its participants from a tightly constrained lens. For example, parents of culturally diverse gifted children are often criticized for their lack of involvement with their children's projects. Interviews with local school psychologists (S. Herd, personal communication, February 12, 1993) reveal that in many minority families each generation becomes better educated than the previous one and, therefore, no one is there to help instruct the children when the children are "stepping out in the field." As a result, these children often feel alone. There may be no one or very few like them in their programs, and their parents, although proud of their children's achievements, may not be actively involved in ways similar to majority children's parents. Culturally diverse gifted children may need different assistance with projects than do their dominant culture classmates. This does not mean that they are any less capable or lacking in ability, or that their parents are less interested in their children's achievements.

Meeting the psychological needs of culturally diverse gifted children is particularly challenging. Most of these children carry with them racial vulnerability. Steele (1992) commented that blacks, like everyone, risk devaluation for a particular incompetence. However, blacks and other visible racial minority groups further risk that their incompetence confirms broader racial inferiority stereotypes by dominant culture. There is really no way to adequately measure the effects of decades of infusing particular racial groups with negative messages that they are inferior and do not measure up. When an African-American, Latino, or Native American child sits down to complete an IQ test, he or she is particularly vulnerable to the effects of negative racial stereotypes.

Creating an evaluation design from a multicultural perspective is an additional challenge. The "goodness of fit" among the educator, the child, and the program is complex. In creating an evaluation design, Southern (1992) considered summary judgment the most dangerous of pitfalls for evaluating program effectiveness. Summary judgment means that rather than evaluating for refinement, improvement, and change, school personnel evaluate for judgment and value. This kind of evaluation design is dangerous because it is very easy for educators to misjudge what they do not know and to devalue what is different. The variations in behavioral indicators of giftedness among and within cultures must be included in effective evaluation schemes.

# CONCLUSION

Often, when people refer to multiculturalism, they understand it to mean addressing the needs of those groups found in fewer numbers than the majority culture. In America, multiculturalism is often a "side issue" that is not examined unless there are people of color involved. American culture presumes by its melting pot image that multicultural values are inherent in its practice. In reality, the values of America are primarily of white European origin. In truth, all people possess a culture and are diverse in a variety of ways. Opening our minds and hearts to the magnitude of cultural diversity is the task for America in the 21st century.

Similarly, developing the talents of and educating gifted children is not a luxury but a necessity in a postindustrial society that demands a highly educated population. The talent pool is vast. Culturally diverse gifted children are found in that pool in increasing numbers. Accepting the challenge of serving their needs provides a wonderful opportunity for personal and professional growth for educators, school psychologists, and school counselors, and an opportunity for the betterment of programs serving *all* gifted children.

# REFERENCES

Baldwin, A. Y. (1984). *The Baldwin Identification Matrix 2 for the identification of the gifted and talented: A handbook for its use.* New York: Trillium Press.

Baldwin, A. Y. (1985). Programs for the gifted and talented: Issues concerning minority populations. In F. D. Horowitz & M. O'Brien (Eds.), *The gifted and talented: Developmental perspectives.* Washington, DC: American Psychological Association.

Baldwin, A. Y. (1991). Gifted black adolescents: Beyond racism to pride. In M. Bireley & J. Genshaft (Eds.), *Understanding the gifted adolescent* (pp. 231–239). New York: Teachers College Press.

Craig, G. J. (1992). *Human development.* Englewood Cliffs, NJ: Prentice-Hall.

Frasier, M. (1987). The identification of gifted black students: Developing new perspectives. *Journal for the Education of the Gifted, 10,* 155–180.

Frasier, M. M. (1989). The identification of gifted black students: Developing new perspectives. In C. J. Maker & S. W. Schiever (Eds.), *Critical issues in gifted education: Defensible programs for cultural and ethnic minorities.* Austin, TX: PRO-ED.

Frasier, M. (1990). Identifying the typical and atypical gifted: A paradigm for the 21st century. In *Education of the gifted in the 21st century. Applying new ideas and innovative approaches to gifted education* (pp. 41–46). Santa Barbara, CA: The Townes Foundation

Frasier, M. (1991a). Disadvantaged and culturally diverse gifted students. *Journal for the Education of the Gifted, 14*, 234–245.

Frasier, M. (1991b). Response to Kitano: The sharing of giftedness between culturally diverse and non-diverse gifted students. *Journal for the Education of the Gifted, 15*, 20–30.

Frasier, M. (1992). Ethnic/minority children: Reflections and directions. *Challenges in gifted education* (pp. 41–48). Columbus, OH: Department of Education.

Garrison, L. (1989). Programming for the gifted American Indian student. In C. J. Maker & S. W. Schiever (Eds.), *Critical issues in gifted education: Defensible programs for cultural and ethnic minorities*. Austin, TX: PRO-ED.

Gay, J. E. (1978). A proposed plan for identifying black gifted children. *Gifted Child Quarterly, 22*, 353–360.

George, K. (1989). Imaging and defining giftedness. In C. J. Maker & S. W. Schiever (Eds.), *Critical issues in gifted education: Defensible programs for cultural and ethnic minorities*. Austin, TX: PRO-ED.

Hasegawa, C. (1989). The unmentioned minority. In C. J. Maker & S. W. Schiever (Eds.), *Critical issues in gifted education: Defensible programs for cultural and ethnic minorities*. Austin, TX: PRO-ED.

Helms, J. E. (1992). *A race is a nice thing to have: A guide to being a white person or understanding the white persons in your life*. Topeka, KS: Content Communications.

Hillard, A. (1976). *Alternatives to IQ testing: An approach to the identification of gifted "minority" children* (Final report). Sacramento: California State Department of Education, Sacramento Division of Special Education. (ERIC Document Reproduction Service No. ED 147 009)

Ivey, A. E., Ivey, M. B., & Simek-Morgan, L. (1993). *Counseling and psychotherapy: A multicultural perspective*. Needham Heights, MA: Allyn & Bacon.

Kaufman, A., & Kaufman, N. (1983). *Kaufman Assessment Battery for Children (K-ABC)*. Circle Pines, MN: American Guidance Service.

Kitano, M. K. (1989). Critique of "Identification of gifted Asian-American students." In C. J. Maker & S. W. Schiever (Eds.) *Critical issues in gifted education: Defensible programs for cultural and ethnic minorities*. Austin, TX: PRO-ED.

Kitano, M. K. (1991). A multicultural educational perspective on serving the culturally diverse gifted. *Journal for the Education of the Gifted, 15*, 4–19.

Lee, S. (1989). *Do the right thing* [film]. Universal City, CA: Universal City Studios.

Maker, C. J., & Schiever, S. W. (Eds.). (1989). *Critical issues in gifted education: Defensible programs for cultural and ethnic minorities*. Austin, TX: PRO-ED.

Matthew, J. L., Golin, A. K., Moore, M. W., & Baker, C. (1992). Use of SOMPA in identification of gifted African-American children. *Journal for the Education of the Gifted, 15*, 344–356.

Mercer, J. (1981). The System of Multicultural Pluralistic Assessment: SOMPA. In *Balancing the scale for the disadvantaged gifted* (pp. 29–57). National/State Leadership Training Institute on the Gifted and the Talented. Ventura, CA: Office of the Ventura County Superintendent.

Mercer, J., & Lewis, J. (1978). Using the System of Multicultural Pluralistic Assessment (SOMPA) to identify the gifted minority child. In A. Y. Baldwin, G. H. Gear, & L. J. Lucito (Eds.), *Educational planning for the gifted* (pp. 7–14). Reston, VA: Council for Exceptional Children.

Ortiz, V., & Gonzalez, A. (1991). Gifted Hispanic Adolescents. In M. Bireley & J. Genshaft (Eds.), *Understanding the gifted adolescent* (pp. 240–247). New York: Teachers College Press.

Raven, J. (1956). *Progressive Matrices*. London: H. K. Lewis.

Raven, J. (1962). *Advanced Progressive Matrices*. London: H. K. Lewis.

Red Horse, Y. (1982). A cultural network model: Perspectives for adolescent services and paraprofessional training. In S. M. Manson (Ed.), *New directions in prevention among American Indian and Alaska native communities* (pp. 173–184). Portland: Oregon Health Sciences University.

Richert, E. (1987). Rampant problems and promising practices in the identification of disadvantaged gifted students. *Gifted Child Quarterly*, *31*(4), 149–154.

Shore, B. M., Cornell, D. G., Robinson, A., & Ward, U. S. (1991). *Recommended practices in gifted education: A critical analysis.* New York: Teachers College Press.

Singleton, J. (1991). *Boyz N the Hood* [film]. Burbank, CA: Columbia Pictures.

Southern, W. T. (1992). Lead us not into temptation: Issues in evaluating the effectiveness of gifted programs. *Challenges in gifted education* (pp. 103–108). Columbus: Ohio Department of Education.

Steele, C. M. (1992, April). Race and the schooling of black Americans. *The Atlantic Monthly*, pp. 68–78.

Tanaka, K. (1989). A response to "Are we meeting the needs of gifted Asian-Americans?" In C. J. Maker & S. W. Schiever (Eds.), *Critical issues in gifted education: Defensible programs for cultural and ethnic minorities.* Austin, TX: PRO-ED.

Tannenbaum, A. J. (1990). Defensible? Venerable? Vulnerable? *Gifted Child Quarterly*, *34*(2), 84–86.

Terman, L. M., & Oden, M. H. (1925). *Mental and physical traits of a thousand gifted children.* Stanford, CA: Stanford University Press.

Terman, L. M., & Oden, M. H. (1947). *The gifted child grows up.* Stanford, CA: Stanford University Press.

Terman, L. M., & Oden, M. H. (1959). *The gifted group at mid-life.* Stanford, CA: Stanford University Press.

Tonemah, S. (1985). *Tribal–cultural perspectives of gifted and talentedness.* Unpublished manuscript (p. 345). (Available from D. Montgomery, Elmhurst School, Oklahoma City, OK 73106.)

Tonemah, S. (1987). Assessing American Indian gifted and talented students; abilities. *Journal for the Education of the Gifted*, *10*, 181–194.

Torrance, E. P. (1977). *Discovery and nurturance of giftedness in the culturally different.* Reston, VA: Council for Exceptional Children.

Torrance, E. P. (1980). Psychology of gifted children and youth. In W. M.

Cruickshank (Ed.), *Psychology of exceptional children and youth* (pp. 150–160). Englewood Cliffs, NJ: Prentice-Hall.

Torrance, E. P. (1982). Identifying and capitalizing on the strengths of culturally different children. In C. R. Reynolds & J. B. Gutkin (Eds.), *The handbook of school psychology* (pp. 481–500). New York: Wiley.

Udall, A. (1989). Curriculum for gifted Hispanic students. In C. J. Maker & S. W. Schiever (Eds.), *Critical issues in gifted education: Defensible programs for cultural and ethnic minorities*. Austin, TX: PRO-ED.

VanTassel-Baska, J. (1989). The disadvantaged gifted. In J. F. Feldhusen, J. VanTassel-Baska, & K. Seeley (Eds.), *Excellence in educating the gifted*. Denver: Love.

Wechsler, D. (1974). *The Wechsler Intelligence Scale for Children–Revised*. San Antonio, TX: Psychological Corporation.

Wechsler, D. (1991). *The Wechsler Intelligence Scale for Children–Third edition*. San Antonio, TX: Psychological Corporation.

Whitmore, J. (1987). Conceptualizing the issue of underserved populations of gifted students. *Journal for the Education of the Gifted, 10,* 141–153.

Woliver, R., & Woliver, G. M. (1991). Gifted adolescents in the emerging minorities: Asians and Pacific Islanders. In M. Bireley & J. Genshaft (Eds.), *Understanding the gifted adolescent* (pp. 248–257). New York: Teachers College Press.

Wong, S. Y., & Wong, P. R. (1989). Teaching strategies and practices for the education of gifted Cantonese students. In C. J. Maker & S. W. Schiever (Eds.), *Critical issues in gifted education: Defensible programs for cultural and ethnic minorities*. Austin, TX: PRO-ED.

# *Part V*

## Intervention Strategies

# Chapter 18

# *Family Consultation as an Approach to Providing Psychoeducational Services to Gifted Children*

### Gerald Porter, Joel Meyers

◆ ◆ ◆

GIFTED CHILDREN PRESENT A RANGE of behaviors, emotions, and problems that can have an impact on their social, emotional, and cognitive development (Davis & Rimm, 1989; Delisle, 1992; Meckstroth, 1991). Systemic perspectives recognize that the child's behaviors, emotions, and problems occur in an environmental context (e.g., the family, the school, the community) and that the child and the environment influence each other. Interventions based on this perspective have a maximum opportunity to help gifted children.

School-based consultation is one approach to intervention with children that relies, in part, on systemic theory (e.g., Curtis & Meyers, 1988). Although school-based consultation has implications for working with parents, previous work on consultation has been limited to approaches for working with teachers and other school personnel. One purpose of this chapter is to illustrate how this model can be extended for work with families, with a particular focus on families with gifted children.

Consultation has been defined as "a collaborative problem solving process in which two or more persons (consultant and consultee(s)) engage in efforts to benefit one or more other persons (client(s)) for whom they bear some level of responsibility within the context of reciprocal interactions" (Curtis & Meyers, 1988, p. 36). The consultant might be a school psychologist, counselor, or other school professional, whereas teachers have been the typical consultees because of their responsibility for the students in their classes. However, parents could also play this role, because they have major responsibility for the social, emotional, academic, and cognitive development of their children. In fact, because of the frequency, duration, and intensity of contact between parents and children, parents are in a unique position to have a powerful influence on their gifted children.

Consultation has several advantages as an approach to intervention with families. First, consultation is a framework that emphasizes prevention as well as remediation. This is particularly important for gifted students who have internal resources that may increase their potential to respond effectively to preventive techniques. Second, consultation is an approach that is used to facilitate the performance of all children, including those who demonstrate no negative symptoms. This can be particularly important for gifted populations whose behavior and learning performance can be facilitated, even when they exhibit no problematic symptoms. Third, consultation is already a significant component of the role of school support personnel, so these individuals are prepared and able to provide consultation to families. Fourth, the systemic framework that underlies consultation can enable effective approaches to increase the interaction between school and family systems. Although this may be important for all populations, it can be particularly important for families of the gifted. Parents of gifted students can profit from school-based suggestions about how to facilitate their children's learning and development, and they are often in a unique position to offer insights that can facilitate the school's efforts to educate these children. Finally, school-based consultation strategies assume a collaborative relationship between consultant and consultee. This can be particularly important for parents of the gifted, who often have unique expertise regarding their children, and who are likely to respond more cooperatively when treated as colleagues who have valuable information and ideas to contribute (Davis & Rimm, 1989; Delisle, 1992; Dettman & Colangelo, 1980; Feldhusen & Baska, 1989; Shore, Cornell, Robinson, & Ward, 1991).

The purpose of this chapter is to introduce consultation as a model for psychoeducational services to gifted children through consultation between school personnel and the family. This chapter contains three primary components. First, research is reviewed that provides an understanding of giftedness that is useful for families and school personnel. Second, research is reviewed that illustrates the impact of family on gifted children. Third, a model of family consultation is presented as a basis for integrating psychoeducational services for gifted children through the home and school.

# UNDERSTANDING GIFTEDNESS

## Understanding the Construct of Giftedness

If parents are to be an effective resource for their child, they need to understand what it means for their child to be gifted in terms of specific strengths and weaknesses (Shore et al., 1991). For the purposes of this paper, being gifted is understood in terms of Renzulli's (1984) three-ring model. According to this multidimensional framework, gifted behavior results from the interaction of three components: above-average abilities (which can be general or specific), high motivation reflected in high levels of task commitment, and superior creativity and problem-solving skills (Davis & Rimm, 1989; Delisle, 1992). This three-ring model has the advantage of providing breadth in conceptualizing a range of factors relevant to giftedness, and it provides sufficient flexibility to allow greater diversity in terms of the proportion of students considered eligible and the types of children identified as gifted. The breadth of this definition increases the probability that females, children from poor families, and children of racial/ethnic minorities are identified as gifted. It also increases the probability that gifted students who do not score exceptionally high on standardized tests of intelligence may still be identified as gifted.

Milgram's (1991) 4 × 4 model of giftedness adds to the three components identified by Renzulli by explicitly considering the degree of giftedness in the context of ecological factors. Milgram identified four categories of giftedness and four levels of giftedness. The four categories of giftedness include (a) general or overall intellectual ability that is usually measured by an IQ test; (b) specific cognitive abilities that are typically assessed by achievement tests, intelligence tests, or school grades; (c) some indication of general ability for creative and ingenious problem solving that might be tapped by tests of divergent thinking; and (d) specific creative talent as evidenced by exceptional performance in a specific area. The four levels of giftedness are hierarchically arranged from nongifted to mildly gifted, moderately gifted, and profoundly gifted. Milgram also considered three settings or environments in which giftedness can manifest itself: school, home, and community. Milgram's explicit consideration of the family setting may make the model particularly useful to consultants who take a systemic or family-centered approach.

The use of a multidimensional model such as Renzulli's or Milgram's can help parents better understand the true nature of giftedness and their child's particular talents. Both Renzulli's three-ring model and Milgram's 4 × 4 model dovetail with Renzulli's (1984) Revolving Door Identification Model (RDIM), which stresses multiple sources for identification and an inclusive talent pool (Davis & Rimm, 1989).

## Identifying Signs of Giftedness
### Parent Participation in Screening for Giftedness

Perhaps the initial way in which parents confront their child's giftedness is through the identification process. In fact, parents are more likely to recognize their children's giftedness than are teachers or other school personnel (Delisle, 1992; Meckstroth, 1991). One investigation found that 87% of the parents surveyed had recognized that their child was gifted by 6 years of age (Gogel, McCumsey, & Hewett, 1985). Parents are sometimes the only source of specific information about the child's extraordinary accomplishments and abilities (Davis & Rimm, 1989).

However, parents often feel that school personnel are not receptive to their efforts to identify and serve their gifted children (Shore et al., 1991), perhaps because educators have negative attitudes toward high-ability children. As a result, many parents are reluctant to approach schools (Meckstroth, 1991). Family consultation offers an approach that encourages schools to work cooperatively with parents. The result should be a reduction in resistance to mutual input from school personnel and from parents of the gifted. Because parents detect giftedness very early in their children's lives, it may be especially useful to involve them in screening preschool children for giftedness by seeking informal nomination by parents (Davis & Rimm, 1989; Feldhusen & Baska, 1989).

### Parent Participation in Assessment of Giftedness

Once potentially gifted children have been identified through screening procedures, parents can be involved in the assessment process through the use of rating scales, questionnaires, and open-ended nomination forms that provide information on a child's self-concept, interests, motivation, and creativity. School psychologists have an obvious role, based on their psychometric expertise in intellectual and achievement testing, in that they can help parents interpret and understand the results of assessment (Seeley, 1989).

It is particularly important that parents understand their child's giftedness and have accurate information about the results of the comprehensive evaluation. Parents need to understand the cognitive strengths of their child as well as abilities in the affective domain and other developmentally significant areas. One reason this understanding is important is that the label "gifted" does not usually characterize all of a child's ability areas. Parents need information about their child's weaknesses as well as strengths. A student may be gifted in one domain but average or below average in others. It can be important for consultants to help in dispelling parents' unrealistic and inappropriate expectations and debilitating stereotypes regarding their gifted child (Meckstroth, 1991). A multidimensional conception of giftedness, such as espoused by Renzulli or Milgram, can be used by evaluators to understand the many types of giftedness (Milgram, 1991), and this type of broad framework can help parents develop appropriate expectations based on their gifted child's actual configuration of abilities (Davis & Rimm, 1989; Meckstroth, 1991).

## Understanding Giftedness in Families that Are Culturally Different

Children from poor families and ethnic/racial minorities are traditionally underrepresented in programs for the gifted and talented (Davis & Rimm, 1989). As with majority families, identification is a major issue confronting minority and economically disadvantaged families with potentially exceptional children.

Conventional identification strategies, especially those overly dependent on the use of IQ testing, are less likely to distinguish talented children from nonmainstream groups. The best approach to maximizing the accurate identification of culturally different and poor children is to employ a variety of identification methods. Renzulli's RDIM incorporates both traditional methods, such as standardized IQ and aptitude testing, and informal identification strategies that may expand the talent pool to 15% to 20% of the school population (Davis & Rimm, 1989). In this model, informal procedures, such as parent, teacher, and even peer nominations, may capture minority children who do not demonstrate their exceptionality in school achievement.

Some research shows that many black students feel that academic success is "acting white" and consequently reject school achievement as contrary to their identity as African-Americans (Fordham & Ogbu, 1986; Ogbu, 1986). This is a misperception of many black youth and an ironic and unanticipated consequence of desegregation that characterizes contemporary black youth culture. Actually, African-American culture has traditionally prized, sought, and valued education (Gibbs, 1989). Even antisocial behavior, however, may be indicative of exceptional creativity among children who are outside the mainstream based on culture or economics (Swenson, 1978).

Gay (1978) reinterpreted 11 characteristics typical of gifted majority students and explained how these are likely to be manifest among gifted black children. For example, many gifted children are sharp and insightful observers of their environment, and this is true of African-American gifted children as well. However, black gifted children and adolescents, according to Gay, may be particularly sensitive (and vulnerable) to racism and consequently feel alienated from school (and mainstream society). As a result, they may manifest their insight by challenging authority or asking the "wrong" questions (Gay, 1978).

Davis and Rimm (1989) argued that programs for the culturally and economically diverse should include components that support cul tural identity; provide cultural enrichment beyond the normal curriculum; and provide training in divergent thinking, counseling, parent education, parent support groups, and career education. Research shows that non–English-speaking children and those with limited English proficiency need bilingual instruction to maximize their achievement (Fillmore & Valadez, 1986; Hakuta, 1986).

Family consultation might be particularly appropriate for some minority and disadvantaged populations because of the particular problems that adversely impact these groups, such as single-parent families, poverty, and inadequate health care, which can indirectly lead to school problems (Allen & Majidi-Ahi, 1989). Early intervention is a particularly effective approach for diverse populations, especially those that are economically disadvantaged. Shore et al. (1991) recommended the development of preschool interventions for the gifted to maximize the development of their potential abilities. They argued that preschool programs and services may be particularly valuable to high-ability, inner-city minority children and gifted children from low socioeconomic backgrounds who may need more environmental stimulus to compensate for disadvantages. Compensatory programs for at-risk preschoolers may be particularly helpful to poor or culturally different gifted children who are more likely to underachieve in later school years.

# IMPACT OF FAMILIES ON GIFTED CHILDREN

## Systemic Theory of Family Functioning

Systemic theories provide one foundation for school-based consultation models (Curtis & Meyers, 1988), and this perspective is at least equally important in family consultation. A systemic framework is particularly important because family consultation represents the intersection of the school system and the family system and provides an opportunity for forging family–school partnerships (e.g., see Paget, 1992). Systemic perspectives recognize that the child's behaviors, emotions, and problems occur in an environmental context (e.g., the family, the school, the community) and that the child and the environment have a reciprocal influence on each other (Christenson, Abery, & Weinberg, 1986; Plas, 1986). Because the family and school are interactive systems, problems are viewed as located within interpersonal interactions rather than within the individual child. Interventions that are developed based on an understanding of this systemic perspective attempt to change systemic interactions rather than individuals (Bertalanffy, 1968; Plas, 1986). This approach is expected to provide a maximum opportunity to help gifted children because interventions are focused on the environments that have an ongoing impact on these children. This focus creates the opportunity to remedy the referral problem and to prevent the development of future problems.

One specific example of a systemic model that has been applied productively to families and to family–school intervention is structural theory (e.g., see Fish & Jain, 1992). Based on Minuchin's (1974) work, this model considers several variables. One is identity, as children establish a sense of belonging to the family group (including its rules) while developing autonomy based on the family's accommodation to the child's needs. A second major variable in this model is the family structures (e.g., parent–child, husband–wife, sibling–sibling), which can affect children based on the degree to which effective boundaries are established between the systems to allow for both family interaction and autonomous individual development. Finally, adaptation refers to the family ability to change productively in response to (a) developmental changes that occur within various subsystems of the family (e.g., growth of the gifted child through various stages of development) and (b) external pressures (e.g., changes in economic circumstances, relocation of the family).

A variety of models of family functioning rely on many of these variables. For example, the Circumplex Model (Olson, Sprenkle, & Russell, 1979) considers family adaptability, cohesion, and communication within the family. This model provides a range of approaches to assess families on these dimensions and, because assessment is a key component of family consultation, this framework is particularly useful.

## Family Dynamics in Families with Gifted Children

Family systems approaches can be used to understand the problems of gifted children and adolescents (Jenkins-Friedman, 1992). One study (Matthews, West, & Hosie, 1986) evaluated 125 families of gifted children, using *The Family Assessment Device*, which measures six dimensions of family dynamics (problem solving, communication, roles, affective responsiveness, affective involvement, behavior control). Gifted families were found to be healthier in all dimensions, except affective involvement.

When systemic problems do occur in families of the gifted, they are often the result of parent efforts to treat their gifted child like an adult or to focus attention on their child rather than their problematic marital relationship (Jenkins-Friedman, 1992). These pressures can lead to child-focused problems, such as underachievement in school or disabling perfectionism, that appear to be isolated in the child, but may be caused or maintained by systemic conditions in the family.

Davis and Rimm (1989) identified a number of double messages or half truths communicated by parents that may be symptomatic of these systemic conditions. One example is the "that's good, but don't think you're gifted" message. Parents who convey this message to their gifted child may be concerned about the child's social–emotional adjustment and may fear that the child's high ability may lead to preoccupation with academic characteristics. As a result, such parents may encourage involvement in nonacademic areas, such as sports or social activities, even at the expense of academic success.

Problematic communication between gifted children and parents who have a troubled marital relationship often occurs when there is competition between parents for their children's affections, for dominance in the family system, or for revenge against the other parent (Davis & Rimm, 1989). This competition and conflict may focus on issues such as discipline or child-rearing practices, but can be manipulated easily by a gifted child, and it can result in a coalition between one parent and the child.

Another difficult problem influencing family dynamics is sibling adjustment (Ballering & Koch, 1984; Grenier, 1985; Kaufman & Sexton, 1983; Shore et al., 1991). Competition between gifted children and their nongifted siblings may be the result of parenting techniques that are perceived by the children as favoring either the gifted or the nongifted sibling, and this can have an impact on either child's self-esteem. This can be particularly difficult when a gifted child has a close-age older sibling who has less ability. Parents may respond to this situation by attempting to protect the esteem of the nongifted child by downplaying the gifted sibling's abilities and achievements. This type of environment can pressure high-ability siblings to hide their talents and to underachieve. For the nongifted child, this familial situation can result in underachievement as well, because the child feels he or she cannot successfully compete. When all children in the family are gifted, there can be high expectations and competition that may be threatening, especially to a child lacking self-confidence (Davis & Rimm, 1989).

## Parent Emotional Needs

Parents may need help coping with the feelings generated by discovering their child is gifted. These feelings may be influenced by negative attitudes or stereotypical ideas about giftedness (Shore et al., 1991), and may include anxiety and guilt over their ability to help their gifted child; feelings of jealousy, resentment, or rivalry (Shore et al., 1991); and bereavement over the loss of their "normal" child (Meckstroth, 1991).

Some parents, in an effort to manage these problematic feelings of inadequacy and guilt, may try to compensate by giving too much attention to the child or by placing inappropriately high performance expectations on themselves and their child. This can result in underachievement and emotional difficulties for the child (Jenkins-Friedman, 1992).

To help parents cope more effectively with these emotional problems, school districts with programs for gifted students might provide parent groups and parent counseling (Conroy, 1987; Meckstroth, 1991; Shore et al., 1991). These groups can also provide education regarding parenting strategies and advocacy skills (Riggs, 1984). Parent groups and workshops can increase parental involvement in their gifted child's educational programming (Wolf, 1987). Such support services can also provide training in effective communication skills that may facilitate the efforts of school personnel to provide family consultation.

## Parental Management Strategies
## for Gifted Children

Educational programs have been suggested to help parents better understand the needs of their gifted children and to develop parenting skills (Cornell, 1989; Davis & Rimm, 1989; Riggs, 1984; Shore et al., 1991; Wolf, 1987). Considerable discussion appears in the literature about the potential importance of parent advocacy to obtain the educational programs necessary to ensure that gifted children reach their potential (Davis & Rimm, 1989; Delisle, 1992; Riggs, 1984; Shore et al., 1991). Dettman and Colangelo (1980) suggested that parents take an active and cooperative role in the design and implementation of effective programming for gifted youth. The active involvement of parents in educational programming increases the probability of effective family consultation.

As alluded to above, however, a particularly pressing need for many parents is to develop the parenting skills needed to cope effectively with their gifted children. Parents of gifted children need to learn how to identify and set appropriate standards for the behavior and academic performance of their gifted children. They also need strategies for communicating clearly the roles of various family members. In addition, due to perfectionistic tendencies of many gifted children, parents must help their children feel valued for themselves rather than their achievements (Meckstroth, 1991). Parents can do this by teaching their children to select appropriate learning activities, breaking tasks down into more manageable parts, and focusing on the process of learning rather than the product.

Parents also need to learn to teach their gifted children to cope with competition and stress. Davis and Rimm (1989) suggested that parents teach their children strategies such as the timely use of humor to relieve tension, identification of the sources of stress, and the cultivation of enjoyable outlets, such as sports or other physical activities. Other approaches recommended for teaching stress management skills include helping gifted children develop close personal relationships, and parental modeling of appropriate reactions to stress. Relaxation strategies, cognitive restructuring, and study skills are also techniques that can reduce school children's stress (Cavallaro & Meyers, 1986).

# A MODEL FOR SCHOOL-BASED CONSULTATION WITH FAMILIES OF GIFTED CHILDREN

The school-based family consultation model has several important components that are presented in this section of the chapter. These include (a) family consultation as an interpersonal process, (b) three distinct approaches to family consultation, and (c) a decision-making framework for family consultation. It is important to recognize that the model of consultation in this chapter is adapted from a model of school-based consultation that has been used primarily with teachers serving as consultees. Therefore, much of the research cited is based on work that has been done with teachers as consultees, rather than with families. Research is needed that documents the efficacy of many of these principles in family consultation.

## Family Consultation as an Interpersonal Process

A consistent characteristic of most models of school-based consultation is that the relationship between consultant and consultee is nonhierarchical, collaborative, and coordinate (e.g., see Caplan, 1970; Curtis & Meyers, 1988; Gutkin & Curtis, 1990; Meyers, Parsons, & Martin, 1979). Generally, this principle has been expressed based on the notion that consultation takes place between two equal professionals, each with a different area of expertise (e.g., Meyers et al., 1979). Although most parents are not "professionals" who have received advanced training in a related professional discipline, they do have unique expertise regarding their family and their children. At the same time, the consultant has unique expertise related to his or her area of training (e.g., school psychologists may have expertise in assessment and behavior management). This principle is implemented in family consultation by viewing parents and other family members as having expert knowledge and skills regarding their family. The purpose of consultation is to ensure that the expertise of both consultant and consultee benefits the child.

This collaborative approach conflicts with other approaches to the consultation process that view the consultant as an expert who will tell the consultee how to resolve a problem. This is a particular danger in family consultation because family members are likely to view the trained professional as having more of the expertise needed to solve their problems.

One way to implement a collaborative consultation relationship with the family is by communicating clearly to the parents that they have the freedom to accept or reject any ideas, suggestions, or recommendations. This principle recognizes the importance of maintaining the consultee's active involvement. The consultee is most likely to implement those ideas that he or she has a role in developing, and is least likely to implement those ideas that are imposed by the consultant. One concrete way to follow this principle is to present ideas and to make suggestions in a tentative manner that explicitly invites the consultee's response.

It is also important that the consultant emphasize the consultee's contributions to success. This emphasis is particularly important in family consultation because it communicates a valuing of the expertise of the family, which reinforces the consultee's use of problem-solving strategies. These ideas continue to be viewed as relevant to the effective practice of school-based consultation (e.g., Gutkin & Curtis, 1990); however, research is needed to document their importance in family consultation. Research that conceptualizes consultation as an interpersonal process by studying the consultation dyad offers a promising direction for research on the process of family consultation (e.g., see Erchul, 1987, 1992; Erchul, Hughes, Meyers, Hickman, & Braden, 1992). This interpersonal framework for researching the consultation dyad has potential to address questions about the nature of interpersonal control, directedness, and collaboration, as well as resistance in school-based consultation. These issues are all equally important in family consultation, and they are suggested as directions for research.

## Three Categories of Family Consultation

The model of family consultation includes three categories of consultation that vary based on how directly services are provided from the consultant to the child. These include child-centered, parent-centered, and family-centered consultation. These three categories of consultation are presented below.

This model is conceptualized in conjunction with school-based consultation, because the consultant providing family consultation (e.g., school counselor, school psychologist, school social worker) might provide consultation services to school personnel regarding the same child. This model is adapted from other writers who have distinguished different types of school-based consultation based on the degree to which services are provided directly to the child (e.g., Caplan, 1970; Meyers et al., 1979), and it is linked particularly to recent efforts that conceptualize three categories of consultation that are analogous to those used in this model of family consultation—that is, child-centered, teacher-centered, and system-centered consultation (e.g., Meyers, 1989; Meyers, Brent, Faherty, & Modafferi, 1993; Meyers & Kundert, 1988).

### Child-Centered Consultation

Child-centered consultation is implemented when the goal is to change the behavior, attitudes, or cognitions of the child. Under these circumstances, the characteristics of the child are viewed as major reasons for the referral, and the approach to consultation is based on data gathered directly by the consultant. These data typically would be gathered using individual diagnostic techniques, such as intelligence tests, projective tests, diagnostic educational tests, interviews, and observations of the child in the school and family setting. Data for this approach to consultation might also be gathered based on the consultant's experience providing counseling to the child (either individual or group counseling). In addition to data reflecting the child's characteristics, child-centered consultation would be based on environmental factors, including parent, family, and school variables relevant to the problem. Sometimes a gifted child may display disabling perfectionism, even though there is no evidence of inordinate pressures from parents or school. In such a case, child-centered consultation would be most appropriate to treat the problem, which is apparently caused primarily by the child's characteristics as a gifted individual.

### Parent-Centered Consultation

Parents are often a key component of the family environment that has an impact on children who are referred. Therefore, there are times when the parents, rather than the child, ought to be the focus of consultation. Parent-centered consultation is implemented when the primary goal is to modify the behavior, attitudes, or cognitions of one or both parents. When this approach to consultation is selected, it is assumed that problems exhibited by the parents are major variables contributing to the observed problems of the child. In these circumstances, changes in key characteristics of the parents (e.g., parenting behaviors, parental emotions) would have a dramatic positive effect on the child so that the need for the referral would be eliminated.

Similar to Caplan's (1970) consultee-centered consultation, parent-centered consultation would seek to increase the parent's knowledge, skill, or objectivity. Interviews as well as observation procedures would be used to determine which of these issues might be the primary concern. Examples of these problems are presented below.

*Knowledge* might be the focus of parent-centered consultation with gifted children when the parents are unaware of key developmental principles with gifted children. In this type of intervention, consultants might provide information to parents about child development and the construct of giftedness, and about how to identify giftedness. Another example of how knowledge can be a factor in parent-centered consultation is when parents are so focused on the child that they leave no time for themselves. Under these circumstances, one goal might be to inform parents that it is important for their child's maximum development that the parents take time to do things socially as a couple.

*Parenting skills* might be the focus of parent-centered consultation when the parents are unsure how to manage the behavior of their gifted child. This can be a particularly important issue with gifted children who require opportunities for input into various family decisions for their development and adjustment to the family (Jenkins-Friedman, 1992; Shore et al., 1991). Parenting skills might be enhanced through training that includes presentation of didactic information concerning the skill, opportunities to observe implementation of the skill, opportunities to implement the skill under observation, and opportunities to practice implementing the skill in the family setting. Such parent training can be provided to parents from a single family or to groups of parents. One important issue in implementing skill training is ensuring ongoing active participation of the parents (Kovachi, 1991).

Parent-centered consultation may often need to be focused on increasing *parental objectivity* in dealing with their children. For example, some parents may lose objectivity because of lack of confidence in dealing with gifted children whom the parents may fear have more intelligence than they do. Also, a range of emotional conflicts for parents of the gifted (e.g., authority conflict, child or parent hostility, parental guilt regarding their ability to help a gifted child, parental jealousy of gifted child) can cause loss of parental objectivity.

Interventions focused on lack of objectivity are similar to those discussed in the literature on consultee-centered consultation, and these techniques are discussed elsewhere in more detail (e.g., Caplan, 1970; Meyers, 1975; Meyers et al., 1979). They include the use of direct and indirect confrontation techniques. Indirect techniques are recommended when direct strategies would stimulate parental resistance. In indirect techniques, the problem is generally discussed as if someone other than the parent had the problem. For example, the consultant might approach the parents' discomfort providing limits and structure for their gifted child as if it were the child's problem. The consultant might say, "As you know, Johnny is bright and is often aware of a range of behavioral options. As a result, he is even more likely to question your rules and behavioral limitations than are many other children. Therefore, it is particularly important that you consistently enforce rules with Johnny once the family has agreed to these rules."

In contrast to indirect confrontation, direct confrontation techniques focus more on the problem as if it were the problem of the parent. As noted above, indirect confrontation strategies are used to avoid stimulating too much parental resistance. An example of direct confrontation might be as follows: "You have described several instances when you were unable to enforce the rules that the family had previously agreed were appropriate for Johnny. Why do you think that this issue presents a difficulty for you?" Direct confrontation strategies must be implemented with great care to maintain a productive relationship with the parents. This strategy has been discussed elsewhere in relation to teacher-centered consultation (e.g., Meyers, 1981; Meyers et al., 1979; Parsons & Meyers, 1984).

### Family-Centered Consultation

Family-centered consultation is implemented when the primary goal is to change key aspects of family functioning. This approach focuses on the family as a system, rather than specifically on parents or the referred child. It is based on the family systems theories reviewed earlier in this chapter. When family-centered variables are relevant, improved family functioning is expected to have a dramatic impact on the child, which would eliminate the need for the referral. The improved functioning would also be expected to have positive effects on the parents, mitigating any need for parent-centered consultation.

When family-centered approaches are used, the consultant relies on interviews, questionnaires, and observations to gather data. For example, questionnaires assessing family functioning, such as the *Family Adaptability and Cohesion and Evaluation Scales* (FACES)

(Olson & Portner, 1983; Olson et al., 1979), the *Family Environment Scale* (Moos & Moos, 1981), and the *McMaster Family Assessment Device* (Epstein, Baldwin, & Bishop, 1983), might be administered to family members. These questionnaires can also be used as a basis for structured interviews. The Circumplex Model has a structured observation technique (Olson & Portner, 1983; Olson et al., 1979) that can be used in conjunction with the FACES.

Family members who would be the focus of these data-gathering approaches include parents, the identified child, siblings, and members of the extended family. Family-centered consultation focuses on issues such as communication patterns, approaches to decision making, family rules, flexibility in developing and implementing rules over time, the degree of closeness between family members, the degree to which individuals' autonomy is fostered, and the clarity of family members' roles. Approaches such as Fish and Jain's (1992) application of structural family therapy to school settings could be used to generate intervention ideas for this approach to family consultation.

## A Decision-Making Framework for Consultants

Other sources have clarified how this consultation model can serve as a decision-making framework to assist consultants in determining which category of consultation is most appropriate to a particular referral during school-based consultation (e.g., Meyers et al., 1993; Meyers et al., 1979; Parsons & Meyers, 1984). When applied to family consultation, the decision-making rule is to choose first the most indirect approach that is appropriate to the case (i.e., family-centered or parent-centered consultation) and to use approaches requiring the most direct contact between consultant and client (i.e., child-centered consultation) as a last resort.

The consultant determines first whether the case can be solved most efficiently through family-centered consultation. If so, then the consultant would use family-centered approaches, hoping that this indirect level of intervention would help to solve family-, parent-, and child-oriented problems. After deciding that family-centered consultation is not appropriate, the consultant next determines whether the case can be solved most efficiently through parent-centered consultation. If so, then the consultant would use parent-centered approaches. In these cases, an increase in the knowledge, skills, self-confidence, and objectivity of the parents is expected to result in more effective education for all children and to remedy the problems of any referred children. Child-centered consultation would be selected only when family-centered and parent-centered approaches have been ruled out.

The most indirect approaches (i.e., family and parent centered) are the priority, because they have the greatest potential to reach a maximum number of students, to reduce referrals of individual children, and to prevent the development of future problems.

# CONCLUSION

A key principle of family consultation concerns the importance of developing a productive school–family partnership. Paget (1992) indicated that systems theory can provide a basis for developing this partnership. This chapter has described a model of family consultation that considers child-centered, parent-centered, and family-centered approaches to working with families. The chapter also makes reference to school-based consultation models that consider child-centered, teacher-centered, and system-centered approaches to consultation in schools. It is important to underscore the intersection between school-based consultation and family consultation, because this may provide a natural vehicle for developing effective school–family partnerships.

In some situations, family-centered, parent-centered, and child-centered consultations are inappropriate because the primary source of the problem is the school. However, even when school-based consultation is viewed as the most appropriate intervention, it is important to maintain involvement of the family through family consultation, which can provide effective ways to involve the parents in the solution of the problem.

Understanding and effectively intervening in the lives of gifted children and adolescents can be enhanced by the use of multidimensional constructs of giftedness that take an ecological view of the factors affecting the gifted (e.g., Renzulli's three-ring model or Milgram's $4 \times 4$ model). Consultants can be particularly helpful to parents (especially parents of girls, the culturally different, or the economically disadvantaged) by facilitating their involvement in the identification of their gifted children. Family consultation can address parents' understanding of giftedness, knowledge of their child's particular talents, and awareness of how to nurture their child's gifted characteristics. Family consultation can also help parents cope with their own feelings and expectations about their gifted child's exceptionality and can help to find ways to facilitate the interaction between gifted and nongifted siblings. The consultation model presented in this chapter reflects the potential contributions of parents and the family system to the social, behavioral, and cognitive development of gifted students, and, as noted above, the school environment can make significant contributions.

However, a range of factors in the wider community, outside of school, can also contribute to the development of gifted children. Consultation models focused on gifted children need to consider these broader influences, which may be just as significant as school or family factors. This is consistent with the systems theories that consider the reciprocal impact of a range of variables in systems relevant to the child.

An important element of all school-based consultation models involves the stages of consultation (e.g., Gutkin & Curtis, 1990), and problem-solving stages are equally important for the successful completion of family consultation. This chapter has not delineated these stages because they are not unique to family consultation with the gifted. However, it is important to recognize that the completion of each stage of consultation (e.g., contract negotiation, problem identification, problem definition, intervention, evaluation) is necessary for consultation to be successful. When resistance is encountered in family consultation, one effective strategy is to review prior stages of consultation to see if resistance is due to the unsuccessful resolution of one or more of the stages (e.g., Meyers, in press).

Family consultation is a model that has the potential to prevent the development of future problems in the gifted child. It can also prevent the development of problems in siblings of the gifted child. Therefore, this model has an advantage over therapeutic models that are geared toward remediating the child's problem, rather than preventing future problems. This benefit is particularly important when considering the potential for implementing this model with gifted children from minority backgrounds. The preventive goals, and the explicit focus on the ecology of those environmental settings that influence the child, have potential to make a significant difference in the lives of minority as well as majority children with gifted potential.

# REFERENCES

Allen, L., & Majidi-Ahi, S. (1989). Black American children. In J. T. Gibbs & L. N. Huang (Eds.), *Children of color: Psychological interventions with minority youth* (pp. 148–178). San Francisco: Jossey-Bass.

Ballering, L. D., & Koch, A. (1984). Family relations when a child is gifted. *Gifted Child Quarterly, 28,* 140–143.

Bertalanffy, L. von (1968). *General systems theory: Foundations, developments, applications.* New York: Braziller.

Caplan, G. (1970). *The theory and practice of mental health consultation.* New York: Basic Books.

Cavallaro, D. M., & Meyers, J. (1986). Effects of study habits on cognitive restructuring and study skills training in the treatment of test anxiety with adolescent females. *Techniques: A Journal for Remedial Education and Counseling, 2,* 145–155.

Christenson, S., Abery, B., & Weinberg, R. (1986). An alternative model for the delivery of psychological services in the school community. In S. N. Elliot & J. C. Witt (Eds.), *The delivery of psychological services in the school community* (pp. 349–392). Hillsdale, NJ: Erlbaum.

Conroy, E. H. (1987). Primary prevention for gifted students: A parent education group. *Elementary School Guidance and Counseling, 21,* 110–116.

Cornell, D. G. (1989). Child adjustment and parent use of the term "gifted." *Gifted Child Quarterly, 33,* 59–64.

Curtis, M. J., & Meyers, J. (1988). Consultation: A foundation for alternative services in the schools. In J. L. Graden, J. E. Zins, & M. J. Curtis (Eds.), *Alternative educational delivery systems: Enhancing instructional options for all students* (pp. 35–48). Washington, DC: National Association of School Psychologists.

Davis, G. A., & Rimm, S. B. (1989). *Education of the gifted and talented* (2nd ed.). Englewood Cliffs, NJ: Prentice-Hall.

Delisle, J. R. (1992). *Guiding the social and emotional development of gifted youth: A practical guide for educators and counselors.* White Plains, NY: Longman.

Dettman, D. F., & Colangelo, N. (1980). A functional model for counseling parents of gifted students. *Gifted Child Quarterly, 24,* 158–161.

Epstein, N., Baldwin, L., & Bishop, D. (1983). The McMaster Family Assessment Device. *Journal of Marital and Family Therapy, 9,* 171–180.

Erchul, W. P. (1987). A relational community analysis of control in school consultation. *Professional School Psychology, 2,* 113–124.

Erchul, W. P. (1992). On dominance, cooperation, teamwork, and collaboration in school-based consultation. *Journal of Educational and Psychological Consultation, 3,* 363–366.

Erchul, W. P., Hughes, J. N., Meyers, J., Hickman, J. A., & Braden, J. P. (1992). Dyadic agreement concerning the consultation process and its relationship to outcome. *Journal of Educational and Psychological Consultation, 3,* 119–132.

Feldhusen, J. F., & Baska, L. K. (1989). Identification and assessment of the gifted. In J. Feldhusen, J. VanTassel-Baska, & K. Seeley (Eds.), *Excellence in educating the gifted* (pp. 85–102). Denver, CO: Love.

Fillmore, L., & Valadez, C. (1986). Teaching bilingual learners. In M. Wittrock (Ed.), *Handbook of research on teaching.* New York: Macmillan.

Fish, M. C., & Jain, S. (1992). Family–school intervention using a structural model. In M. J. Fine & C. Carlson (Eds.), *The handbook of family–school intervention: A systems perspective* (pp. 302–314). Needham Heights, MA: Allyn & Bacon.

Fordham, S., & Ogbu, J. U. (1986). Black students' school success: Coping with the "burden of 'acting white.'" *Urban Review, 18,* 176–206.

Gay, J. E. (1978). A proposed plan for identifying black gifted children. *Gifted Child Quarterly, 22,* 353–357.

Gibbs, J. T. (1989). Black American adolescents. In J. T. Gibbs & L. N. Huang (Eds.), *Children of color: Psychological interventions with minority children* (pp. 179–223). San Francisco: Jossey-Bass.

Gogel, E. M., McCumsey, J., & Hewett, G. (1985). What parents are saying. *G/C/T, 8,* 7–9.

Grenier, M. E. (1985). Gifted children and other siblings. *Gifted Child Quarterly, 29,* 164–167.

Gutkin, T. B., & Curtis, M. J. (1990). School-based consultation: Theory, techniques, and research. In T. B. Gutkin & C. R. Reynolds (Eds.), *Handbook of school psychology* (pp. 577–611). New York: Wiley.

Hakuta, K. (1986). *Mirror of language: The debate of bilingualism.* New York: Basic Books.

Jenkins-Friedman, R. (1992). Families of gifted children and youth. In M. J. Fine & C. Carlson (Eds.), *The handbook of family–school intervention: A systems approach* (pp. 175–187). Needham Heights, MA: Allyn & Bacon.

Kaufman, F. A., & Sexton, D. (1983). Some implications for home–school linkages. *Roeper Review, 6,* 49–51.

Kovachi, A. (1991). Implementation and evaluation of a group educational and support program for parents of preschoolers with handicaps. *Dissertation Abstracts International, 52,* 2302B.

Matthews, F. N., West, J. D., & Hosie, T. W. (1986). Understanding families of academically gifted children. *Roeper Review, 9,* 40–42.

Meckstroth, E. A. (1991). Guiding the parents of gifted children: The role of counselors and teachers. In R. Milgram (Ed.), *Counseling gifted and talented children: A guide for teachers, counselors, and parents* (pp. 95–120). Norwood, NJ: Ablex.

Meyers, J. (1975). Consultee-centered consultation with a teacher as a technique in behavior management. *American Journal of Community Psychology, 3,* 111–121.

Meyers, J. (1981). Mental health consultation. In J. C. Conoley (Ed.), *Consultation in schools: Theory, research and procedures.* New York: Academic Press.

Meyers, J. (1989). The practice of psychology in the schools for the primary prevention of learning and adjustment problems in children: A perspective of the field of education. In L. A. Bond & B. E. Compas (Eds.), *Primary prevention and promotion in the schools* (pp. 391–422). Newbury Park, CA: Sage.

Meyers, J. (in press). A consultation model for school psychological services: Twenty years later. *Journal of Educational and Psychological Consultation.*

Meyers, J., Brent, D., Faherty, E., & Modafferi, C. (1993). Caplan's contributions to the practice of psychology in schools. In W. P. Erchul (Ed.), *Consultation in community, school and organizational practice: Gerald Caplan's contribution to professional psychology* (pp. 99–122). Washington, DC: Hemisphere.

Meyers, J., & Kundert, D. (1988). Implementing process assessment. In J. L. Graden, J. E. Zins, & M. J. Curtis (Eds.), *Alternative educational delivery systems: Enhancing instructional options for all students* (pp. 173–197). Washington, DC: National Association of School Psychologists.

Meyers, J., Parsons, R. D., & Martin, R. (1979). *Mutual health consultation in the schools.* San Francisco: Jossey Bass.

Milgram, R. M. (1991). Counseling gifted and talented children and youth: Who, where, what, and how? In R. Milgram (Ed.), *Counseling gifted and talented children: A guide for teachers, counselors, and parents* (pp. 7–21). Norwood, NJ: Ablex.

Minuchin, S. (1974). *Families and family therapy.* Cambridge, MA: Harvard University Press.

Moos, R., & Moos, B. (1981). *Family Environment Scale manual.* Palo Alto, CA: Consulting Psychologists Press.

Ogbu, J. U. (1986). The consequence of the American caste system. In U. Neisser (Ed.), *The school achievement of minority children* (pp. 19–56). Hillside, NJ: Erlbaum.

Olson, D. H., & Portner, J. (1983). Family adaptability and cohesion and evaluation scales. In E. E. Filsinger (Ed.), *Marriage and family assessment: A sourcebook for family* (pp. 299–315). Beverly Hills, CA: Sage.

Olson, D. H., Sprenkle, D. H., & Russell, C. S. (1979). Circumplex model of marital and family systems: I. Cohesion and adaptability dimensions, family types, and clinical application. *Family Process, 18,* 3–23.

Paget, K. D. (1992). Proactive family–school partnerships in early intervention. In M. J. Fine & C. Carlson (Eds.), *The handbook of family–school intervention: A systems perspective* (pp. 119–133). Needham Heights, MA: Allyn & Bacon.

Parsons, R. D., & Meyers, J. (1984). *Developing consultation skills.* San Francisco: Jossey-Bass.

Plas, J. M. (1986). *Systems psychology in the schools.* New York: Pergamon.

Renzulli, J. S. (1984). The Triad/Revolving Door system: A research-based approach to identification and programming for gifted and talented. *Gifted Child Quarterly, 28*(4), 163–171.

Riggs, G. G. (1984). Parent power: Wanted for organization. *Gifted Child Quarterly, 28,* 111–114.

Seeley, K. (1989). Facilitators of the gifted. In J. Feldhusen, J. VanTassel-Baska, & K. Seeley (Eds.), *Excellence in educating the gifted* (pp. 279–298). Denver, CO: Love.

Shore, B. M., Cornell, D. G., Robinson, A., & Ward, V. S. (1991). *Recommended practices in gifted education: A critical education.* New York: Teachers College Press.

Swenson, E. V. (1978). Teacher assessment of creative behavior in disadvantaged children. *Gifted Child Quarterly, 22*(3), 338–343.

Wolf, J. S. (1987). Workshops for parents of the gifted. *Roeper Review, 9,* 243–246.

# Chapter 19

# Counseling Academically Behaving Adolescents About Wellness

**Paul Michael Janos**

◆ ◆ ◆

INFORMATION ABOUT COUNSELING PRACTICES that are effective with so-called gifted children is scant, and based mostly on clinical work (Myers & Pace, 1986)—in part because the concept of "giftedness" has compromised research (Renzulli & Reis, 1991). To minimize such difficulties, this chapter focuses on adolescent students who have evidenced disciplined and sustained academic *behavior* in the form of uncommonly rapid rates of progress through school grades. It is loosely organized around "wellness," which consists of appropriate development in six dimensions: intellectual or academic, emotional, social, physical, occupational, and spiritual (Hettler, 1984).

## HISTORICAL BACKGROUND

John Stuart Mill was an eminent English intellectual and statesman whose "Autobiography" (Mill, 1961) illustrates many of the issues pertinent to counseling the gifted. Between the ages of 3 and 14, most of his waking hours were spent in rigorous study, written and verbal examination, and debate with his father. At ages 14 and 15, he spent 9 hours daily devoted to "hard intellectual labor, requiring intensive application" (Cox, 1926, p. 708). From age 16, he studied law full time *and* continued to be tutored by his father. Not surprisingly, at age 21, he suffered an emotional crisis, during which he reported taking no pleasure in any human endeavor.

For present purposes, Mill's wellness may be said to have been beset by his father's unrelenting academic demands, emotionally repressive behavior, and discouragement of relations with age-mates. These moved Mill to publish cautions about "the power and practice of analysis" and to advocate "due balance among the faculties" (Mill, 1961, p. 89). The practical implication is for counselors of gifted adolescents to critically examine the degree of effective support accorded to each dimension of wellness.

Empirical studies support Mill's admonitions. Terman and Oden (1947), for example, reported that what one might call "severe" academic behavior (markedly early entrance to college) temporarily diminished wellness for 52.2% of females and 76.7% of males. The Fund for the Advancement of Education (1957) reported similar results for 58% of one cohort to enter college early and 65% of another. Clinically, Terman stressed the need to avoid one-sided development (Janos, 1986), as did Pressey (1949) regarding the Fund's subjects.

Consistent with these findings, but on a more intimate level, Hollingworth's (1939) work with children with IQs above 180 led her to believe that, as a general rule, "training in attitudes, emotions, and drives" was "even more important" than intellectual training (p. 585). She targeted the following issues: (a) to find enough hard and interesting work at school, (b) to suffer fools gladly, (c) to keep from becoming negativistic toward authority, (d) to keep from becoming hermits, and (e) to avoid the formation of habits of extreme chicanery. As described in Hollingworth (1942), she taught the children to maintain academic momentum while minimizing the tensions inherent in their increasing academic discrepancies from age-mates, to anticipate situations in which such discrepancies might pose problems, to correct any of their own distorted perceptions of social situations, and to apply problem-solving rather than defensive strategies. In essence, she taught perspective taking, self-control, and savoir faire.

# CONTEMPORARY PRACTICES

Finding hard and interesting work remains a primary wellness need of academically behaving youth (Janos & Robinson, 1985). This conclusion found further support in Kerr and Colangelo's (1988) data, collected from tens of thousands of high school juniors and seniors taking the *American College Test*. Barely 8% of students at either the 95th or the 99th percentile desired help with "personal concerns"; however, within the 99th percentile group, 53% desired help with occupational and educational goals, 80% with independent study, and 93% with honors programs. Counselors can support these academic agendas *and* take advantage of teachable moments with respect to additional possibilities for wellness. This bifocal strategy, incidentally, mobilizes counselors to advocate with schools for individually responsive academic programs.

Despite valuing academics highly, students often respond well to initiatives regarding certain traditional counseling issues, including taking control of their own development; deciding when (and when *not*) to specialize; choosing "between" careers and relationships; deferring gratification endlessly into the future; and preparing for life "after school" (Frederickson, 1986). Perrone (1986) supported gifted students' development of personal values and "adult" skills, such as asking meaningful questions, being self-directed, being concerned with the welfare of others, and discovering and defining problems. McMann and Oliver (1988) addressed gifted students' guilt about achievements, perceptions of differentness, doubt, inferiority, depression, and the feeling that they must perform to be accepted.

To address such issues, Janos (1991) recommended that counselors help students to assess how academic behavior may be impacting other aspects of their lives and to make plans for overall wellness that are practical and responsive to feedback. This approach empowers students with information and genuine autonomy, and supports reasonable risk taking.

Although counseling is generally committed to students' allaround wellness, more limited advocacy for development in the academic dimension has become an increasing focus in some circles over the last 20 years, championed by the Study of Mathematically Precocious Youth (SMPY) at Johns Hopkins University (Stanley, 1977). SMPY has advocated removal of arbitrary obstacles to academic progress. Specific recommendations are many, including skipping grades, moving ahead fast in subjects such as mathematics, taking college courses while still in secondary school, leaving high school when ready to enter college (with or without a diploma), taking heavy course loads, and/or combining degree work. SMPY has based its recommendations on selective attention to successful cases of academic behavior (e.g., Mill), reports such as that of the Fund for the Advancement of Education (1957), and educational experimentation with subsets of contemporary students identified through annual academic talent searches (administrations of the *Scholastic Aptitude Test* [SAT] to hundreds of thousands of students, usually seventh graders).

Sawyer (1986) urged freely offering information about talent searches and accelerative programs, helping students prepare for the SAT and interpret test results, and developing educational and support services appropriate for academically behaving students both in

and out of schools. Sawyer also identified specific information resources, such as Duke University's Talent Identification Program's
newsletter, its *Talent Tabloid*, and its *Educational Opportunity Guide*
to many educational programs.

Educational personnel should inform students about all of their
educational options. However, school psychologists and counselors
should also arm students with comprehensive information about the
diverse results of particular choices. Rapid academic progress has obvious merit *with certain students*, but on its own fails to completely meet
even their academic needs, much less their wellness needs in general
(Levine, 1986), and does not reliably increase adult achievement
(Swiatek & Benbow, 1991). Moreover, as mentioned above, *most* students report significant detriments to wellness due to severe academic
behavior (e.g., Fund for the Advancement of Education, 1957; Terman
& Oden, 1947). Even though the literature suggests that such problems are minor, school psychologists and counselors should be alert to
identify cases requiring support; instances are likely to increase as the
romance with rapid academic progress gains momentum, and entrance
barriers to accelerative programs continue to drop.

Contemporary studies have confirmed that, of students whose academic behavior results in early college matriculation, a substantial
minority (between 20% and 30%) may exhibit such symptoms as relatively poor grades, vocational confusion, anhedonia (i.e., inability to
experience happiness), and clinical depression (Cornell, Callahan, &
Loyd, 1991a, 1991b; Janos, Sanfilipo, & Robinson, 1986). Even Stanley's (1985) SMPY sample suggests that approximately 20% may earn
relatively low grades. It stands to reason that there must be pressing
wellness needs among students in any representative group.

For students whose academic progress may have faltered or collapsed, Janos et al. (1986) urged that school psychologists and counselors listen without being judgmental, validate students warmly and
frequently, and encourage the development of enhanced self-esteem.
Such students may simply need support dealing with wellness issues,
such as making ends meet financially, individuating from their families, and expressing themselves sexually.

Ironically, inadequate educational options may be part of the problem. Thus, counselors must step forward to assure the incorporation of
procedures sensitive to overall wellness within *all* educational programs, accelerative or not. Accelerative programs, in particular, beg for
incorporation of bona fide channels for opting out with wellness intact.
To pay more than lip service, it is necessary that clear goals for development in each dimension be set, and that specific strategies and timetables be supported, as have been shown to work (Pressey, 1949).

# IMPRESSIONS FROM A PROGRAM FOR EARLY COLLEGE ENTRANCE

Given the skimpy empirical reports, experiences with the approximately 130 students aged 12 to 14 who had matriculated at a selected state university between 1977 and 1989—academically behaving adolescents by any measure—are also presented. However, the focus here is not intended to be on them in particular (for such information, see Janos, Robinson, & Lunneborg, 1989), but on counseling issues that often arise in association with disciplined and sustained academic behavior.

## Reaching Out

Almost by definition, academically behaving students (and their families) highly value academic achievement. Consequently, the more that they perceive counseling to be a source of useful academic or career information and support, the more actively they will seek it. At the university level, requisite information addresses, in part, specific courses, teachers, majors, competitions, graduate and professional school options, scholarships, grants, financial aid, careers, and so forth. (Similar information may be sought by precollege students.) Additionally, counselors can collect information about (and actively cultivate) potential funding sources, mentors, employers, and so on.

The academic focus of counseling can generally be expanded to wellness because the majority of students, although developing well, have needs that, with a little encouragement, they are eager to discuss. A good example of one's eagerness to do so was the note, taped to our door by a 15-year-old first-year male college student: "I am NOT of sound mind or bawdy. PLEASE ADMIT ME to the nearest mental health facility. I agree to all actions taken."

If counseling is welcomed by students, they typically will be the ones to initiate consultation about the wellness issues attributed to adolescents, such as increasing individuation from families, physical appearance, making and keeping friends, heterosexual and homosexual fantasy and intimacy, contraception, pregnancy and abortion, age-appropriate risk taking (including drug use and antisocial behavior), personal and political values and identity, and financial matters. Vexation with social conditions also often emerges as a bona fide problem.

School psychologists' and counselors' own comfort and nonjudgmental approach is crucial to the free flow of communication. Neither students nor their parents care to be confronted by counselors' personal views on issues. What they seem to appreciate most is valid information (and sources for more), overviews of possible options for action, and outlines of the logical implications and practical consequences of decisions. Fishing for these, one youngster asked, "How would you advise a 4-foot, 300-pound purple space alien on securing nookie with a human female?"

Students empowered with information can be trusted to take action appropriate for their situations. For example, one 15-year-old college sophomore constantly deprecated himself and his peers. He acted arrogant and supercilious during his frequent visits to the counselors' office. He also had disfiguring acne, which he picked. During a visit, the information that there are medicines that can make acne go away for good was off-handedly conveyed. Shortly afterward, the boy's mother reported that her son had talked to her about obtaining the medicine. Several months later, the acne was cured. No youngster passing through the program exhibited a greater increase in wellness!

Counselors often have to convey information to students in the course of inertial action, the product of habit and unexamined notions. It is generally fun for both parties to consider together, "What can underlie behaving in such a fashion?" The pleasure of intellectual exploration, even jousting, and the felt need for cognitive consistency will help students to examine the reasons for their decisions, identify potential shortages of information, and allow them to change their minds, if necessary, to resolve lingering inconsistencies. In essence, this technique slows the action, opens the system, and invites students to apply their intellectual prowess to other dimensions of wellness.

It is safe to assume that gifted students who have problematic imbalances in wellness are aware of them, and looking for chances to talk. However, the students are often sensitive and defensive. Unconditional positive regard goes far with them. One should never assume that one knows what underlies their concerns. Their disproportionate academic behavior *may* be the result of undercultivation of one or more wellness dimensions, or of compensation for frustrations or disappointment in them. However, it may instead stem from intellectual idealism or outright addiction to studies. For example, for several quarters after reading *Atlas Shrugged* (Rand, 1957), a 16-year-old college junior behaved like the fictional Francisco D'Anconia. She worked every waking minute and slept only 3 hours each night. After 3 months of this regimen, she was physically exhausted and became sick. This happened several quarters in a row. She seemed oblivious to experiences of repeated sickness and awareness that the sources of pleasure in her life had dwindled. However, following failure to finish a course (because of illness), she gained control of her study behavior and began to accept her human limitations.

Regardless of how highly counselors value wellness, they must respect students' seemingly disproportionate values and commitments. They should not attempt to force students out of such patterns, or aggressively communicate their personal opinion that the pattern is ill-advised. In fact, possibilities for constructive intervention exist only to the extent that discomfort is felt and remedies are sought *by a student*. Students may share Rilke's opinion of therapy: "I don't want the demons taken away because they're going to take my angels, too" (quoted in Hillman & Ventura, 1992, p. 136). There may be additional legitimacy to students' claims that wellness will be addressed when academic demands diminish. It is, of course, generally appropriate to query statements that lack definition, such as, "I can always catch up socially."

To reach many students, one must first break down negative stereotypes about counselors, such as that they intend to invade students' privacy and change their behavior. It is challenging to provide information to someone who, for legitimate reasons, appears unreceptive at the moment. This often can be accomplished by communicating to students the perspective that counseling consists mainly of providing information, identifying options, and supporting choices. If a student's choice is to limit discussion strictly to academics, or not to discuss anything at all, that choice must be supported. Even the narrowest of paths eventually connects with the royal road to wellness. Moreover, genuinely student-centered counseling necessarily opens a broader diversity of healthy outcomes than do approaches restricted by rigid beliefs.

A practical technique for engaging students is to enliven the counseling site with incentives to consult. These might include a daily "Far Side" cartoon, a blackboard with evolving repartee, student newspapers, or a log for recording student activities and humor. One of the best incentives is to maintain unstructured office hours, featuring animated students and a visibly empty seat waiting for one more participant. One can build rapport by spending non–office time with students, such as walking places together, inviting oneself along to a class event (e.g., a film or guest speaker) that a student enthuses about beforehand, stopping by the student coffeehouse, and attending or organizing birthday parties and dances—provided that one is sensitive to students' responsiveness. Proper supervision of such out-of-office contacts with adolescents is, without question, essential.

## Common Problems

Many academically behaving students view themselves as intellectual impostors, and acutely feel discrepancies between where they "are" and where they imagine they "ought to be." They often attribute characteristics of high achievers (e.g., Einstein, the Curies, John Lennon) to the "stars" among their cohort, against whom they compare their own magnitude. Such comparisons, paired with common experiences of hearing peers labeled "genius" or "prodigy," often result in discouragement or depression. This can be exacerbated by grouping, because in any small group only one or two can shine in within-group comparisons.

Students often show symptoms that inspirational ideals, natural tendencies to make comparisons with peers, and others' loose use of labels have been translated into impossible personal standards for daily measurement. Instead, their own *satisfaction* with activities should be portrayed as more important than how their performance is regarded by others.

The stereotype of pushy or controlling parents has been confirmed only infrequently in our experience with the 130 early college entrants mentioned earlier. However, a few students (who vigorously avoided counseling) ultimately confessed to having been under strict orders from parents to focus on classes, to avoid talk. Among such students, wellness appeared compromised along lines where, it appeared, parents were also compromised. The extreme emphasis on academics was compensatory. Once students sampled experiences in the suppressed dimensions of wellness, they appeared hooked, but families typically communicated disapproval of resultant changes. On the other hand, when students warded off growth experiences outside academics, they appeared to progressively decline in wellness, and the academic dimension ultimately succumbed also. Although long-term assessment of such individuals was the exception, they appeared to remain at risk.

Academically behaving students from significantly disturbed family systems must be relatively rare. However, these families seem to gravitate disproportionately to visible programs for so-called gifted students. (So, too, in my experience, do adults with delusions of brilliance!) Counselors should be prepared to accurately identify and cope with such systems and individuals. Extreme sensitivity and, ultimately, faith in adolescents' immense power to "grow themselves" is, obviously, in order.

In spite of the striking problems of the small minority of students described above, most of the early college entrants had families who seemed able to support their wellness needs and who, by virtue of their vocations and lifestyles, provided good models. Nevertheless, a substantial minority of the students from even these healthy families were, for many developmental reasons, insufficiently motivated at the time to sustain virtually one-dimensional academic behavior. They tended to be made anxious by peers who were. Several plodded on, eventually working things out. Perhaps more common was to become paralyzed by aimlessness and depression and to falter (or collapse) academically. Such students typically experienced years during which, like Mill, they took no pleasure in any human endeavor. They were heavy users of counseling.

The salvation of these students was that they had been congregated with each other, all age-mates roughly matched on abilities and interests, who became soul mates and mutual supporters. This incidental congregating aspect of programs for academically behaving students is probably the most powerful intervention on behalf of wellness that can be provided (e.g., Sawyer, 1986; Janos, 1991; Janos et al., 1989). It has been empirically shown that such students preferentially associate as much as 11 to 19 hours per week (Janos et al., 1988). Such grouping would be more beneficial, however, if not fomented by programmatic duress.

Alarmism over age-appropriate risk taking should be avoided by school psychologists and counselors. In our experience, risks to development stemming from contact with students who are significantly older and more experienced, but not necessarily wiser, are genuine— but constructive overall. For males, the role of brilliant prodigy can too easily become an effective means of avoiding the anxiety-provoking experiences that lead to timely development in the social and emotional dimensions. Consequently, males may benefit much from efforts to make opportunities for such experiences attractive and successful from their perspectives. Females, in comparison, seem relatively aggressive in seeking out social experiences, with which they are often inadequately prepared to deal. Not uncommonly, they suffer emotional, sexual, and other physical injury, from which they usually recover. Obviously, one must be uncomfortable in the face of such findings, but this is insufficient justification for interfering with informed decisions made by students or families. The most appropriate role for school psychologists and counselors seems to be to stand ready as sources of information, reflection, and support—for students, as well as for parents when possible. This calls for delicacy in balancing the needs of several constituencies (student, family, and society), with maintaining students' confidences (except as required by law) a particular concern.

In a chapter ostensibly valuing wellness, it would never do to forget that academically behaving students have physical and spiritual needs. Our experience refutes all stereotypes that they are calculating nihilists, or willowy, pale, bulbous-eyed freaks recoiling in horror or disgust from the athletic fields and hard physical labor. Examples of opposite extremes abound. One young man, who went on at age 26 to join the mathematics and physics faculties at one of the most prestigious universities in the country, was an avid body builder throughout his adolescence. Others devoted themselves to sailing, bowling, cycling, swimming, or golf. Many of the adolescent females danced, ran, or rowed competitively or professionally. We dealt repeatedly with campus police and medical clinic calls to vouch for young males either nabbed at the crest of a perilous rope climb up a multistory stone-faced campus building or recovering from mishaps occasioned by exercising physical capacities.

Spiritual needs, widespread among students, were typically tended by the family, although often shared with the counselor. The youngest boy in one cohort unswervingly prepared for 4 years for a missionary year that could begin only after he turned 18. One of the young women was a champion in competitions of reciting passages from the Bible.

Perhaps worthy of mention as instances of the growth tips of ethical development, campus police received more than one call regarding misapplications of talent, particularly with respect to abuse of others' computer accounts. One student, for example, devised a program to mimic an unused public terminal, but that actually recorded account information entered by anyone luckless enough to log onto it (the "Trojan horse" trick).

Full appreciation of the breadth of wellness mandates that counselors be aware of the special needs of discrete subsets of academically behaving students. It appears particularly worth stressing that youngsters who ultimately identify themselves as lesbian, gay, or bisexual—who were well represented in our program—have unique needs for support. Many such students earned erratic grades when they were coming out. For them, obtaining social support was more crucial than study, and concerns about becoming victims of discrimination absorbed additional energies. Counselors should firmly advocate that schools acknowledge and provide significant support for this vulnerable and all-but-invisible minority.

# CONCLUSION

The literature on counseling academically behaving students is skimpy, but a few conclusions are tenable. One is that academic behavior is usually a foundation of wellness. In extreme cases, however, it can shoulder aside social contact, intimacy, leisure, self-esteem, pleasure, positive mood, rest, physical health, occupational exploration, and purpose in life. Assuring that *each* dimension of wellness receives adequate support, were it possible, would solve this problem.

The consensus is that the educational needs of academically behaving students must be more adequately met and that schools, as a rule, must make the lion's share of improvements. Even academic acceleration programs must broaden their scope to wellness in general, and be accountable for risks to wellness that they increase or introduce. As Pressey (1949) illustrated, these risks can be minimized by adopting clear goals in each dimension, together with definitive strategies and specific (but flexible) schedules for attaining them.

Counselors should be skilled at supporting academic behavior while opening as wide a range of realistic options in every dimension of wellness as possible. They should be willing to empower students to make the ultimate choices as to directions in which to grow, support age-appropriate risk taking, and genuinely value the diversity of unpredictable outcomes that will thereby result. Counselors should be aware of the risks and benefits of congregate academically behaving age-mates: they can both intimidate and support each other.

These conclusions have been informed by considerable feedback from adolescents provided during long-running episodes of academic behavior and, afterward, from the young adults into which they grew. Obviously, such data must yield to more systemic inquiries and to empirical studies. There is need for behavioral description of the dimensions of wellness, and for research regarding the balance of academic behaviors and other dimensions in academic programs. As this work continues, sounder information will accrue to a field that now enjoys no more than a toehold in empiricism.

# REFERENCES

Cornell, D. G., Callahan, C. M., & Loyd, B. H. (1991a). Socioemotional adjustment of adolescent girls enrolled in a residential acceleration program. *Gifted Child Quarterly, 35*, 58–66.

Cornell, D. G., Callahan, C. M., & Loyd, B. H. (1991b). Research on early college entrance: A few more adjustments are needed. *Gifted Child Quarterly, 35*, 71–72.

Cox, C. M. (1926). *Genetic studies of genius: Volume II. The early mental traits of three-hundred geniuses*. Stanford, CA: Stanford University Press.

Frederickson, R. H. (1986). Preparing gifted and talented students for the world of work. *Journal of Guidance and Counseling, 64*, 556–557.

Fund for the Advancement of Education. (1957). *They went to college early*. New York: Research Division of the Fund.

Hettler, R. (1984). Presenting the wellness concept to the uninitiated. In J. P. Opatz (Ed.), *Wellness promotion strategies* (pp. 28–38). Dubuque, IA: Kendall/Hunt.

Hillman, J., & Ventura, M. (1992, May/June). Is therapy turning us into children? *New Age Journal*, pp. 60–68, 139–141.

Hollingworth, L. S. (1939). What we know about the early selection and training of leaders. *Teachers College Record, 40*, 575–592.

Hollingworth, L. S. (1942). *Children above 180 IQ. Stanford Binet: Origin and development.* Yonkers-on-Hudson, NY: World Book.

Janos, P. M. (1986). The socialization of highly intelligent boys: Case material from Terman's correspondence. *Journal of Counseling and Development, 65,* 193–195.

Janos, P. M. (1991). The self-perceptions of uncommonly bright youngsters. In R. Sternberg & J. Kolligian (Eds.), *Perceptions of competence and incompetence across the lifespan.* New Haven: Yale University Press.

Janos, P. M., & Robinson, N. (1985). Social and personality development of the gifted and talented. In F. Horowitz (Ed.), *The gifted and talented: A developmental perspective.* Washington, DC: American Psychological Association.

Janos, P. M., Robinson, N., Carter, C., Chapel, A., Curland, R., Daily, M., Guilland, M., Heinzig, M., Kehl, H., Lu, S., Sherry, D., Stoloff, J., & Wise, A. (1988). A cross-sectional developmental study of the social relations of students who enter college early. *Gifted Child Quarterly, 32,* 210–215.

Janos, P. M., Robinson, N., & Lunneborg, C. (1989). Markedly early entrance to college: A multi-year comparative study of academic performance and psychological adjustment. *Journal of Higher Education, 60,* 514–518.

Janos, P. M., Sanfilipo, S., & Robinson, N. (1986). "Underachievement" among markedly accelerated college students. *Journal of Youth and Adolescence, 15,* 303–313.

Kerr, B. A., & Colangelo, N. (1988). The college plans of academically talented students. *Journal of Counseling and Development, 67,* 42–48.

Levine, N. S. (1986). Comments on "acceleration." In J. C. Maker (Ed.), *Critical issues in gifted education: Defensible programs for the gifted* (pp. 197–208). Austin, TX: PRO-ED.

McMann, J., & Oliver, J. (1988). Problems in families with gifted children: Implications for counselors. *Journal of Counseling and Development, 66,* 275–278.

Mill, J. S. (1961). Autobiography. In M. Lerner (Ed.), *Essential works of John Stuart Mill.* New York: Bantam.

Myers, R. S., & Pace, T. M. (1986). Counseling gifted and talented students: Historical perspectives and contemporary issues. *Journal of Counseling and Development, 64,* 548–551.

Perrone, P. (1986). Guidance needs of gifted children, adolescents, and adults. *Journal of Counseling and Development, 64,* 564–566.

Pressey, S. (1949). *Educational acceleration* (Bureau of Educational Research Monograph #31). Columbus: Ohio State University Press.

Rand, A. (1957). *Atlas shrugged.* New York: Random House.

Renzulli, J. S., & Reis, S. M. (1991). The reform movement and the quiet crisis in gifted education. *Gifted Child Quarterly, 35,* 26–35.

Sawyer, R. (1986). Intellectual challenges and emotional support of the precocious child. *Journal of Counseling and Development, 64,* 593–597.

Stanley, J. C. (1977). Rationale of the Study of Mathematically Precocious Youth during its first five years of promoting educational acceleration. In J. C. Stanley, W. C. George, & C. H. Solano (Eds.), *The gifted and creative: A 50-year perspective* (pp. 75–113). Baltimore: Johns Hopkins University Press.

Stanley, J. C. (1985). Young entrants to college: How did they fare? *College and University, 60,* 219–228.

Swiatek, M., & Benbow, C. (1991). Ten-year longitudinal follow-up of ability-matched accelerated and unaccelerated gifted students. *Journal of Educational Psychology, 83,* 528–538.

Terman, L. M., & Oden, M. H. (1947). *The gifted child grows up: 25 years' follow-up of a superior group. Volume IV: Genetic studies of genius.* Stanford, CA: Stanford University Press.

# Chapter 20

# Counseling Gifted Young Women About Educational and Career Choices

## Constance L. Hollinger

♦ ♦ ♦

COUNSELING GIFTED YOUNG WOMEN about educational and career choices requires an understanding of gender-specific issues underlying their achievement-related decisions. The decisions of gifted young women frequently appear at odds with their actual talents and abilities, as evidenced in standardized test scores, grades, and performance. For example, why does the precocious mathematician decide to drop her advanced placement math course? Why does she decide that she ultimately wants to pursue a career in the performing arts, rather than one in engineering?

Even in the few areas such as mathematics where differences have been found (Maccoby & Jacklin, 1974), sex differences in ability are quite small and have declined in recent years (Hyde & Linn, 1988; Jacklin, 1989). Gifted girls, especially at the elementary level, achieve good grades and experience success in school. Nonetheless, gifted women remain underrepresented among recipients of advanced graduate and professional degrees, in certain career areas such as math and science, and in careers of high status and challenge. Why, despite their abilities and success in the educational system, do gifted girls and young women make the decisions that they frequently make?

In addressing the above questions, this chapter (a) integrates conceptual differences in understanding women's achievements, (b) provides an overview of factors influencing the impact of those conceptual differences upon achievement decisions, (c) examines individual differences among gifted young women in their perceptions of those influences, and (d) provides strategies and suggestions for school support personnel working with this population.

# A CONCEPTUAL FRAMEWORK
# FOR INTERVENTION

Since Terman and Oden's (1947, 1959) longitudinal research on the gifted, the "underachievement" of gifted women has been well documented (Reis, 1987; Reis & Callahan, 1989). Gifted women's educational and career accomplishments have been neither commensurate with their talents and abilities nor comparable to those of their gifted male counterparts. This "failure" of gifted women to realize their potential has been a primary focus of concern for both researchers and those counseling gifted young women. Effective counseling under this paradigm requires an understanding of the internal (intrapersonal), interpersonal, and external (sociocultural) barriers that prevent gifted young women from achieving what their male counterparts have traditionally achieved. The focus is on the gifted young woman and the design of interventions to assist her in overcoming barriers. The implicit goal is that she realizes her potential through attainment of educational and career goals commensurate with her talents and abilities.

Throughout the 1980s, Carol Gilligan (1982; Gilligan, Ward, & Taylor, 1988) and others provided an alternative perspective that called for an examination not of why women "fail," but rather why society "fails" to recognize and value contributions that have traditionally been made by women. Eccles (1987) emphasized the need to understand why women make the achievement-related choices that they make rather than why they "fail" to make other choices. Super (1980), Tittle (1983), and others further drew attention to the fact that academic and career choices are not made in isolation, but rather in relationship to other life spheres such as home and family. Jordan, Kaplan, Miller, Stiver, and Surrey (1991) further endorsed this view by emphasizing the centrality of relationship issues for women (e.g., weighing the impact of their educational and career choices on others) in the decision-making process. Effective counseling under this paradigm emphasizes the sociocultural context and focuses on socializing agents who perpetuate gender stereotypes and biases. A primary goal of intervention is societal understanding, valuing, and rewarding of women's unique contributions, as well as their accomplishments in areas other than education and career.

Those who counsel gifted girls and young women must draw upon both of these perspectives in developing an integrated conceptual framework that avoids biases inherent in both while benefitting from the significant contributions made by each. In doing so, a critical examination of definitions and issues regarding achievement is a prerequisite. The following questions are meant to stimulate critical examination of assumptions or beliefs that might otherwise bias the counseling process.

First, what is meant by and recognized as "achievement"? According to Spence and Helmreich (1983), the study of achievement has been limited to educational and career attainments. Are these the only two life spheres in which an individual achieves? Are accomplishments in other spheres of one's life not considered achievements? As Unger and Crawford (1992) asked, why is the nurturing of the next generation not viewed by society as an achievement? Conversely, as Mednick (1989) suggested, is not acceptance of stereotypically feminine goals and aspirations merely a perpetuation of the gender-biased status quo?

Second, which talents and abilities are to be realized? Many gifted young women possess multiple talents and abilities. How might the precocious mathematician who is also a talented artist with extraordinary interpersonal or relational skills best realize her potential? In the counseling process, are some of her talents and abilities valued over others and, if so, by whom and why? Are talents equally valued regardless of the gender of the gifted individual?

Third, how is counseling effectiveness evaluated? How is the realization of potential determined? The research literature has applied external criteria for evaluating societally valued achievements. One mathematically precocious young woman completes her doctorate and chooses a research career with the National Aeronautics and Space Administration, whereas another equally gifted young woman completes a bachelor's degree in mathematics and chooses to teach high school mathematics. Has only one of these young women realized her potential? In contrast to an external normative evaluation, achievements can be evaluated from the perspective of the individual by focusing on her idiographic definition of achievement and her evaluation of her accomplishments (Hollinger & Fleming, 1992). What does the gifted woman view as her achievements? How do her achievements compare with earlier aspirations?

Finally, what is the ultimate goal of academic and career counseling with the gifted young woman: her contribution to society or her satisfaction with life? Is receiving the Nobel prize for her contributions comparable to retrospective personal satisfaction with her accomplishments?

An integrated conceptual framework for counseling recognizes all accomplishment as achievement; values diverse talents, skills, and abilities equally; recognizes the need to work with socialization agents and gifted males as well as gifted females; values societal contribution and personal life satisfaction equally; and evaluates counseling effectiveness against personally as well as societally defined criteria. Without an integrated conceptual framework that addresses the questions posed above, the subtle, all-pervasive gender biases and stereotypes characteristic of American culture may merely be perpetuated by the counseling process.

# SOCIETAL MESSAGES TO GIFTED GIRLS AND WOMEN

The global, gender-stereotypic societal message is explicitly and implicitly clear: Women are passive, nurturing, kind, and caring. They are *not* to be masculine (e.g., logical, independent, intelligent). The gifted female's immediate network of significant others, however, may communicate mixed and conflicting expectations. While expected to be feminine, she is also expected to achieve and excel—expectations that are stereotypically masculine. If she is further expected to excel in stereotypically masculine domains, such as math and/or science, she is caught in the trap of a three-way interaction of diametrically opposed expectations (Hollinger, 1991a) and confronts the "dilemma of the gifted woman" (Noble, 1987).

From infancy, parents' interaction patterns with female infants differ from those with sons. These patterns foster passivity over agency and independence long before their daughters are labeled gifted. In fact, parents tend to recognize giftedness in their daughters at a later age than they do their sons (Fox, 1982). Even after the gifted label has been conferred, parents communicate lower expectations for their daughters' achievements (Phillips & Zimmerman, 1990). While parents "assist" their sons in solving a problem, parents may "help" their gifted daughters by solving the problem for them (Rand & Gibb, 1989). Even among parents who expect their daughters to achieve academically, many have very traditional career aspirations, expecting that their daughters merely acquire some marketable skills to supplement the family income or support themselves sometime later in life (Fleming & Hollinger, 1979b; Fox, 1982; Walker, Reis, & Leonard, 1992).

The gifted girl is also likely to encounter gender bias when she begins formal education. Minimal effort has been directed toward eradicating gender inequities in the classroom. Curricular materials, teachers' interaction patterns, and even guest speakers perpetuate the cultural norm. Although the girl may be explicitly rewarded for achievement and expected to achieve, the overpowering message typically is one of gender, rather than ability expectations (American Association of University Women, 1992; Sadker, Sadker, & Klein, 1991). Based on their research, Belenky, Clinchy, Goldberger, and Tarule

(1986) suggested that this problem is further exacerbated by traditional pedagogical methodologies that are incompatible with "women's ways of knowing."

Peers, a powerful source of influence, particularly during adolescence, also communicate clear gender-stereotypic messages. Gifted males, in particular, have been found to be less than gender equitable with respect to their expectations for the achievement behavior of their female counterparts, and expect that their future spouses will assume quite traditional feminine roles (Dolny, 1985). Choosing between academic excellence and peer acceptance is difficult for a gifted female!

Even if everyone in her immediate social network were completely free of gender bias, the gifted female encounters subtle, all-pervasive gender-stereotypic messages that reflect the "family values" of the last decade. From television shows and commercials to the print media, women continue to be portrayed in stereotypic terms. Messages regarding the "costs" of violating the feminine stereotype constitute what author Susan Faludi (1991) described as a backlash against women and the progress toward gender equity made in the 1970s.

In addition, the gifted female encounters a lack of clarity with respect to the roles of adult women (McWilliams, 1992). Women in her immediate social network (e.g., mothers, aunts) may be struggling to define or redefine their roles by returning to college or entering the workforce for the first time. Conversely, messages from female role models regarding gender segregation and stratification of careers, salary inequities, sexual harassment, burnout of superwomen, and the "glass ceiling" (that prevents women from advancing to the highest levels of career attainment) may raise serious doubts about the possibilities of "having it all."

Although the normative reality described above may vary, the critical reality is the one filtered through the eyes and ears of the individual, the perceived reality that creates individual differences in awareness of the gender–achievement conflict. Such differences, conceptualized as three developmental stages of awareness (discussed in the next section), must be recognized and addressed in the counseling process.

# GIFTED AND FEMALE: COPING WITH A GENDER-BIASED SOCIETY

Some gifted young women, having internalized gender-stereotypic messages, do not perceive themselves as gifted and may experience minimal conflict. Not until later in life, as evidenced by the gifted women in Terman's study (Sears & Barbee, 1977), do questions arise as to what "might have been" had they pursued career options. In contrast, many gifted women, labeling themselves as both female and gifted, experience the conflict inherent in such mutually exclusive societal labels. Many view the conflict as a lose–lose situation in which a choice must be made between either home and family or career. Still others resolve the conflict by deciding to have it all. Understanding the gifted young woman's perception of societal messages and expectations is therefore the first counseling task.

## Stage 1: Gender-Typed Woman

The gender-typed gifted young woman, having internalized gender-stereotypic messages, perceives and assimilates only that feedback from her environment that is congruent with the feminine stereotype (Bem, 1981). Incongruent feedback, such as praise for her accomplishments in math, science, or any other stereotypically masculine domain, is neither "heard" nor incorporated into her self-belief system. These young women have difficulty accepting and/or identifying with the gifted label. Additional consequences of this selective perception include low self-perceptions of ability, especially in stereotypically masculine achievement domains; low sense of personal competence, social values, and interests; low aspirations for educational and career attainment; and personal behaviors or characteristics that are expressive (e.g., kind, sensitive to the feelings of others) rather than agentic (e.g., independent, assertive) (Hollinger, 1991a).

The above profile influences achievement-related decisions by determining the gifted young woman's perceptions of both the value and the probability of success with various achievement tasks (Eccles, 1985). For example, in deciding whether to pursue advanced placement course work in mathematics, the gender-typed gifted female may perceive such course work as having minimal value. Advanced math has little utility value if her future goals are stereotypically feminine in nature (e.g., full-time homemaker, nurse, teacher) and negative attainment value in that succeeding in math not only fails to affirm, but actually conflicts with, her view of herself as feminine. Second, perceiving herself as having minimal math ability lowers her expectations for success and/or raises her estimates as to the amount of time and effort required to succeed. In simple cost–benefit terms, the gender-typed gifted young woman anticipates excessive investment of effort and/or the likelihood of failure in undertaking an academic task viewed as having minimal, if any, value. Her decision to drop out of the math mainstream therefore makes sense!

Similarly, according to Gottfredson's (1981) developmental theory of occupational aspirations, careers that are incongruent with her gender identity are eliminated during childhood. Once eliminated, such careers are never again considered as possible options. The gender-typed gifted girl would eliminate from consideration any career perceived as being "too masculine." Unfortunately, the vast majority of challenging, high-status careers are stereotyped as masculine.

Counseling the gender-typed young woman must begin with a thorough examination of her self-belief system, including her self-perceptions of talents, abilities, values, interests, and personal attributes. The primary goal of her recognizing and accepting her talents and abilities can be achieved through careful examination of those self-beliefs that are either distorted or completely absent as a function of the gender-stereotypic filtering process. Exploring the origins and past sources of validation for various self-beliefs can identify erroneous or simplistic beliefs in need of correction or refinement. Where did the belief that "I am not good in math" originate? Who or what reinforced that belief? What function or purpose does that self-belief serve? Creating cognitive dissonance by reality testing the belief against her objective performance history and normative data can in turn lead to changed self-perceptions.

Goals and aspirations for the future also require careful scrutiny and reality testing. Few gifted young women are aware of the consequences of dropping out of the advanced mathematics sequence in high school. They are later surprised to discover that these high school math courses are prerequisites for admission to many colleges within a university (e.g., colleges of engineering or business). Many are quite surprised by the amount of math and science involved in even the most stereotypically feminine careers. In career exploration, occupations eliminated from consideration must also be examined. Why would the woman never want to be an engineer? Throughout this exploration, the process of breaking stereotypic, paired association of gender with academic disciplines and careers is begun.

Finally, those not expecting to work outside the home need to explore current divorce and workforce statistics. They might be surprised to learn that among one sample of gifted women graduating in the 1970s, 95% reported working outside the home (Walker et al., 1992)!

## Stage 2: Conflicted Women

Many gifted young women, including those in Stage 1 who move to recognizing and accepting their giftedness, are aware of the conflict between gender and gifted expectations. They see a lose–lose situation requiring an either-or choice: either advanced placement math and physics or popularity and dating, either engineering or home and family. The "flight into femininity" by many gifted young women, coinciding with the increased importance of gender identity during adolescence, is a choice that may, at least temporarily, resolve the either-or conflict. Like those in Stage 1, they opt out of math and science sequences, honors courses, and other stereotypically masculine pursuits, although for different reasons. Unlike their Stage 1 counterparts, they have an awareness of the conflict and losses associated with their choices. The goal of counseling with these young women is twofold: First, break the stereotypic paired associations between gender and academic disciplines, careers, and characteristics critical to the learning process (e.g., intellectual curiosity, logical thinking and reasoning). Second, transcend simplistic either-or thinking.

Through exploration of repertoires of human behavior across contexts, the gifted readily recognize that a person, regardless of gender, can be competitive and aggressive in one context while gentle and kind in another (e.g., a chief executive officer in the corporate office vs. at home playing with children). Simplistic career stereotypes, dependent upon surface and simplistic understanding, can be dispelled through examination of the hidden factors and complementary skills required by various careers. Many stereotypically feminine careers require stereotypically masculine skills and abilities, and vice versa. A nurse must be assertive, analytic, and independent, whereas a physician must be caring and compassionate.

Homework assignments designed for discovery learning about gender socialization and cultural perpetuation of gender stereotypes, combined with reading biographies of women who have succeeded in nontraditional careers, can stimulate further questioning, followed by critical analysis and discussion. Subsequent readings, such as Carol Tavris's (1992) *The Mismeasure of Woman*, provide a conceptual framework that enables the gifted young woman to understand the conflict that she has experienced.

Interviewing a sample of women who combine career, home, and family with avocational pursuits can provide irrefutable data that the either-or choice is neither a necessity nor the norm. Lifework planning, emphasizing the integration of all life spheres, can then enable the gifted young woman to envision and plan for a future that combines, rather than limits, her life choices. Through structured experiences, she can explore options for realizing her many talents and abilities through various arenas of her life. Abandoning either-or thinking, the gifted young woman now faces the challenge of having it all.

## Stage 3: Superwomen

The majority of gifted young women aspire to combining a career with home and family and perceive few, if any, barriers or challenges to this goal (Fleming & Hollinger, 1979b; Smith & Ludec, 1992). The optimism of adolescence obscures the reality of attempting to maintain a neurosurgery schedule, attend parent conferences, and prepare a dinner party for one's spouse's clients all in one day. Her perfectionism and energy enable the gifted female adolescent to excel as a cheerleader, socialite, and advanced placement honors student. However, the costs of perfectionism and the "superwoman syndrome" can be high.

The goal of counseling these young women is threefold: (a) prioritizing goals, values, and investments of time, energy, and talents; (b) developing coping competence for managing life stressors (see Chapter 16); and (c) recognizing that having it all does not mean "doing it all." Again, having the young women interview women who integrate all life spheres is recommended, although with an emphasis on how that integration is managed and the coping strategies employed. Structured experiences in prioritizing (see Fleming & Hollinger, 1979a) can then enable the gifted young woman to make choices on the basis of her own priorities.

Coping competence includes stress and time management training. An additional task is the identification of life spheres and/or situations in which "less than perfect" will be acceptable. Finally, counseling women that having it all does not mean their having to do it all is essential. Recent surveys document that women, regardless of career investment, are still responsible for the majority of tasks central to home and family (Reis, 1987). To avoid the doing-it-all syndrome, gifted young women need to acquire dual decision-making, self-assertion, and negotiation skills.

# FOR ALL GIFTED GIRLS AND YOUNG WOMEN

Whereas the developmental stages of awareness discussed in the previous sections identify counseling needs specific to the individual, several general intervention issues must be addressed (see Hollinger 1991b). First, career counseling must address the complexity of integrating multiple gifts and talents, coping with multiple and frequently conflicting expectations from others, and dealing with the ambiguity of having so many career and lifestyle options from which to choose.

Second, career exploration must move from a simplistic, one-dimensional to a three-dimensional examination of (a) all talents, abilities, and skills required by specific careers (e.g., the interpersonal skills needed by physicians, the math and science involved in glassblowing); (b) the variation within a given career area of skills and abilities required and satisfactions derived (e.g., public defender vs.

corporate tax law, family practitioner vs. thoracic surgeon); and (c) the integration of educational and career plans with other lifestyle goals. Use of standardized, career-assessment measures, in addition to being gender biased, can obscure such career complexities and should therefore be used with caution.

Third, gifted girls and women need to examine and ultimately understand their past academic decisions and the issues implicit in their educational and career aspirations. Eccles's (1985) model can serve as a comprehensive framework for guiding the gifted young woman to such an understanding through exploring her perceptions of past achievement events, her valuing of specific achievement tasks, and her expectations for success.

Fourth, teaching gifted young women about the realities of their culture simply cannot be achieved through lecture. Structured experiences, selected readings, and interviewing of female role models which facilitate data collection for independent examination and analysis empower her by allowing her to draw her own conclusions.

Fifth, many traditional theories of career development were derived and tested on male-only populations. As a result, such theories are limited in their applicability to women's career development. School support personnel are advised to review the more recent work of Astin (1985), Farmer (1985), and Marshall (1989) to understand better the complexities and nuances specific to the career development of gifted girls and women.

Finally, as implied by the integrated conceptual framework, school support personnel must encourage the gifted girl or young woman to recognize and accept all of her talents and abilities. Encouragement of stereotypically masculine competencies must avoid sending implicit messages that devalue stereotypically feminine competencies. Conversely, encouragement and support for stereotypically feminine competencies and aspirations must avoid implicit messages of "preference" for that which is gender "appropriate"! The gifted young woman must clarify, after identifying gender-stereotypic baggage, exactly what she wants.

# SPECIFIC PROGRAMS

Since the late 1970s, a number of general career development programs have been developed specifically for gifted young women. For example, Project CHOICE (Fleming & Hollinger, 1979a) is a diagnostic prescriptive career development program that includes structured group experiences, career information lab activities, and guidelines for role model and mentoring opportunities. Several programs specific to math and science careers are described in *Women and the Mathematical Mystique* (Fox, Brody, & Tobin, 1980) and the special issue of *Journal for the Education of the Gifted*, which describes programs such as Rand and Gibb's (1989) Action Science. Nash, Borman, and Colson (1980) and Shamanoff (1985) provided descriptions of and guidelines for establishing mentoring programs for gifted young women. Programs, strategies, and interventions exist. The greater need is for professionals with an astute and knowledgeable understanding of the gifted girl or young woman who can tailor interventions to meet her unique individual needs.

## COUNSELING SIGNIFICANT OTHERS

Until the significant others in their lives transcend gender stereotypes and biases, gifted girls and young women will need to cope with conflicting gender–achievement expectations. As Bell (1989) observed, "There is something wrong here and it is not me!" Nonetheless, gifted young women continue to wrestle with this conflict created by others. Even those who succeed in realizing their own personally defined aspirations may continue to experience doubt about unmet societal expectations. Nevertheless, with the exception of Kerr's (1986) work with gifted males and EQUALS (Kreinberg, 1978), which focuses on math teachers, few programs focus primarily on those who create the dilemma for gifted young women. Why? Why not replicate Kerr's work with gifted boys and young men to assist them in planning how their career commitments can be integrated with parenting responsibilities and housekeeping responsibilities? Why not run parent groups that assist parents in identifying and transcending their gender stereotypic expectations for their child, female or male? Why not focus on changing curricular materials, classroom interaction patterns, and instructional strategies that perpetuate gender inequity in the educational system? Why not change the focus of intervention so that, in some distant future, there is no longer a need for a chapter such as this one?

## CONCLUSION

Growing up in a gender-biased society, gifted young women encounter a steady stream of messages that define what constitutes achievement and femininity as well as the relationship between these two constructs. Regardless of the extent to which these messages are internalized, gender socialization and bias impact every aspect of the gifted young woman's achievement-related decision making. This influence is manifested in diverse ways, ranging from failure to realize one's potential to the stress-related consequences of the superwoman syndrome. Although direct assistance to gifted young women is essential, intervention efforts designed to eradicate the gender bias endemic in our culture offer the only hope that some day gifted young women will be truly free to realize their gifts and talents.

# REFERENCES

American Association of University Women. (1992). *The AAUW Report: How schools shortchange girls*. Washington, DC: Author.

Astin, H. S. (1985). The meaning of work in women's lives: A sociopsychological model of career choice and work behavior. *Counseling Psychology, 12,* 117–126.

Belenky, M. F., Clinchy, B. M., Goldberger, N. R., & Tarule, J. M. (1986). *Women's ways of knowing*. New York: Basic Books.

Bell, L. A. (1989). Something's wrong here and it's not me: Challenging the dilemmas that block girls' success. *Journal for the Education of the Gifted, 12,* 118–130.

Bem, S. L. (1981). Gender schema theory: A cognitive account of sex typing. *Psychological Review, 88,* 354–364.

Dolny, C. (1985). University of Toronto Schools' gifted students' career and family plans. *Roeper Review, 7,* 160–162.

Eccles, J. S. (1985). Why doesn't Jane run? Sex differences in educational and occupational patterns. In F. D. Horowitz & M. O'Brien (Eds.), *The gifted and talented: Developmental perspectives* (pp. 251–295). Washington, DC: American Psychological Association.

Eccles, J. S. (1987). Gender roles and women's achievement-related decisions. *Psychology of Women Quarterly, 11,* 135–172.

Faludi, S. (1991). *Backlash: The undeclared war against American women*. New York: Crown.

Farmer, H. S. (1985). Model of career and achievement motivation for women and men. *Journal of Counseling Psychology, 32,* 363–390.

Fleming, E. S., & Hollinger, C. L. (1979a). *Project CHOICE: Creating her options in career exploration*. Boston: Educational Development Corporation.

Fleming, E. S., & Hollinger, C. L. (1979b). *Realizing the promise of female adolescents: A diagnostic–prescriptive model*. Final report to the Office of Education, Department of Health, Education and Welfare (Women's Educational Equity Act Program No. G00760497). Washington, DC: Department of Health, Education and Welfare.

Fox, L. H. (1982). *The social processes that inhibit or enhance the development of competence and interest in mathematics among highly able young women: Final report*. Washington, DC: National Institute of Education.

Fox, L. H., Brody, L., & Tobin, D. (1980). *Women and the mathematical mystique*. Baltimore: Johns Hopkins University.

Gilligan, C. (1982). *In a different voice: Psychological theory and women's development*. Cambridge, MA: Harvard University Press.

Gilligan, C., Ward, J. V., & Taylor, J. M. (Eds.). (1988). *Mapping the moral domain*. Cambridge, MA: Harvard University Press.

Gottfredson, L. S. (1981). Circumscription and compromise: A developmental theory of occupational aspirations. *Journal of Counseling Psychology, 28*, 545–579.

Hollinger, C. L. (1991a). Career choices for gifted adolescents: Overcoming stereotypes. In J. Genshaft & M. Bireley (Eds.), *Understanding the gifted adolescent: Educational, developmental, and multicultural issues* (pp. 201–214). New York: Teachers College Press.

Hollinger, C. L. (1991b). Facilitating the career development of gifted young women. *Roeper Review, 13*, 132–136.

Hollinger, C. L., & Fleming, E. S. (1992). A longitudinal examination of life choices of gifted and talented young women. *Gifted Child Quarterly, 36*, 207–212.

Hyde, J. S., & Linn, M. C. (1988). Are there sex differences in verbal abilities? *Psychological Bulletin, 104*, 53–69.

Jacklin, C. N. (1989). Female and male: Issues of gender. *American Psychologist, 44*, 127–133.

Jordan, J. V., Kaplan, A. G., Miller, J. B., Stiver, I. B., & Surrey, J. L. (1991). *Women's growth in connection: Writings from the Stone Center*. New York: Guilford.

Kerr, B. A. (1986). Career counseling for the gifted: Assessments and interventions. *Journal of Counseling and Development, 64*, 602–604.

Kreinberg, N. (1978). EQUALS in math. *Independent School, 37*, 47–49.

Maccoby, E., & Jacklin, C. (1974). *The psychology of sex differences*. Stanford, CA: Stanford University Press.

Marshall, J. (1989). Re-visioning career concepts: A feminist invitation. In M. B. Arthur, D. T. Hall, & B. S. Lawrence (Eds.), *Handbook of career theory*. London: Cambridge University Press.

McWilliams, N. (1992). The worst of both worlds: Dilemmas of contemporary young women. In B. Wainrib (Ed.), *Gender issues across the life cycle* (pp. 27–36). New York: Springer.

Mednick, M. T. (1989). On the politics of psychological constructs: Stop the bandwagon, I want to get off. *American Psychologist, 44*(8), 1118–1123.

Nash, W. R., Borman, C., & Colson, S. (1980). Career education for gifted and talented students: A senior high school model. *Exceptional Children, 46*(5), 404–405.

Noble, K. D. (1987). The dilemma of the gifted woman. *Psychology of Women Quarterly, 11*, 367–378.

Phillips, D. A., & Zimmerman, M. (1990). The developmental course of perceived competence and incompetence among competent children. In R. J. Stornborg & J. Kolligian (Eds.), *Competence considered* (pp. 41–66). New Haven, CT: Yale University Press.

Rand, D., & Gibb, L. H. (1989). A model program for gifted girls in science. *Journal for the Education of the Gifted, 12,* 142–155.

Reis, S. M. (1987). We can't change what we don't recognize: Understanding the special needs of gifted females. *Gifted Child Quarterly, 31,* 83–88.

Reis, S. M., & Callahan, C. M. (1989). Gifted females: They've come a long way—or have they? *Journal for the Education of the Gifted, 12,* 99–117.

Sadker, M., Sadker, D., & Klein, S. (1991). The issue of gender in elementary and secondary education. In G. Grant (Ed.), *Review of research in education* (Vol. 17, pp. 269–334). Washington, DC: American Educational Research Association.

Sears, P. S., & Barbee, A. H. (1977). Career and life satisfactions among Terman's gifted women. In J. C. Stanley, W. W. George, & C. H. Solano (Eds.), *The gifted and the creative: A fifty year perspective* (pp. 28–65). Baltimore: Johns Hopkins University Press.

Shamanoff, G. A. (1985). The Women Mentor Project: A sharing approach. *Roeper Review, 7,* 163–165.

Smith, N. J., & Ludec, S. K. (1992). *Women's work.* Calgary, Alberta: Detselig Enterprises.

Spence, J. T., & Helmreich, R. (1983). Achievement-related motives and behaviors. In J. T. Spence (Ed.), *Achievement and achievement motives: Psychological and sociological approaches* (pp. 7–74). San Francisco: Freeman.

Super, D. E. (1980). Life span, life space approach to career development. *Journal of Vocational Development, 16,* 282–298.

Tavris, C. (1992). *The mismeasure of woman.* New York: Simon & Schuster.

Terman, L. M., & Oden, M. H. (1947). *The gifted child grows up: Twenty five years' follow-up of a superior group.* Stanford, CA: Stanford University Press.

Terman, L. M., & Oden, M. H. (1959). *The gifted group at mid-life: Thirty five years' follow-up of the superior child.* Stanford, CA: Stanford University Press.

Tittle, C. K. (1983). Studies of the effects of career interest inventories: Expanding outcome criteria to include women's experiences. *Journal of Vocational Behavior, 22,* 148–158.

Unger, R., & Crawford, M. (1992). *Women and gender: A feminist psychology.* New York: McGraw-Hill.

Walker, B. A., Reis, S. M., & Leonard, J. S. (1992). A developmental investigation of the lives of gifted women. *Gifted Child Quarterly, 36,* 201–206.

# Chapter 21

# *Consultation Strategies with Gifted and Regular Educators: A Collaborative Approach*

**Dawn P. Flanagan**

◆  ◆  ◆

GIFTED STUDENTS ARE a heterogeneous group representing varying degrees of cognitive and academic abilities, talent, and creativity. When a student is identified as gifted, the label signifies that the student has exceptional capabilities relative to same-age peers. Once the student is identified, however, the effectiveness of service delivery is unclear. Ideally, the collaborative consultation efforts of school personnel and other professionals would culminate in policy and programming that are sensitive to the variations within this population. These efforts would also serve to cultivate students' exceptionalities through challenges designed to meet their unique educational needs. The variation in quality of services provided to gifted and talented students, however, is nearly as great as the variation of abilities represented by these students.

Educators are becoming increasingly concerned with gifted students who are not receiving special education services or who are receiving minimal services. These students are not sufficiently challenged in the educational milieu. In addition, variation among evaluation and identification procedures and adherence to certain myths, such as the assumption of automatic adaptive social–emotional development among gifted students, have resulted in inadequate service delivery. Finally, the lack of individualized instruction in some programs serving gifted and talented students may hinder their ability to investigate and expand in areas of interest in which they excel. This may, in turn, hinder the development of planning and organizational skills (Kress, 1985). It is unlikely that gifted students are achieving up to their full potential given these conditions.

There is a need to establish collaborative support networks within a systems context that will lead to the development of quality programs for the gifted and talented. Through such collaborative efforts, school personnel are expected to promote environments in which gifted students will reach their potential and greatly benefit society.

School personnel and parents concerned with the identification, programming, and social–emotional development of students who are gifted and talented have specific consultation needs. Collaborative relationships designed to identify and solve problems are a useful strategy that is gaining recognition (Parke, 1992). Working effectively with gifted learners requires the implementation of specialized services that necessitate adherence to a collaborative consultation model. According to Parke (1992), "the collaborative process offers the most creative and responsive results because marshalling the talents of many individuals results in outcomes that surpass what any one individual can accomplish" (p. 73). Although collaboration has been shown to be effective in the consultative process, there is little evidence that gifted and regular educators are collaborating.

This chapter presents basic consultation techniques as a premise for building collaborative relationships, as well as specific consultation strategies that have proven effective in the education of students who are gifted. In addition, this chapter discusses several collaborative consultation models that have been offered as frameworks designed to meet the needs of gifted and talented students.

# BUILDING COLLABORATIVE RELATIONSHIPS: BASIC TECHNIQUES

The primary goal of collaborative consultation is to achieve a balance between *expert* and *referent* power. Expert power exists when an individual is perceived as having the knowledge and ability needed to help another attain a specific goal. Referent power exists when an individual is seen as having traits that are similar to another person's and, therefore, is able to identify with that person. Once a balance between these two powers is achieved, a bidirectional (rather than unidirectional) influence process will ensue, thereby allowing the unique contributions of all parties involved in the consultation process to be realized. This emphasis on *mutual power* will ultimately lead to the generation and implementation of specific strategies that will result in positive behavioral, attitudinal, programmatic, or organizational change. Much of the consultation literature, however, has placed primary importance on the role of the consultant, with less emphasis on the consultee and others involved in this process (Parsons & Meyers, 1985).

Parsons and Meyers (1985) suggested several consultation techniques that may prove useful in facilitating the role of the consultee in a bidirectional influence process. These techniques are designed to ensure collaborative consultation and therefore require that the consultee be involved. Active participation will result in a relationship in which the consultee feels useful and responsible for evoking positive change. In the first technique, the consultant must create an environment in which the consultee has the freedom to accept or reject ideas. This will foster cooperation rather than competition. A second technique requires that the consultant encourage the consultee to generate ideas, offer suggestions, and make decisions. This will foster an egalitarian exchange of ideas, rather than a hierarchical exchange in which the consultant exerts power over the consultee. Moreover, consultee decision making and the resultant sense of shared responsibility act to maintain an egalitarian relationship and increase the likelihood of attitudinal or programmatic change. In the final technique, the consultant must recognize the consultee's contributions and emphasize how these efforts have been influential in stimulating change.

Other researchers have emphasized the importance of joint problem solving and indirect assistance to a third party in their definition of consultation (Alpert & Meyers, 1983; Norris, Burke, & Speer, 1990). Dyck and Dettmer (1989) discussed a process consultation model "in which the consultant helps the client perceive, understand, and act upon the problem" (p. 254). In this approach, alternatives may be generated regarding the problem at hand and possibilities suggested for solving similar problems in the future. This approach appears to be an efficient and effective way of addressing problems in a school setting (Dyck & Dettmer, 1989). Regardless of the approach or specific techniques that are used, the foundation for productive consultation and collaboration is active participation and effective communication.

Training in basic consultative techniques notwithstanding, parents and school personnel must understand and appreciate the consultation process to be effective in implementing change. Administrative and systemic support as well as ongoing reinforcement for joint problem solving and program planning are necessary precursors for positive collaborative, consultative relationships between parents and teachers. The literature provides ample confirmations of the positive relationship between parental influence on early development and later life achievements of their gifted children (Jenkins-Friedman & Fine, 1984).

An increasing awareness of the positive impact that parents of gifted youngsters have on their children's developmental, emotional, and intellectual well-being has led many researchers to design strategies to facilitate collaboration between parents and school personnel. Table 21.1 provides a summary of consultation strategies that have

**TABLE 21.1. Consultation Strategies Designed to Meet the Needs of Students Who Are Gifted**

| Source | Target Population | Strategy | Goal |
|---|---|---|---|
| Humes and Clark (1989) | Parents and gifted adolescents | Group intervention with parents (strategies adapted from Gordon, 1976; Miller, Nunnally, & Wackman, 1975) | To increase the gifted adolescent's intrapersonal needs for personal adjustment and self-acceptance |
| Kline and Meckstroth (1985) | Parents of highly (140–160 IQ) and exceptionally (above 160 IQ) gifted students | Professionally guided, ongoing, support groups for parents | To encourage gifted students and promote their development |
| | | Psychoeducational consultant for the family | To provide interpretations that are objective and presented in a preventive manner |
| | | Counseling for parents | To gain skill and courage in becoming tactful and active advocates for their gifted child's appropriate education |
| Seeley (1985) | Parents and gifted children | Ongoing counseling for parents and children provided by school psychologists | To provide objective interpretations and clear directions to both parents and educators of the gifted |

| | | | |
|---|---|---|---|
| Wolf (1989) | Parents who have preschool gifted children | Private consultation prior to the child's entry into a public school system | To facilitate parent decision making regarding school setting, grade placement, enrichment, and so on, as well as parent–school communication |
| Jenkins-Friedman and Fine (1984) | Gifted and regular education teachers | Transactional analysis | To establish operative parent–teacher partnerships that will lead to effective problem solving |
| Walker and Dangel (1992) | Parents of gifted and talented students | Effective problem solving, including problem identification, responsibility/ownership, generation of options, implementation of options, evaluation of effectiveness | To provide parents with useful suggestions to help their children develop effective problem-solving skills |
| Sherman (1982) | Parents of gifted and talented students | Patience, commitment, understanding | To promote positive parent–teacher interactions |

recently been offered as a means to facilitate parent–teacher communication and promote the development of gifted students. Several authors advocate various types of counseling (e.g., problem-solving skill training) as one method of collaborative consultation for parents of the gifted (Humes & Clark, 1989; Kline & Meckstroth, 1985). Seeley (1985) described the role of the school psychologist as instrumental in counseling parents of gifted students. He indicated that the school psychologist's knowledge of assessment could facilitate a parent's understanding of a child's exceptionalities, as well as provide a base for making suggestions regarding educational programming.

Kline and Meckstroth (1985) discussed the role of a psychoeducational consultant for the family, and Wolf (1989) stressed the importance of a private consultant for parents who have gifted preschoolers. In either context, the role of the consultant is to provide objective interpretations and facilitate parent decision making regarding selection of a school setting, grade placement, provision of enrichment activities, and behavior management strategies. The location of local, state, and national support and advocacy groups can also be provided by the consultant. Alternately, Jenkins-Friedman and Fine (1984) discussed transactional analysis as an effective strategy for gifted and regular classroom educators to use as they work together to solve problems. Similarly, Walker and Dangel (1992) offered suggestions to assist parents of gifted children in helping their children develop effective problem-solving skills. Finally, Sherman (1982) espoused patience, commitment, and understanding as the building blocks for positive parent–teacher relationships. Through these collaborative efforts, parents and teachers can gain a better understanding of gifted children, and gifted children can come to acknowledge and accept their unique abilities and similarity to nongifted peers (Allan & Fox, 1979; Colangelo & Zaffrann, 1975; Humes & Clark, 1989).

# CONSULTATION MODELS: EVOKING CHANGE IN GIFTED EDUCATION THROUGH COLLABORATION

School psychologists, teachers, counselors, and administrators regularly confront the responsibility of providing educational and psychosocial services to gifted students (Edwards & Kleine, 1986). The first step in providing these services involves inservice education of school personnel regarding the unique personal, social, emotional, and intellectual needs of gifted students. Training in consultation techniques and instruction in consultative strategies are necessary to ensure that school personnel have the knowledge and skill to work collaboratively in a variety of educational settings. The most difficult task to achieve is for everyone in the school and community environments to recognize the need for, take part of the responsibility in, and work toward the goal of full service delivery to gifted and talented students (Parke, 1992). When school personnel, professionals, and administrators come to understand and value the consultation process, they can work together to adopt a collaborative consultation model that complements their unique talents and fits the nature of their educational environment. Table 21.2 provides a summary of several consultation models that have been proposed for addressing the unique needs of gifted children and adolescents.

Edwards and Kleine (1986) advocated a multimodal model of consultation for working with gifted students, emanating from the work of Lazarus (1976, 1981), that emphasizes the importance of operating within a collaborative, consultative context (Edwards, 1978; Gerler, 1978). In their model, individual performance is assessed vis-à-vis seven modalities of experience: behavioral, affective, sensory, imaginal, cognitive, interpersonal, and physiological (drugs or diet). The acronym BASIC ID symbolizes each area and is used as a framework for addressing referral concerns. Although problems are considered within each modality, a consideration of the interplay among all modalities is necessary (Edwards & Kleine, 1986).

The therapy component of the multimodal model is grounded in learning theory and based on the following postulates: (a) counseling, consultation, and therapy are designed to address the unique needs of each student or situation (Lazarus, 1981); (b) the modalities are dynamic and interactive while at the same time distinct (Lazarus, 1976); and (c) the success of any intervention is a function of the number of modalities included in treatment (Edwards & Kleine, 1986; Lazarus, 1976).

Edwards and Kleine (1986) related several positive features of their model. First, the components of this model may be logically extended to all school personnel working with individuals who are gifted. Second, the multiple-factor approach to needs assessment is consistent with the complex nature of giftedness. Third, the model incorporates current research and clinical experience. Fourth, it allows for assessment and intervention that is tailored to meet an individual's needs. Finally, the model facilitates psychosocial development in gifted individuals through the synthesis of psychological, social, and educational needs. Thus, Edwards and Kleine's model provides a multidimensional, conceptual framework for assessing client problems that has applicability for all school personnel who work with gifted adolescents.

In addition, there is a need for collaborative interventions with

**TABLE 21.2. Specific Consultation Models Designed for Working with Students Who Are Gifted**

| Source | Target Population | Type of Model | Positive Features |
|---|---|---|---|
| Edwards and Kleine (1986) | Gifted adolescents | Multimodal collaborative consultation approach | Incorporates current research |
| | | | Provides a multidimensional, conceptual framework for analyzing client problems |
| | | | Tailors assessment and intervention to each client's individual needs |
| | | | Allows for synthesis of psychosocial and educational needs through collaborative efforts |
| VanTassel-Baska (1991) | Gifted students who are learning disabled or physically impaired | Three-level collaborative consultation approach | Addresses treatment of problems associated with learning disabilities in conjunction with interventions associated with giftedness |
| | | | Emphasizes establishing collaborative relationships within the community in an effort to increase resource availability |
| | | | Employs case management procedures as part of the school-based team |
| | | | Parents are included in educational decisions regarding comprehensive planning strategies |

| | | | |
|---|---|---|---|
| Dyck and Detmer (1989) | Gifted students who are learning disabled | Consulting teacher model: an indirect service delivery approach | Results in a "multiplier" effect that enables teachers to more clearly identify student needs and more competently teach in ways that are beneficial to all learners<br><br>Significantly reduces the amount of time that gifted students spend outside of the regular education setting |
| Parke (1992) | All gifted and talented students | Collaborative planning and service delivery within a systems context | Places student needs at the center of all educational decisions<br><br>Emphasizes a multiprogramming approach based on the distinctive learning characteristics of gifted students<br><br>Bases educational decisions on the input of an interdisciplinary placement and review team<br><br>Emphasizes collaborating in curriculum development, evaluation, and student well-being |

gifted individuals who are learning disabled. This population is perhaps one of the most neglected and underserved groups in the education system today. Gifted individuals who are learning disabled often go unnoticed because their disability (as determined by a significant discrepancy between expected and actual achievement) is not severe enough to be detected by performance in the regular classroom or on standardized tests (VanTassel-Baska, 1991). Consequently, most of the services provided to this population are delivered in the regular classroom and are supplemented with general instructional strategies (Dyck & Dettmer, 1989). Collaborative consultation models designed for working with gifted students with disabilities have been proposed in an effort to gain a better understanding of these learners and involve the expertise of professionals across a variety of fields.

VanTassel-Baska (1991) presented a consultation model for delivering services to gifted learners with disabilities (i.e., learning or physical disabilities) through educational collaboration. She offered several reasons for using collaboration as a means of facilitating service delivery to these students. First, few programs are designed to meet the needs of gifted students who are learning disabled or physically impaired, and treatment of problems associated with a specific disability is addressed separately from interventions associated with giftedness. Second, the educational needs of these students demand more than the regular classroom can offer. Programs for these students require educational decision teams and comprehensive planning strategies that include the parent as a participant. Third, because individualized programming involves many resources that may extend beyond what the school can provide, there is a need to establish collaborative relationships within the community in an effort to increase resource availability. Fourth, available funding may not be sufficient to cover the cost of specialized programs for gifted students with disabilities. Therefore, collaboration at local and state levels is necessary and facilitates access to broad-based resources. Finally, it is necessary to consult with other professionals who are more knowledgeable in this specialized area (e.g., specialists in handicapping conditions, school psychologists) in an attempt to broaden the professional's knowledge base.

VanTassel-Baska (1991) described a three-level collaborative consultation model for program development for disabled gifted students. At the first level, collaboration is described as a one-to-one relationship between the student and a significant other (e.g., teacher, older student). This level of interaction has the benefit of offering disabled gifted students personalized treatment of specific problems or concerns. The second level involves collaboration among a team of school personnel working toward a common goal. The benefits at this level include the use of assessment for creating appropriate interventions, development or adaptation of curricula, and evaluation of program effectiveness (VanTassel-Baska, 1991). The third level of this model involves collaboration among various institutions regarding shared concerns and results in a wider spectrum of resources to meet the educational needs of these students.

Although several levels of collaboration are important in developing and implementing programs to meet the needs of disabled gifted learners, VanTassel-Baska (1991) described level two as the critical level for case management. She suggested that a leader be appointed from the members of the school-based team. This individual would be responsible for obtaining and synthesizing comments and suggestions offered by team members and devising a plan based on their input. In the process of creating a plan, levels one and three would be included in the collaborative effort. Ultimately, the plan would "aggregate perspectives of various team members in such a way that the resulting program and services are multi-dimensional and sufficiently rich to meet the needs of individual learners" (VanTassel-Baska, 1991, p. 260).

Another approach for serving gifted students with learning disabilities has been offered by Dyck and Dettmer (1989) and involves consultation between special and regular education teachers within the general education classroom. In their approach, "services for the gifted student who also is learning disabled can be provided through consultation among the gifted program facilitator, the learning disabilities specialist, and the classroom teacher, with input and involvement from parents and the student as well" (p. 255). Dyck and Dettmer described a seven-step consultation process designed to assist teachers in introducing, implementing, and following through on opportunities to engage in collaborative consultation.

According to Dyck and Dettmer (1989), planning is the first step of the collaborative consultation process. During the planning phase, individuals must concentrate on the area(s) of concern, prepare any materials that may be needed, generate several action alternatives, and organize meeting times and locations that are convenient to all participants. Initiating is the second step of the consultation process and involves rapport building, organizing an agenda, and addressing concerns that were stated tentatively in the planning phase. Steps 3 and 4 involve gathering information and specifying concerns, respectively, in an attempt to focus more clearly on pertinent issues. Collaborative problem solving is the goal of Step 5. During this phase, several options are generated and reviewed and the most reasonable alternatives are selected. At Step 6, goals are outlined, role responsibilities are identified, and individuals are selected to be involved in classroom modification or other suggested interventions. This step ultimately leads to the generation of evaluation criteria to determine the effectiveness of plans, programs, and interventions. Follow-up is the focus of the last step in this process and involves examining data, analyzing results, and determining whether to continue a previous plan or devise a new one. This final step also necessitates routine reviews and assessment to determine if goals were met and to monitor progress.

Dyck and Dettmer (1989) discussed several benefits that the consulting teacher approach can offer students and school personnel who work with gifted students with disabilities. For example, this approach has a powerful "ripple" or "multiplier" effect that affords teachers the opportunity to more effectively address the needs of *all* students and instruct them in ways that are beneficial. In addition, this approach significantly reduces the amount of time gifted students with learning disabilities spend away from the regular educational setting. Gifted students, with their special talents in areas such as art, music, science, mathematics, and language arts, can make important and significant contributions in the general education setting. In the absence of proper support and intervention in the regular classroom, however, these students may be at risk for developing a handicapping condition by the time they enroll in high school or college. If gifted students with learning disabilities do not participate regularly or feel a sense of belonging in the regular education classroom, their talents may go unnoticed or unnurtured and, subsequently, their potential benefit to society may be significantly curtailed (Dyck & Dettmer, 1989). Thus, Dyck and Dettmer's seven-step collaborative consultation model shows great promise as a tool for helping regular and special education teachers effectively address student needs. Moreover, this can be done without depriving the student of opportunities for stimulation and socialization that are provided regularly in the general education milieu (Idol-Maestas & Celentano, 1986).

Most recently, Parke (1992) proposed a full-service model for programs involving students who are gifted and talented. This approach includes components of all the models mentioned above and emphasizes the importance of collaboration in planning and service delivery within a systems context. Parke's conceptualization of full service for gifted and talented students includes the following postulates: (a) all decisions regarding gifted education and programming are made by an interdisciplinary placement and review team; (b) student needs represent the focal point from which all decisions regarding program design are made; (c) the provision of services to gifted and talented students emanates from a multiple-programming approach to ensure that the needs of this diverse population are met; and (d) collaboration occurs on a regular basis among all team members and school personnel to guarantee the longevity and success of this approach.

Parke's (1992) collaborative planning and service delivery model includes seven key components. The first component involves collaboration among general education professionals. Basic to the process of education is the notion that all educators work to challenge intellectually all students, including those who are gifted, in an effort to meet their individual educational needs. Educators specifically trained in providing services to gifted and talented students must be willing to accept the skills and broader viewpoint that regular educators bring to the educational process. Through understanding, mutual respect, and shared responsibility emerges a powerful team capable of accomplishing more than a single member could achieve (Parke, 1992).

The second component of Parke's model involves collaborating in the student selection process. A collaborative team representing a variety of professions is necessary to achieve wide-range acceptance and agreement regarding the nature of the population being served and to maximize program effectiveness. A team that includes parents, school psychologists, administrators, policymakers, regular and gifted educators, and other school personnel is likely to devise effective student selection and program delivery plans because it "reflects the culture" in which these plans will be implemented (Parke, 1992).

Collaborating in program design and placement are the third and fourth components of Parke's model, respectively. Collaboration in program design must include an emphasis on programs that incorporate a variety of content areas—not only mathematics and language arts—in which students demonstrate exceptionality. Programs that include a broad array of academic possibilities will promote student exploration of high-interest topics and ensure that the diverse needs of the gifted are adequately met. Following the identification of student needs and the development of a program plan, decisions concerning program placement can be made. These decisions often revolve around questions or concerns regarding grade acceleration, amount of time spent with same-age peers, and the student's desire to enroll in special programs. The collaborative efforts of the members of a school-based team can help to clarify these issues, as well as a multiplicity of others that may arise during this phase of planning and delivering services to gifted and talented students (Parke, 1992).

The final three components of Parke's model include collaborating in curriculum development, evaluation, and student well-being. Collaboration in curriculum development is integral to the success of any program designed for gifted students because it assures that these programs are paced appropriately and broadens the possibilities for interdisciplinary study, community projects, mentorships, and so forth. Collaborating in evaluation of programs is an equally important and challenging task. The effectiveness of any service provided to gifted and talented students must be evaluated by addressing several important questions, such as the following (Parke, 1992): How will success be defined and measured? What criteria do students value in determining their success in special programs? What evaluation procedures should be instituted? Who will conduct the evaluation? Finally, collaborating for student well-being is necessary in order to create educational environments that are safe and accepting of individual differences and that value excellence. In addition, school psychologists, counselors, and social workers can play an instrumental role in helping gifted students maintain positive self-perceptions by providing support, teaching strategies, and offering individual guidance to these students as they meet the many challenges that confront them throughout their educational careers (Parke, 1992). Parke's full-service model emphasizes the potentially powerful effects of collaborative consultation on educational decision making and shows great promise for effectively meeting the educational needs of students who are gifted and talented.

## COLLABORATIVE CONSULTATION MODELS IN PERSPECTIVE

Evidence is accumulating regarding the positive effects that collaboration has for educational decision making, instructional planning, and service delivery for students who are gifted and talented. At the base of all the consultation models presented in this chapter is the notion that mutual respect, shared responsibility, and ongoing collaboration at all levels of the consultative process are necessary to incur positive changes. The component parts of each consultation model presented above are consistent with the complex nature of giftedness. Edwards and Kleine (1986) offered a multimodal collaborative approach that allows for the synthesis of both psychosocial and educational needs of gifted adolescents and is consistent with level two of VanTassel-Baska's (1991) model—that is, employing a school-based team to address the unique needs of gifted children through conducting multifaceted assessments, devising interventions, and modifying programs. Whereas Edwards and Kleine's (1986) model is geared toward working with adolescents, the collaborative consultation steps outlined by VanTassel-Baska (1991) and Dyck and Dettmer (1989) are more general and address the special needs of gifted students of all ages. Both approaches employ a school-based team to address the unique needs of gifted children through conducting multifaceted assessments, devising interventions, and modifying programs. VanTassel-Baska's (1991) three-level model is most similar to Parke's (1992) model in that it advocates collaboration among the student, school system, and larger community. Finally, although VanTassel-Baska (1991) and Dyck and Dettmer (1989) designed their models to address specifically the needs of gifted students with disabilities, both Edwards and Kleine's (1986) and Parke's (1992) models could be adapted easily for this purpose. Regardless of the model employed, if true collaboration is achieved within the educational community, richer environments for all gifted students will ensue.

# CONCLUSION

The effectiveness of service delivery to students who are gifted and talented has yet to be proven. There is increasing concern regarding the appropriateness of evaluation and identification procedures for these students. The lack of effective identification and programming for gifted students who are disabled is even more alarming. There is a growing need to establish collaborative support networks within a systems context in an effort to promote environments in which gifted students can reach their full potential. This is by no means an easy task. As stated earlier, for collaboration to occur, all individuals involved in the process of education must be willing to assume responsibility for and work toward a common goal of full-service delivery for gifted and talented students.

A first step in achieving this crucial element involves inservice education focusing on the unique needs of gifted students, consultation techniques, and specific instruction in consultative strategies. Universities must also provide specialized training in the collaborative consultation process. Once school personnel receive training and instruction, they may feel more confident and better equipped to work collaboratively to identify and solve problems in a variety of educational settings. A second step is to organize a school-based team that will be responsible for addressing concerns regarding the identification, programming, and placement of students who are gifted. This team may include school psychologists, counselors, social workers, regular and special educators, administrators, parents, and any other individuals concerned with the education of the gifted. Once a team has been assembled and is working together toward a common goal, decisions can be made regarding which collaborative consultation model is most appropriate for addressing the unique needs of the gifted students within that educational environment. Professionals and educators may select one of the models presented in this chapter or choose to develop their own framework by building on the component parts of these models. Regardless of the consultation model, careful planning, ongoing support for collective problem solving, and routine evaluation of program effectiveness are necessary for successful collaboration to occur in the schools.

# REFERENCES

Allan, S. D., & Fox, D. K. (1979). Group counseling the gifted. *Journal for the Education of the Gifted, 3* 83–92.

Alpert, J. L., & Meyers, J. (1983). *Training in consultation.* Springfield, IL: Charles C. Thomas.

Colangelo, N., & Zaffrann, R. T. (1975). *Counseling the gifted student.* Madison: University of Wisconsin Press.

Dyck, N., & Dettmer, P. (1989). Collaborative consultation: A promising tool for serving gifted students with learning disabilities. *Reading, Writing, and Learning Disabilities, 5,* 253–264.

Edwards, S. (1978). Multimodal therapy with children: A case analysis of insect phobia. *Elementary School Guidance and Counseling, 13,* 23–29.

Edwards, S. S., & Kleine, P. A. (1986). Multimodal consultation: A model for working with gifted adolescents. *Journal of Counseling and Development, 64,* 598–601.

Gerler, E. R. (1978). The school counselor and multimodal education. *School Counselor, 25,* 166–171.

Gordon, T. (1976). *P.E.T. in action.* Ridgefield, CT: Wyden Books.

Humes, C. W., & Clark, J. N. (1989). Group counseling and consultation with gifted high school students. *The Journal for Specialists in Group Work, 14,* 219–225.

Idol-Maestas, L., & Celentano, R. (1986). Teacher consultant services for advanced students. *Roeper Review, 9,* 34–36.

Jenkins-Friedman, R., & Fine, M. J. (1984). A useful framework for parent–teacher contacts. *Roeper Review, 6,* 155–158.

Kline, B. E., & Meckstroth, E. A. (1985). Understanding and encouraging the exceptionally gifted. *Roeper Review, 8,* 24–30.

Kress, M. (1985). Vanguard: Focus on the gifted learner. *Teaching Exceptional Children, 17,* 122–125.

Lazarus, A. A. (1976). *Multimodal therapy.* New York: Springer.

Lazarus, A. A. (1981). *The practice of multimodal therapy.* New York: McGraw-Hill.

Miller, S., Nunnally, E. W., & Wackman, D. B. (1975). *Alive and aware.* Minneapolis, MN: Interpersonal Communications.

Norris, D. A., Burke, J. P., & Speer, A. L. (1990). Tri-level service delivery: An alternative consultation model. *School Psychology Quarterly, 5,* 89–110.

Parke, B. (1992). Collaboratively planning and delivering services to gifted and talented students. In *Challenges in gifted education.* Columbus: Ohio Department of Education.

Parsons, R. D., & Meyers, J. (1985). *Developing consultation skills: A guide to training, development, and assessment for human services professionals*. San Francisco: Jossey-Bass.

Seeley, K. (1985). Facilitators for gifted learners. In J. Feldhusen (Ed.), *Toward excellence in gifted education*. Denver, CO: Love.

Sherman, W. M. (1982). The importance of parent/teacher cooperation in gifted education. *Roeper Review, 5*, 42–44.

VanTassel-Baska, J. (1991). Serving the disabled gifted through educational collaboration. *Journal for the Education of the Gifted, 14*, 246–266.

Walker, J. J., & Dangel, H. L. (1992). Helping parents help their gifted child: Developing problem-solving skills. *Challenge, 51*, 15–17.

Wolf, J. S. (1989). Consultation for parents of young gifted children. *Roeper Review, 11*, 219–221.

# *Part VI*

# Current Issues

————————— **Chapter 22** —————————

# What Gifted Education Can Offer the Reform Movement: Talent Development

**Sally M. Reis**

————————— ◆ ◆ ◆ —————————

IN THE CURRENT, seemingly endless discussion about educational reform, many involved in gifted education have noted the similarities between the recommendations of the "reformers" and the basic principles of educating gifted and talented students. Key ideas such as thinking skills, product development, product and portfolio assessment, higher standards, teaching to students' strengths and interests, flexible instructional grouping, and so forth, have been suggested by leaders in educating high ability students for over two decades (Marland, 1972; Renzulli, 1976a, 1976b; Torrance, 1962). The major recommendations of the reform movement have been discussed repeatedly in every education journal and at every major education conference in the United States. Recently, Larry Cuban (1990) offered a compelling analysis of why the "reform movement" has been repeated so many times in this century in public education. To illustrate this repetition, Cuban used three examples of recurring school reforms: teacher-centered instruction (as opposed to pupil or child centered), the academic versus the practical curriculum, and the centralized versus decentralized authority in governing schools. In his historical analysis, Cuban argued that the recurrence of these and other reforms throughout the 20th century suggests that efforts at reform have failed to remove the problems the reforms were intended to solve.

It seems apparent that some of the suggestions being offered in the current national dialogue about educational reform will undoubtedly create other problems for all students in general, and for high ability students in particular (Renzulli & Reis, 1991). For example, a standardized national curriculum may actually result in the specification of minimum standards for able youth. The use of heterogeneous classes all of the time in all subject areas may deprive high ability students of the appropriate challenge they so desperately need. The misuse of cooperative learning may result in high ability students tutoring other students, to the detriment of their own achievement gains. The use of group grades in a cooperative learning situation may result in lower grades for high ability students.

In this chapter, the necessity to provide differentiated services for high ability students is discussed, as is current research relating to the curricular and instructional practices currently used in classrooms for high ability students. Numerous suggestions are also offered about the ways in which gifted education can serve as a model for school reform, and a suggestion is offered for replacing the current emphasis on remediation and skill work with an emphasis on talent development.

# THE NEED TO PROVIDE SERVICES FOR HIGH ABILITY STUDENTS

## The "Dumbing Down of Textbooks"

One reason that so many average and above average students become bored in school and demonstrate mastery of the curriculum is because contemporary textbooks have been "dumbed down," a phrase used in 1984 by Terrel Bell, former secretary of education. Chall and Conrad (1991) concurred with Bell's assessment, documenting a trend of decreasing difficulty in the most widely used textbooks over a 30-year period from 1945 to 1975. "On the whole, the later the copyright dates of the textbooks for the same grade, the easier they were, as measured by indices of readability level, maturity level, difficulty of questions and extent of illustration" (p. 2). Kirst (1982) also commented that textbooks have dropped by two grade levels in difficulty over the last 10 to 15 years. Most recently, Philip G. Altbach (Altbach, Kelly, Petrie, & Weis, 1991), noted scholar and author on textbooks in America, suggested that textbooks, as evaluated across a spectrum of assessment measures, have declined in rigor.

Researchers have discussed the particular problems encountered by high ability students when textbooks are dumbed down because of readability formulas or the politics of textbook adoption. Bernstein (1985) summarized the particular problem that current textbooks pose for gifted and talented students:

> Even if there were good rules of thumb about the touchy subject of textbook adoption, the issue becomes moot when a school district buys only one textbook, usually at "grade level," for all students in a subject

or grade. Such a purchasing policy pressures adoption committees to buy books that the least able students can read. As a result, the needs of more advanced students are sacrificed. (p. 465)

Chall and Conrad (1991) also cited particular difficulties for the above-average student with regard to less challenging reading textbooks:

Another group not adequately served was those who read about two grades or more above the norm. Their reading textbooks especially provided little or no challenge, since they were matched to students' grade placement, not their reading levels. Many students were aware of this and said, in their interviews, that they preferred harder books because they learned harder words and ideas from them. Since harder reading textbooks are readily available, one may ask why they were not used with the more able readers, as were the easier reading textbooks for the less able readers. (p. 111)

## Repetition in Content

Recent findings by Usiskin (1987) and Flanders (1987) indicate not only that textbooks have decreased in difficulty, but that they incorporate a large percentage of repetition to facilitate learning. Usiskin argued that even average eighth-grade students should study algebra, because only 25% of the pages in typical seventh- and eighth-grade mathematics texts contain new content. Flanders corroborated this finding by investigating the mathematics textbook series of three popular publishers. Students in Grades 2 through 5 who used these math textbooks encountered approximately 40% to 65% new content over the course of the school year, which equates to new material 2 to 3 days a week. By eighth grade, the amount of new content had dropped to 30%, which translates to encountering new material once every $1\frac{1}{2}$ days a week. Flanders suggested that these estimates are conservative because days for review and testing were not included in his analysis, and concluded, "There should be little wonder why good students get bored: they do the same thing year after year" (p. 22).

Repetition in content is also reflected by the scores students attain on pretests taken *before* they open their textbooks. For example, a study conducted by the Educational Products Information Exchange Institute (1980–1981), a nonprofit educational consumer agency, revealed that 60% of fourth graders in certain school districts were able to achieve a score of 80% or higher on a test of the content of their math texts before they had opened their books in September. In a more recent study dealing with average and above readers, Taylor and Frye (1988) found that, among fifth and sixth graders, average and above average readers could pass pretests on comprehension skills before they were covered by the basal reader. The average students were performing at approximately 92% accuracy, while the better readers were performing at 93% on comprehension skills pretests. The mismatch between students' capabilities and current knowledge, and the curricular materials they are expected to study becomes even more disturbing when one considers the heavy reliance on textbooks and their declining challenge level.

## The Mismatch Between Student Ability and Instruction

Students should be matched with curriculum that is appropriate for their ability level. For learning to occur, instruction should be above the learner's current level of performance. Chall and Conrad (1991) stressed the importance of the match between a learner's abilities and the difficulty of the instructional task, stating that the optimal match should place the instructional task slightly above the learner's current level of functioning. When the match is optimal, learning is enhanced. However, "if the match is not optimal (i.e., the match is below or above the child's level of understanding/knowledge), learning is less efficient and development may be halted" (Chall & Conrad, p. 19). Clearly, the current trend of selecting textbooks that the majority of students can read is a problem for high ability students.

A mismatch seems to exist between the difficulty of textbooks, the repetition of curricular material in these texts, and the needs of high ability learners. A reasonable conclusion is that many of these students spend much of their time in school practicing skills and learning content they already know. All of these factors may be causing the most capable children to learn less and may be encouraging their underachievement.

## Meeting the Needs of High Ability Students in the Regular Classroom

Three recent studies have analyzed whether the needs of high ability students can be met in classroom settings. This research presents a disturbing picture of what happens to high ability students in their regular classrooms.

The Classroom Practices Survey (Archambault et al., 1992) was conducted by The National Research Center on the Gifted and Talented to determine the extent to which gifted and talented students receive differentiated education in regular classrooms. Six samples of third- and fourth-grade teachers in public schools, private schools, and schools with high concentrations of four types of ethnic minorities were randomly selected to participate in this research, and over 51% responded to this national survey. Sixty-one percent of public school teachers and 54% of private school teachers reported that they had never had any training in teaching gifted students. The major finding of this study is that classroom teachers make only *minor* modifications in the regular curriculum to meet the needs of gifted students. This result holds for all types of schools sampled and for classrooms in various parts of the country and in various types of communities.

The Classroom Practices Observational Study (Westberg, Archambault, Dobyns, & Salvin, 1992) extended the results of the Classroom Practices Survey by examining the instructional and curricular practices used with gifted and talented students in regular elementary classrooms throughout the United States. Systematic observations were conducted in 46 third- and fourth-grade classrooms. The observations were designed to determine whether and how classroom teachers meet the needs of gifted and talented students in the regular classroom. Two students, one gifted and talented or high ability and one of average ability, were selected as target students for each observation day. The *Classroom Practices Record* (CPR) was developed to document the types and frequencies of differentiated instruction that gifted students receive through modifications in curricular activities, materials, and teacher–student verbal interactions.

Descriptive statistics and chi-square procedures were used to analyze the CPR data. The results indicated little differentiation in the instructional and curricular practices, including grouping arrangements and verbal interactions, for gifted and talented students in the regular classroom. Across five subject areas and 92 observation days, gifted students received instruction in homogeneous groups only 21% of the time, and, more alarmingly, the target gifted and talented or high ability students experienced no instructional or curricular differentiation in 84% of the instructional activities in which they participated. A content analysis was also conducted on the 92 daily summaries completed by the trained observers. The most dominant theme in this content analysis involved the use of identical practices for all students. Phrases such as "no differentiation" and "no purposeful differentiation" appeared on 51 of the 92 daily summaries. Anecdotal summaries such as the following provided poignant glimpses into the daily experiences of high ability students: It should be noted that the targeted high ability student was inattentive during all of her classes. She appeared to be sleepy, never volunteered and was visibly unenthusiastic about all activities. No attempt was made to direct higher order thinking skills questions to her or to engage her in more challenging work. She never acted out in any way.

The Curriculum Compacting Study (Reis et al., 1993) examined the effects of escalating levels of staff development on the teaching practices of elementary school teachers throughout the country as they implemented a plan called curriculum compacting (Renzulli & Smith, 1978; Reis, Burns, & Renzulli, 1992) to modify the curriculum for high ability students. Three treatment groups of second- through sixth-grade teachers from across the country received increasing levels of staff development as they implemented curriculum compacting. Three steps are used in curriculum compacting: (a) assessing the content area that demonstrates student proficiency; (b) eliminating content that students have already mastered; and (c) substituting more appropriate alternatives, some of which are based on student interest. A control group of teachers continued with normal teaching practices. Four hundred thirty-six teachers participated in this study, as did 783 students.

Students in both control and treatment groups took the next chronological-grade–level *Iowa Test of Basic Skills* in both October and May. When classroom teachers in the treatment groups eliminated 40% to 50% of the regular curriculum for high ability students, no differences were found between treatment and control groups in reading, math computation, social studies, and spelling. In science and math concepts, students in the treatment group whose curriculum was compacted scored significantly higher than their counterparts in the control group. Accordingly, teachers could eliminate as much as 40% to 50% of material without detrimental effects to achievement scores. In some content areas, scores were actually higher when this elimination of previously mastered content took place.

## Recent Research Relating to Grouping Practices and Program Elimination for High Ability Students

James Kulik (1992) and Karen Rogers (1991) recently completed two meta-analytical studies on the effects of ability grouping on gifted students. Their conclusions are similar and provide a sound basis for an examination of instructional and ability grouping. The current attention being paid to the elimination of tracking obscures two major issues: (a) tracking and grouping are not the same and (b) what happens within the group (termed curricular adjustment by Kulik) is as essential as (if not more essential than) how the group is formed.

According to Kulik's (1992) meta-analytic review, some grouping programs have little or no effect on students, others have moderate effects, and still others have major effects. Kulik found that, for talented students, enrichment and acceleration have the largest effects on student learning:

In typical evaluation studies, talented students from accelerated classes outperform non-accelerates of the same age and IQ by almost one full year on achievement tests. Talented students from enriched classes outperform initially equivalent students from conventional classes by four to five months on grade equivalent scales. (pp. 6–7)

Kulik summarized the effect of schools' eliminating the use of grouped programs:

The damage would be greatest, however, if schools in the name of detracking, eliminated enriched and accelerated classes for their brightest learners. The achievement level of such students falls dramatically when they are required to do routine work at a routine pace. No one can be certain that there would be a way to repair the harm that would be done if schools eliminated all programs of acceleration and enrichment. (1992, pp. 6–7)

In another recent study, Purcell (1993) examined the perceived effects of the elimination of an enrichment program on the students who had participated in the program. In this study, 19 parents were interviewed and 27 parents completed a survey about how they thought eliminating the program would affect their children. Ninety-five percent of the parents identified both short- and long-term academic and social effects on their children as a result of the elimination. Over 60% of the parents said they expected that their children would be bored with the traditional curriculum.

# WHAT GIFTED EDUCATION CAN OFFER THE REFORM MOVEMENT

*The New York Times* recently named as standard bearers in education nine persons who are nationally known for innovation. Included was Hank Levin, who developed the Accelerated Schools Model. In a recent interview, Ron Brandt (1992), the editor of *Educational Leadership*, asked Levin, "What makes the Accelerated Schools Model different from some other programs for at-risk students?" Levin responded, "What may be most unusual is that we believe the teaching–learning approach that works best for at-risk kids is a 'gifted and talented' strategy, rather than a remedial approach." Levin recalled his initial work on the Accelerated Schools Model:

I started to do a lot of reading in the research literature, and in the literature on gifted and talented programs and I was convinced that if we exposed all children to the richest experiences . . . we could bring kids into the mainstream. And we'd find that a lot of these kids *were* [emphasis in original] gifted and talented; even in the traditional sense. (p. 20)

The extension of activities originally designed for high ability students to *all* students is not a new idea. In the 1970s, Renzulli (1976a, 1976b) advocated the use of various enrichment activities as a way to identify strengths and potential interests in all students. He also stressed the use of general enrichment experiences and group training activities for all students in the original Enrichment Triad Model (Renzulli, 1977). He and his colleagues further extended the services normally reserved for gifted students to all students with the Revolving Door Identification Model (Renzulli, Reis, & Smith, 1981). This model included provisions for much more flexible identification procedures, the involvement of all students in enrichment opportunities, and a possibility for more intensive follow-up by any student who showed an interest.

A recent federal report (Ross, 1993) on the status of gifted education in the United States calls attention to the role that the "gifted field" has played in education, that of being a "laboratory" for creative teaching techniques, instruments such as product evaluation scales, model programs, and innovative curriculum projects. Programs such as Future Problem Solving, Odyssey of the Mind, Great Books, Talents Unlimited, and Young Inventors have often been initiated by enrichment specialists or gifted coordinators who are not confined by the demands of the "regular curriculum."

In its relatively short history, the field of gifted education has achieved a rather impressive "menu" of exciting curricular adaptations, thinking skills programs, independent study skills, and numerous other innovations. For example, enrichment specialists who use the Schoolwide Enrichment Model (Renzulli & Reis, 1985) concentrate on identifying students' interests and learning styles. They then provide challenging curriculum experiences to students who need specific services, instead of providing identical experiences to all students in a classroom, regardless of their previous knowledge of the curriculum. Because of the experience gained in the use of these exciting techniques, many benefits exist when a good enrichment program is implemented. First, exciting opportunities can be made available to *all* students. For example, in the Schoolwide Enrichment Model, many enrichment opportunities are provided to all students in an effort to identify those young people in whom a potential exists for talent development. Second, the techniques used for high ability students by gifted education specialists can often be extended to a much wider circle of students, and to all students in some cases. In the curriculum compacting study cited earlier (Reis et al., 1992), teachers who had participated in the staff development program and subsequently implemented curriculum compacting originally targeted one to two students for the curriculum compacting process. However, once they had modified curriculum for these targeted students, they were able to use this strategy with other students who were not identified as gifted. In many instances, the teachers were able to use compacting with as many as 10 to 15 students in their classrooms. In the four sections that follow, specific suggestions are made regarding how curricular and instructional strategies often used with gifted students have been or can be extended to a broader population of students.

## Creative Alternatives in Curriculum and Instruction

For the last two decades, specialists in education of the gifted have been developing innovative curriculum units and extending the regular curriculum to include a wide variety of creative alternatives. The use of these units and strategies is documented in the professional journals and includes, in addition to curriculum units, thinking and process skills, independent study skills, research skills, and problem solving. Two well-known approaches that are often implemented in gifted education programs are now used with a much broader range of students: Talents Unlimited (developed from Taylor's, 1967, multiple talents theory) and The Enrichment Triad (Renzulli, 1977; Renzulli & Reis, 1985).

Calvin Taylor (1967) and Carol Schlichter (1979) suggested the use of various types of thinking skills for all students. The multiple talent approach to teaching, defined by Taylor (1967) and operated by Schlichter (1979) and linked to Guilford's (1967) research on the nature of intelligence, is a system for helping teachers identify and nurture youngsters' multiple talents in productive thinking, forecasting, communication, planning, decision making, and academics. In this approach, traditional academic talent helps students to gain knowledge in a variety of disciplines, while the other five talents assist students in processing or using the knowledge to create new solutions to problems. Schlichter (1979) cited four assumptions that underlie the multiple talent approach: (a) people have abilities or talents in a variety of areas; (b) training in the use of these thinking processes can enhance potential in various areas of talent and, at the same time, foster positive feelings about self; (c) training in particular talent processes can be integrated with knowledge or content in any subject area; and (d) the multiple talents are linked to success in the world of work.

The Schoolwide Enrichment Triad Model (SEM) evolved after 15 years of research and field testing by both educators and researchers (Renzulli & Reis, 1985). It combined the previously developed Enrichment Triad Model (Renzulli, 1977) with a much more flexible approach to identifying high potential students called the Revolving Door Identification Model (Renzulli et al., 1981). This combination was initially field tested in 12 school districts of various types (rural, suburban, and urban) and sizes. Research studies were conducted that indicated positive growth for students, even those who were not identified for gifted program services (Reis, 1981). These and other field tests resulted in the development of the SEM (Renzulli & Reis, 1985), which has been widely adopted throughout the country.

In the SEM, a talent pool of 15% to 20% of above average ability/high potential students is identified through a variety of measures, including achievement tests, teacher nominations, assessment of potential for creativity and task commitment, and other alternative pathways of entrance (self-nomination, parent nomination, etc.). High achievement and intelligence test scores automatically include a student in the talent pool, enabling those students who are underachieving in their academic work to be included.

Once students are identified for the talent pool, they are eligible for several services, which are also extended to other (nonidentified) students in numerous situations. First, interest and learning styles assessments are used with talent pool students. Informal and formal methods are used to create and/or identify students' interests and to encourage students to further develop and pursue their interests in various ways. Second, a service provided to all eligible students is curriculum compacting, in which the regular curriculum is modified by eliminating portions of previously mastered content. Third, the Enrichment Triad Model offers three types of enrichment experiences. Types I, II, and III enrichment are offered to all students; however, Type III enrichment (see Figure 22.1) is usually more appropriate for students with higher levels of ability, interest, and task commitment.

Type I enrichment consists of general exploratory experiences, such as guest speakers, field trips, demonstrations, interest centers, and audiovisual materials, designed to expose students to new and exciting topics, ideas, and fields of knowledge not ordinarily covered in the regular curriculum. Type II enrichment includes instructional methods and materials that are purposefully designed to promote the development of thinking, feeling, research, communication, and methodological processes. Type III enrichment is the most advanced level in the Enrichment Triad Model. Whereas Types I and II enrichment and curriculum compacting should be provided on a regular basis to talent pool students, the ability to revolve into Type III enrichment depends on an individual's interests, motivation, and desire to pursue advanced-level study. Type III enrichment is defined as investigative activities and artistic productions in which the learner assumes the role of a first-hand inquirer, thinking, feeling, and acting like a practicing professional, even if this involvement is pursued at a more junior level than the adult researcher or artist.

---

TYPE III ENRICHMENT

## "Bobby Bones"

| by Jerry Beach | Eric Chadwick | *Grade 4* |
| Allison Roxby | Rebecca Christian | *East School* |
| Donny Capnano | Stephanie Durstin | *Torrington, Connecticut* |
| Merri Petrovits | | |

### Brief Description

Bobby Bones is a life size model of the human skeletal structure with a taped mini-course designed to be presented to other youngsters. Thomas Hébert, the resource teacher who provided managerial assistance to the students, indicated that he was delighted with the "ownership" involved in the completion of this Type III. The physical education teacher in East School, Janet Beck, supervised the building of the skeleton and helped Tom to coordinate the entire project. The students' classroom teacher, Steve Ksenych, compacted the curriculum for the entire school year, enabling the project to be completed. The art teacher, Elaine Towne, provided advice and helped the students build Bobby Bones. Another classroom teacher who had outstanding talent in music, helped the students to write a song that accompanied the mini-course in anatomy that was developed after the skeleton was built. This Type III required two years to complete and was subsequently presented to every third grade classroom in Torrington as a Type II mini-course in conjunction with the third grade health curriculum.

(*continues*)

---

**Figure 22.1** Type III Enrichment. From *The Schoolwide Enrichment Model* by J. S. Renzulli and C. M. Reis, 1985, Mansfield Center, CT: Creative Learning Press. Reprinted by permission.

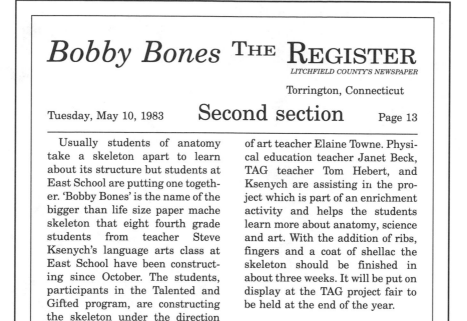

*Bobby Bones* THE REGISTER

*LITCHFIELD COUNTY'S NEWSPAPER*

Torrington, Connecticut

Tuesday, May 10, 1983          Second section          Page 13

Usually students of anatomy take a skeleton apart to learn about its structure but students at East School are putting one together. 'Bobby Bones' is the name of the bigger than life size paper mache skeleton that eight fourth grade students from teacher Steve Ksenych's language arts class at East School have been constructing since October. The students, participants in the Talented and Gifted program, are constructing the skeleton under the direction of art teacher Elaine Towne. Physical education teacher Janet Beck, TAG teacher Tom Hebert, and Ksenych are assisting in the project which is part of an enrichment activity and helps the students learn more about anatomy, science and art. With the addition of ribs, fingers and a coat of shellac the skeleton should be finished in about three weeks. It will be put on display at the TAG project fair to be held at the end of the year.

**Figure 22.1.** continued

## Modification of the Regular Curriculum

Because many high ability students need their curriculum modified in some way, gifted education specialists have developed a number of strategies that can also be used with other students. Besides curriculum compacting (Reis et al., 1992), which has been successfully used with a much broader segment of the population, a number of other strategies often implemented for high ability students can be extended to all students. Kaplan (1986), for example, advocated the use of thematic units and developed a system for using a grid to develop these units. The underlying theme (e.g., power, conflict) can be expanded, and more complex extensions can be made for students interested in pursuing advanced content, processes, or products. This type of content acceleration becomes even more appropriate when the dumbing down of curriculum and the amount of repetition are considered.

## Alternate Means of Assessment

Many of the recommendations regarding assessment suggested by those involved in the reform movement have been used frequently in gifted education for the last two decades. Product and process assessment, as well as academic and artistic portfolios, have all been common. Gifted education specialists have also used developmental identification, teacher nomination of talents and curriculum strengths, and individual education plans and programs to enable teachers to identify student strengths as opposed to weaknesses.

One example of product assessment that has been used in the development of student product portfolios is the *Student Product Assessment Form* (Reis, 1981). This assessment instrument was developed for both students and teachers to evaluate progress on student products. The form is discussed with students prior to beginning their work on a product. Student work is assessed on 15 separate indicators of project quality, with half related to the process used and the other half evaluating the overall quality of the product. The cover sheet of the instrument is designed to be copied and filed in students' permanent record folders to enable a record of productivity to be compiled from primary grades through high school graduation.

## Talent Development

The focus of education of the gifted has always been the identification *and* development of talent in young people. The field has emphasized the *development* of student strengths and the encouragement of student interests. Specialists in education of the gifted have stressed the use of Individualized Education Programs to eliminate work that students have already mastered and to find the time for them to pursue their individual interests and talents. Others who are not directly involved in the gifted field are now suggesting the use of many strategies developed by researchers and practitioners in gifted education as a method of school improvement (Brandt, 1992). Rather than allowing the reform movement to institute practices that would have a negative impact on high ability students, such as the elimination of all grouped classes, professionals need to suggest how the programs and practices in gifted education can be used to benefit all students. One way that this could occur would be the creation within each school of a position for an enrichment specialist who would provide direct services to high ability students half of the time and serve as a catalyst for all types of enrichment services to the entire school the rest of the time. The possible benefits are listed in Table 22.1.

The need for an emphasis on talent development in the schools and

## TABLE 22.1. Benefits to the School When an Enrichment Program Exists

1. Enrichment experiences (assemblies, performances, speakers) are often organized by the enrichment specialist.

2. Mini-courses and advanced training opportunities are often scheduled for a wider range of students than are normally identified in the enrichment program.

3. Curriculum materials, computer software, and equipment are often supplied to classroom teachers by the enrichment specialist to provide exciting work opportunities for all students in the classroom.

4. Staff development for classroom teachers is often provided by the enrichment specialist to benefit all students in areas such as creative thinking skills, research techniques, and critical thinking.

5. Model lessons in a variety of areas (creativity training, thinking skills) that benefit both teachers and students are often taught in classrooms by enrichment specialists.

6. Enrichment specialists encourage high ability students to present to classrooms the products they have developed in the program. After seeing these products, other students often become interested in pursuing similar work under the supervision of the classroom teacher.

7. When enrichment programs such as Future Problem Solving and Odyssey of the Mind are introduced by the enrichment specialist, other students and teachers often become involved.

8. When classroom teachers learn to modify regular curriculum (including eliminating curriculum that students already know) for high ability students, other students benefit.

9. Classroom teachers are often encouraged to use more challenging work to meet the needs of high ability students, and the challenge often benefits other students.

10. Textbooks with more advanced content are often advocated by enrichment specialists. These books offer more appropriate challenges to all students.

11. A philosophical belief may emerge, because of the presence of the program, that one major goal of education is the identification and development of talent in all children.

for personnel to plan and carry out the various opportunities that will facilitate developing talents is crucial. With the elimination of programs for gifted and talented students, the positions of many of the persons directly responsible for these innovative strategies have been eliminated and/or these persons have been reassigned to other full-time teaching positions. When these positions disappear, the "spark plug" who organized and implemented these exciting alternatives also disappears with the program. Accordingly, all educators must be committed to the advocacy necessary to continue creating and maintaining programs and practices that can serve as models of standards that can be accomplished by not only the most talented students, but many other students as well.

# CONCLUSION

In conclusion, some of the recommendations put forth by the school reform dialogue can create problems for gifted students. Current research indicates that their academic needs are not frequently addressed in regular classroom settings and that some forms of instructional grouping may be necessary if these students are to realize their potential. Many strategies and programs that have been used in gifted programs can be used to improve general education and by shifting the focus to *developing talents*, a more exciting learning environment can be created for all students.

# REFERENCES

Altbach, P. G., Kelly, G. P., Petrie, H. G., & Weis, L. (1991). *Textbooks in American society*. Albany: State University of New York Press.

Archambault, F. X., Westberg, K. L., Brown, S., Hallmark, B. W., Emmons, C., & Zhang, W. (1992). *Regular classroom practices with gifted students: Results of a national survey of classroom teachers*. Storrs, CT: National Research Center on the Gifted and Talented.

Bernstein, H. T. (1985). The new politics of textbook adoption. *Phi Delta Kappan, 66*, 463–466.

Brandt, R. (1992). Building learning communities: A conversation with Hank Levin. *Educational Leadership, 50*, 19–23.

Chall, J. S., & Conrad, S. S. (1991). *Should textbooks challenge students? The case for easier or harder textbooks*. New York: Teachers College Press.

Cuban, L. (1990). Reforming again, again, and again. *Educational Research, 19*, 3–13.

Educational Products Information Exchange Institute. (1980–1981). *Educational Research and Development Report, 3*.

Flanders, J. R. (1987, September). How much of the content in mathematics textbooks is new? *Arithmetic Teacher, 35*, 18–23.

Guilford, J. P. (1967). *The nature of human intelligence*. New York: McGraw-Hill.

Kaplan, S. N. (1986). The Grid: A model to construct differentiated curriculum for the gifted. In J. Renzulli (Eds.), *Systems and models for developing programs for the gifted and talented*. Mansfield Center, CT: Creative Learning Press.

Kirst, M. W. (1982). How to improve schools without spending more money. *Phi Delta Kappan, 64*, 6–8.

Kulik, J. A. (1992). *An analysis of the research on ability grouping: Historical and contemporary perspectives*. Storrs, CT: The National Research Center on the Gifted and Talented.

Marland, S. P. (1972). *Education of the gifted and talented: Report to the Congress of the United States, U.S. Commissioner of Education*. Washington, DC: U.S. Government Printing Office.

Purcell, J. (1993). The effects of the elimination of gifted and talented programs in our most able students and their parents. *Gifted Child Quarterly, 37*(4), 177–186.

Reis, S. M. (1981). *An analysis of the productivity of gifted students participating in programs using the revolving door identification model*. Unpublished doctoral dissertation, The University of Connecticut, Storrs.

Reis, S. M., Burns, D. E., & Renzulli, J. S. (1992). *Curriculum compacting: The complete guide to modifying the regular curriculum for high ability students*. Mansfield Center, CT: Creative Learning Press.

Reis, S. M., Westberg, K. L., Kulikowich, J., Caillard, F., Hebert, T., Plucker, J., Purcell, J., Rogers, J. B., & Smist, J. M. (1993). *Why not let high ability students start school in January? The Curriculum Compacting Study*. Storrs, CT: The National Research Center on the Gifted and Talented.

Renzulli, J. S. (1976a). The enrichment triad model: A guide for developing defensible programs for the gifted and talented (Part I). *Gifted Child Quarterly, 20*, 303–326.

Renzulli, J. S. (1976b). The enrichment triad model: A guide for developing defensible programs for the gifted and talented (Part II). *Gifted Child Quarterly, 21*, 237–243.

Renzulli, J. S. (1977). *The enrichment triad model: A guide for developing defensible programs for the gifted and talented*. Mansfield Center, CT: Creative Learning Press.

Renzulli, J. S., & Reis, S. M. (1985). *The schoolwide enrichment model*. Mansfield Center, CT: Creative Learning Press.

Renzulli, J. S., & Reis, S. M. (1991). The reform movement and the quiet crisis in gifted education. *Gifted Child Quarterly, 35*, 26–35.

Renzulli, J. S., Reis, S. M., & Smith, L. H. (1981). *The revolving door identification model*. Mansfield, Center, CT: Creative Learning Press.

Renzulli, J. S., & Smith, L. H. (1978). *The compactor*. Mansfield Center, CT: Creative Learning Press.

Rogers, K. B. (1991). *The relationship of grouping practices to the education of the gifted and talented learner* (Report No. 9101). Storrs, CT: National Research Center on the Gifted and Talented.

Ross, P. O. (1993). *National excellence: A case for developing America's talent*. Washington, DC: U.S. Department of Education.

Schlichter, C. L. (1979). The multiple talent approach to the world of work. *Roeper Review, 2*, 17–20.

Taylor, B. M., & Frye, B. J. (1988). Pretesting: Minimize time spent on skill work for intermediate readers. *The Reading Teacher, 42,* 100–103.

Taylor, C. W. (1967). Questioning and creating: A model for curriculum reform. *Journal of Creative Behavior, 1,* 22–23.

Torrance, E. P. (1962). *Guiding creative talents.* Englewood Cliffs, NJ: Prentice-Hall.

Usiskin, Z. (1987). Why elementary algebra can, should, and must be an eighth-grade course for average students. *Mathematics Teacher, 80,* 428–438.

Westberg, K. L., Archambault, F. X., Dobyns, S. M., & Salvin, T. J. (1992). *Technical report: An observational study of instructional and curricular practices used with gifted and talented students in regular classrooms.* Storrs, CT: National Research Center on the Gifted and Talented.

# Chapter 23

# Building Advocacy and Public Support for Gifted Education

**Peggy Dettmer**

◆  ◆  ◆

> Give me a lever that is long enough,
> and a place to stand, and I can
> move the world.
>
> —Archimedes

ADVOCACY IS AN ESSENTIAL PART of providing appropriate education for gifted and talented students. *Advocacy* can be defined as giving active support to a cause, putting out a call to take a position on an issue, and acting to see that it is resolved in a particular way. *Political advocacy* provides the leverage, or power and pressure, that forms attitudes and influences decision making. *To advocate* is to speak in favor of a cause, recommend a position on an issue, or plead as intercessor on another's behalf.

Advocacy for gifted programs is emerging as a vital part of gifted education. Strong advocacy efforts create the leverage needed for obtaining the curriculum and resources gifted students must have to develop their potential. Effective advocates influence neutral and reluctant groups to place high priority on serving educational needs of very able students.

Advocacy may be organized or spontaneous, and directed to groups and individuals or focused on the general public. *An advocate* can act individually or join with others to form an advocacy group. Spontaneous, informal advocacy for gifted programs occurs when proponents interact with others about their convictions toward individualized and differentiated instruction for very able students. Organized advocacy involves actions of school personnel, national and state organizations, and parent groups to create a climate of supportive attitudes for the differentiated curriculum that challenges highly able students.

Gifted education has not been particularly popular in egalitarian societies, and probably never will be. Public interest and support for gifted education tend to ebb and flow, reflecting a fundamental ambivalence toward the issue of providing special programs for students who have superior ability and are believed capable of succeeding in school on their own (Gallagher, 1988). Where education is perceived as an entree to success and power, demands for democratic equality are keen. The issue becomes volatile when proponents fear exploitation by the very able (Freehill, 1982). Some resist targeting money for an exclusively select group of gifted students, particularly when programs are perceived as little more than curricular frills. As budget constraints and personnel shortages threaten existing programs, knee-jerk advocacy efforts mushroom to save programs temporarily, and die down when the crisis has passed. Thus, an advocacy-by-crisis attitude prevails in gifted education (Dettmer, 1991).

Several philosophical and practical concerns underscore the need for advocacy efforts to combat the resistance toward gifted education. The major concerns include equity issues, underrepresentation of low-income and minority students in gifted programs, financial constraints, pressures of educational reform movements and trends, and benign neglect.

To be an effective advocate, one has to believe sincerely in the cause (Gallagher, 1986) and stay with that cause year after year. An advocate for gifted programs must present investment in appropriate education for gifted children as one of the most constructive acts a society can undertake on its own behalf. Gifted programs must be accepted as a vital, integral part of basic academic programs and not a reward for high ability. Advocates need to be involved in all major educational movements, including restructuring, school reform, and school improvement. To bring about such revolutionary changes, gifted education must escape from its marginal position to take an active place in the center of the educational conversation (Ross, 1989). Supporters of gifted education must think of themselves as programming for the giftedness in students rather than as special advocates of a narrowly defined, small subset of students (Treffinger, 1991).

Special education personnel have become skilled advocates for students with disabilities, and gifted education supporters can learn much from them. However, the parameters of their causes are not the same. High ability, talent, and creativity simply do not elicit the compassion, concern, and collective guilt that disabilities do. In an age where professional sports figures and performing arts entertainers earn astounding wealth and accolades from spectators and fans, excellence in other areas of ability tends to spawn envy and distrust. Leyden (1985) candidly illustrated such attitudes toward exceptional ability in a wry description of her introduction to Katie:

> Katie was a startlingly pretty child with a mass of auburn curls, huge blue eyes, and dimples. She sang with a true, clear voice, took dancing and guitar lessons, and enjoyed writing stories. She was an avid reader. She was also an outgoing child, very much at ease in the company of adults, whom she liked to entertain with bright social conversation. She was confident in manner, even a little gracious. Her parents adored her; I disliked her on sight. For Katie was only 3 years old. Poor Katie. Apart from her doting parents, no one felt comfortable in her presence. *Everything about her jarred one's expectations* [emphasis added]. (p. 1)

Advocacy for serving the needs of gifted and talented students must include efforts to educate the general public, and key role groups in particular, about the characteristics, needs, and curricular implications for very able children like Katie who jar others' expectations.

# ENLIGHTENED SELF-INTEREST AND CHILD ADVOCACY

During times of social unrest, the line of tension stretching between poles of individual excellence and group equality is taut and resonant with dialogue. However, it slackens during crises in which progress and products are needed, such as the years immediately following Sputnik. Harrington, Harrington, and Karns (1991) made the case that, although there have been no Sputniks recently, U.S. congressional and White House factions seem receptive to funding that focuses on improving the country's weakened economic position.

Gallagher (1991) described such thinking as *enlightened self-interest*, in which the public is willing to invest in specialized education for gifted and talented individuals when all others stand to benefit significantly. Until very bright children reach an age at which their potential becomes useful, however, their presence continues to jar societal values. As Gallagher succinctly put it, it is natural to be resentful of those who can accomplish things easily, and "We are rarely eager to help those whom we resent" (Gallagher, 1988, p. 112).

Nevertheless, democracy is served best by educating all people so they can more nearly reach their potential (Greenlaw & McIntosh, 1988). The opportunities for gifted programs to serve the needs of learners like Katie (child advocacy) while building a better world for all others (enlightened self-interest) must be promoted through strong advocacy efforts.

Without the organizational strength of lay advocacy groups, gifted education could collapse in many areas where it is in a fragile state (Tannenbaum, 1986). Many communities have lost existing programs in the face of shrinking budgets and escalating priorities. Strong advocacy programs that address enlightened self-interests and collective needs of society, *and* promote child advocacy by serving students' special needs must become integral parts of gifted education.

# A LONG, STRONG LEVER FOR ADVOCACY

The responsibility for gifted program advocacy until now has fallen primarily upon two groups—gifted education personnel in schools and universities, and families of identified gifted students. These groups provide the "load arm" upon which gifted program momentum depends (see Figure 23.1). Their tenacity and perseverance are responsible for bridging the polar extremes of societal concerns and individual needs to attain current levels of program funding and development. However, their advocacy efforts are often viewed by skeptics, cynics, and budget-crunchers as little more than protection of professional positions or vested interest in their own child's advancement. Too few other role groups are involved in meaningful ways. The absence of a large, dedicated cadre of general education professionals who affiliate with gifted education has limited gifted education programs (Renzulli, 1987).

When Archimedes proposed to move the world, he stipulated having a place to stand *and* a very long lever, or "effort arm." An effort arm comprising many role groups and extending beyond the fulcrum point of societal self-interests and child interests is the power force needed to compel action for gifted programs. Gifted education advocates, like Archimedes, also need a firm place on which to stand and apply the leverage that produces program momentum. This place to stand should be a united front that consolidates and coordinates the purposes and practices of special education, gifted education, and general education personnel toward serving needs of all students (B. Clark, personal communication, January 12, 1993).

Four types of activity are needed for gifted program advocacy: (a) emphasis on ways in which societal needs (enlightened self-interest) and individual needs (child advocacy) can be served through effective gifted programs; (b) development of support for gifted education among many different role groups; (c) strengthening of the sup-

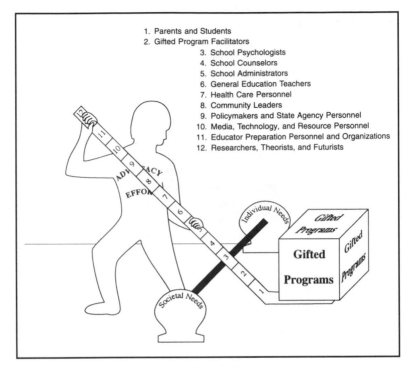

**Figure 23.1.** Role group advocacy for gifted education.

port levels within role groups; and (d) use of appropriate strategies for advocacy. Such activity requires a broad base of advocacy that includes parents, students, and school personnel.

## Parents, Students, and Gifted Program Facilitators as Advocates

Parents and caregivers are the child's first and best advocates (Silverman, 1993). They are concerned about many issues, including quality of school curriculum, safety of the learning environment, identification of student abilities and talents, academic challenges, social and personal effects of the gifted label on students, career and higher education counseling, grading and evaluation policies, and demands and pressures on students. However, parents must expand their interests in education beyond concerns for their own children to study all social movements, legislative actions, and debates about educational topics. Each school policy and practice affects gifted education in subtle as well as obvious ways. Parents of gifted students must promote excellent education for *all* persons as the bedrock of a solid community, the foundation of a strong nation, and the cultural preservation and advancement of society.

Organized parent groups are effective vehicles for gifted program advocacy. Legislators, school board members, and other policymakers do listen to parent constituents. Keys to the success of parent groups are a unifying purpose for the organization; excellent leadership; open meetings with an agenda for each meeting (particularly one that focuses on all education, not only gifted programs); an advisory board with multirole membership; and widely representative participation that includes school personnel, community members who do not have children in the gifted program, and gifted students. Advocacy often boils down to the positive use of accurate, helpful information presented by a large number of concerned people (Riggs, 1984). Newsletters, conferences, presentations to policy-making groups and fundraisers for schools are activities that parent groups have used effectively (Kraver, 1981).

Gifted students can be effective as their own advocates. They deliver credibility to programs when they address administrators, policymakers, and teachers. Advocacy agendas should include opportunities for them to speak on their own behalf (Gallagher, in Buescher, 1984). Students who have graduated from school are especially convincing when they return to share their views about strategies and alternatives that nurtured their potential or did not serve their interests and needs (Dettmer, 1991).

Gifted program facilitators must become involved in all aspects of school programs and policies. The reform movements and collaborative approaches of the 1990s now offer a window of opportunity for integration of gifted education concepts into the general classroom and the community beyond school walls (Dettmer, 1993). Through teamwork and collaboration among gifted education personnel and general education personnel, those who are neutral or even negative toward gifted education may become more supportive of differentiated learning programs for gifted students.

## School Psychologists as Advocates

The school psychologist has a vital role in determining special needs of high ability students and helping to plan differentiated curriculum for those needs. Few school psychologists, however, have taken any formal course work in gifted education (Davis & Rimm, 1989). Educators of gifted individuals must help school psychologists improve service to gifted students by interacting with them frequently and providing information about assessment, programs, and educational interventions.

It is important for school psychologists to allow sufficient time in their schedules to test for gifted behavior and performance. Gifted students typically require more examination time than do nongifted students. Ample time also is needed for interpretation of test results to gifted program facilitators and classroom teachers. These facilitators, teachers, and school psychologists, working as a team in a collaborative setting, then use the data to design meaningful learning experiences and environments that provide challenge and enrichment for each student.

The school psychologist role is ideally suited for addressing under-referral of minority populations and low-income students to gifted programs. Psychologists can assist counselors in administering and interpreting instruments to help gifted students plan their postsecondary education and select meaningful career goals. They also need to become comfortable with alternative assessment techniques, such as portfolio, creativity measures, sociograms, and self-esteem inventories. They will want to explore ways of determining students' preferred learning styles and interests.

Input by school psychologists during preassessment, comprehensive evaluation, staffing, and reevaluation conferences provides the opportunity not only to support gifted programs, but to advocate for the rights of all students to participate in learning programs that cultivate their potential. Difficult questions may arise. For example, parents may question, "Why was my child gifted in Central City, but not here in Southwest City?" and teachers may ask, "Should this student really be placed in the gifted program while flunking math?"

As consultants to various school committees, school psychologists are invaluable in helping with selection of materials, development of identification systems for gifted programs, implementation of teacher inservice and staff development programs, and formulation of gifted program policies (Brown, 1982). One overlooked area of contribution by school psychologists is providing input toward ideas for class activities that address the student's strengths and needs as identified by assessment instruments. A staff development possibility is to conduct an information session on problems inherent in teacher referral systems, such as the halo effect, errors of generosity, severity and central tendency, and personal biases that affect reliability and validity of teacher nominations for gifted program placements.

## School Counselors as Advocates

School counselors serve a vital role in the support of gifted students and their educational programs. However, like school psychologists, they seldom have formal training in gifted education (Davis &

Rimm, 1989). This is unfortunate, because they should be working directly with teachers and other school personnel to recognize the unique talent of highly able students and facilitate their learning needs. Counselors can help generate ideas that provide opportunities for enrichment and acceleration. They should participate in curriculum development, textbook selection, and other programmatic activities to ensure that appropriate guidance permeates all academic components for gifted students. Their services also are valuable in evaluating the gifted program and recommending improvements. When counselors are advocates for gifted students and are knowledgeable about their characteristics and needs, they can help students work to capacity and reduce the discrepancy between ability and achievement. Gifted students very much need role models and adult confidants who are neither judgmental nor directive.

Counselors are pivotal in establishing a bond between parents and schools. This bond is particularly important for parents of culturally diverse children, who sometimes do not receive needed information on gifted programs and identification procedures (Colangelo, 1985). In a social institution that must operate in many ways to encourage conformity, counselors are appropriate spokespersons for respect of individuality and encouragement of abilities and talents.

School counselors support gifted students when they guide and advise on matters of postsecondary education and training, career goals and aspirations, financial aid for advanced schooling and degree programs, family dynamics, peer relationships, and personal characteristics such as perfectionism, procrastination, overscheduling, and time management. Their counsel is essential in assisting needs of gifted girls, underachievers, social isolates, and other educationally disadvantaged populations. They can help students cope with dilemmas, such as making career decisions when they are talented in many fields, learning to manage long years of preparation in rigorous disciplines, or combining their dedication to careers and productivity with aspirations for having a family and serving their communities.

Students typically identified as gifted tend not to display behaviors that bring them to the attention of the counselors (Safter & Bruch, 1981), and many gifted students never avail themselves of counseling (Greenlaw & McIntosh, 1988). Nevertheless, many do experience pressures, confusion, ostracism, and periods of underachievement that warrant the support and involvement of the counseling staff. Counselors assist gifted students by setting aside time to help them sort out and deal with parent, teacher, and peer pressures that often accompany high ability. Their input is invaluable in understanding causes of underachievement and dropping out among the gifted student population.

School counselors communicate the need for differentiated service for a population that others too often assume can and should take care of themselves. Counselors can be highly influential advocates for gifted programs by participating in inservice and staff development for gifted education and contributing to the flow of information about gifted students' behaviors and learning needs.

## School Administrators as Advocates

Administrators have overwhelming responsibilities as school executives. They cope with pressures from parents, demands for school reform, dwindling resources and shrinking budgets, teacher shortages, and escalating burdens upon schools to function as service institutions for a wide range of social needs. Although they also are in the ideal position to support and encourage gifted programs, until now too few have added the considerable weight of their influence to this effort. When administrators take a firm, positive stand as leaders for gifted education, most of the other role groups become involved at a practical, productive level.

First and foremost, administrators must ensure intellectual safety and security within the school climate, for in many schools it is not very safe or "smart" to exhibit love of learning and demonstrate high achievement. School executives can support gifted education by making clear statements of policy about gifted programs and providing helpful information to legislators about program needs and benefits.

As instructional leaders, building administrators should seek training and acquire information to ensure that very able students in their schools are not "curriculum disabled" or "school impaired." They will need to clarify the roles of gifted program personnel in relation to other school staff, and encourage their school personnel to take risks in providing curricular alternatives and learning options. It is crucial that they not only promote, but *participate* in staff development for gifted education. They might devote a segment of staff meeting time periodically to build public relations toward programs for all students at risk, including those who are gifted and talented. They should be particularly conscientious in commending staff who work together to serve the special needs of gifted and talented students. When interviewing prospective teachers, it would be good to ask candidates how they would address the needs of the school's brightest and most talented students.

## General Education Teachers as Advocates

Gifted students spend the major portion of their school days in general classrooms. Numerous studies comparing teacher understanding of gifted behaviors with teacher attitudes of support toward gifted programs report that the more teachers know and learn about gifted-ness, and collaborate with gifted education personnel, the more likely they are to have positive attitudes about gifted student participation in special learning programs (Wyatt, 1982). Teachers who address needs of gifted students by soliciting assistance from gifted program person-nel and community resources must not be perceived as less than com-petent because they utilize support personnel and outside resources (Dettmer, Thurston, & Dyck, 1993).

## Health Care Personnel as Advocates

Medical personnel are valuable but underused members of advo-cacy groups and advisory boards. With their interest in promoting the health and well-being of the whole child, they can support educators in determining unidentified needs that are creating psychological and physical problems for their young patients. Furthermore, advocacy for gifted education can be extended through vehicles as uncomplicated as placing pertinent reading material in medical center offices and wait-ing rooms.

## Community Leaders as Advocates

An African proverb states that it takes an entire village to educate a child. Students with exceptional ability and talent need resources that extend beyond school walls. Business leaders in many commu-nities support the development of high potential by providing intern-ships and mentor programs, displaying student work, hosting competi-tive activities, contributing funds, and serving as content experts or product evaluators. This cooperation must be encouraged and expanded. Key business leaders can provide helpful influence and promote impor-tant contacts. Community leaders can serve on school advisory coun-cils and planning committees to contribute their expertise. Senior citi-zens, who are community leaders by virtue of their experience and wisdom, often are delighted and eager to assist in a variety of ways.

## Policymakers and State Agency Personnel as Advocates

Legislators, school board members, state department of education personnel, and other policymakers and program regulators are power-ful forces affecting education. As public leaders, they are influential in creating general awareness of the crises in education. State coordina-tors for gifted programs, in particular, have a crucial role in building legislative support for gifted education. If legislators are to lend their support, they will need information that state department personnel can provide.

## Resource Personnel as Advocates

Librarians, media specialists, and technologists are among gifted students' best resources and supporters. They assist with special projects, skills of searching for information, and research and inquiry techniques. They inform teachers about new developments in media for students who are capable of working beyond conventional learning systems. Textbook authors and materials specialists have not yet contributed to gifted education programs as much as they can and should. The lack of challenge in basal materials for very able students has been cited by every major content group in the United States (Renzulli & Reis, 1991). When publishers recognize the benefits of including enrichment ideas, curriculum compacting tips, and accelerative techniques in the texts used by schools, they will have additional incentive for becoming actively involved in gifted education (Dettmer, 1991).

## Professional Development Personnel as Advocates

Educators for teacher preparation and for staff development coordinators comprise another essential but underinvolved group in gifted education advocacy. Undergraduate students and graduate students in teacher preparation programs must have course work that cultivates positive attitudes toward gifted students and encourages use of teaching methods and clinical practices that are appropriate for gifted students. Few education majors take courses focusing specifically on education of gifted students. Therefore, gifted education personnel in universities and schools should collaborate with methods instructors of teacher preparation courses to provide information in all teacher education classes about the needs of gifted students.

Staff development specialists can help educators avoid teaching techniques and materials that are busywork and disincentives for bright students. When these specialists acquaint teachers with methods that challenge students, allow teachers to experience success with the methods, and provide follow-up contacts to reinforce those methods, they are serving the special needs of this unique population. They also are enabling teachers to be effective advocates for the rights of gifted students to have differentiated curriculum in heterogeneous school settings.

State and national organizations that advocate for gifted and talented individuals are becoming increasingly effective as support systems. One example of outreach and networking is the National Association for Gifted Children (NAGC) advocacy movement. In reaching out to other organizations, such as the National School Boards Association, the Middle Schools Association, and the Association for Supervision and Curriculum Development, NAGC conveys its important message to groups that can compound the support of gifted programs through the ripple effect. In 1992, the Ad Hoc Public Relations Committee was formed by NAGC to reach out to influential public and professional colleagues outside gifted education. NAGC hosted an innovative Advocacy and Education Conference for affiliates in the spring of 1993 and, in collaboration with the Office of Gifted and Talented in Washington, D.C., conducted a leadership workshop involving representatives from major organizations in the field. To create advocacy through technology, a bulletin board on gifted education was set up in 1992 as part of SpecialNet, the electronic bulletin board service from GTE Directories Education Services of Dallas. This service, designed to reach more than 40 boards and 6,500 members, presents timely information on advocacy issues, announcements from national and state organizations, updates on important research, teaching ideas, and links with others in the field of gifted education.

## Researchers, Theorists, and Futurists as Advocates

As discussed earlier, much of the difficulty in cultivating positive public relations for gifted education emanates from societal convictions about values such as egalitarianism, heterogeneous grouping in schools, and equity of social programs. Gifted program personnel need much more information and reflection upon social issues such as those identified by Howley, Howley, and Pendarvis (1986) as legitimation, socialization, and normalcy. Theorists and researchers contribute to gifted program advocacy when they develop hypotheses and generate new knowledge about giftedness and learning. Visionaries for the future support gifted education and advocate for gifted students by helping educators anticipate shifts in support, enabling them to function more effectively as change agents for the future.

# BUILDING LEVELS OF SUPPORT FOR GIFTED EDUCATION

Advocacy for a cause is a value-laden, attitudinal process. Although some proponents for gifted education may paint the canvas of their advocacy plans with rosy colors by expecting everybody to be an ardent supporter with a bit of encouragement and a few success stories, that is not a realistic approach. The processes of advocacy and public support are much more complex than that.

Advocacy for gifted education should be approached as a process composed of three levels and nine stages subdivided among those three levels (see Figure 23.2). Level One includes the three stages of *attention, interest*, and *participation*. The first two of these three stages are more attitudinal, whereas the third stage begins to involve action. In Level Two, a *concern* stage nudges those who are moving from Level One to be concerned, enter an *involvement* stage, and then begin to provide *support*. The stages of this second level contain more action than attitudinal growth. Level Three stages are all primarily action based because the attitudes now are acceptant and supportive. In this third level, the *commitment* stage directs the supporter of a cause into active *advocacy* and finally into intensive *promotion* of the cause.

It would be myopic to expect everyone in the world to adopt a particular cause and advocate for it at the very highest stage of action. However, proponents for gifted education can begin with present attitude or action stages of their target role groups and work to increase momentum with as many as they can, as far as possible.

Reis and Renzulli (1988) determined that the most successful gifted programs are comprehensive programs in which all instructional staff are aware and, in varying degrees, involved. In similar fashion, when more role groups are participating at higher stages and taking stances as integral parts of the total education scene, gifted program advocates, like Archimedes, can "move the world" to provide effective education for gifted and talented students.

# A 10-STEP PLAN FOR EFFECTIVE ADVOCACY

Successful advocacy is assured when the long arm of leverage by many role groups is in place and functioning; role groups are escalating through the attitudinal and action stages of support; and advocates are adhering to a simple, 10-step plan of action. These steps are as follows:

*Step 1*: Work hard in all social and educational arenas so that gifted education becomes an integral part of the conversations about effective schools, effective teaching and learning, student growth, and professional development. Take an interest in all aspects of education and cultures.

*Step 2*: Explain the rationale for providing differentiated learning environments and experiences to very able, talented, and creative stu-

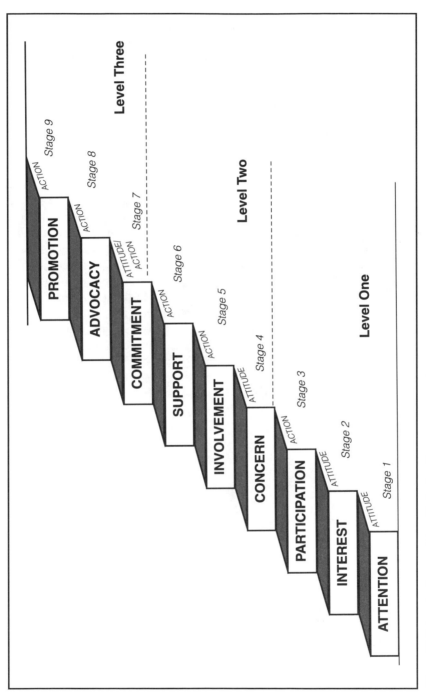

**Figure 23.2.** Levels of support for gifted education.

dents within an egalitarian society and indicate the high price of failing to provide meaningful school experiences for this population. Do so by using words and techniques appropriate for each target audience.

*Step 3*: Present the facts about gifted education. Many gifted education source books and journals include comprehensive summaries of primary events in gifted education history, major philosophies, influential theorists, and current practices in the field. Prepare concise fact sheets designed in formats that suit each target audience best. Include salient information but avoid overkill.

*Step 4*: Highlight positive outcomes from existing gifted programs that have most successfully met gifted students' academic, social, and personal needs.

*Step 5*: Describe the major benefits that gifted programs can provide for *all* members of the schools and communities.

*Step 6*: Be candid and realistic about problems inherent in providing gifted education. Acknowledge that only when programs are evaluated, shortcomings and pitfalls are pinpointed, and corrective measures are taken will advocates truly be able to promote their cause. Invite input from all knowledgeable, interested parties and share the results of evaluations and follow-up activities that address identified problems.

*Step 7*: Thank all those who support gifted programs and education in the larger context, with phone calls, letters, and face-to-face interactions. When appropriate, and with their consent, commend outstanding efforts through the public media.

*Step 8*: Cultivate collaboration skills and develop networks with people and organizations who are sources of information, advice, and support. Remember that networking is not manipulation of others. It is two-way service and support between each pair of networking groups.

*Step 9*: Abandon advocacy-by-crisis approaches, and dismantle bandwagon vehicles of support that include only gifted program facilitators and parents of gifted students.

*Step 10*: With consistency and direction, maintain commitment and momentum over time for the advocacy and support of excellent education that serves the educational needs of gifted students.

# CONCLUSION

Proponents of gifted education must always be about the business of strong political advocacy to build public support for the programs. The field needs sophisticated public relations, advertising strategies, and media techniques to awaken the conscience of communities, states, and nations from the lethargy about this issue in which it has languished (Abraham, 1986).

> There is no farm community, small town, city or metropolitan area which would not benefit from identifying and educating their gifted children, but their awareness has to come first. . . . Each of us devoted to this field can provide "the light in the darkness" to get the movement that is needed. (Abraham, 1986, p. 222)

Gifted education advocates must select a firm place on which to stand with conviction, and then provide powerful leverage through the involvement of many roles. They must nurture growth from beginning stages to advanced stages of advocacy, and engage in conscientious practice of basic advocacy principles. With these elements in operation, schools and communities will be providing the motive and the momentum that can "move the world" to serve the unique educational needs of gifted individuals.

# REFERENCES

Abraham, W. (1986). From Goddard to Gallagher—and beyond. *Roeper Review*, *8*, 218–222.

Brown, P. P. (1982). The role of the school psychologist in gifted education. *Roeper Review*, *4*, 28–29.

Buescher, T. M. (1984). What do the national calls for reform mean for the gifted and talented? An interview with James Gallagher. *Journal for the Education of the Gifted*, *7*, 229–237.

Colangelo, N. (1985). Counseling needs of culturally diverse gifted students. *Roeper Review*, *8*, 33–35.

Davis, G. A., & Rimm, S. B. (1989). *Education of the gifted and talented* (2nd ed.). Englewood Cliffs, NJ: Prentice-Hall.

Dettmer, P. (1991). Gifted program advocacy: Overhauling bandwagons to build support. *Gifted Child Quarterly*, *35*, 165–171.

Dettmer, P. (1993). Gifted education: A window of opportunity. *Gifted Child Quarterly, 37*(2), 92–94.

Dettmer, P., Thurston, L. P., & Dyck, N. (1993). *Consultation, collaboration, and teamwork for students with special needs*. Needham Heights, MA: Allyn & Bacon.

Freehill, M. F. (1982). *Gifted children: Their psychology and education* (2nd ed.). Ventura, CA: Ventura County Superintendent of Schools Office.

Gallagher, J. J. (1986). Equity vs excellence: An educational drama. *Roeper Review*, *8*, 233–235.

Gallagher, J. J. (1988). National agenda for educating gifted students: Statement of priorities. *Exceptional Children*, *55*, 107–114.

Gallagher, J. J. (1991). Programs for gifted students: Enlightened self-interest. *Gifted Child Quarterly, 35,* 177–178.

Greenlaw, M. J., & McIntosh, M. E. (1988). *Educating the gifted: A sourcebook.* Chicago: American Library Association.

Harrington, J., Harrington, C., & Karns, E. (1991). The Marland Report: Twenty years later. *Journal for the Education of the Gifted, 15,* 31–43.

Howley, A., Howley, C. B., & Pendarvis, E. D. (1986). *Teaching gifted children: Principles and strategies.* Boston: Little, Brown.

Kraver, T. (1981). Parent power: Starting and building a parent organization. In P. B. Mitchell (Ed.), *An advocate's guide to building support for gifted and talented education* (pp. 24–30). Washington, DC: National Association of State Boards of Education.

Leyden, S. (1985). *Helping the child of exceptional ability.* London: Croom Helm.

Reis, S. M., & Renzulli, J. S. (1988). The role and responsibilities of the gifted program coordinator. *Roeper Review, 11,* 66–72.

Renzulli, J. S. (1987). Point counterpoint: The positive side of pull-out programs. *Journal for the Education of the Gifted, 10,* 245–254.

Renzulli, J. S., & Reis, S. M. (1991). The reform movement and the quiet crisis in gifted education. *Gifted Child Quarterly, 35,* 26–35.

Riggs, G. G. (1984). Parent power: Wanted for organizations. *Gifted Child Quarterly, 28,* 111–114.

Ross, P. O. (1989, November). *Keynote address.* Presentation at the National Association for Gifted Children Convention, Cincinnati, OH.

Safter, H. T., & Bruch, C. B. (1981). Use of the DGG Model for differential guidance for the gifted. *Gifted Child Quarterly, 25,* 167–174.

Silverman, L. K. (Ed.). (1993). *Counseling the gifted and talented.* Denver: Love.

Tannenbaum, A. (1986). Reflection and refraction of light on the gifted: An editorial. *Roeper Review, 8,* 212–218.

Treffinger, D. J. (1991). Critical issues in gifted education. *Educating Able Learners, 16,* 4–8.

Wyatt, F. (1982). Responsibility for gifted learners—A plea for the encouragement of classroom teacher support. *Gifted Child Quarterly, 26,* 140–143.

# Author Index

# Subject Index

♦ ♦ ♦

*McMaster Family Assessment Device,*
317
Media specialists, 399
Medical personnel, 398
Memory enhancers, 212
Men. *See* Gifted boys and men
MENSA, 231
Mentors, 230
Metacomponents of intelligence,
34–36
Middle school, 7–8, 107, 109, 111
Middle Schools Association, 400
MIDIs. *See* Musical Interface Digital
Interfaces (MIDIs)
Minilabs in classrooms, 168
MiniTab, 158
Minority gifted, 59–61, 285–297,
307–308
*Mismeasure of Women, The* (Tavris),
344
*Monitor Test of Creative Potential,*
77
Moral development, 19–20, 27, 261,
332
Multicultural issues
assimilation, 285–287, 294
definition of, 286
developing a multicultural identi-
ty, 287–289
family's understanding of gifted-
ness, 307–308
identification of minority gifted,
59–61, 289–293
research on, 285–286
Multimedia software, 159, 163,
166
Multiple assessment, 91
Multipotentiality, 260
Musical Interface Digital Interfaces
(MIDIs), 165–166

NAGC. *See* National Association for
Gifted Children (NAGC)
*Nation at Risk, A,* 173
National Association for Gifted Chil-
dren (NAGC), 252, 400
National Association of School Psy-
chologists, 49

National Council of Teachers of
Mathematics, 164
National Research Center on the
Gifted and Talented, 279,
374–375
National School Boards Association,
400
National standards for achievement,
94
National/State Leadership Training
Institute for the Gifted, 136–137
National testing movement, 9
Native Americans, 60, 285, 289, 292,
295, 296
Neurocognitive characteristics, of
learning disabled gifted stu-
dents, 207–209
*New Jersey Test of Reasoning Skills,*
86
Nonsuccess, 260
Northwestern University, 225
Novelty, coping with, 37
NSF-NET, 158

Object-oriented programming lan-
guages, 159
Odyssey of the Mind, 378
Office of Gifted and Talented, 131,
400
*Otis-Lennon Mental Ability Test,*
53–54
Out-of-level assessment, 87–88
Overexcitabilities (OEs), 20–21

Pacific Islanders, 60–61, 292
Parent-centered consultation,
314–316
Parents. *See also* Family
advocacy by, 393–394
assessment and, 306–307
characteristics of, 244
communication with teachers,
181–183
consultation with, 276–277,
303–319, 353, 356
double messages communicated
by, to gifted children, 310
emotional needs of, 310–311

SAT. See *Scholastic Aptitude Test* (SAT)
Saturated classrooms, 167
*Scales for Rating the Behavioral Characteristics of Superior Students*, 103
*Scholastic Aptitude Test* (SAT), 103, 219, 325
School counselors. See Counselors
School personnel. See also Counselors; School psychologists; Teachers
  in Autonomous Learner Model (ALM), 149–152
  as catalysts, 117–118
  curriculum involvement by, 123, 132
  guidelines on educational services for support personnel, 113–118
  helping gifted females cope with stress, 275–279
  highly gifted and, 235–237
  preparation of, 12, 136–137, 141, 155–156
  role of, in evaluation of instructional outcomes, 95–96
  specialness perspective and, 253
  and stress management for gifted, 265–266
  underachievement syndrome and, 173–174
School psychologists
  advocacy by, 394–395
  in Autonomous Learner Model (ALM), 149–152
  and evaluation of instructional outcomes, 95–96
  helping gifted females cope with stress, 275–279
  highly gifted and, 235
  and identification of gifted, 49–50
  and stress management for gifted, 265–266
School-within-a-school programs, 231
Schoolwide Enrichment Model, 95, 378–379

Schoolwide Enrichment Triad Model (SEM), 380–382
Science software, 162, 165
Screening. See Identification
Secondary education. See High school
Selection of environments, 39–40
Self-contained classes, 230–231
Self-directed learning. See Autonomous Learner Model (ALM)
Self-efficacy, 205–206
Self-esteem, 21–22, 212
Self-interest, enlightened, 391–392
SEM. See Schoolwide Enrichment Triad Model (SEM)
Senior Seminar, 135–136
Sensitivity, 23
*Sex Role Inventory*, 277
Sex-role socialization, 269–272, 275–277, 340–341
Shaping of environments, 39–40
Siblings, 184, 244–248, 310
SIT. See *Slosson Intelligence Test* (SIT)
Site-based management, 8
*Sixteen Personality Factor Questionnaire*, 93
Skill deficiencies, correction of, 186, 187–188
*Slosson Intelligence Test* (SIT), 54
SMPY. See Study of Mathematically Precocious Youth (SMPY)
Social skills. See also Peer pressure; Peer relationships; Peer support groups
  difficulties in, 19, 205
  lack of attention to assessment of, 86–87
  poor peer relationships, 259
  training in, 212
Socialization. See Sex-role socialization
Software, 158, 159, 161–167, 212
*Something About Myself*, 78
SOMPA. See *System of Multicultural Pluralistic Assessment* (SOMPA)
Specialness of gifted, 252–253

# About the Editors and Contributors

◆  ◆  ◆

***Marlene Bireley*** has taught elementary school, learning disabled and developmentally handicapped children; served as a school psychologist; and taught various topics in special education and school psychology at the Ohio State University. In 1969, she joined the faculty of Wright State University as coordinator of (and the first faculty member in) special education. In that capacity, she developed programs in special education, gifted education, and school psychology. Since her early retirement in 1988, she has continued to teach, write, and consult in these three areas of interest. She co-edited *Understanding the Gifted Adolescent* with Judy Genshaft and authored the 1993 publication *Crossover Children: A Sourcebook for Helping the Learning Disabled / Gifted Child.*

***Judy L. Genshaft*** is the dean of the School of Education at the University at Albany, State University of New York. Prior to this position, Genshaft served as professor and chairperson of the Department of Educational Services and Research at The Ohio State University. In addition, she has been a visiting professor at the University of British Columbia, Vancouver, Canada. Before holding an academic position, Genshaft worked as a therapist in a community mental health center. She has written numerous journal articles and chapters focusing on such issues as mathematical anxiety in female adolescents, improving study skills, professional ethics and practice, and assessment of intellectual abilities. Her recent book, edited with Marlene Bireley, *Understanding the Gifted Adolescent*, was published in 1991. Genshaft has received several awards and honors for her leadership for women and for her contributions to the National Association of School Psychologists. She is a member of the board of trustees of Support for Talented Students.

***Constance L. Hollinger*** is professor of psychology and coordinator of the School Psychology Program at Cleveland State University. Prior to her current position, she was dean of students at Lake Erie College for Women. Her research interests include the longitudinal study of gifted and talented women, with particular focus on the realization of potential and self-perception. She also conducts research in the area of assessment of intellectual ability. Hollinger has published numerous journal articles and is co-author of *Project CHOICE: A Diagnostic–Prescriptive Model of Career Education for Gifted Young Women*. She also serves as a consultant bank member for the National Research Center on the Gifted and Talented.

***George T. Betts*** is director of the Center of the Education and Study of the Gifted, Talented and Creative and associate professor of special education at the University of Northern Colorado in Greeley, Colorado. Betts is also on the Executive Board of the National Association for Gifted Children, and president of the Colorado Association for the Gifted and Talented. He is also the co-developer, with Jolene Knapp Kercher, of the Autonomous Learner Model (K–12), which is now being implemented in over 500 school districts in the United States and Canada.

***Susan Borovsky*** is completing her Ph.D. at the Ohio State University in gifted education with an emphasis on gifted women and their achievements. Borovsky has taught for 21 years at levels ranging from nursery school to the university. Additionally, she has owned and operated small businesses dealing with the arts.

***Carolyn M. Callahan*** is a professor in the Department of Educational Studies in the Curry School of Education, University of Virginia, and associate director of the National Research Center on the Gifted and Talented. Currently, she teaches courses in the area of education of the gifted and is executive director of the Summer Enrichment Program. She has published more than 40 articles, 10 book chapters, and several monographs on the topics of creativity, program evaluation, and the issues faced by gifted females. In 1988 she was selected Outstanding Faculty Member in the Commonwealth of Virginia, and in 1989 received the Distinguished Scholar Award from the National Association for Gifted

Children (NAGC). She is a past-president of the Association for the Gifted, second vice president and member of the Executive Board of NAGC, and on the editorial boards of *Gifted Child Quarterly, Journal for the Education of the Gifted*, and *Roeper Review*.

**Mary Ruth Coleman** has served as associate editor of the *Journal for the Education of the Gifted* for over 7 years, and has put together two special issues—the first on gifted girls and women, and the second on underserved gifted. She is the associate director for the Gifted Education Policy Studies Program. Prior to this, she developed and chaired a new department at Chowan College designed to address the needs of special populations—disabled, culturally different, and economically disadvantaged college students. Her teaching experiences include public and private elementary schools for 5 years, with both regular classroom and gifted program assignments. She has taught for 3 years as an adjunct faculty at East Carolina University, and has been a guest lecturer at the University of Virginia at Charlottesville and the College of William and Mary. In addition to teaching, Coleman has presented numerous seminars, workshops, and staff development programs on a variety of topics. She serves on the board for The Association for Gifted (TAG) and the board for the National Association for Gifted and Talented (NAGT), and chaired the 1993 and 1994 TAG Symposiums. The NAGC recognized her with the 1992 Early Leader Award.

**Gary A. Davis** is professor of educational psychology at the University of Wisconsin, where he teaches courses in creativity, gifted education, and other areas. He has served on the Wisconsin State Superintendent's Committee on Gifted and Talented and on the Board of Directors for the Wisconsin Council on Gifted and Talented. He currently is consulting or reviewing editor for the *Journal of Creative Behavior, Gifted Child Quarterly*, and *Creativity Research Journal*, and is named on the editorial board for the *Creative Child and Adult Quarterly*. Some books he has authored include *Education of the Gifted and Talented*, with Sylvia Rimm; *Handbook of Gifted Education*, with Nicholas Colangelo; *Creativity Is Forever*; *Effective Schools and Effective Teachers*; *Creative Teaching of Values and Moral Thinking*; and *Creative Thinking and Problem Solving* (Apple II computer disk and manual).

**Peggy Dettmer** is professor of educational psychology and special education, and chair of the Counseling and Educational Psychology Department at Kansas State University in Manhattan, Kansas.

She directs advanced degree and certification programs in gifted education and educational psychology. Dettmer is immediate past-chair of the Professional Development Division of the National Association for Gifted Children, and prior to that office served as chair of the Inservice/Staff Development Committee of the division for several years. She serves on the NAGC Ad Hoc Committee for Public Relations, and the NAGC Professional Standards Committee. Recent publications include the book *Consultation, Collaboration, and Teamwork for Students with Special Needs* as senior author, and "Gifted Program Advocacy: Overhauling Bandwagons to Build Support" as guest editor for the fall 1991 *Gifted Child Quarterly* topical issue on advocacy for gifted programs.

**John F. Feldhusen** is the Robert B. Kane Distinguished Professor of Education and director of the Gifted Education Resource Institute at Purdue University. He is author of 223 articles, 45 book chapters, and 25 monographs and books. He is currently interested in the concept of talent development in gifted education.

**Dawn P. Flanagan** is an assistant professor of school psychology at St. John's University in New York City. Her research interests include the professional role and function of school psychologists, cognitive assessment and intervention, and social skills development in preschool children. She has presented at national, regional, and local conferences and published journal articles in these areas.

**James J. Gallagher** is Kenan Professor of Education at the University of North Carolina at Chapel Hill. He is the director of the Gifted Education Policy Studies Program, housed in the Frank Porter Graham Child Development Center (FPG). From 1967 to 1979, he served as the first chief of the Bureau of Education for the Handicapped in the United States Office of Education. He was the director for the FPG center from 1970 to 1987. In addition to over 100 published articles, chapters, and reviews, Gallagher is author of *Teaching the Gifted Child*, which is out in its fourth edition (this edition was co-authored with his daughter, Dr. Shelagh Gallagher). Gallagher is an active lecturer and, in addition to numerous U.S. presentations, he has also presented in Russia, Finland, Sweden, Australia, the Middle East, and China. Gallagher is the president of the National Association for Gifted Children, and the editor of the *Journal for the Education of the Gifted*.

**Steven I. Greenbaum** is a researcher who lives in upstate New York. He is a supporter of the gifted and his affiliations include membership in the groups Support for Talented Students and Parents for Excellence.

***Michael J. Hoover*** is certified as a school psychologist and special education administrator in the state of Colorado and is a nationally certified school psychologist. He is currently employed as a pupil services coordinator at Weld School District #6 in Greeley, Colorado. Hoover is also an adjunct professor at the University of Northern Colorado (UNC) and has been on the faculty of the Summer Enrichment Program for the Gifted and Talented at UNC. He has also been involved in crisis intervention on the local, state, and national levels.

***Richard D. Howell*** is currently a faculty member of the Special Education program, Department of Educational Services and Research in the College of Education at The Ohio State University. His teaching responsibilities include graduate-level courses and doctoral seminars in computer applications in education and training, technologies for students with disabilities, adaptive design and rehabilitation for the severely handicapped, robotic devices as cognitive aids, and interactive devices and computer courseware design. Howell has published and presented extensively throughout the United States and Europe concerning his research in the design of assistive devices and educational robotics for students with disabilities. Presentations on current research using new and emergent assistive technologies include the annual meetings of the Association for the Advancement of Rehabilitation Technologies, the Technology and Media Division of Council for Exceptional Children, and the Invitational Research Symposia on Special Education.

***Paul Michael Janos*** worked as psychologist for the Early Entrance Program at the University of Washington from 1980 to 1989. He has published 14 papers related to that work, one designated Research Paper of the Year (1985) by the National Association for Gifted Children. Janos is currently a psychologist with Northwest Youth and Family Services.

***Elizabeth Maxwell*** has over 15 years of teaching experience in the language arts and gifted education fields. Currently, she is associate director of the Gifted Child Development Center in Denver, Colorado. A co-founder of the Institute for the Study of Advanced Development (ISAD), she is its vice president. In 1991 she served as the guest editor of *Advanced Development Journal*, ISAD's annual juried journal, using her background in psychosynthesis to augment its focus on the self. Maxwell is also certified within the field of psychosynthesis psychotherapy, having received this recognition in 1986 from the Psychosynthesis Training Center of High Point Foundation in Pasadena, California. She uses this holistic psychology together with her knowledge of giftedness in her practice as a psychotherapist.

**Joel Meyers** is a professor in the Department of Educational Psychology and Statistics and director of Programs in School Psychology at the University at Albany, State University of New York. He has published on topics such as school-based consultation, mainstreaming, school psychology, and the primary prevention of learning and adjustment. In 1992, Meyers was appointed editor of the *Journal of School Psychology*.

**Sidney M. Moon** is a visiting assistant professor of educational psychology in the Department of Educational Studies at Purdue University and a certified family therapist. She has been active in the field of gifted education for more than 10 years in various capacities, including those of parent, teacher, administrator, counselor, researcher, and professor. She is especially interested in theory, research, and clinical practice that addresses the unique dynamics of gifted family systems.

**Beverly N. Parke** is the author of *Gifted Students in Regular Classrooms* (1989). Interest in the topic stems from her years working with gifted and talented students as a classroom teacher, program supervisor, and teacher trainer. She has numerous publications to her credit on topics such as creativity, assessment issues, self-instructional programs, and standards for teacher training. Recent works include a computer program, *The G/T Planner* (1990), which matches problem behaviors with teacher strategies for their remediation, and articles on classroom management. Parke has served as president of The Association for Gifted and as editor of *The Journal for the Education of the Gifted*. She has traveled throughout the United States and Canada working with educators in pursuit of bringing full service to gifted and talented students. She served as an associate professor of Special Education/Gifted Child Education (1979–1991) at Wayne State University.

**Deborah L. Plummer** is a licensed psychologist in the state of Ohio. Currently she is employed as an assistant professor in the Psychology Department at Cleveland State University. Plummer has been a psychologist at the Oberlin College Counseling Center.

She has been a consultant with many universities, schools, and institutions on the topic of diversity and cross-cultural issues. Her research and publications center on the issues of diversity and becoming culturally competent.

**Gerald Porter** is an assistant professor in the Programs in School Psychology at the University at Albany, State University of New York. Before that, Porter was a psychologist for the New York State Department of Correctional Services and the Division for Youth. He is interested in the social–emotional adjustment of exceptional children.

**Sally M. Reis** is an associate professor of educational psychology at the University of Connecticut, where she also serves as principal investigator of the National Research Center on the Gifted and Talented. She was a teacher for 15 years, 11 of which were spent working with gifted students on the elementary, junior high, and high school levels. She is the coordinator of Confratute, the summer institute at the University of Connecticut. She has traveled extensively across the country conducting workshops and providing inservice for school districts designing gifted programs based on The Enrichment Triad Model and The Revolving Door Identification Model. She is co-author of *The Revolving Door Identification Model*, *The Schoolwide Enrichment Model, The Secondary Triad Model*, and *The Triad Reader*. Sally has written and co-authored many articles on gifted education, served on the Editorial Board of the *Journal for Education of the Gifted* and *Gifted Child Quarterly*, and is on the Board of the National Association for Gifted Children.

**Sylvia B. Rimm** is a psychologist specializing in working with gifted and creative children who are not performing up to their ability in school. She directs the Family Achievement Clinic with four offices in Wisconsin. She has taught graduate courses in the areas of gifted and talented, creativity, and underachievement, and is the author and researcher of several internationally validated creativity instruments, including *Group Inventory for Finding Talent, Group Inventory for Finding Interests,* and *Preschool and Kindergarten Interest Descriptor*, and three inventories for the identification of underachievement patterns (*Achievement Identification Measure, Group Achievement Identification Measure, Achievement Identification Measure–Teacher Observation*). She is the co-author of *Education of the Gifted and Talented*, and author of *Underachievement Syndrome: Causes and Cures; Guidebook—*

*Underachievement Syndrome: Causes and Cures*; and *How to Parent So Children Will Learn*. She speaks and publishes nationally on family and school approaches to working with gifted, creative, and underachieving children.

**Linda Kreger Silverman** is a licensed psychologist and director of the Gifted Development Center in Denver, Colorado. In addition, she founded and directs the Institute for the Study of Advanced Development, and is editor of two journals: *Advanced Development* and *Understanding Our Gifted*. She has published extensively in the field of gifted education; *Counseling the Gifted and Talented*, which she edited, was recently released. She began studying gifted children in 1958, and has experience as a resource teacher, teacher trainer, counselor, psychometrist, researcher, author, and lecturer. For 9 years, she served on the faculty of the University of Denver in counseling psychology and gifted education, and coordinated the gifted education graduate program. Beginning in 1979, the Gifted Child Development Center has assessed over 1,700 gifted children under her supervision.

**Robert J. Sternberg** is IBM Professor of Psychology and Education in the Department of Psychology at Yale University. The author of many books and articles, he was named one of the top 100 "Young Scientists in the U.S." by *Science Digest* and was listed in the 1986 *Esquire* magazine register of "Outstanding Men and Women Under 40." His most recent book, *Beyond IQ*, received the Outstanding Book Award from the American Educational Research Association in 1987. He is the recipient of numerous grants and awards, including a John Simon Guggenheim Fellowship, and is a Fellow of the American Psychological Association. He lives in Mt. Carmel, Connecticut.